The Anthropology of News and Journalism

T0344230

THE ANTHROPOLOGY OF
NEWS
& JOURNALISM

GLOBAL PERSPECTIVES

Edited by S. Elizabeth Bird

Indiana University Press | Bloomington and Indianapolis

This book is a publication of
Indiana University Press
601 North Morton Street
Bloomington, IN 47404-3797 USA

http://iupress.indiana.edu

Telephone orders   800-842-6796
Fax orders   812-855-7931
Orders by e-mail   iuporder@indiana.edu

The paper used in this publication meets the minimum
requirements of American National Standard for
Information Sciences — Permanence of Paper for Printed
Library Materials, ANSI Z39.48-1984.

Manufactured in the United States of America

Library of Congress Cataloging-in-Publication Data

The anthropology of news and journalism : global
perspectives / edited by S. Elizabeth Bird.
     p.   cm.
   Includes bibliographical references and index.
     ISBN 978-0-253-35369-6 (cloth : alk. paper) — ISBN 978-
0-253-22126-1 (pbk. : alk. paper) 1. Mass media and
anthropology. 2. Communication in anthropology.
3. Anthropology in popular culture. I. Bird, Elizabeth.
   P96.A56A56   2010
   302.23 — dc22   2009021547

1 2 3 4 5   15 14 13 12 11 10

For my father, Tom Bird

CONTENTS

ACKNOWLEDGMENTS

For several years, I have been working at the intersection of anthropology and media studies, with a special interest in news and journalism. This book was finally an opportunity to bring the fields together in a way that has only become possible recently, as more scholars have begun addressing journalism from a cultural perspective.

First and foremost, I acknowledge all the contributors to this book for their commitment to the project and their patience as it developed. Many colleagues and friends, whether they know it or not, have provided encouragement, helping me believe that this project was needed and important. In particular, I thank Barbie Zelizer, Mark Pedelty, and my longtime friend and collaborator, Bob Dardenne. Thanks also to the graduate students from anthropology and communication at the University of South Florida, who have taken my classes and found value in the melding of our two disciplines. Jennifer Hunsecker and Sue Regonini, both USF anthropology doctoral students, helped me compile the bibliography that emerged from all these chapters.

And as always, thanks to my husband, Graham Tobin, and my sons, Dan and Tom, for their love and support.

The Anthropology of News and Journalism

Introduction

The Anthropology of News and Journalism: Why Now?

S. ELIZABETH BIRD

After decades of interdisciplinary scholarship on news and journalism, is there anything new that anthropology can bring to the table? My colleagues and I seek to answer that question in this book. My hope is that it will speak not only to fellow anthropologists but also to our colleagues in communication and journalism studies who share our belief that to grasp the complexities of meaning construction in today's world, we need to explore the many ways in which "truth" is negotiated through news. And I also hope the essays in this book will speak to journalists themselves and to those who teach not only the profession of journalism but also how to reflect upon it.

So what is an anthropological perspective on news and journalism? Briefly put, it is a way to explore the nature of news as a form of cultural meaning making — its creation, content, and dissemination. The preferred method is ethnography, which has long been the cornerstone of anthropology, although now taken up enthusiastically by social scientists across disciplines. Wolcott (1999: 76) argues that, although ethnography is not in itself a clearly defined "method," a "central and unifying" principle of all ethnographic work is "a commitment to cultural interpretation" through a close, personal engagement with the people and phenomena studied. This is the perspective from which the authors in this book explore news and journalism, although their work shows how complex ethnography has become in a world where the local can no longer be understood without reference to the global. A further strength of anthropology is its commitment to see cultural phenomena comparatively, never assuming that "my way" is intrinsically more definitive than "your way." This global, comparative perspective is one of the key dimensions that anthropology can offer to journalism scholarship, which has tended to assume that "news is news," wherever we might find it. By seeing how news operates in specific and variable circumstances, these ethnographers problematize easy assumptions about what news means and does across cultures.

Journalism and the Anthropology of Media

Anthropologists who explore news and journalism are among the many who agree that to understand the contemporary world, we must grasp the role of media in constructing and maintaining that world. Our discipline came late to the field of media studies, but today the anthropology of media has come of age, as more anthropologists move away from bounded notions of local culture, necessitating consideration of global processes, such as the dynamic "mediascapes" defined almost 20 years ago by Appadurai (1990). Spitulnik's comment that there "is as yet no 'anthropology of mass media'" (1993: 293) has fortunately become outdated, as a growing body of literature has appeared (e.g., Askew and Wilk 2002; Ginsburg, Abu-Lughod, and Larkin 2002; Coman and Rothenbuhler 2005). Mark Peterson, in his fine analysis of the relationship between anthropology and mass communication, outlines the rise of an anthropology of media that is "theoretically eclectic, freely borrowing concepts and theoretical language from communication studies, British cultural studies, and literary criticism, as well as from theoretically sympathetic strands of social theory and political science" (2003: 56).

The impulse to study media comes out of an increasingly urgent sense that anthropology today can no longer dismiss media as external forces acting upon distinct "cultures," but rather that they are inextricably embedded in culture, reflecting and reshaping it in an ongoing process. For instance, in her introduction to her co-edited collection on anthropology and the media, Kelly Askew writes that "it is CNN, Hollywood, MTV, and other global media that now present and represent cultures to the majority of the world" (Askew and Wilk 2002: 1). And because it purports to describe reality, news is clearly a crucial force in representing and shaping public culture. Nevertheless, while acknowledging the global reach of CNN, internet news, and other forces, until recently few anthropologists explored *news* as a cultural phenomenon, focusing instead on entertainment media — TV, film, music, and so on. None of the essays in Askew and Wilk's collection nor in another recent volume (Ginsburg, Abu-Lughod, and Larkin 2002) address news or journalism except peripherally.

We now have a fairly extensive and sophisticated body of literature, emanating from inside and outside anthropology, on the reception of television programming cross-culturally, both in terms of non-Western cultures' readings of Western media and in terms of the importance of specifically local TV, film, music, and so on. Yet there remains a significant gap in the anthropological understanding of media, because we have neglected the role of news in constructing reality and the constitution of public culture. Zelizer (2004) in an influential call for the academy to "take journalism seriously" argues that although there is a significant body of scholarship that approaches journalism from a cultural perspective, the rise of cultural studies, with its overwhelming focus on entertainment media, has tended to marginalize the study of news as a cultural phenomenon. Anthropologists looking for theoretical guidance in media studies have tended to take their cue from cultural studies, rather than from the more quantitative approaches traditionally favored in journalism studies, and thus have focused primarily on entertainment media. To be sure, several anthropologists have produced important ethnographies of journalists, such as the groundbreaking studies of war and foreign correspondents by Pedelty (1995) and Hannerz (2004a), respectively, and of the press in Ghana by Hasty (2005). These ethnographies shed light on the daily routines of news making, broadening the field from such U.S.-based studies as those of Tuchman (1978), Gans (1979), Fishman (1980), and the UK-based studies of Schlesinger (1991) and Born (2005). They have explored the very notion of what "news" is in different cultural contexts, examining the strategies through which news is defined, created, and disseminated. As Zelizer (2004: 176) writes, "Cultural inquiry assumes that journalists employ collective, often tacit knowledge to become members of the group and maintain their membership over time ... yet presumes that what is explicit and articulated as that knowledge may not reflect the whole picture of what journalism is and tries to be." She points to the need to expand the global scope of news ethnographies, as we are attempting in this volume.

Less common have been anthropological contributions to both the textual content of news and the reception and circulation of news in everyday life. Outside anthropology and cultural studies there is a significant literature that either employs quantitative content analysis to reveal patterns in journalistic texts or uses sociological and psychological methods to study audience response to news. However, in many respects, these are precisely the kinds of approaches that cultural studies vehemently rejected, because they were seen as inadequate to capture the complexity of the way media texts actually circulate in the real world. Cultural studies explicitly rejected the traditional linear model of communication, which suggested a flow of information from producer, through text, to audience. As Johnson (1986) explained in a definitional article on cultural studies, a goal of the movement was to define this flow as much more complex, more accurately seen as circular rather than linear. In practice, studies that encompassed the range of producer, text, and audience are quite rare (my own 1992 study of U.S. supermarket tabloids being one attempt), but a cultural approach to media at the very least attempts to acknowledge and capture the fluidity with which media act within culture. As anthropology became more engaged with media studies, the emphases that seemed most compatible were ethnographies of production or reception and only occasionally analyses of content, although news and journalism received little attention at all. On the other hand, the academic study of news and journalism, as represented in such key journals as *Journalism and Mass Communication Quarterly,* focused heavily on quantitative content analyses and social scientific studies of audience response. Somehow the cultural turn in media studies did not connect well with the traditional field of journalism studies until quite recently (Zelizer 2004).

Anthropology and Journalism as Related Endeavors

Thus the neglect of journalism by ethnographers to some extent reflects these disciplinary methodological differences. However, I believe anthropologists have also shied away from the cultural study of journalism because in considering it, we necessarily find ourselves thinking about the sometimes uncomfortable parallels between ethnography and journalism as ways of describing and understanding reality. As Shankman (2001: 49) writes, journalism is often "suspect in academic circles"; peer reviewers are known to dismiss ethnographies they dislike as "journalistic," meaning they are superficial or glib. Journalists, meanwhile, take pride in their ability to tell the story accurately and engagingly in a very short time, observing that anthropologists may take months or years to do their "reporting," and then write their "stories" in dense and impenetrable style. Nevertheless, we all know that ethnographers and journalists are both in the business of gathering information about people and constructing narratives about what they learn for an audience. In cultural anthropology, descriptive and interpretive approaches have always been at the core, epitomized in the ethnographic method, through which a "thick description" of culture is attempted, with the goal to see "from the native's point of view." These days, anthropologists recognize that ethnographic methods, developed to achieve a complete picture of small, isolated societies, must be adapted to the realities of a globally interconnected world, with ethnographers developing many new techniques, often resembling journalistic methods, and applying them in familiar societies (see e.g., Abu-Lughod 2000; Marcus 1998). Meanwhile many forms of journalism, known variously as "cultural," "new," or "public" journalism, can look very much like ethnography. Today there are many books that began life as journalistic accounts. Is a book like Dennis Covington's *Salvation on Sand Mountain: Snake-Handling and Redemption in Southern Appalachia* (1996) a work of journalism or ethnography? The line is not clear; nevertheless, anthropologists tend to take a "holier-than-thou" stance toward journalists, as Jennifer Hasty discusses in this volume.

So it is perhaps risky for anthropologists to venture into the "field" of journalism and news making and claim to offer insights about what journalism is and does. As a profession, anthropologists have not taken well to being "studied" by journalists, as the uproar over Patrick Tierney's book *Darkness in El Dorado* suggests (2000). While many of Tierney's accusations about the conduct of anthropologists working with the Yanomami people in the Amazon proved unfounded, he also offered a serious critique of some ethnographic practices (Borofsky 2005). If we wish to create an "anthropology of journalism," we should be prepared to engage with a "journalism of anthropology" in return.

This is not to say that the two professions are the same (see Bird 2005a). They have different missions, and they work in different environments and under different constraints, as Awad (2006) suggests in her discussion of both the intersections and divergences of ethical expectations in both fields. Journalists traditionally do not owe their allegiances to their "sources," as anthropologists do; they have the added burden of the public's "right to know." For journalists, developing rapport with people they cover is generally to be avoided, as hindering their ideal of objectivity. Anthropologists never quite settle on whether to be a "stranger or friend," needing a little of both. Yet the goals of anthropology and journalism are enough alike that some mutual appreciation is surely desirable. I hope this collection is a step in bringing the fields together with mutual respect.

Production, Content, and Reception: Anthropological Contributions and Absences

The most established tradition in the nascent field we call "anthropology of news and journalism" involves the ethnography of journalists, partly driven by an awareness that ethnography and journalism are related enterprises. Although media reception is now quite frequently on anthropologists' agendas, very few have tackled the reception of *news*. The essays in part 2 of this volume begin to address that gap. Even fewer anthropologists have explored the *content* of news, and before introducing this volume's authors and their work, I would like briefly to explore why I believe it would be worthwhile for more ethnographers to do so. Although the relative neglect of media content by anthropologists is understandable, a cautious return to the textual study of news is potentially valuable. Today we live in a mediated world; much of what cultures "know" about each other is learned from media, with news being a key conduit. News is unique among media forms in that it purports to be (and is often received as) an accurate reflection of reality, even though we know that news is a cultural construction that draws on narrative conventions and routine practices.

As Peterson (2003) shows, there actually was a fledgling "anthropology of media" movement in the mid-twentieth century, and one of its elements was an interest in using media texts as a way to "decode" cultural values. His overview shows that anthropologists studied commercial movies, other media such as soap operas, and (occasionally) journalistic texts. Perhaps most famous was the mid-twentieth-century "culture at a distance" approach, used in an attempt to understand societies that could not easily be studied ethnographically, such as Benedict's famous study of Japan, in which she used Japanese films, books, and other texts as cultural indicators (Benedict 1946). Such approaches meshed well with an interest in the "texts" of oral cultures, such as myths and folktales, drawing particularly from the field of folklore studies, which has a heavy literary influence. Later, as Peterson points out, such textually based approaches fell out of favor in anthropology, with occasional exceptions, such as Drummond's 1996 analyses of blockbuster movies as cultural "dreams." One reason for this was a decline of interest in the nation as a useful cultural unit, as well as a growing awareness that texts of this kind are likely to represent the values of those in power rather than "ordinary" people. In addition, anthropologists in the second half of the century were eager to shed vestiges of the "armchair anthropology" of earlier times, in which often decontextualized texts could serve as surrogates for ethnographic observation and study. Firsthand engagement with everyday life, always a hallmark of anthropology, became of primary importance; as Gupta and Ferguson (1997a) suggest, being "in the field" was the gold standard for real anthropology. Then in media studies, the rise of qualitative analyses of media audiences in the 1980s, often drawing on ethnographic models, also downplayed the importance of the text, focusing increasingly on creative audience responses (see Alasuutari 1999 for overview of audience studies).

However, as Zelizer (2004) discusses, in the United States there did arise a significant movement within journalism studies, inspired largely by the work of James W. Carey, who had argued for the role of news as a symbolic system that helped make meaning in culture, drawing heavily on the symbolic anthropology of Geertz (1973, 1983). The work of Carey and his followers advocated a culturally contextualized approach to news, while focusing primarily on qualitative interpretation of text, rather than on traditional content analysis or ethnographic studies of reception. A key theme in such work has been a reconceptualizing of news as a form of cultural storytelling (Bird and Dardenne 1988, 2008). Zelizer (2004: 181) provides a comprehensive assessment of the body of scholarship in this area through the 1980s and 1990s; current representative work of this kind includes several studies by Kitch (2000, 2003), whose work focuses on the role of news in defining shared cultural narratives, such as national mourning. Much work in this tradition explicitly draws on the analysis of themes in the myths and legends of oral cultures, something once common in traditional anthropological work but less relevant today, for obvious reasons. Perhaps the most extended use of the myth analogy is Jack Lule's (2001) work on the mythical themes discernible in the *New York Times*. Lule shows how "objective" news stories are framed and constructed around themes like "the victim," the "hero," and so on. I argue elsewhere (Bird and Dardenne 2008) that the problem with such approaches (most apparent in the work of Lule, who relies very heavily on Jungian archetypal theory rather than the more ethnographically sound approaches of symbolic anthropology) is that they can easily fall into the trap of invoking supposed archetypal themes, while ignoring real cultural context — why these themes, these stories in this specific culture? This, I believe, is one of the areas in which anthropologists might make a contribution. One of our central goals has been to "translate" cultures, and the stories told in news can tell us a great deal about specific cultural circumstances.

So it is perhaps ironic that interpretive textual analysis, the area of journalism studies that most explicitly invokes anthropology, is the approach that anthropologists have largely eschewed. Most of the authors in this book do not use textual analysis as a significant tool in understanding news; rather, they focus on how texts come to be and how they circulate. My own work (Bird 2003) has also predominantly focused on the circulation of meaning among audiences, although I have ventured into textual interpretation. Nevertheless, I believe anthropologists might profitably address more attention to texts, in addition to production and reception.

Finnish media scholar Alasuutari (1995) discusses how during the 1994 elections in Finland, a TV station asked people in the street what they thought about the public images of the presidential candidates, focusing on the question "Have the media influenced your images of the candidates?" Most of us are familiar with that kind of question, and with the usual responses, as people assert that they make up their own minds about such things and are not influenced by media (although, of course, "other people" often are). As Alasuutari points out, "None of the interviewees nor the journalists pointed out how absurd the question actually was. Hardly any ordinary citizen would have any means to form an image of the candidates *outside* or irrespective of the media. Still the interviewees were able to regard it as a basically sensible question" (89). The larger point here transcends political campaigns. People typically deny media influence — and, of course, the media do not have a simple predictable "effect." But media, especially news media, do have enormous power to shape the reality experienced by readers and viewers. As Philo (2008) argues, audiences, however active, cannot make an infinite number of meanings from the texts they are given.

For anthropologists, this is clearly significant. More anthropologists than ever are working in communities in their own countries, often on pressing social issues such as poverty, health disparities, education, and disasters. All these issues are defined by media; news does not merely report "the facts," but actively shapes reality into acceptable stories. To fully understand such issues, surely any anthropologist (even those primarily conducting more traditional, local ethnographies) should have an idea of how these issues are framed by the news media? Yet while it is quite common for anthropologists to use newspaper archives to trace local events and histories, it is much less common for them to do systematic media content analysis to develop a picture of the dominant "stories" that shape everyday reality.

Similarly, anthropologists working abroad are finding it increasingly valuable to explore not only how local and national media in their study countries frame events, but also how those nations' affairs are represented in international media. The inclusion of media content analysis, while still relatively rare, has become increasingly visible in the context of the multisited ethnographies that are becoming the norm. Anthropologists like Abu-Lughod (2000) have written about the need to add media analysis to their methodological toolkit in order to understand national and international processes. Edwards (1994) writes that traditional ethnography did not seem adequate to grasp the situation of people he worked with in Afghanistan. To produce a more multifaceted picture, he combines traditional "field" accounts with discussion of news narratives both from and about the country, as well as virtual ethnography of the internet communication among displaced Afghanis, all in an attempt to put the actual experiences of his field participants into their global context.

So, in addition to asking how journalists make news, and how people use news, an important question is: What are the stories that people in any given society are being offered as tools to make meaning? Occasionally, anthropologists have touched on these questions. Kottak (1990), for example, contrasts national television news in Brazil with news in the United States. He shows how both focus on civics, the nation-state, and international affairs, but that the balance is different. Furthermore, he points to a particular theme in Brazilian news — stories about the United States that focus on some (often unwelcome) aspect of technology in U.S. society, such as reproductive technologies. He argues that this theme confirms for Brazilians "the stereotype of American society as developed but flawed. . . . American culture sometimes carries its . . . inventiveness to inhumane extremes. Such stories appeal to Brazilians because they suggest that power, influence, and technology are insufficient to warrant full international respect" (92).

Kottak's admittedly cursory look at Brazilian news thus identifies themes, but he does not go on to ask why, for example, stories about U.S. technology are structured in this way and what that might tell us about Brazilian worldviews and senses of cultural identity. This area is ripe for deeper anthropological analysis — how are particular topics turned into stories, framed in culturally specific ways? Some very useful anthropological work has begun to appear in this area. For example, Peterson (2007), well known for his ethnographic work on both journalists and news reception, has also offered close readings of specific news texts, such as Danish news coverage of Islam in the wake of the 2005 publication of cartoons that depicted the prophet Muhammad and caused outrage in many Muslim countries. He concludes:

> The point here is that through these textual operations, a particular perspective is overcoded. Readers are invited to see the events following the publication of the cartoons as a single global event in which rational Western actors engaged in a democratic practice are met with a hostile global response by undifferentiated "Muslims" whose protests are not characterized as forms of democratic expression but as irrational actions. (2007: 254)

Peterson does not claim that all members of the Danish news audience necessarily see events exactly like this. This is not a return to the overly simplistic view that there is one unproblematic "national character." Rather, the particular framing "invites" audiences to take this view — a much more subtle position. Similarly, Briggs (2007) offers an analysis of Venezuelan press coverage of infanticide, practiced by desperate people in poverty. He explains that this analysis is part of a much larger ethnographic project, during which he realized that in order to understand public and official attitudes to the issue, it was essential that he learn how it was framed in the news media, which were the source of everyone's information. He concludes,

> As each infanticide story transformed a few broken bodies into national discourses on social bodies (especially of poor communities) and the body politic . . . press coverage offered elites a chance to confirm their sense that the poor in general partook in the brutality, irrational, and subhuman qualities of monster mothers and fathers at the same time that working-class citizens could attempt to distance themselves from the images and accusations and enter the space of the good citizen — to which they enjoyed so little access — by creating (for reporters), revoicing, and identifying themselves with the vox populi. (2007: 337–38)

Too often, I think the discussion of news content gets bogged down in wondering what is the "real truth" about a particular event, a question that seems to suggest that journalists really could be completely objective recorders of mere facts, if only, somehow, they could get it right. More interesting, I think, is the question of which story is being told about any event. Why one story over another, and how does the story then become part of the commonsense reality in specific cultural contexts? Most of us, for instance, are very aware that the story of the Iraq war is deeply contested. We can scour the internet and find accounts of events that differ radically. If we have time (a lot of it!) we might sit down, sift through it all, and reach some kind of conclusion about the "truth." Most people in most societies don't have the time or the resources to do that — they have little choice but to engage with the stories that predominate in their daily experiences. And, of course, it is not just the information but the language, the choice of words, the images — the entire frame of the news coverage. For instance, the U.S. press, in the early years of the Iraq war, presented a "sanitized" view, "free of bloodshed, dissent, and diplomacy, but full of exciting weaponry, splashy graphics, and heroic soldiers" (Aday, Livingston, and Hebert 2005: 18). In other countries, even in nations that ostensibly supported the war, "the story" was framed differently. Ravi (2005), for example, compared news coverage in the United States, United Kingdom, India, and Pakistan, concluding that "newspaper coverage seems to reflect notions, values, and ideas that resonate within particular societies" (2005: 59), a point echoed by Dimitrova and Strömbäck (2005), comparing Sweden and the United States. While we cannot know for sure how real audiences were affected by the differences, any anthropologist studying on the ground would do well to know the dominant frames of reference for such events. The texts themselves hold important, symbolic meaning and constitute significant cultural narratives, as Postill (2006) suggests in his study of the media's role in framing Malaysia as a nation, allowing the Iban to "become" Malaysian.

Postill's work, like that of Peterson and Briggs, does not rely on textual analysis alone, but incorporates such analysis into larger ethnographic studies. This, I believe, is where anthropologists can make significant contributions. Linguistic anthropologists have already applied techniques of discourse analysis to media texts (e.g., Cotter 2001). And their unique perspective, in contrast to that of many literary-trained analysts, is their realization that texts must be interpreted in the context of their creation and reception. This point is made forcefully by Schroder (2007), who points out the decontextualized nature of much media discourse analysis, and argues the need for genuine ethnographic work to test and elaborate on the textual interpretations. Richardson, speaking specifically about journalism, makes a similar point, arguing that "journalistic discourses are always socially situated, therefore analyzing them requires more than a list of text-linguistic concepts" (2008: 153). He goes on to write that the complex context of journalistic texts remains the least developed aspect of the growing study of language and journalism. And as Gürsel reminds us in this volume, the "story" is more than just words; perhaps now more than ever, reality is constructed through images. So far, visual anthropologists, many of whose interests include the analysis of ethnographic images, have paid little attention to news photographs; this is an area ripe for anthropological interpretation.

From this brief overview, it should be apparent that there is indeed value in analyzing the content of journalistic texts, and that anthropologists, with their sensitivity to context and larger connections, are poised to join media studies scholars and interdisciplinary discourse analysts in interpreting the power of news stories to shape reality.

Nevertheless, textual analysis alone cannot tell us everything we need to know, as several decades of qualitative audience research has clearly shown. We cannot study a text, read off its meaning, and conclude that audiences will react in predictable ways. Texts do carry dominant meanings — news sets the agenda. But in everyday life, readers and viewers interact with those texts in a multitude of ways. Yet when it comes to news, especially news in cultures other than the West, we know very little about how the narratives of journalism actually enter daily life and consciousness, and that's where I believe we need some detailed ethnographic work. Kottak confidently says that the stories of U.S. technology "appeal to Brazilians," but do we really know that? Do Brazilians talk about these issues, and if so, in what context? Similarly, I might argue that for British people, in contrast to Americans, the Iraq war was framed more in terms of civilian tragedies than military success, because that is how the media framed it. But is that really translated into everyday perceptions and action?

As I have discussed, most ethnographic audience analyses have focused on specific media genres, and in part that is because it is relatively easier to do it that way. Anthropologists can frame observation and interviews around TV shows, as Miller (1992) has done with the reception of U.S. soap operas in the West Indies, or Mankekar (1999) with Indian viewers of native programming, showing how audiences use these texts to interrogate everything from gender roles to ethnic identity. An early pioneer in this field was Eric Michaels, whose important work on responses of Australian aboriginal audiences is collected in Michaels, Langton, and Hebdige (1994). News is harder to handle: it is received sporadically and is not even defined precisely. In a small project I did on audience reception and understandings of news in the United States (reported in Bird 1998, 2003), I found there was not even agreement on what news is. For some people, news includes talk shows, late-night comedians, parody news shows, or reality TV, while for others it is confined to "straight news" and does not even encompass magazine shows like *60 Minutes*. As Pedelty and others argue in this volume, "news" may flow through channels far outside journalism as such. I am sure that in other cultures, notions of what constitute news are likely as varied, but perhaps in different ways.

However, my clearest conclusion was that culturally, news is not really even about text — it is about process. In my study, I invited readers and viewers to talk, in a kind of contrived natural setting, about the news. People found it very difficult to talk about specific texts in detail, but rather used the texts to frame a "story" that emerged in conversation. As we work to make sense of news, we involve others in the negotiation of meaning. Explaining this process, a participant said, "When you watch by yourself, a lot of times you have ideas that you have unsolved because you can't converse with other individuals." Another agreed: "It helps others in the community feel a part of the news world. The community or the listeners get to contribute to the story and make the news effective and be part of the results." The rise of the internet and its multiple forums for such sharing has greatly expanded and complicated this process, of course.

Thus the cultural significance of news emerges through everyday interaction, and people pay attention to news very selectively. In my 2003 study, I found that some news stories were especially significant because they spoke to people of different demographics in different ways. In an analysis of online discussion of a story about revelations that the Rev. Jesse Jackson had fathered an illegitimate daughter, I concluded that the story was used not as a "text" with a clear meaning but as an opportunity to interrogate issues, from morality, to religion, to race. People do not evaluate news stories in isolation but incorporate them into their already established worldviews. Participants' gender, nationality, ethnicity, and life experiences all play a role in reception, showing that textual analysis alone cannot reveal the complexity with which news stories are received. These observations are in line with the direction of much recent media audience scholarship, as the emphasis has moved from a direct text/response focus to an interest in audience practices — for instance, how people talk about media, how they organize activities around media, or how they use media images to provide "scripts" for behavior (see Bird forthcoming). This kind of approach is intrinsically anthropological, with its emphasis on connections and the teasing out of a subtle relationship between text and audience that has little to do with cause and effect. In anthropology, it is perhaps best exemplified in the work of Abu-Lughod (2004). Hobart, for example, describes his realization that in order to understand the role of media in Balinese life, he needed to explore practices that "only partly overlap with direct engagement in the medium (reading the newspapers, watching the box) and have as much to do with anticipating, chatting about, criticizing, understanding, and so on. Such practices also include Balinese commenting on their own practices" (Hobart 1999b: 12). The embrace by anthropologists of this approach is demonstrated in a collection (Postill and Bräuchler forthcoming) that brings together several anthropological discussions of media practices. Even this collection, however, pays scant attention to practices around news; the few current qualitative studies of news reception have come from communication and cultural studies (e.g., Martin 2008) and focus almost exclusively on Western contexts. Here is where the contributions in this volume are especially important.

Thus my hope is that more anthropologists will become involved in cultural studies of news, inserting a comparative perspective that is sorely lacking. We need detailed, ethnographic studies of how news is received in specific cultural circumstances, and we also need a better understanding of what news is, and is perceived to be, across cultural contexts whose circumstances may be very different. Some critics suggest that in contemporary U.S. society, journalism's increasing triviality is transforming us from informed citizens into distracted consumers, while others argue that technology now offers an alternative route to citizenship in an affluent "wired" society. We know little about how news circulates in non-Western cultures, where local political, social, and economic realities will be reflected in very different ways, changing the relative importance of media such as newspapers, TV, radio, and the internet.

About a decade ago, I participated in an international colloquium on the phenomenon of "tabloidization." As the event began, many of us thought we understood the subject we were gathered to discuss. Most of us from Britain and the United States held some kind of notion that "tabloidization" was a negative process that was "dumbing down" journalism and discouraging rational discourse. However, we also learned that in some contexts, such as Mexico and the former Eastern bloc, apparently similar trends in journalism — a loosening of controls, snappier, more accessible writing, concern about engaging the reader — were acting as positive forces for social change and democratic participation (see Sparks and Tulloch 2000). By the end of three days, the meaning and the implications of "tabloidization" were no longer so clear. The lesson is that to understand the meaning of news, we must understand context; journalism emerges from and responds to cultural specificities. Even in two societies as apparently similar as Britain and the United States, we do not always appreciate this.

Thus questions I and others have explored in the West may seem important here but may be completely irrelevant elsewhere. Here, we tend to forget that while we worry about the effects of addiction to computers and a surfeit of information, millions of people worldwide cannot even communicate by telephone. In a country where we agonize about political apathy, low voter turnout, and the role of journalists in changing this, we forget about nations where people put themselves at risk for the right to vote or to read uncensored news.

There is a world of difference between a news audience thirsty for information and one saturated with it. Journalism has multiple meanings in many contexts. My hope is that more anthropologists will start joining colleagues across the disciplines in this comparative exploration. This enterprise should include analyses of particular texts, because these texts clearly set the agenda for discussion. But it should also continue to explore the creation of news through ethnography and the meaning of news in everyday life, while somehow holding these together and demonstrating their connections.

The Anthropology of News and Journalism: The Book

This volume is thus unified by a focus on cultural context, a concern with how meaning is created and circulated, and a commitment to understand the real implications of this in a global setting. In a broader sense, we are debating how "truth" is defined and contested in a world where control over information determines who holds power, whether at the local or national level. The study of news and journalism is inherently multidisciplinary, approached from fields as diverse as quantitative sociology, communications, history, linguistics, semiotics, and various branches of psychology. All ask different questions, and sometimes they do not intersect well with each other. An anthropological (or cultural) approach to journalism sees news as embedded in everyday practices. It may focus on the way real people — professional journalists or newsmakers in the broadest sense — are able to turn events into stories. Do they act as autonomous agents or as actors constrained by an ideological system? Or both? It may also explore how news circulates and is received, as stories take on new meanings in the telling. Or it may focus on news narratives and a discussion of what meanings come to dominate in particular settings. And perhaps more than other scholars of news, anthropologists are open to see news as a process that operates in forms outside the traditional definitions of journalism.

The essays collected here are all published for the first time, and they represent some of the most established scholars in the area, as well as newer researchers whose work is pushing scholarship in exciting new directions. Most identify as anthropologists; others come from communications and cultural studies. The essays were selected to represent a range of geographical locations, taking the reader out of the familiar comfort zone of journalism as it operates in the United States and Europe. Many of the authors reflect at some level on how their role as ethnographer is both similar to and different from that of the journalist.

We begin with chapters that primarily address the production of news (although the reader will quickly recognize that several chapters could comfortably move between sections). How are events turned into news, and how does this news move into cultural circulation? Karin Wahl-Jorgensen sets the scene; a communications researcher whose methods are strongly ethnographic, she offers a cogent critique of what she calls "newsroom-centricity." She points out that while there now exists extensive scholarship using ethnographic approaches to journalism, most scholarship addresses the "workplace" — that is, the newsroom of often large and elite news operations. She argues that this focus on elite journalistic communities, working in very organized environments, tends to erase the more diffuse work done in local news, alternative media, non-Western countries with fewer resources, and the new virtual environment. She suggests that anthropologists, espousing a multisited, multi-method approach to "the field" and more disciplinary tolerance for extended fieldwork, are perfectly positioned to fill these major gaps in our knowledge.

Some of the following chapters do retain a focus on the newsroom, with productive results, while others take up the challenge to explore journalism in a more unconventional setting. The chapters by Zeynep Gürsel and Amahl Bishara both address how international news about the infamous Israeli-constructed barrier came to be created. Gürsel focuses on the negotiations at a U.S. news magazine about which of the available stories and photos will appear in print and thus will help define the issues for U.S. audiences. Bishara discusses the strategies used by Palestinians and others to gain international news coverage of their issues; this dimension of news construction represents a continuing struggle to be noticed by journalists and thus get on the news agenda. Both expose the "commonsense" fallacy that news is a given — that events somehow move from "out there" to print in a clear, organized fashion. Rather, news emerges from a constant struggle over who is permitted to define the reality of the barrier and the lives of the people it impacts. And while the focus here is the story, the photos, and the people who make and select them, the audience is also ever-present, as an imagined target. By the time the stories and photos reach the audience, they will be shaped in predictable ways that take into account the anticipated worldview of that audience, thus helping to both represent and reinforce that worldview in a continuing, circular process.

Our next two chapters move the discussion onto the working of journalism's professional ideologies in specific circumstances. Manzella and Yacher use the context of Hugo Chávez's Venezuela to explore how a community of journalists negotiates the very meaning of journalism in a politically constrained environment. While often expressing a commitment to a North American ideal of an unfettered, "objective" press, many are also torn in terms of their duty to support the government (as, of course, are many of their North American and European colleagues in times of crisis). Schwenkel's field is far from the conventional newsroom, but also addresses the journalistic norms and values of Vietnamese press photographers during the U.S. war in Vietnam, as recalled through ethnographic interviewing. She argues that they clearly saw their role not as impartial observers but as active participants in a patriotic war. At the same time, her work problematizes the easy Western depictions of a repressed press under socialist conditions. Both chapters remind us that journalists form particular "interpretive communities" (Zelizer 1993) in specific environments.

Ursula Rao's chapter takes us to India to explore how events become news in a distinctive context — the local native language press. Rao shows how different this model of journalism is from the more elite English language press, which works within a Western paradigm. Here, the press is the focus of continuous jockeying for position among local interests, as news is created from locally generated texts. Here, as Wahl-Jorgenson has suggested, we see a much more theoretically "messy" form of news gathering, where distinctions between journalist, audience, and newsmaker do not fit the conventions.

Jonathan Skinner's chapter is the most textually based study in the volume, analyzing British press coverage of the disastrous volcanic eruption on the island of Montserrat. He shows how journalists in the distinctly partisan context of the UK worked to frame this "international" story as primarily a political problem for the British government, in contrast to its coverage in the U.S. magazine *National Geographic.*

Part 1 concludes with a provocative essay about the relationship of journalism and anthropology by one of the pioneers in the ethnographic study of journalism in a non-Western setting, Jennifer Hasty. Against the backdrop of her extensive fieldwork in Ghana, Hasty interrogates the parallels between doing ethnography and doing journalism, taking the discussion in fascinating new directions. In particular, she examines why anthropologists, with their traditional affinity for the powerless, have preferred not to engage closely with the world of journalism and its uncomfortable but unavoidable accommodations with those in power.

The focus of the second part is on how news is circulated and received. First, Kerry McCallum, from a communications background, uses a form of discourse analysis to look at how news on indigenous affairs is received by Australians. She shows that a rich reading of textual framing is necessary, but incomplete without an equally careful reading of the frames employed by news audiences. Her subtle approach shows how media frames are understood but transformed and added to by the everyday talk of people who are both media audiences and members of their own discursive communities. Next, Mark Peterson analyzes news-related practices in urban Delhi. He shows how much can be learned by moving almost completely away from news texts themselves and into the lives of people in the community. Here, the emphasis is not so much on what people read but on what it means to attend to particular news genres over others, and how news reading fits into one's daily routine. In so doing, we learn a great deal about how dominant meanings are circulated and the interrelationship of news, politics, class, caste, and many more facets of urban life.

The next three authors offer studies of how news "works" in three very different cultural settings. Essentially, all problematize traditional definitions of what news really is, rooted as they are in mainstream elite journalism. Debra Spitulnik takes us to Zambia, her long-term field site, where, rather like Rao, she explores the complexity of what "news" really is in a radio environment where "urgent private announcements" about funerals and other events have traditionally been a major part of the news landscape. Do people wanting to make these announcements constitute news makers or news audiences, or are they advertisers who should be expected to pay for airtime? How (if at all) is the circulation of such personal news connected to the news of the elite that we associate with journalism? This context is clearly far from traditional notions of journalistic professionalism and news objectivity; indeed, many of the terms that are central to standard discussions of news are simply not relevant here.

Next, Dorle Dracklé's discussion of the intersection of gossip, local, and national news in Portugal also subverts traditional distinctions about news production, dissemination, and reception. She looks at "media amateurs" who take up from the traditional circulation of news and gossip in the town square, describing a complicated public sphere to which is now added the world of blogs and other virtual news outlets, an area explored in more detail in part 3. Finally, Mark Pedelty takes us almost completely out of the realm of "news" as traditionally conceived. In his discussion of the circulation of political information through music, he reminds us of the messy origins of news in folklore, ballads, and broadsheets, before professional journalism came to define scholarly definitions of news.

Pedelty's piece leads nicely into part 3, which explores the transformations of news in a new digital media environment, whether in Germany or the United States. Dominic Boyer and Maria Vesperi both address newsrooms of traditional news organizations, where journalists are finding that old routines are radically different, as they are bombarded with digital information, often assembling stories rather than writing them. Meanwhile, the audience for traditional news is eroding, and newspapers are having to develop ways to compete with bloggers and self-defined internet journalists. It is hardly surprising that many Western journalists (and journalism scholars) perceive the entire field as being in crisis: some see the new news environment as threatening the very basis of journalism (Henry 2007), with the proliferation of cable TV, the internet, cell phones, citizens' news sites, and alternative and independent (indy) news sources transforming the media landscape.

Finally, Adrienne Russell presents a case study that suggests the potential of online journalism that actually embraces this new environment—the rise of Salon.com. Contrary to predictions that the digital environment signals the end of intelligent analysis, her work suggests that it can actually foster thoughtful journalism, if the online publication can create and "brand" a type of news that reaches a loyal audience, although perhaps one that is smaller than the "masses" once reached through traditional news. Russell discusses the delicate balance between encouraging audience participation and production and maintaining the authority of Salon's journalists as professionals.

THE TIME IS RIGHT for more anthropologists to participate in the systematic analysis of the role of news in culture, and this volume is offered as a way to bring together many of those active in that endeavor. It is not that scholars in other disciplines have ignored the cultural dimensions of news; a significant body of work exists. But as Curran and Park suggest, much of this has been "self-absorbed and parochial" (2000: 3), assuming that theories about the role of journalism and news in the West (primarily the United States and Great Britain) can be unproblematically applied in a non-Western setting. Anthropologists may be able to prove this is not the case. As Boyer notes in this volume, anthropologists are often parochial, too. Many are now discovering media, and they may not always understand how many of their exciting questions have already been explored by media and journalism scholars. As newcomers, we should remain humble and acknowledge the work that has gone before. However, the study of news and journalism is an inherently interdisciplinary enterprise, and we should not be reluctant to participate. In today's world, as Appadurai (1990) argued, anthropologists must acknowledge and engage the global "mediascape." News may help to empower and transform—or to oppress and obfuscate. Either way, news and journalism play a significant role in the construction and maintenance of culture at the local and global levels, and anthropologists have a place in interpreting that role.

PART ONE

ETHNOGRAPHY OF NEWS PRODUCTION

1

News Production, Ethnography, and Power

On the Challenges of Newsroom-Centricity

KARIN WAHL-JORGENSEN

Since the 1970s, ethnographic research has contributed tremendously to knowledge about news production processes and newsroom cultures, providing a rich description of journalists' ways of life and work. Ethnographers of news production have charted the cultures of newsrooms and the production processes unfolding within them, and shed light on the routines, values, and professional practices of journalists.

As Born (2005: 15) observed, in studies of media and beyond, ethnographic fieldwork has been "a sharp tool for discerning not just the unifying features but the divisions, boundaries, and conflicts of the society being studied." On the one hand, it has highlighted the ways in which journalists can constitute "interpretive communities" (Zelizer 1993) central to the creation of a form of news culture (Allan 2004). Ethnographers of news production have suggested that journalists of all stripes share certain cultural orientations and experiences. Harrison (2000: 108–37), in her work on television newsrooms, found similarities across news organizations in a set of "formulas, practices, normative values, and journalistic methodology." Others have pointed to the ideal of objectivity (Soloski 1999), the thrill of the deadline, a disregard for authority, and a genuine desire to serve the public as unifying features (e.g., Cottle 2003: 15). On the other hand, news organizations are shaped by complex professional hierarchies, structures, and power relations that challenge any claims of unity (cf. Tunstall 2001), and these diversities and cleavages have been thoroughly mapped by news production ethnographers. As Cottle (2007) pointed out, the ethnography of news production has provided an invaluable corrective to a slew of generalizations that have circulated in media and journalism studies, including

(1) *instrumental* arguments about elite control over news media and output, (2) *media conspiracy* claims involving media complicity, (3) *social compositional* accounts of media performance based on the demographic

characteristics of journalist recruitment, (3) political economy arguments about how the news is shaped and limited by market forces, (4) cultural studies theorization of the discourses and identities embedded into news texts, as well as (5) postmodernist speculation about the implosion of meaning via mediated spectacle. (Cottle 2007: 1)

By offering scholars more nuanced descriptions of the forces that shape journalism, the ethnography of news production has thus complicated our accounts and cautioned against easy generalizations, contributing to a more rigorous field of scholarship. Indeed, it remains one of the most fruitful avenues for obtaining a nuanced understanding of both journalism and journalists.

However, the news production ethnography tradition has evolved under a specific set of constraints and circumstances, which means that it has emphasized particular production practices and environments over others. This chapter looks at the consequences of a key methodological feature in the ethnography of news production: its reliance on the locality of the newsroom, or its "newsroom-centricity." Put slightly differently, most anthropological work on news production has revolved around the material space of the newsroom, the "factory floor" of journalism. This chapter demonstrates some of the consequences of newsroom-centricity. In particular, the concrete trajectory of this research tradition has resulted in an emphasis on certain types and categories of news work, coinciding with convenient and prestigious locations for ethnographic observations. The chapter ultimately suggests that we ought to be reflexive about the power relations that shape our approaches and paradigms as newsroom ethnographers.

A Brief History of Newsroom-Centricity

The ethnography of news production has always been an interdisciplinary endeavor, situated at the intersection of media and journalism studies, anthropology, and the sociology of work. In common with the disciplines of anthropology and sociology from which it has taken both inspiration and key figures, it draws heavily on ethnographic methods (Abbott 1993; Lounsbury and Kaghan 2001), but it also departs from ethnographic preoccupations in significant ways. Here, I would like to chart some of these affinities and departures and their consequences for the production of knowledge about the work of journalists.

Like other ethnographic research endeavors, the anthropology of news production has been structured by a particular methodological presumption: that we can capture the object of study by focusing on particular discrete sites or "fields." Like other field sciences, anthropology engages in the "detailed study of limited areas" (Gupta and Ferguson 1997a: 6), on the basis that such an approach can give us meaningful information about the practices of particular "tribes" living and working in these limited areas. Such an approach is clearly not without its problems, associated with the assumption that "different cultures inhere in discrete and separate places" (Gupta and Ferguson 1997a: 35). Ever since the reflexive turn of the 1970s, ethnographers have debated, and reflected upon, such problematic aspects of their approach. Despite this reflexivity, it remains an inescapable methodological fact that ethnographers cannot do their work without material "anthropological locations." Ethnographies require the construction of a "field" that is defined as exotic and strange when juxtaposed with the comfort and familiarity of "home." As Gupta and Ferguson (1997a: 5) observe, the field is an overdetermined setting for the discovery of difference, involving a conceptual segmentation of the world into particular cultures, areas, and sites. In the case of the ethnography of news production, scholars have tended to focus on journalists' culture as it emerges within the limited areas of newsrooms and other centralized sites for news production, usually paying scant attention to spaces, places, practices, and people at the margins of this spatially delimited news production universe.

There are sound reasons for the focus on the newsroom, which I here refer to as "newsroom-centricity." The newsroom is the most obvious place to seek out cultures of journalism because news production, as a professional practice, has been centralized and concentrated there. As Nerone and Barnhurst (2003: 435) observed:

> Communication scholars understand the press as an institution that originates its most significant activity in the space of the newsroom. Ethnographic studies of newspapers begin there, of course, but content studies also focus on newsroom output, and even audience studies track responses to what emerges from the newsroom. The newsroom thus receives scrutiny as a work zone that leaves its tracks in the form and content of newspapers and in the conditions of reception for the audience.

Indeed, the history of the newsroom is closely tied to the history of journalism itself. The invention of the newsroom coincided with the emergence of a professionalized and commercially viable press that was fiercely competitive and reliant on advertising (Tuchman 1978: 19). As such, the newsroom was born alongside the idea of a professional culture with distinct work practices. In North American and European contexts, this development occurred over a relatively short period in the late nineteenth and early twentieth centuries. Høyer's study of the emergence of newsrooms in Scandinavia provides a compelling description of the news production routines at *Morgenbladet,* the most influential early Norwegian newspaper, at the end of the 1850s. *Morgenbladet* had one newsroom, which was primarily occupied by subscriptions and printing personnel. The editor had a desk in a small back room, but "conducted most of his business walking about the town, wearing his top hat, between the library, government office, the university, the parliament, and the offices of lawyers and doctors, or he received visitors at home. He stored all the collected manuscripts in his top hat and unloaded them in the composing room" (Høyer 2003: 457). Although many of the sites and individuals that were then deemed newsworthy remain part of today's "news net" (Tuchman 1978), the formalization of physical location for the organization of news gathering did not occur until later in the nineteenth century.

By this time, European and American newspapers had begun to organize their production processes within the physical space of the newsroom, in arrangements that were fairly similar to those prevailing in today's media organizations. Wilke's study of the development of the German newsroom demonstrates that while, in the early 1800s, the printing houses that owned newspapers started to dedicate space to editorial activities, it took until the end of the century before a more extensive, functionally specialized area had been introduced. Here, the term *newsroom* is shown to be profoundly misleading, insofar as it is usually not taken to mean just *one* room devoted to news production but several distinct spaces — usually (both historically and in the contemporary context) in the form of open-plan offices. For example, by 1906, the newsroom of the *Münchner Neueste Nachrichten* had rooms dedicated to the editorial staff specializing in trade, local news, Bavaria, politics, the military, and art and culture (Wilke 2003: 470).

The development of the newsroom occurred at similar times elsewhere in Europe and the United States, with the amount of space and degree of specialization increasing over the course of the twentieth century (e.g., Høyer 2003; Nerone and Barnhurst 2003; Sanchez-Aranda and Barrera 2003). However, to some extent the newsroom, while a dominant fixture in European and North American media organizations, depends upon the availability of generous financial resources, and in many corners of the world, from Russia to Sierra Leone, even relatively prominent newspapers operate entirely without centralized spaces of news production (Wahl-Jorgensen and Cole 2006). Nevertheless, within the national contexts — particularly the United States and the UK — that have dominated journalism ethnography, there are practical reasons for the prevailing definition of the newsroom as "the field."

But the newsroom is at the same time a historically specific and dynamic construction, the ever-shifting meaning of which newsroom ethnographers have sought to describe and interpret. Here, I argue that the ways in which the practices of journalists have rubbed up against the cultures of journalism ethnographers in the context of newsroom-centricity have contributed to an emphasis on routinized and controlled forms and aspects of news work, rather than on the spontaneous and unpredictable elements favored by the professional mythology of journalists.

The Ethnography of News Production

As Cottle (2000b) has suggested, a "first wave" of classical newsroom ethnographies, including the work of scholars such as Epstein (1973), Fishman (1980), Tuchman (1978), Golding and Elliott (1979), and Gans (1979), charted the cultural milieu and professional domains of journalists. Early ethnographic studies of news production were frequently conducted by sociologists informed by anthropological approaches rather than by journalism scholars (cf. Wahl-Jorgensen and Franklin 2008). These researchers were drawing on paradigms emerging within their disciplines and have been highly influential in shaping later work, including the preoccupations of today's news ethnographers. In particular, sociologists of work have traditionally operated on the assumption that a fixed physical workplace is the locus for professional cultures and practices (e.g., V. Smith 2001), and the ethnography of news production is no exception. Through studies of workplaces or "factory floors," this approach has been particularly interested in delineating the relationship between routines and creativity in work contexts—whether it be in the case of doctors, factory workers, or restaurant waiters. It has sought to understand "the daily negotiations through which structure is produced and reproduced in everyday workplace settings" (Lounsbury and Kaghan 2001: 28). From this perspective, the resonance of the metaphor of the news factory (e.g. Bantz, McCorkle, and Baade 1980) is perhaps not surprising, because its language describing the assembly line of news production fits into the framework set up by sociologists of work. Likewise, Golding and Elliott's (1979) conclusion that the news production process is a "highly regulated and routine process of manufacturing a cultural product on an electronic production line" (cited in Golding and Elliott 1999:119) and Fishman's (1980) interest in "manufacturing the news" have reverberated throughout both early and contemporary work on news production. So, for example, another classical study, Philip Schlesinger's 1978 ethnography of BBC News, uncovered a "stop-watch culture" at the public service broadcaster, focusing on "how the production of news is controlled day-to-day and minute-to-minute" (Schlesinger 1978: 48–49). Similarly, Gaye Tuchman's long-term study of news production across four sites in print and broadcast formats in major metropolitan areas took an interest in how news work "transforms occurrences into news events" (Tuchman 1978: 12) through the creation of rhythms of work, including the structured dispersion of reporters and editors in time and space. These work processes help to "routinize the unexpected" and "tame the news environment" (Tuchman 1973). Indeed, an ethnographic approach to news production has made a tremendous contribution to understanding that although journalists often see their work as creative, exciting, and unpredictable, based on the adrenaline rush of uncovering spontaneously breaking news stories, the everyday realities of news work are often based on the hard graft of routine labor (Golding and Elliott 1979; Brennen 1995). In this sense, the preoccupation of ethnographic methods with the routine, ordinary, and everyday (cf. Malkki 1997) rubs up against the idea of news as the extraordinary, unpredictable, singular, and unexpected.

Overall, the ethnography of news production has uncovered how the newsroom structure itself allows for careful planning, rather than primarily facilitating the unleashing of creativity. Such observations are embodied in the metaphor of the "news factory" and captured in the ample writings about journalistic routines (cf. Golding and Elliott 1999). It is therefore not surprising that newsroom-centric ethnographies, in their preoccupation with charting patterns in journalists' ways of life and the rules governing their professional activities, have rubbed up against the discourses and self-understandings of journalists. At the same time, as Cottle (2000b) stressed, the emphasis on routine and patterned ways of life has often meant that newsroom ethnographers have been more likely to "see" homogenization over differentiation. As I shall argue, this structural blind spot in the ethnography of news production is further reinforced by the privileging of particular "ethnographic locations" over others.

Power and "Studying Up"

If newsroom ethnographers have followed the lead of their home discipline in terms of (a) the reliance on ethnographic location of "the field" as the site for the production of scientific knowledge and, within that, (b) an emphasis on patterns, routines, and structure, they have also departed from conventional ethnographic approaches in one significant way: the classics of anthropology, which have shaped dominant research traditions in the discipline, are based on the principle of relatively powerful Western academics studying relatively powerless and culturally and geographically distant "tribes" (Hannerz 2001). Indeed, as Hannerz (1986) suggested, anthropologists have tended to direct their scholarly gaze at "the most other of others." Or, in Nader's (1972) terminology, they have "studied down." However, the macho ritual of studying the exotic "other" and gaining power and prestige from the distance, discomfort, and foreignness of the field (Gupta and Ferguson 1997) is entirely at odds with the tradition of newsroom ethnographers. If anything, the paradigm here is one of cultural proximity over distance; of "making the familiar strange." Indeed, researchers have noted the similarities between the endeavors of anthropologists and journalists, suggesting that they "use similar methods and . . . produce a similar kind of knowledge" (Awad 2006: 922; see also Hannerz 2004a; Malkki 1997). Using language that describes journalists as collaborators and equals, they have sought to understand what ethnographers can learn from the professionals they study. Indeed, many anthropologists or sociologists of journalism are "lapsed journalists" with a lasting sympathy for the profession. There are clear advantages to studying one's own society, in terms of access to sites and languages, cultural capital and understanding, familiarity and empathy, even if it also makes it more difficult to attain the analytical distance that remains central to some conceptions of the anthropological encounter (Palriwala 2005: 155–58).

If anything, the cultural distance between researchers and researched in newsroom ethnography derives from the practice of "studying up" or engaging in "elite research" (Conti and O'Neil 2007), by paying a disproportionate amount of attention to elite individuals, news organizations and journalistic practices within them. The practice of studying up has profoundly shaped which types of professional practice are best documented within the ethnography of journalism and which are neglected. Studies have tended to focus on work in large, often national, television and newspaper newsrooms. The pioneering UK and U.S. studies all took place at national or metropolitan broadcasters and newspapers. This tradition has continued up to this day. For example, in Britain, there have been several high-profile recent studies of the BBC, which have charted the changing organizational culture of the renowned public service broadcaster. Georgina Born's long-term study, published in her magnum opus, *Uncertain Vision* (2005), is a case in point. Through fieldwork conducted over almost a decade, starting in the mid-1990s, she meticulously charts key trends that have shaped the world-famous public service broadcaster. Among other things, she studies the emergence of a managerial culture focused on rationalizing news production and content, and increasingly relying on a casual and multiskilled workforce. These trends, however, are not unique to the BBC. They reverberate across the landscape of news production, but have been most extensively documented within prestige newspaper or broadcast national media organizations.

As such, the emphasis on the routines, cultures, practices, and processes of elite, national newsrooms might serve to ignore those of less glamorous journalistic workplaces, which are nevertheless dominant in terms of both the number of employees, the quantity of output, and audience sizes. The scholarly neglect of a majority of the occupation it proclaims to study is particularly problematic because the working conditions of journalists vary hugely depending on economic, political, technological, and social conditions. The emphasis on particular forms of journalistic production means that we have gathered an impressive body of evidence about particular journalistic tribes, while almost completely ignoring others. In the absence of competing accounts, the tribes whose lived experience has been amply documented by ethnographers come to stand in as the universal(izing) and authoritative descriptions of what journalism is all about.

The professional practices of local journalists have been particularly neglected. In the UK and the United States, most journalists work in local or regional media (Franklin 2006). For example, the most recent UK figures suggest that only 11 percent are employed in national media (Journalism Training Forum 2002). In the British context, even ethnographic studies that ostensibly focus on local and regional media have often actually been focused on regional production sites of national news organizations with a heavy emphasis on the BBC (Cottle and Ashton 1998; see also Aldridge 2007). However, this is not to suggest that local news practices have been completely ignored by researchers with ethnographic affinities. For example, Ursula Rao's chapter in this volume takes an ethnographic look at local newspapers in India, examining how urban citizens enter the news. She argues that "the expansion of local news making and the open-door policy of editorial teams has opened up the press as a resource to a wide range of people, who invest in press relations as a ray of hope, a desire for communication, a road for populist politics, or a strategy for the manipulation of leadership issues." My own ethnographic work on how local newspapers in the San Francisco Bay Area deal with letters to the editor (e.g., Wahl-Jorgensen 2007) similarly demonstrates how local editors valorize the voices of "ordinary people" in their communities and highlight the significance of good relationships with their readers. If anything, then, such work suggests that local media are characterized by distinctive newsroom cultures, shaped by closer relationships to their audiences. However, most studies of local news making have been based on interviews with news workers, rather than on sustained ethnographic observation (e.g. Kaniss 1991; Franklin 2006).

The focus on elite, national, or metropolitan media organizations can, to some extent, be explained by the political economy of publishing and the academy. Researchers may be more likely to gain institutional approval and prestige, grant money, publications, and promotions by studying well-known national and elite news organizations than by examining more marginalized media practices.

Also, while the relatively small number of elite national news organizations may serve as a more comfortable basis for generalizations and statements suggesting a "shared culture" (Harrison 2000), such claims are much more difficult to make for the vast diversity of local, alternative, or specialist media practices. As Kaniss (1991: 9) complained:

> The problem with trying to understand local news coverage . . . is that it is a far more difficult task than looking at the role of the national news media. Where many studies have conveniently selected a network television news program, or a weekly newsmagazine, or a national newspaper . . . in order to analyze the media's impact on national elections or policy, the local news media embrace thousands of newspapers, television, and radio stations, city magazines, and other forms of localized media in markets throughout the country.

Yet such complication might be exactly what is necessary "given the differentiated nature of the journalist 'tribe(s)' nomadically wandering through today's news ecology . . . [which means that] it no longer seems plausible to presume a generalized view of 'journalism' as an undifferentiated culture or shared professional canon" (Cottle 2000b: 24). Certainly, studying the lived experience of journalists in under-researched media, occupational roles, and regions could add hugely to the study of journalism and anthropology. This is all the more important as a pedagogical intervention: many scholars teach present and future journalists from areas where journalistic work is so different that they find little to recognize in the existing literature. It is also important because while some of the trends that newsroom ethnographers have identified are probably shared by journalists across the board, others are unique to their contexts and deserve recognition as such.

In this respect, the neglect of journalistic practices marginalized within the newsroom is particularly alarming. That is to say, newsroom-centric research tends to overlook particular categories of news workers. It predominantly charts the professional cultures of privileged full-time reporters over stringers and freelance journalists. This is the case despite the fact that the journalistic workforce is increasingly based on short-term employment and a reliance on freelancers. For example, the UK's National Union of Journalists has reported an explosion in the number of accredited freelance journalists (Bew 2006: 201). This trend reflects both the increasing use of occasional employees at established news organizations, the growth of specialist magazines, and the ease of setting up one's own website or blog in a time of citizen journalism. Nevertheless, if freelance journalism has always strongly contributed to journalistic cultures and content, there is little ethnographic research reflecting those realities. If, as one journalist reflected in an interview with Stephen Hess (2001: 163), freelance "correspondents, even the most professional and relied upon, are treated terribly by news organizations, both financially and editorially," this power relationship is once again inscribed in the (lack of) attention of researchers. Freelance journalists are, by definition, structurally excluded from the "field" of the newsroom, and their tenuous connection with the centralized and routinized forms of news production means that they are often invisible as members of the journalistic tribes.

Other forms of journalistic production that operate at the peripheries of the newsroom—even though they may be an integral part of the content put out by news organizations—are equally neglected by ethnographic researchers. This is particularly true of specialisms which are removed from the excitement of the news-gathering process and frequently occupy the lower rungs of the newsroom hierarchy. As a result, the work of arts journalists, music critics, and features reporters has received little attention (Harries and Wahl-Jorgensen 2007). Similarly, scholars have failed to pay attention to the large numbers of news workers occupied in business journalism, a specialty area that is growing ever more expansively (Journalism Training Forum 2002) and whose success is linked to larger social trends, including the globalization of capital. Popular forms of journalism, despite their broader appeal, have also received scant attention. Here, an exception is Elizabeth Bird's study of supermarket tabloids. She shows that tabloid writers, whose stories are often denounced as sensationalist fabrication, claim allegiance to ideals of objectivity (Bird 1992: 92), since they, like other journalists, are simply reporting the words of their sources.

When specialists *have* been studied from a sociological-anthropological paradigm that has taken an interest in professional cultures, this research has often used interview and survey research methods, rather than ethnographic fieldwork, and focused on the prestigious end of the professional spectrum by looking at the work of groups such as specialist correspondents for national news organizations (Tunstall 1971) and foreign correspondents (Hess 2001). Reflecting the power hierarchies of news production, the best-studied specialist professional subcategory is that of political journalists (e.g., Seymour-Ure 1968; Tracey 1977). Michael Tracey's 1977 book, *The Production of Political Television*, is one of a few such studies to draw on ethnographic fieldwork. Tracey studied political journalists at UK national broadcasters ITV and BBC to understand the making of programs involved in the policy-making process, focusing on how government and commercial organizations attempt to influence coverage. In keeping with the newsroom-centric approach, those forms of specialist reporting that have been well studied by newsroom ethnographers are usually ones that have dedicated spaces within functionally specialized newsroom environments.

Nevertheless, more recent ethnographic studies conducted by journalism and media scholars are beginning to redress this lack of attention to journalistic subcultures by focusing on more specialized and hitherto under-researched forms of news production. Examples includes Julian Matthews's 2003 ethnographic work on children's television, Simon Cottle's examination of natural history programming (2004a), and Eamonn Forde's 2003 studies of music journalism. Such studies often combine interviews with relatively brief newsroom observation periods, which manage to capture the workings of well-defined specialist areas. However, in their prevailing focus on prestige media outlets, they do not challenge the power relations reinforced by the newsroom-centric tradition, and they continue to revolve around the newsroom as the "field" that defines journalistic cultures.

Journalistic work that takes place entirely outside the newsroom environment is particularly difficult to trace. For this reason, alternative journalism practices have only recently started to attract the attention of journalism scholars. Alternative media are often produced in informal spaces that are more challenging to learn about and access, including private homes, community centers, schools, and pubs. And the individuals who produce alternative journalism rarely see themselves — and are rarely seen be others — as journalists (e.g., Atton 2008).

The methodological problems of relying on evidence gathered at nodal points within the newsrooms of elite media organizations might, to some extent, be addressed by conducting comparative, multisited ethnographies in different types of media, as well as in different geographical and cultural contexts (Cottle 2007; Marcus 1995). However, the practice of conducting multisited ethnographies is both more resource-intensive and time-consuming than traditional single-sited research and is therefore even less likely to receive institutional support, particularly in media, communication, and journalism studies departments, which have conventionally had less of a tradition of the long-term fieldwork engagement practiced by anthropologists. The resource-intensive nature of ethnographic fieldwork has also meant that it has conventionally been easier to undertake for academics in resource-rich contexts and countries. As already mentioned, this has meant that the majority of locations for ethnography have been large cities in the Western world, especially in the United States and the UK, while we know relatively little about journalism cultures outside this axis, reflecting a more general need to de-Westernize media research in a context where global resource and power inequalities are reflected in the academy (cf. Curran and Park 2000).

As Schwenkel points out in her chapter for this volume, there has been a particular emphasis on the workings of journalism in capitalist societies, to the virtual exclusion of scholarship on socialist journalism cultures. Her work on photojournalism during the Vietnam War provides an important exception in this regard, demonstrating that socialist photographers operated in similar ways to ethnographers, hence providing the "viewer with deeper ethnographic insights into how war and revolution shaped daily life practices, capturing the multifacetedness of society under constant threat of violence." She contrasts this approach to that of Western correspondents, whose adherence to the ideal of objectivity ultimately resulted in a "dehumanizing and objectifying" focus on the spectacle of dead bodies and violence.

International and comparative studies of news production, using an ethnographic framework, have certainly contributed to complicating nation-centered approaches to news production and recognizing the increasingly globalized nature of news (e.g. Volkmer 1999). For example, Hannerz's study of foreign correspondents for major news organizations in key cities (2004a) was part of a deliberate political project to seek out the roots of a cosmopolitan imagination, by identifying how the stories of gifted journalists can engender a sense of human compassion and responsibility for the lives of others. Yet this was clearly — and explicitly marked as — a study of global elites, which implied that we have something to learn from journalistic practices of excellence. As such, it underscored the elitist impulse underlying the tradition of studying up. Similarly, when Cohen, Levy, Roeh, and Gurevitch set out to study "global newsrooms, local audiences" (1996), they focused on the Eurovision news exchange, a pan-European news service based on the coming together of national broadcasters. They wished to understand the "'gatekeeping' function performed by a relatively small number of journalists — men and women who day in and day out coordinate the dissemination of a large volume of television news, exchanged among the world's broadcast organizations by satellite" (1996: vii). As such, they were implicitly heeding Nader's (1972: 284) call for elite research, on the grounds that "never before have so few, by their actions and inactions, had the power of life and death over so many members of the species." Pedelty's (1995) painstaking ethnography of war correspondents in El Salvador compellingly documented the professional rituals and practices of a corps of journalists for elite European and North American news organizations.

Jennifer Hasty's (2005) ethnography of the foremost private and state-owned newspapers in Ghana shows that although the journalists she studied considered themselves cosmopolitan professionals who drew on the Western rhetoric of objectivity, both types of newspapers were, discursively and in practice, distinctively Ghanaian. To her, these newspapers are ultimately "the products of specific historical conditions and are responsive to particular cultural notions of political authority and legitimacy as well as sociality and exchange" (Hasty 2005: 164).

Overall, these studies helpfully move away from an overwhelming focus on

Anglo-American journalism cultures, and reflect an increased interest in the global operations and cultures of news production, but they have not challenged the dominant power relations reflected in the prevailing nation-centered newsroom-centric tradition.

On the Disappearance of the Newsroom

However, the days of the newsroom as a central ethnographic location may be numbered. One of the most fundamental challenges for today's newsroom ethnographers lies in the disappearance of the material space of journalistic labor in a time when 'liquid media' are the order of the day (Deuze 2007). We need to come to terms with the fact that (a) news production is increasingly taking place in and through virtual spaces, (b) news work is becoming increasingly decentralized, and (c) journalism is increasingly reliant on casual labor that is not tied to particular locations. As Cottle (2007) has observed:

> In this interpenetrating communications environment news production no longer takes place within any one organizational centre of production but has become increasingly dispersed across multiple sites, different platforms and can be contributed to by journalists based in different locations around the world or on the move. With journalists and editors based in different locations but all working on the same story and able to access, transmit and edit the same news materials clearly this poses considerable challenges to today's ethnographer.

New technologies are challenging the centralization of news work in the physical site of the newsroom, and enabling "electronically based forms of editorial organization" (Wilke 2003: 474). Newspapers around the world are experimenting with virtual environments for news production. Wilke (2003) gives the example of the German paper *Regioblick,* which is

> the first regional daily newspaper published only on the internet. *Regioblick* does not have a central newsroom. The editorial offices are located wherever the editor works. "We read each other's work every day," members of the staff announced in an interview; "we talk to each other once a week [online], and we meet in person once a month."

Among other things, such practices physically decentralize and desocialize news work, making it a much more diffuse and slippery object of ethnographic study. Of course, the methodological challenges of an emerging virtual world are not unique to journalism scholars, even if our endeavors, because of their technology-intensive subject matter, have been at the forefront of the encounter with this new reality (cf. Wittel 2000). But just as anthropologists have begun to think through methodological issues associated with "virtual ethnographies," these challenges will be central for ethnographers of media production. To get beyond newsroom-centricity, ethnographers must look toward "socio-political locations, networks, and multi-sited approaches" (Wittel 2000: 8). The classical ethnographic methods of observing activity in a fixed locality will have to be supplemented by approaches that take these changes into account.

Newsroom-Centricity and the Need for a Reflexive Turn in Journalism Studies

This chapter has sought to understand some of the consequences of journalism ethnographers' reliance on the newsroom as a "field" and to trace some of the consequences of the particular forms of newsroom-centricity that have prevailed in ethnographies of news production. In particular, I have argued that while conventional anthropological practice relies on "studying down" by focusing on less powerful and privileged "others," newsroom ethnography is predominantly a discipline that studies up, often focusing on privileged journalistic practices to the exclusion of more marginalized ones. While there are good reasons for this intellectual trajectory, it has had real consequences for the production of knowledge in the field, insofar as the power relations prevailing in the world of news work have been reproduced in the attentions of the academy.

The elite-focused approach that has been the result of the "studying up" practices of newsroom ethnography has, to some extent, meant that up until recently we have known much about the producers of news but little about its consumers. However, more recent ethnographic work on news audiences, building on approaches developed within audience research traditions, provides a promising opening in this direction and demonstrates that the anthropology of journalism can go beyond an exclusive focus on the "factory floors" of news organizations (see Bird 2003; Madianou 2005).

Nevertheless, the prevailing power relations that have shaped newsroom-centric research remain woefully underexamined. While anthropology has undergone a "reflexive turn" a generation ago, the anthropology of *journalism* has only recently gained the maturity to even begin the process of reflecting upon its practices. This chapter has represented one small step in this direction. But clearly, to do justice to the diversity of journalistic cultures and practice, we need to place questions of the hierarchies of power in journalism and the academy, as they intersect in our research, at the center of such a reflexive turn.

2

U.S. Newsworld

The Rule of Text and Everyday
Practices of Editing the World

ZEYNEP DEVRIM GÜRSEL

The Battle for Real Estate

On a cold January morning in 2004 in the daily 10 AM meeting, a usually even-tempered senior editor at an American news magazine, *U.S. Newsworld*, exclaimed, "We're turning into a picture book! There's no room for my stories anymore. It's a news magazine — or at least it's *supposed* to be a news magazine. We hardly have any stories. We don't have any *space* for news."

"There are a lot of sacrifices made on the visual side, too," replied the senior photo editor. "All we do is one-picture stories. We all have to give blood equally!"

The trigger for this unexpectedly heated exchange was an image that was going to take up more than a page — the implication being that the news for which there was no space was in the text, not the image. The issue was not the specific image but rather a much larger philosophical difference about the role that visuals play in journalism, one that I observed often during my fieldwork on photojournalism. In fact, arguments over concrete space in the magazine's layout often revealed disagreements over how much abstract value any single element of the story — photograph, illustration, or text — was perceived to have. Many word people saw visual elements as illustrative of the story conveyed in the writer's text, necessary gimmicks to break up blocks of text and keep the reader's attention, whereas visual people saw visuals as journalistic contributions in their own right.

Another day a magazine photo editor I was shadowing explained: "It's about real estate. Trying to get space." Later she added, "The ideal situation is a marriage of words and images, *not* a battle for real estate." But during my fieldwork in 2003 and 2004, I observed very little marital bliss and many battles for real estate. In this chapter I detail the particulars of this battle over physical space on the page in order to underline power relations that shape the production and circulation of visuals that are part of knowledge production about the world and hence powerful tools of worldmaking. According to Nelson Goodman (1978), worldmaking consists of processes of composition and decomposition, processes that are consolidated by identification labels. Goodman underlines that all representations contribute to the understanding and building of realities in which we live. By focusing on visuals that circulate as "references" to "real events" in journalistic contexts, I aim to investigate the creation and diffusion of knowledge about various people and cultures that is marked by the additional authority invested in representations presented as truthful or transparent.

Let me begin by explaining the real estate being fought over: space on "the wall." The wall at *U.S. Newsworld* is a physical wall on which the week's magazine is displayed page by page. As Mary, an experienced art director, pointed out, "First you start with how many ads have been purchased and where they are [in the layout] so that you can calculate how many singles and spreads [two consecutive pages that will be visible together] you have." One wall I saw punctuated this for me as the advertisements were marked by bright orange sheets. In the battle for real estate, the wall is the scoreboard that is constantly being updated. Furthermore, in a production site where labor is divided not only by function, such as writer or photo editor, but also according to corresponding sections of the magazine — Arts, Nation, Science — the wall is a concrete reminder that the magazine is a package, a unified bound publication. The one person who always thinks about the magazine as a package is the editor-in-chief, who makes decisions about how the pages work together. For example, in one morning meeting I heard a visually savvy editor-in-chief ask his staff, "Should we have a male or female in the illustration for that story? It seems a very male image–dominated magazine this week. Is that wise? Is that something we care about?"

At the morning meeting, attended by both word (writers and editors) and visual people, (photo editors, graphic designers, art directors), everyone sits around one large table, although the word people tend to be much more talkative. The word people also often sit closer to the editor-in-chief than the visual people. Although there is a jovial atmosphere, it is clear that there is a hierarchy of opinion, and most jokes are made by a handful of word people. The visual people tend to be very quiet. The meeting functions by the various sections of the magazine pitching their stories and trying to win pages from the editor-in-chief. The answer to the often-asked question "What size story is it?" is either given in lines or pages — for example, 60 lines or four pages. As the editor-in-chief curries favor and favor is doled out in pages, it is the text side that dominates the talk, even if some of the talk is about images.

After the meeting, the senior photo editor communicates what work is needed to each of the photo editors responsible for particular sections, such as World, Nation, Arts, and Health. I focused on the section of the magazine responsible for international news.[1] This organization of news into categories of nation and world is common in news publications around the globe. One consequence of this is that nation is reified as an organizing principle around which to investigate the world. Moreover, in addition to being a convenient way to divide labor, this separation also confirms the impression that the publication is bringing the reader all of the newsworthy world.

Rather than analyze a single object of mass media — a particular set of photographs, for example — I did fieldwork at various nodes of production, distribution, and circulation in the international photojournalism industry and focused on documenting the network through which international news photographs "move" to understand the structural limitations and possibilities that shape these images and their use in contemporary ways of worldmaking. I use the term *nodes* deliberately because I am interested in points of intersections between various actors and institutions, junctions in a system where choices have to be made, such as which image to select, which photographer to assign a particular story, or whether or not to buy a specific photograph being offered. My informants were various "brokers of images," who act as mediators for literal "views of the world." *U.S. Newsworld* was one of several nodes I studied.

The art directors, text editors, writers, photographers, designers, and photo editors all act as mediators in collectively editing the world section of the magazine. In a Chinese silk factory, Lisa Rofel explains that "labor processes are processes of cultural interpretation through everyday practice" (1992: 96). Indeed, during my fieldwork, by following the production and circulation of images, I observed how news images were interpreted by those involved in the collective labor process of visual knowledge. Yet is there something particular about journalistic labor processes? Stuart Hall argues that the key is a difference in relationship to ideology:

> There is a specificity to those practices whose principal object is to produce ideological representations. They are different from those practices which — meaningfully, intelligibly — produce other commodities. Those people who work in the media are producing, reproducing, and transforming the field of ideological representation itself. They stand in a different relationship to ideology in general from others who are producing and reproducing the world of material commodities — which are, nevertheless, also inscribed by ideology. (Hall 1985: 103)

What drew me to photojournalism was the potential to investigate the brokering of news images, visual commodities with ever-widening digital distribution networks, as simultaneous processes of production of representations and reproduction of particular worldviews. In making their various decisions, the image brokers I studied relied on how they imagined populations — both those represented in the photographs and potential viewers — as well as their views of others in the exchange network. Images and imagined communities then are produced, reproduced, and circulated together.

I offer the term *formative fictions* as a way of thinking about how expectations of what something should look like — the manner in which it is anticipated to be imagined by others — informs the selection of images in institutional settings through everyday discursive interactions and practices of image brokers. By focusing on moments of selection as critical sites to investigate the brokering of images as an everyday practice of imagination, I attempted to understand how categories of people are produced through images that then inform how that category is defined and imagined in the future. In the context of the world section of a news magazine, formative fictions are constructed representations that reflect current events yet simultaneously shape ways of imagining the world and political possibilities within it. In other words, these are images that have a certain force because they circulate in journalistic circles and may be published in a news publication of some sort. Amahl Bishara's chapter in this volume superbly details how the anticipation of this force and its international scope plays into the planning and execution of a local political event.

Practices of Mediation

In order to demonstrate the power struggle between text and image in the preparation of a weekly news magazine, I focus on the preparation of a particular 2003 photo-essay about the separation barrier being built in Israel.[2] A photo-essay is a story that is composed primarily of photos and usually spreads over four to six pages. They do not appear every week nor on any type of regular schedule. They are a reversal of the usual hierarchy in a news magazine because they are not prompted by the decision of the text-side to do a story that then needs images to illustrate it. Photo-essays are initiated by the photo department once they have received either an intriguing proposal from a photographer or a completed project ready to be published. They appear as stand-alone stories themselves and hence are often the pride and joy of the photo department (and therefore sometimes the bane of the text side). They are the antithesis of the *one-picture story* bemoaned by the photo editor in the contentious meeting mentioned at the beginning of this chapter. In other words, multiple images are used, usually from a single photographer, and so photographs are given the space to be the primary vehicle for the story rather than illustrations subservient to the text. Sarah, a senior text editor, explained, "When we're looking at

35–36 pages of editorial material, every page is incredibly valuable. If a photo-essay is four pages, that's one-ninth of the magazine—it better be damned relevant!"

Photo-essays underscore the differences between how various people in a publication view the merits of visual knowledge. Photo editors emphasized that photos are about emotion. Jen, a photo editor, explained, "The purpose of a photo is to intrigue a reader. The photo is going to decide whether or not people read a story. I think that's how I can have impact on a story." And several photo editors complained that while the text people are interested in what illustrates a story, they are not thinking about what would make the reader read the story. Sarah was a correspondent before she became the text editor of the world section, and yet she is known as being one of the more visual-friendly word people in her current role. "Photography has to sell the story because the reader perceives the photo first. . . . Before, I would have regarded the photo as an intrusion on my space. As a correspondent I am responsible for writing the best story, but I'm not necessarily thinking about what's the best way to tell a story, as I only know one way to do that—in writing! But as an editor I am responsible to my reader, not to my story." Responsibility toward the reader meant thinking about the big picture. "Jen is responsible for thinking only about the photos, and her interest lies with the photographer, not the big picture. Whereas Mary, the art director, has to marry the words and images."

As Sarah's comments reveal, discussions around photography in news magazines highlight the multiple mediations that constitute the everyday practices of editing the world. News photographs that appear in journalistic publications are palimpsests of imaginations—a layering of choices made by several individuals.[3] The editor is mediating between the writer and the other editors, the photo editor is mediating between the photographer and the text editor, as well as between the photographer and the writer, the art director is mediating between text and image, and so on. Moreover, there is a hierarchy of mediation where senior editors in each section of the magazine mediate between their section and the editor-in-chief, and everyone is anticipating the reception of certain images. One photo editor complained that photographers tone down their imagery to fit what they perceive as the magazine's style, which is particularly frustrating in a digital age when the photographers only send images that they believe the editors will want.[4] In fact, almost all the photographers I interviewed, whether freelancers or wire agency photographers, both in the United States and in Europe, regularly looked through the photographs published in a handful of news magazines that have traditionally made room for documentary photography (very few said they read the articles) and took note of each magazine's visual style. Moreover, all those involved in the production and selection of images anticipate the interpretation of the reader in order to best mediate between the story and the audience. On my first day of fieldwork at one magazine, Marc, an experienced photo editor, drew my attention to the specter of the reader. "They often invoke the name of the reader around here, usually to say he won't understand."

In fact, the reader was invoked in many ways. On the one hand, photo editors regularly quipped sarcastically about the "stuff of real substance" they worked on merely to please the reader such as "Best things to buy for Christmas." Yet readers were discriminating enough so that they had supposedly grown accustomed to the magazine's style, and this style needed to be upheld. While the editor-in-chief might joke that "putting Clay Aiken on the cover is like printing money," readers were also viewed as "curious," as proven by the fact that covers focusing on human origin stories had also done well.[5] I often heard comments in which the assumption was that readers had national allegiance and that, as Americans, they would be "more interested in a story if there's an American connection." Yet even approaching the first anniversary of the Iraq war in 2004, editors had started worrying about how to continue generating interest in a war that had lost its novelty. This anxiety, which only grew with the continuation of the war, was illustrated in a meeting in which editors debated which cover story to run. One group pitched "Why War? A story on war throughout human history delving into the motivations behind violence." Another group suggested a story on obesity as a matter of personal responsibility and the burden of obesity on health care insurance providers. A senior editor, worn out by continuously looking for fresh approaches to the war in Iraq, immediately perked up: "I think we should pander to the audience." Imagining the cover, he continued, "Fat? Not your fault!" and chuckled, "We'll sell a million copies!" So while the reader is constantly being imagined, what the reader is imagined to desire seems highly variable.[6]

Sarah, a senior text editor, saw photography as a critical teaching tool. "The images get the reader's attention. Which is vital, especially with news. . . . Most readers are apt to feel that foreign news is a bit like homework. They are intimidated by it, they don't know the characters, they don't know where these countries are. So we try to make it easier and more appealing. We show you who the characters are so that you can attach a face to a name, and we'll show you where the country is on a map. We try to show people, so readers can attach to a person."

So the task of laying out a story is about wielding emotions in order to "bring the story closer" and educate the reader. Novelty of emotional reaction becomes important to photo editors because even with a story the reader might already be assumed to know, a photo-essay is meant to supply an emotional connection that might have been absent in the reader's previous encounters with the story. While much international news goes unvisualized in publications,[7] certain stories, such as ongoing wars, get a lot of exposure, which can make finding novel emotional angles challenging. So whether the story is new or needs to be portrayed in a new light, the photo editor's task is to determine what can be visualized and then to find ways to photograph it.

Watching Sarah and Jen work with Mary, the art director, on a potential photo-essay made apparent how the reader's interpretation is anticipated while each individual is interpreting images and then trying to articulate suggestions to the others. One particular story looked at Israeli and Palestinian youth growing up in Hebron and Ramallah, respectively.

> Mary, art director: "I have this idea about doing pairs, spreads." [In particular she mentions juxtaposing a photo with balloons in it with another showing a kite.]
>
> Senior photo editor: "I like that thinking. This work has never been published in the United States. I like how this photographer made an effort to stay balanced, unlike [another photographer working on the topic], who had such an opinion."
>
> Jen, photo editor: "These kids are willing to die for their cause. It doesn't have to run this week, but we need to make a commitment to the agency selling the work on behalf of the photographer."
>
> Sarah, text editor: "I have a concern about pairings. We should try to be fair, but that's not always the same as being balanced. So I'm not sure about having one page on Palestine and then the opposite page show Israel. The Palestinian side will be bad guy killers, and then these [pointing to the Hebron photographs] are obviously innocent children. Whereas settlers in Hebron are not innocent. I mean, children are always innocent, but these folks have gone into a city and forced themselves into the center. They are colonialists in the worst possible way. They take all the water and make life miserable for these people. So I am uncomfortable with any kind of equivalency."
>
> Mary: "It wasn't conceived that way."
>
> Chris, photo editor: "Through the youth's divided eyes, this shows visually what the problems are. If we don't run this, our competitors will, and we'll lose it."
>
> Sarah: "Plus, the lay reader can't tell a Palestinian from an Israeli."

In the everyday practice of designing a layout for the photo-essay, each individual's interpretation is part of the collective act of worldmaking for the reader, in the sense that what is being prepared is part of what will be presented as "the world" for the reader in a specific issue. Each labor process above is simultaneously an act of cultural interpretation. In the comments above—all of which are part of the labor behind the photo-essay—the content of the images are simultaneously interpreted in terms of politics, aesthetics, news value, and business strategy. Mary's suggestion about pairing images is graphically motivated: the balloons and kite form a nice contrapuntal visual. This pairing is interpreted by the senior photo editor as a way of underscoring the photographer's commendable balanced approach. Whereas Sarah, the text editor, objects to the pairing because she sees this layout as suggesting equivalence between Palestinian youth and children of settlers in Hebron. Yet she does not believe that lay readers will be able to distinguish a Palestinian from an Israeli, in which case readers would not perceive the layout as suggesting equivalence. Moreover, in tandem with the production of this particular photo-essay, the team is aware of producing the magazine's own reputation as an internationally important magazine. That they have never been published in the United States adds value to the images, and when the text editor seems unconvinced, another photo editor highlights the threat of a competitor running the images. Hence what is simultaneously produced is the concrete weekly world section of the magazine, the reputation of the magazine and its ability to bring the reader all the week's most relevant news, and a representation of the world and the political possibilities in it for the reader.

My research did not extend to the reception of these images by readers, but what I hope to emphasize here is how the anticipation of readers' interpretations is a key factor in decisions at this point in production. Jen, one of the photo editors, was always trying to see all the images available on a topic even if she had already assigned the topic to a particular photographer. "You don't want to look like you missed something, yet you want to provide fresh material. The wire photographs appear in local newspapers, so you want something no one has seen before," she explained. This concern with finding novel angles to stories is especially a concern in weekly news magazines, which risk looking like they are presenting stale news because their production cycle means they cannot cover breaking news. Marc, the photo editor at a competing magazine, concurred, "You can't panic. The whole system is based on panic and the fear that your editor will see what they had and will say why didn't we have this?" And yet balancing fresh material with visuals that endorse the view that the reader is really getting the world in one site is a constant challenge, involving complex choices. For instance, when choosing an image for a story on Shia uprisings in Iraq, Marc compared a portrait of Sistani, the senior Shia cleric in Iraq, with a crowd shot taken at a recent protest. "The Sistani photo has been in every publication in the country. The demonstration photo is not as strong, but it shows that we had a photographer there." He then selected the crowd shot.

Illustrating the Wall

It was in a morning daily editorial meeting that I first heard of the photo-essay concerning the wall. The news peg was the United Nations' October 21, 2003, condemnation of the wall being constructed by Israel in the West Bank and the release of a report detailing the negative implications for Palestinian livelihood. Once the editor-in-chief agreed that there might be room for a photo-essay in that week's issue, Sarah, the text editor who had worked for several years as a correspondent in Jerusalem, Mary, the art director, and Jen, the photo editor, went to work. The dialogues reproduced below emphasize how various brokers approach the task of illustrating the wall, from choosing illustrations to visualize the wall mentioned in the report to visually documenting the impact on those living in areas around the wall. The photographer had sent the panoramic black-and-white prints from sites in Gaza and the West Bank to Jen, who had made an initial selection. She then showed this selection to Mary and Sarah.

> Mary: "I like the feel of that one. That one is good for compositional difference."
> Sarah: "The dustiness of the background, everyday life. . . . Which of these photos do you like?" (She shows two separate photos of women crossing the wall.) "Here is a traditional woman, a working woman, so the empathy factor is higher." (She then looks at an image showing an unveiled pretty young blonde in jeans.) "I'd be very shocked if that was a Palestinian woman."
> Jen: "Why?"
> Sarah: "She looks so modern."
> Jen: "According to the caption, she's Palestinian. But I'll check."
> Sarah: (Reaching for another image.) "Here you see old women and children, so obviously these are not the elements to cause trouble in the world. So you get the sense that this wall is just a total inconvenience. Then I like this one because you have every type of person in it."
> Jen: "You can see how they are living in this desolate landscape. To me the checkpoint is a more familiar image, so it's not surprising."
> Mary: "That one's a bit graphically difficult for me because it's a different shape, but I can practically hear what's going on."

The art director, text editor, and photo editor all act as mediators as they perform their weekly duties in collectively editing the world section of the magazine. The text editor represents the opinion of the writer, whether the writer is down the hall, in the office, or somewhere in the field. The photo editor represents the photographer, and the art director mediates between the text editor's desires and the photo editor's desires. In the above example, as in the story on youth in Ramallah and Hebron, Sarah verbally captions the images. She inserts a narrative, and her manner of codifying what she sees then guides how the images are laid out to tell a story. Jen physically handles the prints, attempts to represent the photographer, and also comments on the images' relation to other imagery on the topic (e.g., "the checkpoint photo is more familiar," implying we have seen images like this in comparable publications).[8] Mary voices concerns over the shape of images, as well as their compositional elements, which is understandable given that she will be responsible for actually sizing the images and designing the final layout of the photo-essay.[9] In the battle for real estate, she is ultimately the broker of solutions, finding ways to marry image and text. Furthermore, because real estate needs are constantly changing—Mary says trying to understand which cover might run the night before going to press "is like reading tea leaves"—her job as art director is to try to anticipate visual products for all possible decisions.[10]

In the dialogue above, Sarah anticipates how the reader will react to various images, and this anticipation of their reception informs her choice in images. What is inferred from her comment comparing the two women climbing over the wall is that the photograph showing the slim younger woman wearing a loose headscarf and a knee-length skirt will be more empathetic to the American reader than the older woman with a tighter headscarf and loose dark clothing. Sarah spent many years working in the Jerusalem bureau, so she may be drawing from that experience when she identifies the younger woman as a "working woman," but she anticipates that the average reader will make the same identification. The categories anticipated in the imagination of the reader are "traditional woman" vs. "working woman, more like one of us." Yet her very next comment underscores that there is a limit to how much familiarity is desirable. The attractive young blonde in jeans is *too modern* to be Palestinian.[11]

The lay reader is presumed by Sarah to be unable to differentiate between Palestinians and Israelis, but able to distinguish which of the women works outside the home. The reader is then anticipated to empathize with the woman with whom she can identify. So these image brokers imagine what traditional and modern look like, respectively, as they represent a particular place for a journalistic publication and anticipate how their readers will imagine this place and relate or not to the people in the images. Hence the photographs become formative fictions.

When Joel, Sarah's boss and one of the most senior text editors at the magazine, walked in, Sarah had to verbalize the rationale for the photo-essay. Joel suggested using an aerial of the wall, to which Jen responded, "Much of the wall is in no-man's-land, so in that sense the wall alone is boring."

Sarah: "To make the best use of this photographer's work, you would really need to expand the theme beyond the wall."

Joel: "The wall is a nice focus, though, because once you get away from the wall, it gets fuzzier. One aerial shot that wasn't by him wouldn't steal the thunder or mood too much, would it?"

Jen: "Well, he really proposed a story on the wall in the sense that a wall is a metaphor for isolation."

Sarah: "It's a metaphor for the strangulation of Palestine."

Jen: "To me it's a metaphor for the end of the peace movement."

Joel: "I am more inclined to look at what the wall actually is: a story of the have and have-nots."

Sarah was concerned that the photographer was not showing the actual fence being evaluated by the United Nations. The team discussed the option of finding aerials to augment the selection of images before them. Sarah reminded the others, "Barriers have existed in Israel since the Intifada." Jen tried to make a case for the scope of the photographer's work: "You can tell a lot about what it will be like" living with these walls. Mary drew attention to a particular image taken in Rafah, Gaza, showing residents returning to homes destroyed in an Israeli invasion. All the images from Rafah and the Gaza Strip were technically outside the scope of the segment of the wall that had drawn criticism from the United Nations that week — the wall in the West Bank. The UN report — the news peg that made this story relevant at this moment — stated concern that the wall might cause disruption of livelihood and further humanitarian hardship for the Palestinians; hence it addressed the impact of the wall on living in the region. What is interesting is that the geographical specificity of the report was mentioned several times to emphasize why the scope of the essay should not extend beyond the West Bank, whereas the emphasis on life around the walls being the focus of the report did not get repeated. Mary clearly appreciated an image from Rafah, but believed it did not fit the story. "Can we number this photo?" This allows it to be entered into the magazine's system and potentially used at another time even if not as part of this photo-essay. "It reminds me of a period movie that shows the nastiness of life in those times."

Joel: "Yes, it looks very premodern."

Jen called the photographer to verify that the blonde actually was Palestinian, and during the conversation she asked several questions about how each image fit into the story that the photographer was trying to tell about the wall. Jen, who tries to ensure that photographers' opinions are taken into account, repeatedly asked which of the images he felt were the strongest. This is another example of a node of production as two actors involved in different production processes negotiate selections among all possible images.

Jen: "I'm not very knowledgeable about the area. I've never been there. So I'm going to ask again. How do the Rafah pictures relate to the wall?"

Photographer: "Well, the wall takes many forms. I mean, the wall along the Egyptian border has been going on for some time now. . . . It's part of a process of walling off a country. . . . Physically it is impossible for the Egypt wall to be connected to the main wall. . . . But I mean the idea is not new. The concept of the wall has been going on for a number of years."

Jen: "I am having a hard time making an argument for the entire selection because Sarah thinks it gets fuzzy if you go beyond the West Bank issue."

Photographer: "Is it just about illustrating a news peg, or is it about good photography and showing the psychology of walls? I am a photographer. I show what something feels like, not what it looks like! All she has to do is caption them very clearly."

Jen: "Her argument is that the walls are not something new except what's happening in the West Bank."

Photographer: "It's a very literal approach to the topic."

Jen: "She wants to show what is new to the reader."

Photographer: "But this is new to the reader; I'll bet my life on it. People don't know about these walls. They don't even know what settlements are. . . . Yes, it's a metaphor, but it is also a very linear thing: the wall is a part of the expansion of the settlement."

Jen turned the conversation to the image of the blonde, verbalizing Sarah's interpretation as her own: "Is she an Israeli woman or a Palestinian? She just doesn't seem typical of a Palestinian woman."

Photographer: "Look, as photographers we tend to photograph the exotic — the woman in the burka, etc. But Ramallah is a very European town. A lot of international Palestinians go to the Ramallah area. It is very Westernized and very modern. . . . I would go for the best picture. Anything that needs to be harmonized or clarified, just clarify it. . . . I know what it's like. Your editor is sitting there with an idea in her head that she wants, but there's nothing there but a ghost. Basically you want images to speak for themselves. . . . It's a photo-essay, so if I were you, I wouldn't let it be driven by linear analysis. . . . There's nothing wrong with writing a story to go along with it. Writing a story to say that this is a way of life we are looking at, a condition of humanity."

Once off the phone, Jen told me she was glad to have had the conversation and repeated what she had said to the photographer. "The current peg is this wall, but there's life around the walls we should be looking at." She explained, "What I am trying to do is represent the photographer's opinion as clearly as I can because he's not here. I'm trying to translate." Indeed, she had to do a lot of translating between the metaphors of the photographer, who was trying to convey what living with the wall *felt like,* and the literal questions of the text editors concerning what the new parts of the wall being erected in the West Bank and those specifically mentioned in the UN's report *looked like.* When Sarah and Joel reviewed the images once again, Joel stopped at the photo of the young woman, now confirmed as a Palestinian. "She's lovely, but what does she have to do with the wall?" Jen replied, "She's just passed through a checkpoint." But the image did not make it into the photo-essay. In fact, all seven images in the final photo-essay showed a portion of the wall and hence focused on the wall — what the wall looks like rather than what life around it or even what observing life around it *felt* like at a particular moment. People were not absent in the final selection, but each image showed a portion of the physical wall itself.

Once the team had reached a layout they were comfortable with, they collectively walked it over to Joel's office. The hierarchy of office space dictates that the text editor's office is much larger and more central than those of the photo editor or art director, so Mary and Jen usually take the images to Sarah's office first, then Joel's. Eventually all four take it to the editor-in-chief. "Have you noticed how much we all walk around in this place?" Joel asked me one day. Even though his post is senior enough that most people go to *his* office these days, I suppose he's clocked in thousands of kilometers of hall strolls over the years. So collectively they walked to the editor-in-chief and showed the piece. Sarah, the text editor, narrated the photo-essay and turned to Jen, the photo editor, only when further clarification was necessary. Jen had translated the images for Sarah, a text person, and now a text person gave voice to the images in front of the ultimate decision maker. Ultimately it is the *talk* about and around images that determines what gets visually represented and what does not.

The editor-in-chief liked the images, so Sarah asked if he would like to run the photo-essay that week. "I just don't think we have the space. But if we change covers tomorrow (the day the magazine closes), then we'll need something else." Although nothing explicit was said, it was understood that he had liked the wall piece *enough* so that it had a good chance of running — even if not that week — and that in any case they should prepare it for publication. The photographer was thrilled that the piece might run. He implored Jen to use only the best pictures, adding, "Don't let the word people rule. Visual people unite!" Later that night Mary posted the tentative pages alongside the rest of that week's content and rejoiced with Jen: the fence is on the wall!

Silence, Voiceovers, and the Art of Negotiating for Visuals

Perhaps in reaction to the fact that text editors often become the voiceover for the images, silence plays an important role in the everyday practices of photo editors — as if the goal is to keep the editor-in-chief from pronouncing a negative decision. Any indication that a set of images might be usable even if not immediately or any reaction other than a direct no is considered a good sign. Silence is a photo editor's friend; it's a *non-no,* which is a potential yes. One morning during the week in which the wall essay was prepared, Sarah, the text editor, asked Mary and Jen, "Did you notice how cranky he [the editor-in-chief] was? I decided within five minutes of the meeting starting that I was not going to say a word." Mary replied, "You know, I decided the same thing." The irony was that Mary almost never speaks at the morning meeting unless responding to a question. But this was completely lost on Sarah, who seemed not even to register Mary's comment as a joke. The text editor had been silent by choice, whereas the art director had been silent out of habit and well-established protocol. This is not to imply that the image people are not respected, but rather to underscore that there is a protocol that the voices heard in the daily meeting often belong to those who are responsible for those producing and editing the words in the magazine.

W. J. T. Mitchell (1994) claims that "the interaction of pictures and texts is constitutive of representation as such: all media are mixed media, and all representations are heterogeneous; there are no 'purely' visual or verbal arts, though the impulse to purify media is one of the central utopian gestures of modernism" (5). However, these narratives suggest that at the sites of production of mass mixed media publications, power relations are not heterogeneous and power is not always mixed mediumwise. Power may not be inherently textual by nature, but despite constant claims that we live in a world awash with images and much rhetoric around the power of images, at the sites of production of U.S. news magazines, it appears that power is very much textual. I found that within their own publications, photo editors inhabit a very liminal space, in which they are constantly mediating between text and image — or the word people and the visual people. Many photo editors express tremendous frustration at being ruled by the text people and being seen as auxiliary. Photo-essays are one of the few opportunities they have to initiate a project that tells a story visually and supports the work of photographers working on long-term projects. These are the long-awaited, patiently earned opportunities to display all the photo department's capabilities and the depth that visuals can bring to a story. The photo-essays are the reward for finding countless headshots, agreeing to photo-illustrations, and watching innumerable favorite photos get left on the table week after week. A senior photo editor with more than 20 years' experience editing "the world" for magazines likened working at text-driven magazines to living in a wasteland and explained the critical importance of collaborations with photographers that result in photo-essays. "I live in a wasteland, but I dream of banks of wild flowers. I live in the desert, but I dream of the forest." As if to underscore this dilemma, Sarah, the text editor, told me, "The visual people see poetry, but we are not a poetry magazine. We're a news magazine."

Visual Journalism as an Anthropological Object

News images are cultural products that circulate as commodities but are also representations coated with complex truth claims about populations and historical events. While news images operate as formative fictions by circulating, they are also situated — geographically, institutionally, and culturally — fictions, and their potential for deployment in myriad contexts makes them compelling sites to explore both how communities are formed and how difference is conceived, whether around race, gender, nation, or ethnicity. In fact, what makes news photographs particularly interesting as an anthropological object of study is that they are fixed images that circulate as truths but can also accumulate or jeopardize their authenticity, value, and credibility through their circulation. In this visual *kula* of images, the more an image circulates in journalistic networks around the world, the more it is validated as much for journalistic credibility as for aesthetic or political force. Remember how important it was for the team that they not lose a strong photo to a competitor. In other words, it can damage a magazine's reputation to be perceived as lacking specific imagery deemed critical for that week's coverage. Conversely, an image or set of images that runs in *U.S. Newsworld* becomes highly visible and will often get picked up by other publications and hence circulate further due to its appearance in the magazine.

Just like the performative function of certain utterances detailed by Austin (1980), Bourdieu (1991), and Butler (1997), the institutional conditions of the production and reception of news photographs are critical to any understanding of their meaning and force. The power vested in the photographers also comes from the reputation of the organization for which they are working. Not only do they need to be the appropriate person, but often they will only get access to certain events if they are attached to certain institutions or publications.[12]

The formative force of documentary images lies in how they interpellate individuals and groups, both those viewing and those fixed within representations. In *Excitable Speech*, Judith Butler (1997) draws on Austin's theory of performativity to analyze how certain utterances interpellate subjects: she analyzes how this sort of interpellation precedes and forms both the subject who utters performatives and the person who is interpellated. It is certainly possible to speak of "hate photographs" as Butler speaks of "hate speech." Just like repeated sexual or racial slurs, repeatedly imaging a certain population in a particular way interpellates the members of that population in a particular way as well as other audiences who come to identify those populations by characteristics highlighted in the representations.

Moreover, journalistic use of photographic representation forces one to rethink visual representation because each photograph is highly singular and indexed to a particular individual, and yet many of the bodies in news photographs are to be seen as stand-ins for large numbers of bodies sharing the same condition. For example, Steve McCurry's famous "Afghan Girl" image, which appeared on a 1985 cover of *National Geographic,* is an indexical representation of Sharbat Gula, an Afghan girl who had moved to Pakistan as a refugee. Her image initially appeared with no identifying name; she was merely one of 2.4 million Afghan refugees and one of 350 female students at a school mentioned in the article. As evidenced by the biometric technology used to identify her irises in 2002 and confirm that a particular 30-year-old woman was indeed the girl in the famous *National Geographic* photograph, that image indexed only her, and yet it also represented Afghan refugees in general. In this way, news photographs are at once truthful visual documents and points of departure for imagining collectives that are represented but not indexed.

The Palestinian blonde in the selection sent to *U.S. Newsworld* was too modern and did not fit Sarah or Joel's image of a typical Palestinian woman. Yet even the photographer admitted that part of the reason for the proliferation of certain images of Palestinian images is photographers' preference for "the exotic," despite their lived experience of a place. So while the lay reader might be presumed to not differentiate between an Israeli and a Palestinian, image brokers perpetuate a certain image of a Palestinian by editing out images that do not match images of Palestinians they have seen before. Effectively these image brokers police the category of Palestinian through mediated representations.

Furthermore, certain parts of the world have certain overdetermined story lines (Hannerz 2004a). Particular geographies are always photographed in relation to the issue of AIDS or genocide or illegal immigrants or starvation. This is a photographic counterpart to how, until quite recently, a fragmented geographical world was often represented in anthropology with certain topics always being studied in certain geographies, such as honor in the Middle East

(Appadurai 1990; Gupta and Ferguson 1997b). Moreover, because some international attention is often better than no attention, less than flattering images, like Butler's hate speech, that nonetheless constitute the social and discursive existence of an interpellated subject are "purchased with the price of guilt" (1997: 24). If news photographs are what Trouillot might term "savage slots," one reason for their prolific production, reproduction, and circulation is that they are one way, and sometimes the only way, to purchase visibility (Trouillot 1991: 27).

Rather than see reception as an activity occurring once a finished product is available to be consumed by a public, my fieldwork focused on practices of reception by various subjects at all the points of decision making prior to the appearance of the image for an end consumer. For, at the moment when a photo editor is perusing dozens of wire service images to choose one to accompany an article, she is imagining the reaction of the viewer, the collective identity of her publication, and how competing image producers/circulators will represent the event. Attention paid to moments of selection renders visible the choices and cultural and political interpretations involved in the everyday labor processes behind the production and circulation of representations. These international news images produce a reassuring (if false) visual narrative asserting that the publications that promise to inform do indeed, at least photographically, have the capability to grasp "the world" in its entirety as a picture and thus to help us grasp the world by seeing what is happening elsewhere. The World section of a news magazine is an imagined seeing "in totality."

Notes

In accordance with the University of California, Berkeley's Committee for the Protection of Human Subjects' guidelines, all my research was conducted anonymously, which is why I have used pseudonyms in all written accounts of this work for both individuals and publications. All information presented here is based on fieldwork and/or interviews I conducted at *U.S. News & World Report, Time,* and *Newsweek* in 2003 and 2004. *U.S. Newsworld,* the title of the magazine described in this article, is a pseudonym, and all information is based on the aggregate of my fieldwork on news magazines. However, dialogues presented here are copied from my transcriptions of actual conversations as they happened during my research. This fieldwork was supported by a Wenner-Gren Individual Research Grant. I am grateful for the suggestions of Elizabeth Bird, Amahl Bishara, Nelson Graburn, Stephanie Sadre-Orafai, and Janelle Taylor, who commented on earlier versions of this chapter.

1. Of course, these are not mutually exclusive categories. When Mars Exploration Rover Spirit, NASA's robotic geologist, landed on Mars and successfully submitted images to Earth in January 2004, one photo editor asked her boss, "Is Mars a national

or international story?" To which he responded, "That's a tough question and a funny question, since I suppose, if you take the viewpoint of the United States, it's a domestic issue."

2. I am aware of the political ramifications inherent in referring to this structure as a security fence rather than a separation barrier or any number of other labels. Yet in the following I have tried to stick to the terms used by my informants, who often used these terms interchangeably, depending on whose opinion they were mediating.

3. I have discussed photographs as palimpsests of imagination in greater detail elsewhere (Gürsel 2006).

4. Photographers used to send in their film without having seen it themselves, and the photo editors would be the first to edit the images. Now photographers are the first editors. One veteran photo editor lamented, "We'll never see what a photographer doesn't want to show. . . . Before, I could see someone thinking [as I edited], I would see how they felt, and I would go through the emotional process [with them while looking through their film]. It's less intimate now."

5. Clay Aiken is an American pop singer who rose to fame in 2003 on the television show *American Idol*.

6. An art director told me about her frustration with a focus groups that her magazine had conducted with readers to better understand what they appreciated: "The reader's understanding of a predominance of war photography is that it's not fun to look at, it's necessary. The groups were fairly discriminatory, and they picked out good images, but I had problems with the moderator because she didn't express that photographs in and of themselves could be newsworthy. She kept asking them to evaluate based on visual attractiveness."

7. A photo editor told me that in her first job her boss had told her, only slightly in jest, that there were countries that matter, countries that don't matter, and countries that matter a little bit and that she should make her edits accordingly.

8. One text editor mentioned visual similarities to other historical moments as a strength for images, such as "This has a Somalia feel of general discontent to it," or "I love this one. It is totally Vietnam looking." Yet she is hesitant to showcase work that is too similar to another photographer's. A story's being reminiscent of another's work is usually an argument against using a set of images, because they are perceived as being unoriginal.

9. In the wall example, the art director was interested in a photo where the subjects were all clustered in the middle of the image.

10. How many options are worked on simultaneously also has to do with a magazine's budget. Two tracking — preparing two cover stories and slightly different magazines — might be typical at a magazine with a large production budget, whereas another magazine might only be able to afford a 10 percent "kill rate," referring to the percentage of images that are prepared for publication but not used.

11. In Bishara's terms, this is one category of person being *unmade* in the process of making another category. In other words, the category of working Palestinian woman is reinforced with the selection of the photograph of the supposedly working woman crossing the wall, but the category of modern Palestinian woman is unmade by the image of the blonde being left out of the selection.

12. In other words, being on assignment for a news magazine might increase a photographer's access to the site of an event. Yet an interesting twist occurs when photographers require visas. A photographer with a valid visa might have a better chance of getting an assignment from a news magazine to cover that story in the first place. Of course, there are also stories of a photographer becoming persona non grata because his or her images were perceived as undesirable to the nation granting the visa. For this reason, publications sometimes cite security concerns and choose not to credit certain images to a photographer.

3 Covering the Barrier in Bethlehem

The Production of Sympathy and the Reproduction of Difference

AMAHL BISHARA

Studies of Western corporate media coverage of international events have tended to focus on institutional structures, textual analysis, or the experiences of foreign correspondents. An ethnographic approach to journalism that examines the social and political contexts of journalistic practices in foreign locations yields a distinct perspective on the by-products of Western journalism. This approach demonstrates that the same sites at which news stories and photographs are produced for global audiences are also sites of local cultural production. News is not the product of a narrow, unified ideology; it is shaped by journalism's on-the-ground and collaborative — though by no means egalitarian — exchanges. Journalists, government officials, and activists all take part in news production, and they bring their own goals and perspectives to this work.

In this chapter, I focus on Palestinian expectations from and involvement in producing Western news coverage of protests against the separation barrier in the West Bank town of Bethlehem. Palestinians organize demonstrations against the barrier in part to attract Western news coverage and thereby generate sympathy for their cause. In Bethlehem, political activism about the barrier and Palestinian perceptions of "Western journalism" contribute to the shaping of the important local categories of the "Palestinian Christian" and the "Palestinian refugee." The broad category of Western journalism should be taken here as closely related to a salient Palestinian term, *al-sahaafa al-duwaliya* (the international press).[1]

Christians are an important minority group in Palestinian society. Middle Eastern minorities' views of themselves have often been refracted through Western perceptions of both the minority group and Muslim Arab majorities (J. Goodman 2005; K. Hoffman 2002; Kaufman 2001; Kosnick 2004; Silverstein 2002). Writing about Berber culture in Algeria, Jane Goodman characterizes the formation of Berber political identity as occurring within a network of branching interconnections that have included Arab Algerians and the French.

Goodman aptly views identity formation as a process that takes place within a complex network that cannot be reduced to a unidirectional flow from the West to the Middle East, but rather entails much more intricate circulations of media, meaning, and social power.

Palestinian Christians' views of themselves — and other Palestinians' views of Palestinian Christians — have likewise hinged on both global and regional flows of power and systems of meaning. While Berbers move frequently among their villages, Algerian cities, and France, Palestinians face serious movement restrictions. However, they also have a complex understanding of the power of external — especially Western, and most especially U.S. — recognition. The Palestinian case is distinct also because, unlike some Middle East minorities, many Palestinian Christian activists are committed to a larger nationalist cause. Palestinian Christians have been an important part of the imagined Palestinian nation from its beginnings. Although Bethlehem has historically been predominantly Christian, Muslims, many of them refugees, constitute the majority today.[2] Palestinian refugees' identity is also influenced by refugees' assumptions about how they are represented in Western journalism.

In his analysis of processes of social construction, Ian Hacking (1999: 161) suggests that social processes are implicated in "making up people," or creating categories of people that become legally, socially, or politically effective in the world. Hacking (2000) asserts that we must distinguish between *concepts* that are socially constructed and the *objects* — including people — with which these concepts are associated, because some kinds of objects, like people, can affect the concepts that define them. Hacking's argument about these looping processes of social construction suggests the prospect that actual Palestinian Christians and refugees might be able to respond to the ideas or concepts that have sedimented to define them and thus change those concepts. But, of course, they would do so in relation to the social context that surrounds them. In this case, the key concepts of the "Palestinian refugee" and the "Palestinian Christian" are constructed in relation to at least three distinct social contexts, or what Hacking would call matrices: Bethlehem society, Palestinian nationalism, and the Western media. These matrices are themselves interrelated but in ways that reflect enduring asymmetries of power among them.

This chapter examines many Palestinians' presumption that Western sympathy gathers around one category, the "Palestinian Christian," and analyzes how this presumption can tend to sideline the importance of the other category, the "Palestinian refugee." I highlight a different kind of outcome to the process of making up people, the possibility that not only are categories of people potentially in the making but that they can also be caught in processes of *unmaking*. Through the endeavor of producing Western news, Palestinian refugees in Bethlehem contributed to the making of the "Palestinian Christian" as a key category of Palestinian nationalism that produces Western sympathy for Palestinians. Yet these refugees were also sometimes implicated in processes of unmaking the concept of the "Palestinian refugee." This was not because these refugees did not believe in refugee rights. Indeed, these people actively promoted what they considered to be the fundamental right of Palestinian refugees to return to their home villages inside present-day Israel. However, they let this claim take second priority as they protested the latest crisis, the barrier. In doing so, they also reproduced their own marginality and alterity. It is essential to note that just as social categories are always in the making and never fully made or completed, processes of unmaking are also not absolute. It is not that the category of the "Palestinian refugee" disappeared. Nonetheless, it is worthwhile to catch these categories in flux, in order to examine how processes of Western journalism can affect national and local politics in the West Bank.

Unfolding the History of a Photograph

My central example in this chapter is a news photograph that appeared in a local Palestinian newspaper and also in the Yahoo! slideshow of the Middle East conflict, which visually documents the news of the last few days from this international "hotspot." The slideshow is an important source because it mirrors the photographs that news agencies make available for publication to their subscribers around the world. This Agence France-Presse (AFP) photo (fig. 3.1), taken on August 8, 2004, by a Palestinian photojournalist, depicts a Palestinian Christian priest holding a poster that shows children breaking down the separation barrier with a giant key. The beginning of the caption reads: "Palestinians march in the West Bank village of Beit Jala near Bethlehem to protest against the construction of part of Israel's separation barrier in the area." Having attended this protest, observed journalists covering various protests, and done ethnographic fieldwork with nonjournalists in Bethlehem in order to understand how they think about Western news, I am able to analyze the social and political relations embedded in this photograph.

In this approach, I travel a similar path as other scholars of cultural production who work to recover initial meanings and contexts that become unavailable as layers of mediation accumulate and as media travel across geographic and cultural distances (E. Edwards 1992; Feld 1996; Lippard 1992; Pinney and Peterson 2003; Silverstein 1996). Each form of mediation has its own epistemologies and norms that structure how intercultural incorporations may be framed. In processes Steven Feld describes, Central African BaBenzélé singing ends up as a sample in a Madonna song by way of ethnographic recordings and

Figure 3.1. Agence France-Presse photograph, taken on August 8, 2004, by a Palestinian photojournalist, shows a Palestinian priest at a protest against the Bethlehem separation barrier. He holds a poster of Palestinian children breaking down the barrier with a key, a symbol of the right of refugees to return to their villages. Photographer: Musa al-Shaer; distributed by AFP Collection/Getty Images. Used by permission.

jazz classics. In this brief musical sample, or quotation, these BaBenzélé sounds are separated from their source entirely in order to produce a culturally unspecific exotic mood (Feld 1996). In this pop music world, it seems, the identity of the people who sang these songs is not important; what is important is that they give the effect of the foreign and the primitive.

News media, on the other hand, can reproduce a homology between a group of people and a place with the ideology of objectivity. One assumption of this ideology, which remains important in U.S. journalism, is that news represents facts and ideas that are out there in the world, rather than possibly constituting these facts through processes of journalistic production (Peterson 2001). By referring to people and places as though these categories or concepts are objective facts, news tends to produce and reproduce the naturalized quality that national and ethnic identities often have on the world stage. The ideology of objectivity does not generally make room for audiences to recognize that these texts might be constitutive of concepts of people and places, rather than just referential to preexisting concepts. This is why news texts can be so influential in processes of social construction or, as Hacking terms it, making up people. Photojournalism especially can seem to have a transparent relationship with objective truth because of the photograph's indexical and iconic relationship to its object.

Yet photographs are anything but unmediated. The photograph of the Palestinian priest encloses several media and other kinds of social processes. Studying these complex and interrelated social processes by way of ethnography illuminates a "media world" (Ginsburg, Abu-Lughod, and Larkin 2002). I highlight here three of these interrelated social processes in turn, starting from the widest frame, the production of the photograph itself, then the organization of the protest, and finally the production of the poster being held by the priest.

How Was This Photograph Produced?

It might be surprising that a rather unassuming protest of perhaps 75 people garnered international news coverage. This kind of coverage was made possible by the institutional structures and day-to-day practices of journalism in the West Bank. During the second Intifada, a Palestinian uprising against Israeli occupation, international news agencies' demands for Palestinian photojournalists skyrocketed. From September 29, 2000, the first day of the second Intifada, through at least the end of 2002, there was a constant stream of events that could generate compelling — and saleable — images from the West Bank and Gaza. Images of protest were visually interesting because they could capture conflict and embodied political performance. Most Intifada images were produced by Western wire service agencies, most notably the Associated Press, Reuters, and AFP, and sold to newspapers and magazines around the world. Yet hundreds of physical restrictions to movement, like checkpoints and roadblocks that Israel erected in the West Bank, prevented journalists from expeditious travel between Palestinian cities (Bishara 2006). As a result, the news agencies hired Palestinian photographers, often as stringers paid by the day, in each city to cover breaking news. In the West Bank, an area slightly smaller than the state of Delaware, a news agency might have relationships with photojournalists in six cities. This is one example of how the political and geographical contexts of knowledge production have a profound effect on what is created.

Both journalists and protesters were pleased that protests warranted coverage. Photojournalists were always looking for material, especially since they were paid by the day. Covering demonstrations fulfilled many journalists' nationalist commitments, as well as their professional need for images. For protesters, the presence of journalists working for Western news organizations made demonstrations seem worthwhile. Protesters made this evaluation according to an important local political calculus. Many Palestinians had ascertained, most recently through their experience during the construction of the separation barrier, that they had no voice in Israeli policy decisions and that their own government, the Palestinian Authority (PA), was powerless on many matters of concern. For this reason, Western media assumed importance as Palestinians attempted to sway powerful segments of the international community. Many Palestinians perceived the U.S. media as the most important of the Western media because of the great power that the United States wields in the region. Given the tight social networks of the West Bank, activists might complain to a journalist who did not cover such a protest.

The separation barrier was itself a hot topic for Western news. It had generated headlines as soon as Israeli prime minister Ariel Sharon announced the idea, in April 2002, of building a barrier to prevent Palestinian suicide bombers from entering Israel. It was the barrier as spectacle — with a proposed length of about 400 miles, made of electrically monitored fences and eight-meter concrete walls — that attracted Western journalists' attention. The barrier inspired comparisons to the Great Wall of China and Hadrian's Wall (Barr 2002; R. Cohen 2002; Dao 2002). Some were amazed that in an era of satellite phones and missiles, issues of national security could be so low-tech and so concrete. Once construction began, the spectacular quality of the barrier continued to attract journalists' — and especially photojournalists' — attention. Yet, as with many other media spectacles, this approach obfuscated key issues as much as it elucidated them. Photographs of the barrier's physical qualities did not necessarily shed light on debates about security or the long-term consequences of the barrier.

This photograph's focus on the priest is consistent with the narrative proclivities of Western journalism about Bethlehem. In part, the priest may have been selected because photojournalists around the world often focus on the most visually distinctive aspect of an event and one that seems to evoke the local color of a particular place (Pedelty 1993). Aside from the priest, everyone else was in mundane street clothes. This decision to photograph the priest also reflects long-standing Western interest in Israel and the Occupied Territories as the "Holy Land." Ulf Hannerz (2004a) has found that foreign correspondents cover the world through regional narratives that reflect their associations with a particular place. He found that Japan is covered as a site of a quirky alternative modernity, while Africa is covered as a site of chaos and disorder. Israel and the Palestinian territories are often covered by way of religion. These news frameworks are linked to much older kinds of cultural production. In nineteenth-century travelogues and fairs (Davidson 2001; McAlister 2001; Obenzinger 1999; Shepherd 1987) and in early-twentieth-century anthropology (Rabinowitz 2001), Palestinians were represented as relics of biblical times. This is another example of what Johannes Fabian (1983) identified as a tendency of those in the West to think of other places in the world as existing in their own past.

Especially around Christmas, Bethlehem, famous as the birthplace of Jesus, was frequently covered in relation to its place in Christian history, even when the latest news might have seemed unrelated to religion. The 2005 Christmas season was the first year that a substantial amount of the barrier around Bethlehem had been completed; the barrier became the subject of the Christmas article for several newspapers. On December 22, the *Christian Science Monitor* emphasized how the wall had become an obstacle to Christian rituals:

> Every year on the morning of Dec. 25, the Latin Patriarch and a host of Church dignitaries head southward from Jerusalem via an ancient road to Bethlehem. But this year, the procession will pass through a metal gate topped with rolls of barbed wire, normally closed but opened briefly so as not to impede the tradition. (Mitnick 2005)

The *Chicago Tribune* described the trend of Christian emigration out of Bethlehem as an effect of the barrier (Greenberg 2005), as did the *Financial Times* (Morris 2005). The *Times* of London quoted biblical passages and provided a glimpse at the contemporary version of the biblical route from Nazareth to Bethlehem (Farrell 2005). While all of these articles expressed sympathy for Palestinian suffering, and although Bethlehem received much more coverage than many other towns around the world that faced political crises, this kind of recognition was troubling to some Bethlehem residents. As the mayor of Bethlehem commented to the *Times,* "We are remembered one day a year. On Christmas Eve all the world speaks of Bethlehem, but they give nothing to us."

At the same time, a local Palestinian organization was also promoting coverage of the barrier by way of the city's place in Christian history. In November 2005, the Open Bethlehem project began to advocate tearing down the separation barrier around the city. Its leaders used a cautious politics of religion to attract audiences to the issue. Leila Sansour, the chief executive officer of Open Bethlehem, suggested that Bethlehem's Christian character made it a city that embraces universal liberal values, stating that Bethlehem "confounds the stereotype of Palestine seen in the news cycles. It is a modern and dynamic society — though one caught in the torpor of imprisonment. Bethlehem is a city of highly educated, multilingual people." She emphasized the importance of maintaining Bethlehem's Christian community: "Bethlehem is the anchor of Christian community in Palestine. Almost half of Palestinian Christians live in our city. If Christianity cannot survive in the Holy Land with its 2,000 years of uninterrupted tradition, it has very little chance of surviving elsewhere in the Middle East" (Open Bethlehem 2005). Sansour was quoted in some of the Western media coverage that year (Harris 2005; Morris 2005). Foreign correspondents' frameworks had, in this case, the support of some activist NGOs.

Returning to the broader question of how this photograph of protest was created, it is clear that the journalist's presence at the demonstration had to do with the local practices of international journalism at this particular time of crisis that made it possible for relatively small protests to be covered by Western news agencies. He may also have covered this protest because of the established interest of the Western media in the separation barrier. His decision to take and his editor's decision to publish this photograph, rather than one featuring another protester, was related to Western frameworks for representing Bethlehem by way of its Christian community.

How Was the Protest Produced?

The Beit Jala protest was organized by the Bethlehem branch of the Emergency National and Islamic Committee, a multiparty coalition established to coordinate political activities like protests and martyrs' funerals. It brought together sectors of Bethlehem society in a way that overcame social divisions between Christians and Muslims, refugees and nonrefugees. The Bethlehem metropolitan area comprises three towns, including Bethlehem and Beit Jala, all of which have historically been home to predominantly Christian residents. Three refugee camps in the area were founded in the aftermath of the 1948 war when people from nearby villages, almost all of them Muslims, fled conflict zones and gathered on the outskirts of Bethlehem. All three towns have also become home to significant Muslim populations since 1948, as some refugees have moved out of the camps. The refugee population has been growing faster than that of the Christians because they tend to have larger families and because many Christians have emigrated to the Americas or Europe. Only about one-third of the population of the metropolitan area, including the three towns and the three camps, is now Christian. However, the Bethlehem area maintains its Christian quality in that churches support many important institutions, such as schools and hospitals. Moreover, local political power remains largely in the hands of Christians. As stipulated by a PA law meant to provide representation for minorities, the mayors of the three towns in the Bethlehem area must be Christian. Palestinian refugees living in the camps are more likely to be living in poverty. The 2006 Palestinian census found that in the West Bank and Gaza as a whole, 38.6 percent of camp residents lived in poverty, compared with 29.3 percent of urban residents (Palestinian Central Bureau of Statistics 2007: 29).

The social context in Bethlehem must be understood in terms of intersecting religious, social, and political identities. Although Palestinian Muslims and Christians have long cherished their good relationships with each other, over the past few decades there has increasingly been tension between the two religious groups (Bowman 2000). In Bethlehem, religious divisions have only been compounded by strained relations between refugees of the camps and nonrefugees. Tensions between long-term residents and refugees are common, both in Palestinian contexts, such as Gaza (Feldman 2007), and in other global refugee crises. In Bethlehem, visitors like me occasionally were admonished by nonrefugees not to visit the camps, lest one be exploited in some way. Some Christians felt refugees had changed social norms in the city for the worse, and sometimes they resented the financial costs of hosting the refugee population. Refugees resented their marginality to local political and economic power, as well as others' negative characterizations of their communities. Existing low-level strains had intensified at the beginning of the second Intifada. Palestinian militants, who were disproportionately refugees, took advantage of the high mountains of the Christian town of Beit Jala to fire on the neighboring Israeli settlement of Gilo. This precipitated Israeli attacks that destroyed many houses, including a few prominent mansions. Some Christians saw this damage as a consequence of militants' disregard for them and of militants' lack of clear strategies. Refugees sometimes asserted that Christians were, on the whole, less politically committed than they were.

These are some of the ways in which refugees and Christians related to and thought of each other in Bethlehem. The concepts of both the Palestinian Christian and the Palestinian refugee have also had complex roles to play in Palestinian nationalism. Especially in the 1960s, 1970s, and 1980s, Palestinian leaders emphasized the existence of a Palestinian Christian community in order to demonstrate their own secularism and openness to religious difference. Increasingly, elite Palestinian politics has oriented itself around Western support, rather than leftist Third World support, and the religious framework for the Palestinian-Israeli conflict has become more dominant. With these developments, Palestinian leaders, and especially Palestinian Christians, have deployed nationalist arguments related to Christianity in a variety of ways, drawing on Christian liberation theology, Christian history, or an ancestral connection between Jesus and his disciples and present-day Palestinians.

The concept of the Palestinian refugee in Palestinian nationalism has also shifted over time. For decades, refugees were at the symbolic heart of Palestinian identity, both because of their suffering and struggles and because the restoration of their rights seemed to be essential to fulfillment of Palestinian national rights. Yet the image of the refugee was also seen as somehow undercutting Palestinians' assertions that they were a national group, ready for modernization and progress. Rashid Khalidi, a prominent Palestinian political analyst, summarizes this irony: "In 1967, the adjective *Palestinian,* if used at all, served primarily as a modifier for *refugees.* . . . A precondition for any achievements on the levels of international legality and world public opinion was that the Palestinians change the image of themselves as refugees" (Khalidi 1987: 7). Contemporarily, although many Palestinians still believe that the refugees' right to return is at the core of the Palestinian national claim, key PA officials and other leaders have hinted that Palestinians will have to relinquish that right. Despite renewed refugee advocacy, this political trend has weakened the centrality of the category of the Palestinian refugee to Palestinian nationalism on the world stage.

If religion, politics, and class have divided Christians and refugees in Bethlehem, the separation barrier is just one aspect of Israeli occupation that has connected them, in this case quite literally. The path of the barrier connects Aida Refugee Camp and Beit Jala, both of which are on the northern edge of Bethlehem. The part of Beit Jala where the barrier was to be constructed, and where the protest was held, had already been transformed by the architecture of occupation. In the late 1990s, Israel built a network of bypass roads so Israeli settlers could drive through the West Bank without going through Palestinian cities. One of these roads was built under Beit Jala, by way of a tunnel constructed through one of Beit Jala's mountains. The road emerged in the middle of a valley, on both sides of which were Beit Jala neighborhoods. Despite going under the Palestinian town, Israel restricted Palestinian drivers from using this road. Years later, the separation barrier was to be built in order to protect this bypass road, and this is where the protest was held.

The director of the Emergency Committee was a refugee who lived with his extended family in Beit Jala in a handsome but simple house that overlooked the road. He had ties in both Aida Refugee Camp and Beit Jala and saw the benefits of bringing the communities together for this Sunday afternoon protest. He invited religious leaders, church groups, and also a youth center from Aida Refugee Camp to attend this demonstration. Churchgoers came in dresses and dress pants, and about 25 teenagers and adults arrived wearing white T-shirts emblazoned with the logo of the youth center. Also mixed into the group were a number of Europeans and North Americans.

So it was that this modest but motley assembly embarked together from the center of Beit Jala, through the narrow streets of the town, and toward the construction site. Some of the teenagers from different parts of town inspected each other with wary curiosity. Others just socialized with their own friends as they casually held signs that said things like "No for the Annexation of Our Lands." Many people held the poster of the children breaking down the wall. Some of the teenagers from the camp, who were regular participants in stone-throwing demonstrations against the barrier near their own homes, were ready for action. But having a few days earlier been involved in a demonstration that ended in shouting matches with soldiers, tear gas, and sound grenades, they had been told to keep things calm.

The group walked across the backyards of people whose olive trees were being cut down because of the barrier, and international visitors stopped to take pictures of green branches strewn around trunks with severed limbs. The group descended about two-thirds of the way into the valley, as far as they could go without breaching a chain-link fence that provisionally kept Palestinians from the bypass road. With their megaphones, the leaders called out slogans against the barrier, and the crowd called back. People hung their signs on the fence, but because of our elevation, there was no way that Israeli drivers below would actually see the signs. The only way for protesters to voice their views to outsiders was by way of the journalists who covered the event. Having gathered and displayed their signs, protesters had little else to do. Protesters milled about and soon departed. To sum up, the protest was the result of alliances that united neighboring communities for the sake of national politics. Due to the structure and location of the protest, Western media presence was an important barometer for organizers' sense of their success.

How and Why Was This Poster Produced?

Having examined the journalistic infrastructure that led to the taking of the photograph, and the political relations inside Bethlehem that led to the organization of the protest, we can now examine the production of the poster itself, a media reframed by the photograph. The youth center that brought about 25 people to the protest had produced this poster for its annual international work camp, in which volunteers from the United States and Europe came to do a service project and learn about Palestinian society. The youth center had printed hundreds of the posters to publicize their summer camp, and they were hanging all around Bethlehem. One of the most active volunteers at the center, who I will call Rashid, worked in advertising, so he knew the value of making a name for the youth center. Indeed, this was why he had instructed the protest delegation to wear their T-shirts. And he was especially happy that so many people, even those with no association with the refugee camp or the youth center, like the priest, were holding the poster.

The poster incorporated a number of important Palestinian political symbols: the village, the church, the mosque, and most notably the key. The key represents Palestinian refugees' right to return, because in 1948 many Palestinians fleeing conflict left their homes and took their keys with them expecting to come home soon. Palestinian refugees have held onto these keys, and today they bring them out when they describe their home villages for their grandchildren —or for visiting reporters and photographers. The refugee issue was significant to the youth center not only because the group served refugee children from Aida Camp but also because its founders strongly believed in the right of Palestinian refugees to return to their home villages. Rashid, who had commissioned the poster, explained to me that it was meant to make a connection between the right of return and opposition to the barrier. He said it suggested that despite the separation barrier, these Palestinian children were determined to build better lives for themselves and their community by carrying out the right of return.

In the youth center's poster, the village, with the limestone and domes of Palestinian vernacular architecture, can be seen behind the barrier, indexing an idyllic past that the children struggle to revitalize. The skyline of this village includes both a mosque and a church. While there were mixed Muslim and Christian villages before 1948, and there still are such villages, this is not the norm. The use of these two symbols asserts that both groups play an integral role in Palestinian society. This poster is evidence of these Palestinian refugees' conviction that Christian-Muslim harmony is an important political value, a part of Palestinian tradition, and a foundation for a better future.

The youth center had chosen to focus on the barrier for its poster because the barrier was affecting the lives of people in the camp quite dramatically, even though the barrier was not yet complete. Construction of the eight-meter wall had brought soldiers and armed guards along with earthmovers and cranes to the camp. Teenagers staged protests, which Israeli soldiers tried to repress. Tear gas settled in the camp almost daily, and some teenagers had been injured by rubber bullets and live ammunition. Tens of teenagers were also arrested and imprisoned by the army, most often for throwing stones at Israeli jeeps and watchtowers during protests. Such arrests had wide-ranging social effects (Cook et al. 2004). Residents knew that if the barrier were to be completed, it would cut them off from the only open space to which they had access, an olive grove owned by the Armenian Church. For decades, the Church had hired camp residents to harvest olives, and residents also used this land to gather herbs and greens and to graze goats and sheep. Notably I found no U.S. news stories written about the effect of the barrier on this community. Nonetheless, for refugees of Aida Camp, construction of the barrier was a pivotal political development of 2004. Thus the poster combined long- and short-term political aims of this community and fulfilled the significant goal of publicizing the youth center itself.

On the surface, this news photograph seemed like a successful end result of the protest. For local audiences who saw the picture in a Palestinian newspaper, it demonstrated Palestinian dedication to resisting the barrier in Bethlehem and steadfastness on the refugee issue. It documented a moment of collaboration between Christian leaders and refugees, which, while hardly unprecedented, would be seen as a constructive move. For those who had seen the youth center's posters up all around town, the picture also implicitly promoted their work even though the center's name and logo were cut off. Local activists involved with the event surmised that this news agency–produced image would travel to international audiences, as it did on the Yahoo! slideshow of the Middle East conflict. Another active adult volunteer in the youth center, Jawad, perceived this as a positive image for global circulation. Jawad told me, "For us, children signify the future, hope, human dignity, and real peace. In contrary, the wall means despair, cruelty, antipathy, inhumanity. In short, the poster carried by the priest was made to say: 'We, the Palestinians, Muslims, and Christians, believe that the Wall does not destroy our lives only; it threatens our children's also.'" The message about the right to return drops out as the image circulates outside of Palestinian contexts, because an international audience is less likely to know about the meaning of the key, or even to see the key, as the image is reproduced in small formats. Jawad's interpretation takes for granted the fact that refugees' presence is erased in exchange for critical representations of the barrier and that priests are good publicity for Palestinians.

Photographs like that from the Beit Jala protest, along with the news articles I discussed, suggest that news representations of the barrier in Bethlehem, produced by way of these complex collaborations among different kinds of activists and journalists, create sympathy for Palestinians facing the barrier by displaying the presence or suffering of Palestinian Christians or alluding to Christian history or values. Because Palestinians themselves are sensitive to and aware of

Western media predilections, these patterns also shaped Palestinian political practice in ways that solidified shifts in Palestinian nationalist priorities and marginalized refugee rights.

The Politics of Framing the Barrier

On Palm Sunday, 2005, a Bethlehem Christian organization led a children's march against the barrier in coordination with an international Christian delegation that was visiting the region. The protest was organized around the idea that the barrier cut off Bethlehem from Jerusalem and thus severed important biblical routes. The protest incorporated a number of Christian symbols, including palm fronds, donkeys, and the child as the harbinger of peaceful redemption. It was meant to resonate more broadly than would the image of Palestinian children breaking down the wall and returning to their families' villages. It also suggested that a Christian ethic of nonviolence was the route to justice. The youth of Aida Refugee Camp were invited to this protest, since they could turn out good numbers and since the residents of Aida certainly agreed with the Christian organization about the barrier.

While there were many internationals and Palestinian journalists there with cameras, I am not sure to what extent this event generated international news coverage. However, this is beside the point, which is that Palestinians' awareness of the proclivities of political audiences abroad authorized certain kinds of political action. It helped to structure a kind of politics in which the Christian organization could call up the refugee youth center and invite children to a Christian-themed protest, but no association from the refugee camp could do the reverse as successfully. The camp was both a riskier place to protest — where one would almost surely encounter Israeli soldiers — and also a less appealing place in which to frame Palestinians' arguments against the barrier. These dynamics changed Palestinian refugees' views of their own local forms of political action.

Since the completion of the wall immediately next to the camp in the summer of 2005, more children and young men have been injured. One, Jawad's 12-year-old son, was shot in the stomach by Israeli soldiers posted in one of the watchtowers in the separation barrier as he played with his cousins on the balcony of his house during an otherwise calm afternoon. Because of such incidents, the barrier is a constant source of anxiety. Walking through the streets of the camp, or sitting outside, one is always aware of whether or not one is in view of the watchtowers.

Even in these difficult circumstances, many refugees seemed hesitant to talk to international visitors and journalists about the breadth of their own experiences because they doubted their experiences would be moving to these audiences. In the summer of 2007, after Jawad's son was shot, a British journalist came to the camp to do a story about the barrier. Jawad, in helping to coordinate the journalist's visit, brought two young men who had spent time in prison because of their protests against the barrier to talk to the journalist about their experiences. Before the journalist arrived, Jawad, a seasoned activist, told them they should not shy away from discussing the active resistance they had engaged in by throwing stones during protests. Yet, when it came time for the youths to speak, they told only the stories of their terrifying arrests and of the deprivations they endured while they were in prison. That is, they told stories of being victims rather than activists.

Having spent a good amount of time with these youths in less formal settings, I knew there were other stories they could have told. They often spoke with pride about how they, fortified only with stones, confronted armed soldiers and guards in armored jeeps who had come to their neighborhood to build a restrictive wall. Their pride sprang from their belief that an Intifada based on popular resistance like their own would be more beneficial to their cause than a series of suicide bombings and from their knowledge of a long history of such popular resistance in the refugee camps. While youths throwing stones were a key positive image of Palestinians in Western news during the first Intifada, which lasted from 1987 through 1993, the concept of youths throwing stones, even against soldiers in armed jeeps, generates less sympathy in the 2000s. They also could have told a historical narrative many in the camp shared, that upon the establishment of Israel, their grandparents had become refugees, pushed out of their villages, and that now, with the building of the barrier, Israel was cutting them off from the small bit of land they had known all their lives.

These young men could have told compelling stories of activism as refugees. Yet these men who were otherwise insightful political thinkers did not consider it prudent to narrate that story for the international audience they perceived to be most important, that of the U.S. and European corporate media. If Christians were associated with peaceful protests and nonviolence, they knew that they, young male refugees, were associated with chaos and violence. These preconceptions were powerful both locally and internationally. Through their failure to find a way to communicate effectively with outsiders except as victims of Israeli oppression, a stance connected to human rights arguments rather than political claims (Khalili 2007), they were also in a sense contributing to the unmaking of the Palestinian refugee as a political category.

Conclusion

Collaborations between journalists working for Western media and Palestinian activists have yielded stories and images sympathetic to Palestinian suffering due to the separation barrier. However, these media tend to eclipse class, religious, and political differences within Bethlehem and to further marginalize the experiences and political claims of Palestinian refugees. To understand how the concepts of the Palestinian refugee and the Palestinian Christian take on changing associations, we must examine influential Western views of these concepts, their places in Palestinian nationalist discourses, and how actual Palestinian Christians and refugees have viewed each other and themselves in specific places like Bethlehem. Especially because Palestinians are highly aware of trends in Western media representation, Palestinian Christians and refugees may contribute to the reshaping of the categories that define them. While making the case against the newer disaster of the separation barrier in Bethlehem, Palestinian refugees may sometimes be unmaking the Palestinian refugee as a key concept and political issue in Palestinian nationalism, at least temporarily. The Palestinian case is by no means unique. Activists around the world are concerned with how they are represented by U.S. and European media. They are cognizant of the deep influence that U.S. and European policies have on their societies. Thus anthropologists of journalism must be on the lookout for how local identities and politics transform in periods of crisis when journalists working for Western media arrive.

Studying journalistic production in broad social context — tracing out a world of media production — requires analyzing how media processes can frame and reframe each other, and how media production relates to other kinds of social processes. This anthropological approach helps us to understand the complex meanings that might be obscured as processes of cultural production fold into each other and as media travel across great cultural and geographic distances. Through ethnographies of journalistic production, social transformations — in this case, shifts in identity politics and nationalist discourses — can be tracked as they are caught up in the processes of media production. These approaches allow us to analyze how and why locations of Western journalistic production are also important sites of local cultural production that can reinforce both local and global hierarchies.

Notes

I am grateful to Elizabeth Bird, Summerson Carr, Hussein Agrama, Robin Shoaps, Lori Allen, and Zeynep Gürsel, who read and gave insightful comments on drafts of this chapter, and to audiences at Macalester College, Tufts University, the University of California at Davis, and Northwestern University for their thoughtful feedback. I am thankful that I was able to conduct research with support from the Lichtstern Research Fund from the University of Chicago and a Fulbright-Hays Dissertation Research Fellowship.

1. Palestinians saw the Western media as a single, albeit diverse, category for several reasons. The "international media" of local parlance consisted largely of big, wealthy media organizations from Europe and North America, which is why I refer to them in this chapter as the Western media. This is still, of course, a very broad term, but one that becomes relevant in part because of global media conglomeration (McChesney 1999). From a Palestinian perspective, it was not always clear where a journalist's work would be published or broadcast, because Palestinians often encountered Palestinian journalists working for international media outlets. Indeed, the photograph I discuss in this chapter — taken by a Palestinian journalist, for a French news agency, but appearing on the website of a U.S.-owned company — speaks to the complexity of the category of the Western media. When protesters saw the Palestinian journalist at the Beit Jala demonstration where this photograph was taken, they likely knew he worked for an international news agency. However, they did not necessarily know which agency. For protesters, the differences among various news agencies were less obvious and less important than those among Arab satellite news stations. From a Palestinian perspective, Arab satellite news stations fell somewhere between the category of "their" media and "international" media. My own characterization of the "Western media" follows in part from this West Bank vantage point. While I read mostly U.S. and British media, I had a sense of what other European journalists were covering because I encountered them covering the separation barrier while we were all working in the West Bank.

2. According to Loren Lybarger's analysis of Palestinian Authority statistics from the 1997 census, Christians constitute 61 percent of the population of the three neighboring towns of Bethlehem, Beit Sahour, and Beit Jala, but less than 17 percent of the Bethlehem Governorate, which includes refugee camps that are part of the Bethlehem metropolitan area and nearby villages. Within the city of Bethlehem itself, 42 percent of the population is Christian (Lybarger 2002: 111).

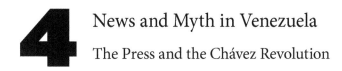

News and Myth in Venezuela

The Press and the Chávez Revolution

JOSEPH C. MANZELLA AND LEON I. YACHER

In the summer of 1993, there were three presidents of Venezuela in as many weeks. It was a pivotal time for one of Latin America's most stable democracies (Neuhouser 1992: 177), which had been plunged yet again into a political crisis. The crisis began with the ouster of President Carlos Andres Pérez, a popular liberal politician who was caught Watergate-style in a morass of corruption and cover-ups. It was also a pivotal time for Venezuelan journalists. It was the corps of reporters of Caracas that weathered intimidation and imprisonment to uncover the Pérez scandal. Thus for the Caracas news community, this moment was not just great but also seminal. Venezuelan journalists had equaled the success of the much-admired American journalists of the Watergate era. And they had confirmed that the press could be a force for change and not a lapdog for the political system.

The events of 1993 helped bolster the notion that the raison d'être of the press was to be a watchdog on the abuses of power, a concept with deep roots in Western press ideology. Implied in the watchdog schema of news is the notion that politicians are innately duplicitous, that authority is not to be trusted, and that government is inherently corruptible. So infused with these notions, influenced in part by U.S. journalism, the Caracas news media emerged from those political crises more powerful than ever.

In the spring of 2007, however, the political revolution of Hugo Chávez had all but silenced oppositional press voices through overt actions supported by the manipulation of cultural symbols embodied in the national mythos surrounding the nation's greatest hero, Simón Bolívar. Marshall Sahlins (1981) explains how events and people become mythologized and then are reproduced and transformed as a new reality, eventually becoming templates for the operating principles of sociopolitical systems. In the context of Venezuela and the rise of Hugo Chávez, the notion of re-creating and transforming myth is particularly critical, especially as it serves multiple functions, including the suppression of what has been a national press notable for its ability to check the powers-that-be.

This chapter argues that in the pivotal years for the Venezuelan press, specifically 2006 and 2007, Chávez neutered an aggressive watchdog Western-style press by re-creating the myth of his nation's founding in the form of a Bolivarian revolution. He accomplished this by positioning himself as a champion of the poor and an opponent of a media elite, which is perceived as ideologically linked to the United States and which Chávez views as a hegemonic empire (Hellinger 2003: 46). Thus Chávez linked himself to Venezuela's history and to the national hero Bolívar, who fought Spanish colonialism in the early nineteenth century. Consequently, Chávez has created a protective shell that the journalistic community has not been able or willing to overcome. It also suggests that the watchdog model of the press, once established, is difficult to entirely suppress because it represents a strong counterideology based on a particularly resilient occupational culture or, as Zelizer suggests, an interpretive community (1993). Through a common discourse about events (Zelizer 1993: 234), such journalistic communities tend to share a distinct way of framing reality (Tuchman 1978).

The material for this chapter is based on in-situ fieldwork in Venezuela, both in the capital, Caracas, and in other locations during the politically tumultuous year of 1993 and in 2006 and 2007. Related fieldwork was conducted in Havana, Cuba, in June 2007 and the Kyrgyz Republic in 2003, 2005, and 2006 (Manzella and Yacher 2005). Structured interviews and newsroom observation in 1993 and 2006–2007 involved editors and reporters at print organizations, whereas broadcast venues were included in the 2006–2007 interviews. Organizations cooperating in this study included the newspapers *El Nacional, El Universal, Últimas Noticias, Diario VEA, El Nuevo País,* and *La Verdad*.[1]

The Rise of Chávez

Chávez refers to his regime as part of the "Bolivarian revolution," and the use of the term *revolution* was in itself both a break from recent political traditions and an incorporation of earlier caudillistic traditions embodied in the mythos of Bolívar, the early nineteenth-century Venezuelan-born military leader venerated in several Latin American countries, including Colombia, Ecuador, Peru, and Bolivia.[2]

Although Hugo Chávez Frias's rise to near-dictatorial power was more evolutionary than revolutionary, there were indications of what was to come shortly after the elections of 1998, when Chávez was elected president by taking 56 percent of the vote just a year after the polls had shown virtually no support for his presidential bid (Trinkunas 2002: 64). One of his first actions was to propose a National Assembly (ANC) that would write a new constitution inclusive of all Venezuelans and through which the poor, in particular, would benefit most. After all, the poorest had reached a nadir in living standards in an oil-rich exporting country that was earning a considerable amount of income on a daily basis. Few expected that Chávez would succeed in his plan to introduce a new constitution, but the appeal of his populist agenda, which tapped into the spirit of Bolivarianism, was, especially for the disaffected, a welcome alternative. Voting for the two primary political parties would have been to select the status quo, an uninviting thought for a sizable population that clearly was without representation (Roberts 2003; Ellner 1996).

In July 2000, Chávez was reelected president after a controversial and confrontational series of events. In part, the vagueness of the new constitution favored the incumbent (John Carey 2003: 130). The opposition resisted, and in April 2002, over half a million people took to the streets demanding Chávez's resignation. The events were chaotic, with more than 20 killed and 100 injured. Chávez was taken into custody, but by April 14, loyalists had returned him to power. The opposition called for a general strike that affected the country's economy for about a month. By February 2003, both sides had agreed to a recall referendum, and on August 15, 2004, Chávez won the vote by 59 percent, which was immediately contested by the opposition. Under a new constitution, Chávez won election on December 3, 2006, by a plurality of 63 percent, which he and his followers interpreted to be a mandate by the people for him to lead by decree. That same day, he declared that his election signaled the end of the transitional period of his leadership and that the "new Bolivarian socialist revolutionary era" had begun (Garrido 2007: 1–6). Shortly after the inauguration ceremonies were completed in early January 2007, Chávez was granted the power to preside at will through what came to be known as the "enabling law."

More important for the future of the news media was the involvement of several news organizations in the failed coup of April 2002. With Chávez temporarily out of power, Venezuela's interim president, Pedro Carmona, summoned several broadcast and print news organizations, including *El Nacional* and *El Universal,* to his office. Carmona agreed to allow the media to handle the new government's communication strategy (Gott 2005: 234). This represented a major victory for the media, which were credited with playing a major role in the April coup (Lemoine 2002). Not surprisingly, with the almost immediate return of Chávez, the news media's position had considerably weakened, moving from a position of information hegemony to evolving liminality.

By January 2007, Chávez had reached the height of power, a coming-of-age so to speak, with his appeal at a zenith, as was his confidence, which some saw as audacious and arrogant. Meanwhile, Chávez developed close ties to Cuban leader Fidel Castro and has effectively been at the forefront of a movement in Latin America to elect leftist-oriented leaders, while encouraging a broader Latin movement against American imperialism (Castañeda 2006). His support of the newly elected leftist presidents of Bolivia, Ecuador, and Nicaragua has been widely covered, and Chávez attended the inauguration ceremonies of each.

It is in the role of a Latin David against an American Goliath that Chávez has successfully reenacted the struggle of Simón Bolívar against Spanish colonialism in the early nineteenth century. Bolívar, called El Libertador, led military liberation movements in Venezuela and several South American nations, including Ecuador and the nation named for him, Bolivia. Thus Bolívar became the heroic archetype for South American politicians who cast themselves as pan-nationalists. Like Bolívar, Chávez seemingly has created a trans-Latin resistance to the perceived neocolonialism of the United States. This heroic frame has resonated both with Venezuelans, especially the underclasses, and with other Latin politicians. However, as Valencia Ramírez (2006: 179) observes, the Chavista movement can also be understood as a "movement of the multitude" that cannot be reduced to a single identity. In this sense Chavistas, primarily of the lower classes, work symbiotically rather than with political verticality with the Chávez regime. This replacement of vertical political parties employs "a model based on direct popular participation in decision making at the local level," albeit with a powerful executive whose authority is unchecked (Ellner 2001: 5).

Chávismo and News Cultures

As Chávez's popular support has grown and he has obtained the "power to lead by decree," his relationship with both the sociocultural and economic sectors of Venezuela has changed and in some cases been transformed. He has said he intends to run for reelection and has predicted a win in 2013 or until his "Bolivarian Socialist Revolution" is complete (Peñaloza 2007). The issue of his presidential permanence is not a matter of public discourse among the poor; it is considered de facto. As one young man told one of the authors, "Those who are rich do not need more—we do!" echoing a populist approach exercised by the Left throughout most of Latin America (Castañeda 2006). As a consequence, critics have arisen among Venezuelans, including academics. Historian Margarita López Maya has warned that the "enabling law" has in effect caused the ANC to become useless and that "traditionally the Left disdains representative institutions" (Moleiro 2007: A2).

In the early 1990s, the major newspapers in Caracas were *Últimas Noticias*, an independent newspaper with a daily run of 320,000 copies, *Meridiano*, with

300,000 copies, and *El Mundo, El Nacional,* and *Diario 2001,* all independent dailies with a circulation of approximately 150,000. *El Universal,* which used to be among the top Caracas dailies, had fallen to a circulation of 140,000 by 1990. By the early years of this century, some of these papers, particularly *El Universal* and *El Nacional,* were hostile to Chávez. Though they do not dominate the circulation wars, *El Universal* and *El Nacional* were — and still are — significant in that they reflect the broader Western journalistic community and the prestige organizations within the nation's media culture. Both newspapers remain heavily influenced by U.S. media ideologies and echo the middle- and upper-class values of their readers. *El Nacional* reporters, in particular, were instrumental in bringing down one regime in 1993.[3]

According to British journalist Richard Gott, the result was a "steady drip of venom" that seeped into the foreign press in Europe and the United States (2005: 246). Gott notes that broadcast institutions were even more subversive, a problem for Chávez that reached a climax later in the virtual banning of Radio Caracas Televisión (RCTV), discussed below. Furthermore, he says the newspapers downplayed the extent of Chávez's popularity especially among the poor, who were not their audience. Among the lower classes, Chávez held the appeal of a Bolivarian caudillo, and gradually as the extent of his popularity became more evident and Chávez's hold on power more secure, Caracas journalists adopted new editorial strategies. These have included tempering overt opposition and have allowed newspapers such as *El Universal* and *El Nacional,* which early in his presidency Chávez called "poisonous" and "a disgrace" (Chávez 2001), to continue publishing while walking an editorial tightrope.

In the clash of newspaper ideologies vs. the Bolivarian revolution, socioeconomics counts for much. It was the virtual neglect of the lower classes that placed the newspapers in opposition to the revolutionary zeitgeist that has fueled the Chavistas and in turn Chávez's popularity. As *New York Times* reporter Simón Romero (2007) notes, "Mr. Chávez's partisans often say critical coverage of the government illustrates elitist and racist sentiments, while dissidents say the news media are their only outlet for expression, since other institutions are controlled by Mr. Chávez." Thus by mid-2006 the journalistic community of Venezuela, particularly Caracas, found itself contending with a progressively more authoritarian regime that drew strength by tapping into the older pan-Venezuelan cultural tradition that includes the veneration of a revolutionary strong man or a caudillo, who wraps himself in Bolivar's myth. There is a certain irony to this. The first newspaper, *Gaceta de Caracas,* was founded in Venezuela in 1808, coinciding with the arrival of the first printing press and as Bolívar's war of independence was approaching. The paper was published by a small group of intellectuals that sought to secede from Spain. The October 24 issue included an editorial rejecting any form of censorship: "The publishers will omit nothing as long as it benefits all, and it would give us great satisfaction to include as many ideas as are communicated to us" (Hernández 2005, our translation). In 1811, when Venezuela was briefly in the hands of Francisco de Miranda, a revolutionary precursor of Bolívar, the Caracas legislature passed a decree abolishing "all forms of censorship" (Hernández 2005).

By 1821 several other print media had appeared in the capital city, and the *Correo Nacional* was founded in the city of Maracaibo, state of Zulia, to the west. These papers addressed a small readership. Literacy rates in the country were low, and the media were primarily vehicles for the elite to discuss their viewpoints. Most of the early newspapers did not survive long, but they set the pace for the future of the country's media. Caracas emerged as the center of power, dominating virtually every facet of the country's socioeconomic and political life. Even as the successful exploration of oil provided the city of Maracaibo with leverage, its influence remains regional in character. Thus media of Maracaibo (and for that matter other parts of Venezuela) are mostly ignored in Caracas.

Then and now, government advertising supported and/or subsidized newspapers directly or indirectly. For most of Venezuela's history, a few families owned the largest daily newspapers, and all major political parties published at least weeklies, each positing their respective views. The media were considered sensationalist, and journalists routinely and tirelessly pursued corruption and incompetence in the government. Other than to attack Simón Bolívar, the country's hero, the media have been among the most free in Latin America. Only in times of emergency would the press be affected by limited censorship. By 2007, however, the fear of censorship forced the major dailies to retreat. Early that year, in interviews at both *El Nacional* and *El Universal,* journalists emphasized neutrality in their work, suggesting only that their "bent" toward oppositional journalism is tempered with caution and restraint.

There are differences between the two newspapers. *El Universal* is formal, serious, and intellectual in its approach and language. On the other hand, *El Nacional* is not above using colloquialisms and/or vulgar terminology. At *Últimas Noticias,* similar in some respects to some American metropolitan tabloids, there is tentative general acceptance of the Chávez regime. As in the past, the newspaper emphasizes murders, robberies, domestic scandals, and other sensationalist stories, except on the editorial pages, where domestic and international coverage shows the serious side of *Últimas Noticias.* On the other hand, *Diario VEA* is strongly and unapologetically pro-Chávez, while *El Nuevo País* is on the other side of the political continuum. Unlike *Últimas Noticias,* the two latter papers decry sensationalism, while professing a duty to be the social conscience of the country. They do not wish to address only the lowest social classes, identified in Venezuela as *chusmas,* for the sake of selling newspapers. These papers also appeal to the middle classes.

Survival Strategies

As mentioned earlier, journalists have had to adopt new editorial strategies to deal with what many perceive as a revolution against them. Indeed, Chávez's rhetoric against the opposition media has escalated, particularly since from the middle of 2006. By the first quarter of 2007, his words were confrontational and antagonistic and appeared in most papers, whatever their political bent, on a daily basis. Predictably, journalists, such as those at *El Nacional* and *El Universal* and other oppositional media, view the Chávez agenda as dangerous and intimidating. Most agree that self-censorship is essential for survival. Venevision, a leading television station, went further. They removed all political programs from their schedule.

Often, in the opinion pages of newspapers, commentaries avoid mentioning Chávez's name and/or anything that relates to his government or government activities. A case in point is a 2007 opinion piece that appeared in the *El Nacional* by Simón Alberto Consalvi, a distinguished former member of the government and a highly respected journalist. The essay, published on the January 23 editorial page and entitled "1957, Venezuela Was One Full Happy Conspiracy" (author's translation), describes a series of events in 1957–58. Although the article makes no reference to the present day, to us the parallels to current political conditions are unavoidable. It recalls that events climaxed on January 23, 1958, when dictator Marcos Pérez Jiménez left the country after ignoring the results of an earlier plebiscite in which he received a vote of no confidence. After extensive rioting, he was overthrown, and pro-democracy figure Rómulo Betancourt took office. Although no mention of the Chávez administration was made, such indirect stabs at the Chávez government belie the more politically aggressive press of the early Chávez years. In an interview (January 12, 2007), Consalvi also noted that the closing of media outlets is a direct result of their antigovernment reporting, and as a result, even moderates have been censoring their own stories. Sensitive issues are dealt with only indirectly. He added that for 63 years *El Nacional* reporters functioned without any limitations or self-censorship and were always free to critique the government.

While it is true that under the new order, journalists minimize risk by avoiding conflicts with the government through tactics such as metaphorical critiques, some journalists recognize that watchdog values still undergird the profession. Armando Avellaneda from *El Nacional* (interviewed January 12, 2007) acknowledged the need for caution, but also unambiguously noted that the role of the journalist is to inform, educate, and provide the tools that would allow readers to make up their own minds about events. When asked if he was being told by the *El Nacional* editors to temper his reporting and avoid controversy, Avellaneda said that in his case "nothing of the sort ever happens." Although he agreed that the role of journalist is to be a watchdog, he noted that this was not reality in 2007.

Other reporters, like Jaime Granda from the *La Verdad* (The Truth), echoed Avellaneda, saying that to do the job properly, a reporter cannot be "married to the government and for that matter to any sector of society" (interviewed January 18, 2007). Granda added that the media are "the conscience of the nation." With a sense of sadness he noted, "Venezuela is terribly divided at this time, and the new generation has been seduced by new fads that in turn have affected the journalism and in particular the print media." Ernesto Ecarri Hung, political and national editor of *El Universal,* emphasized the need to provide balanced reporting so that readers are allowed to draw their own conclusions (interviewed January 10, 2007). He said that perhaps 20 percent of Venezuelans are politically moderate, while the rest are at either extreme of the political spectrum.

Other reporters interviewed in 2007 also felt this was a very difficult period for journalists in Venezuela, particularly because Chávez maintains hegemony over the flow of government information, ensuring virtually no leaks. For example, when giving a speech at the inauguration of Nicaragua's Daniel Ortega, Chávez proclaimed that he was forgiving a $32 million (USD) loan to Nicaragua as a gesture of friendship and solidarity. No one in the press or even members of the government knew the loan existed.[4]

In addition to control over the flow of information, the legal system is being gradually transformed to constrain oppositional news. A recent law was passed further preventing the press from publishing any statement defaming the president or any member of the government. Previously other regulations were put into effect that were designed to shield government officials from a (perceived or real) media attack. In December 2004, the Law of Social Responsibility was passed, protecting the president from any direct or indirect attack from the press, followed by further amendments on March 16, 2005, that extended the law to guard other officials and members of the military as well. In May 2003 the "Tascon list" appeared, listing names of those considered members of the opposition. Some Venezuelans refer to this list as the beginning of "Bolivarian McCarthyism," according to the newspaper *Tal Cual* in a May 2, 2005, article. In October 2003, Chávez himself added to the fear factor by saying that "those who sign against Chávez will sign against the fatherland and will be registered for all history, as they will have to provide their name, surname, signature, identification number, and fingerprint" (Chávez 2004). The speech referred to a then forthcoming recall referendum signature drive scheduled for 2004.

The results of the December 2006 elections gave Chávez such license that he is considering holding a referendum that would close any opposition media that he would consider subversive (Associated Press 2006). The foreign press, too, feels the Venezuelan president's pressure. Since early 2006, visas have been renewed with much difficulty, and access to information has become increasingly more limited (International Crisis Group 2007: 14).

Power and Ideological Shifts

Despite the pressures on oppositional journalists in the early Chávez years, it was an action announced in December 2006 and carried out in May 2007 that most altered the landscape for Venezuela's news media. Taking advantage of a legal technicality, Chávez did not renew the broadcasting license of the nation's most popular and most venerable station, RCTV, which had been a vocal Chávez critic (Lilibeth da Corte 2006). Prior to that, other news media had been closed, such as smaller regional newspapers like *El Impulso* of Barquisimeto and *El Progreso, El Expreso, El Diario de Guayana,* and *Nueva Prensa,* all presumably in retaliation for publishing editorials against the Chávez government (ICG 2007: 14). However, because of RCTV's size and influence, the anticipation of the effective shutdown of the station on May 27, 2007, sent shock waves through the news community and beyond, sparking mass protests both for and against the station. For its part, the government insisted on the right to grant access to free air time, arguing that nonrenewal is the privilege of a sovereign state.

This event further chilled the atmosphere in the journalistic community, which by then had been partitioning into factions moved by both ideology and pragmatism. On the one side, there was the traditional media establishment, represented by newspapers such as *El Universal* and *El Nacional.* But for some journalists, the rise of Chávez meant that traditional news values, such as the belief that the press is society's check on power, began to fall away, and as Simón Romero noted, "a media elite" emerged. This new elite rejected the older ideological schema of news for the notion that journalists serve, in effect, as instruments of social order. This schema embodies what Western observers would characterize as a propagandistic or authoritarian model of journalism (Siebert, Peterson, and Schramm 1963), a step closer to the Cuban media frame. Indeed, it is no secret that the Chávez administration draws inspiration from Cuba. Likewise, interaction between Cuban media and the Chávez regime was ongoing in June 2007, when the authors discussed the Venezuelan news media situation with Orlando Oramas León, subdirector of Havana-based *Granma*. Oramas recounted his trip to Venezuela, where he said he visited a number of newspapers and praised the Chávez media-related actions as moving in the right direction.

Thus by 2007, with the financial support of the Chávez government, a number of newspapers appeared throughout the country, each strongly supporting the regime. In Caracas the daily *Diario VEA* is such a newspaper, in which reporters and editors take strong pro-government positions. In a January 12, 2007, interview, an editor, Mercedes Ortuño, said the purpose of a newspaper is to tell the truth and to support its government by reporting the "positive." She added, however, that on occasion it is necessary to report a negative story, but only if it is handled professionally and truthfully. For example, the newspaper has reported on very high crime rates in the capital city, an issue that even the government has acknowledged. The newspaper also has reported on the lack of cleanliness in Caracas and the prevalence of graffiti throughout the city. Such reporting so angered the mayor of Caracas, who is a Chavista, that he has not since granted interviews to *Diario VEA* journalists. Ortuño reaffirmed her position that reporting the truth is the most important responsibility of the press. Echoing her stand was reporter Luis Enrique Arauto (interviewed January 11, 2007). He repeatedly emphasized that the president is the country's leader and that he is doing the right thing. Between the lines, Arauto's message was that Chávez is untouchable and he is to be respected.

Editors and reporters of the newspaper *Diario VEA* said in early 2007 interviews that they fully supported Chávez's revolutionary agenda, a position visually reinforced by pictures hanging on the walls inside the VEA building of Ché Guevara, the international symbol of the Cuban Revolution, next to Simón Bolívar. The juxtaposition of Guevara and Bolívar underscores the imagined historical connections between the Cuban and Bolivarian revolutions. Significantly, the daily newspaper was founded in September 2003 with financial support directly from Chávez and thus has always backed the regime's positions (Grioni and Iacobeli 2004). *Diario VEA* continues to be subsidized by the government in a variety of ways, predominantly through the purchase of a generous number of ads. A condition for gaining employment includes signing a form showing personal commitment to the revolution and its principles. Not following such an edict is reason for dismissal (Sal-Ari 2007). In addition to the Guevara portrait, there are other icons sympathetic to the Bolivarian revolution hanging throughout the newspaper's reading room.

It could be argued that Venezuela's largest newspaper, *Últimas Noticias,* also receives significant support from the government. Government-paid ads can be found throughout the paper on a daily basis. The paper tends to be sympathetic to Chávez policies, and its readers are mostly middle and lower income. The executive editor, Eleazar Díaz Rangel, said in a January 11, 2007, interview that his paper provides positive, albeit critical, support of the government. The country, he added, "needs stabilization," and the media need to show a "journalistic balance" in their reporting of governmental activities. Díaz Rangel emphasized that Venezuela under Chávez is experiencing a greater period of freedom of speech than in previous periods. It should be noted that Díaz Rangel and *Diario VEA*'s Servando Garcia Ponce, a member of the publication's board of directors and its information editor, were jailed during President Rómulo Betancourt's second term in the early 1960s (Grioni and Iacobeli 2004). Indeed, Betancourt closed many newspapers during his term as president.

Comparative News Communities

The contest between the Chávez government and Venezuela's traditional media communities has inexact parallels in several other places. Of particular importance to the Venezuelan situation is the Cuban media circumstance because of the close informal and formal ties between Cuba and Venezuela and between Castro and Chávez. Of course, there are substantive differences between the two media systems and their journalistic cultures.

A not-entirely-inaccurate description of the Cuban media would be that there are no widely distributed independent media on the island.[5] On the other hand, official media, such as the national newspaper *Granma,* do more than simply espouse the government's position. Although it is true that Cuban national media "tend to confuse the concepts of information and propaganda, and to dissolve into the latter what is specific to the journalistic discourse," as Prieto (2004: 69) notes, that does not fully explain the frame itself. A product of the Communist Party, not the government, *Granma* functions as both a vehicle for the official party line and a well-informed window on world events. Subdirector Oramas said that as a representative of the Communist Party, *Granma* criticizes the government when things run poorly or inefficiently. *Granma* freely uses reports from foreign news organizations, such as the *New York Times,* the *Los Angeles Times,* the *Miami Herald, Le Monde,* and Agence France-Presse. Fidel Castro's lengthy column is also regularly published. Ironically, *Granma* is printed on paper acquired from the United States through a loophole in the embargo that allows certain sales to Cuba in the wake of a devastating 2002 hurricane. Above all, Oramas said, *Granma*'s duty is "to defend the principles of the revolution."

If there is a trend toward adapting a Cuban approach to media in Venezuela, evidence may be found in newspapers. *Diario VEA* regularly publishes articles written by Cuban reporters on international affairs, including pieces that emphasize missteps of American policy. Such pieces tend to be highly accurate in their depictions of the American foibles, although such material is often without a larger context, skewing the reports in the direction of commentary by selectivity in factual reporting.

The connections between Chávez and Castro run deep, and Chávez visits Cuba regularly. As recently as June 2007, he helped inaugurate a monument dedicated to Venezuelan hero Francisco de Miranda in a prominent location along Havana's Malecon (promenade). The visit included a six-hour conversation with Castro and a televised speech to the Cuban leadership. The speech, shown live and rebroadcast on Cuban television at least twice, was mostly tailored to show the brotherhood between Cubans and Venezuelans. The program was shown not only on Venezuelan television but also on the Caracas-based TeleSUR news network,[6] which is geared toward pan–Latin American coverage and is partially funded (51 percent) by the Venezuelan government.[7] The Cuban show *Mesa Redonda* (Roundtable) is regularly shown on TeleSUR.

Indeed, if Chávez is seeking to re-create the Cuban media experience, a redefinition of the role of news in Venezuelan society is needed. Under such a redefinition, the duties of the press would be to create social stability and reassurance in the face of the perceived threat of a new colonial power, i.e., the United States. In this regard the press becomes part of a popular revolutionary resistance and, by extension, the legacy of Bolívar. This, of course, is contrary to Western press ideologies in which value is placed on an unfettered media whose primary role in presenting theoretically (though not as praxis) objective news provides a check on the abuse of authority.

Venezuelan journalism under Chávez resembles in some respects the U.S. journalistic community in the wake of 9/11, in which the external threat moved the press voluntarily and in some cases with elements of psychological coercion toward becoming a tool of government propaganda in the form of tacit acceptance of government information without the requisite questioning. In this sense, another aspect of journalistic culture came to the fore: newspeople tend to be drawn to centers of power and to the powerful even as they strive to "take them down." To an extent, one's status as a journalist is determined in part by whom one can "get to" for an interview or "bring down" in a story. So it was that in the United States, mainstream journalists in general suspended their critical role as government watchdog and as a result elevated the nation's leadership to the next level. Immediately after 9/11, notions of "leadership" became a symbol of national unity and in that sense began to resemble, however briefly, the *caudillismo* (strong man or authoritarian rule) that seems to be so attractive to many Venezuelans. Although much has changed since 2001, the U.S. news community, with notable exceptions, took years to look beyond the mythos that had been created around 9/11 (Zelizer and Stuart 2002) and to begin to reopen its critical and analytical eyes.

Conclusion: Betwixt and Between

There are several contradictory forces at work in Venezuela. On the one hand, traditional journalists feel they are facing both unobtrusive and overt censorship with the myth of a new Bolívar that is gradually disabling the power of news to check governmental excess. This has threatened the independence of news organizations and has significantly constrained journalistic activities. Chávez is perceived by these journalists (as by the middle and upper classes they reflect) as moving toward authoritarian rule. As such there is a fear of the imposition of an authoritarian model of news work and even state control of news. Within Venezuela, opposition to Chávez has also come from university students, who in May 2007 took to the streets of Caracas to challenge the president's actions with signs reading, "No to Silence" (Associated Press 2007). Chávez answered with an intimidating display of police and military in the city's main streets. This fear of authoritarian rule has touched the international press, which has vigorously reported on the RCTV case, and some believe this presages the future.

On the other hand, the Chávez regime seems to believe that the duty of the press is to maintain social order by serving the interests of the state. The dominant media — the traditional news organizations — at the beginning of the Bolivarian revolution represented the interests of the Venezuelan elite, the middle and upper classes of Caracas. As such they were tied to U.S. interests and U.S. models of news work. Consequently, the media did not reflect, and to their critics virtually ignored, the interests of the general populace, or "the people" defined here as the lower classes. In this sense, the traditional news organizations were not only elitist but racist, a perception that cuts to the heart of contemporary Chavismo, which is supposed to represent the nation's majority black, mestizo, and Indian populations (Gott 2005: 250). Likewise, to many less affluent Venezuelans, Chávez is a liberator of sorts, who stands against the socioeconomic elites and the United States, the perceived partner of that elite. This attraction to Chávez in a deeper sense metaphorically reproduces the conditions under which Venezuela became an independent state in the nineteenth century, and thus Chávez becomes the new Bolívar. As Sahlins notes: "Granted that history is much more than the doings of great men, is always and everywhere the life of communities, but precisely in these heroic polities the king is the condition of the possibility of community" (1983: 519).

What this means in the context of a so-called continuing revolution is that the traditional news media organizations exist in what Victor Turner (1969) would call a state of betwixt and between their own system of values and beliefs and the demands of the new order, a liminal phase in which the normal rules based on Western ideologies are suspended for the sake of survival and perhaps also because of a real ambivalence about what the paramount role of the press should be, in terms of supporting or opposing the state. In place of those rules, improvised forms of news writing, in which criticism is indirect or metaphorical, are practiced as the news media find their role in Venezuela's new order an inversion of their role in the pre-Chávez era. Whatever the outcome of the Bolivarian revolution, the news media will emerge on new ground because their former pre-Chávez information hegemony has been challenged in a way that will make the political system more adept at constraining journalists. Likewise, journalists will be more aware of the minefields that politicians can lay and the strategies needed to protect themselves.

Ultimately, the struggle between Hugo Chávez and the press and the internal struggle within the Venezuelan journalistic community over occupational ideologies metaphorically reproduce a larger contest within that nation that involves not only politics and economics but also class and race.

Notes

Leon Yacher acknowledges support from a CSU Research Grant that facilitated the trip to Venezuela, and he thanks Patricia Zibluk and the Sponsored Program Research Office staff for partial support for the Cuba visit.

1. Talks with some broadcast journalists were informal and strictly off the record, as were those with people in diplomatic circles. Those who wished to remain anonymous were cited accordingly. More often than not, those who chose to remain anonymous supported the information provided by those who agreed to have their names included.

2. Caudillos may be described as regional strongmen; they were men of action who frequently had military or quasi-military backgrounds (Kent 2006: 127).

3. Although Venezuela has no domestic news agency, several foreign agencies maintain offices in Caracas. These include the Italian News Agency (ANSA), Associated Press (AP), United Press International, and Reuters. Until the collapse of the Soviet Union, TASS contributed to several of the local newspapers. Much remains the same today, except that in 2007 at least one newspaper was visited by members of the Syrian press seeking to exchange editorials of "mutual interest and benefit."

4. We attempted to meet with several ministers, in particular the minister of communications. With the latter we were repeatedly asked to return at another time or told that he was not available.

5. Other national newspapers are *Juventud Rebelde* (Rebellious Youth), published by the Union of Young Communists, and *Trabajadores,* a trade union publication. There are three radio stations, a state television broadcaster, and educational stations.

6. TeleSUR began broadcasting full-time on October 31, 2005.

7. Other countries' investments include Argentina (20 percent), Cuba (19 percent), and Uruguay (10 percent). On April 6, 2006, President Evo Morales committed Bolivia to buying a 5 percent share of the network. Additional countries from Latin America are expected to join.

5 "The Camera Was My Weapon"

Reporting and Representing War in Socialist Vietnam

CHRISTINA SCHWENKEL

Victimization or Victory

"The Vietnam War." For people in the United States, this phrase typically conjures up images of graphic violence, suffering, and destruction that were frequently published in newspapers and magazines during the U.S. intervention in Vietnam. Indelible photographs of napalmed children, spontaneous executions, and village massacres, once widely disseminated through print media, continue to travel in social, political, and artistic circuits, often as a critique of the U.S. war on terror and a reminder of the egregious failures and violent excesses of past and present U.S. foreign policy.[1] These enduring iconic images, deeply engraved in U.S. memory, have also continued to shape dominant national narratives and historical knowledge of the war as a struggle (gone wrong) to obstruct the spread of communism. Moreover, this visual record, largely produced by international photojournalists working for Western press agencies, has circulated far beyond U.S. borders to incorporate much of the capitalist world into a global imaginary of "Vietnam."

On the contrary, in Vietnam (where the phrase "Vietnam War" has little meaning), hegemonic narratives situate the war against the United States within the broader context of a 30-year struggle for independence and liberation from French colonialism and U.S. imperialism, defensive actions considered entangled and continuous. The repertoire of images of the "American War" produced by liberation war correspondents, as they were called, brings attention not only to U.S. imperial violence and the subjection of Vietnamese people at the hands of "foreign invaders," but also to the active roles and everyday routines of participants in the revolution (Schwenkel 2008). These images, which were also broadly disseminated through national and transnational socialist circuits, are less known to U.S. and other Western viewers, yet have forged a competing global historical memory of the war, based less on visual narratives of victimization and more on a pictorial history of survival and victory.

This chapter focuses an ethnographic lens on the Vietnamese photojournalists who produced this visual history. Much has been written about Western media representations of the U.S. war in Vietnam.[2] But Vietnamese news production has received scant attention.[3] Moreover, journalism in a socialist media system has rarely been the subject of sustained ethnographic observation (see, however, Latham 2000), although anthropologists have examined changing media landscapes in *postsocialist* contexts (e.g., Boyer 2005) and have used historical ethnography to understand *former* socialist practices of media representation and knowledge production (Wolfe 2005; Boyer 2003). Anthropological studies of journalism have more typically addressed the production of capitalist, market-driven news, often by foreign (largely Western) correspondents and press agencies. Archetypal representations of international journalists have frequently employed masculine metaphors of fast-paced and risky mobility, including images of parachutists (Pedelty 1995: 109–12; Hannerz 1998a: 115) and firemen (Hannerz 1998b: 553) who are addicted to danger and disaster and who hurriedly cross the globe covering one "newsworthy" event after another.

The Vietnamese war photographers who constitute the focus of this study worked for the socialist revolutionary press in various capacities and possessed a very different relationship to the war and its representation as "news" than journalists working for the international capitalist press. As such their journalistic methods, motivations, and practices of representation differed significantly. Their work was not primarily event-driven and did not exhibit similar patterns of global hopping — common characteristics of Western news reporting that foster a distanced and detached position from photographic subjects. During the war, Vietnamese photojournalists were indeed mobile, at times traversing national borders as they followed the dense jungle paths of the Ho Chi Minh Trail through eastern Laos and Cambodia. Yet they also remained for long periods in frontline villages and battlefields. Whether itinerant or stationary, they were immersed in the daily lives and struggles of the people with whom they lived, worked, and fought for the duration of the war. Moreover, their work was concerned more with process than event, and they recorded the war as it impacted the everyday routines of their photographic subjects, commonly choosing (for cultural, political, and moral reasons) to capture life over death. This can be contrasted with event-driven news and war photography in the West and the importance of death and bodily remains to its journalistic values and practices. Mark Pedelty's innovative ethnography demonstrates this in its opening pages with a story of a journalist's excitement over the discovery of a corpse: "No body, no story," Pedelty quotes from Michael Massing as a "basic rule" of international journalism (1995: 3).

The similarities between anthropological and journalistic methodologies and modes of knowledge have been noted by scholars (Malkki 1997: 93). Hannerz, for instance, writes that "[t]he work of foreign correspondents . . . parallels that of anthropologists, in that both report from one place to another, often across cultural as well as spatial distances" (1998b: 548). Yet the notion of ethnography as the study of *another* distant culture evokes an older disciplinary paradigm of Euro-American anthropologists studying exotic Others, a paradigm that has gradually become unsettled as increasing numbers of anthropologists carry out fieldwork at "home" (Gupta and Ferguson 1997: 17–18). In this chapter, I argue that Vietnamese photographers were akin to postcolonial ethnographers (whose anthropological project was not Otherness) because of their application of fieldwork methodologies that consisted of long-term immersion and participant observation to produce situated visual ethnographies of the war mediated through the camera. Like anthropologists, they were attentive to the mundane and often intimate aspects of human existence and survival, documenting enduring social and economic practices under conditions of war in the fields of agricultural and industrial production, education, health, family, leisure and entertainment, as well as combat and defense. Unlike the "objective" distance between Western photojournalists (or archetypal ethnographers) and their subject matter, Vietnamese photographers, similar to more recent anthropological practice, stressed their deep connection to and involvement in local communities and social groups. As such, their images provide the viewer with particular (and likewise partial) ethnographic insights into how war and revolution shaped daily life, capturing the multifaceted experiences of society under constant threat of violence.

My arguments are based on three years of ethnographic fieldwork conducted between 1999 and 2007 on visual practices of memory in Vietnam. One component of this project involved interviews with photojournalists who spent years in the field recording the war. I also draw on research with archived newspapers in the National Library in Hanoi, participant observation in museums, and visual analyses of photographic collections to gain insights into Vietnamese news and truth-making practices. In many ways, this chapter is a work of historical ethnography that reflects upon news production through an analysis of the memories that photographers chose to recall and the selection of works they desired to show me. One of the strengths of ethnographic methodology is the "insider" interpretation of sociocultural practices it provides, which may challenge established cultural frameworks and assumed knowledge practices. The use of ethnography to study Vietnamese war photographers allowed me to gain a deeper and more nuanced understanding of how my interlocutors made sense of their professional histories, how they worked through their trauma from the war, and how they negotiated their complex and shifting relationships to cultural production and to the Vietnamese state. Their stories and memories, often painful and guarded, revealed an intimate "emotional economy of the everyday" (Stoler 2002: 168), in which enduring sentiments and affective attachments, particularly toward the people with whom they lived, worked, and fought, shaped their recollections of news production and their personal and professional lives today. Like anthropologists, many of these photojournalists have returned to "their" villages to reconnect with the individuals in their images and to discover their wartime and postwar fates.

Using ethnography to emphasize the immersive, sensorial, and participatory dimensions to Vietnamese war photography, I aim to provide a more complex picture of "socialist journalism," that, like Thomas Wolfe's (2005) historical ethnography of the Soviet press, transcends conventional discussions of "propaganda" and "ideology" and challenges commonplace assumptions that knowledge production in a socialist context is the "soulless" work of servants of the state. I show how photographers' self-positioning as artists and historical agents, in their quest to represent particular truths about the war through a more ethnographic and humanistic approach, called into question the often dehumanizing and objectifying tendencies of detached "objective journalism" as practiced in the West.

Wartime News Production and Representation

A common perception in the West holds that journalism in capitalist and socialist societies is based on fundamentally dissimilar and contradictory practices. Popular formulations in public discourse include a series of contrasts that give authoritative credence to journalists in capitalist contexts denied to their socialist counterparts: while the former is associated with free speech, a democratic press, objectivity, and the presentation of balanced truths, the latter signifies state repression, thought control, ideology, bias, and partiality (Wolfe 2005: 10–11). It is easy to recognize problems with this simplistic model that implicitly links press freedoms to liberal capitalism. As Dominic Boyer has shown, such overwrought generalizations have had a devastating impact on the lives of East German journalists who now struggle professionally and economically in reunified Germany. Those who were considered "too red" (that is, beyond the ability to grasp democratic media practices and values) were forced into retirement after reunification in 1990 (Boyer 2001a: 427). Others who managed to find jobs in Western media institutions have at times had to contend with colleagues who typecast journalists from the East as incompetent "subprofessionals" who had "problems thinking independently and critically because they had been trained to be obedient to authority figures" (Boyer 2001b: 473, 474). The values and practices of journalists engaged in news production in socialist media systems thus fail to meet the professional standards set by the Western press. In effect, they are presumed to be mere propagandists rather than legitimate experts and producers of bona fide knowledge.

In his ethnography of war correspondents, Pedelty discusses journalist perceptions of news propagandists as those who "purposely disseminate false positions and facts in order to support what they consider 'higher' truths" (1995: 227). It would be a professional insult to Vietnamese photojournalists to identify the images and information they produced during the war as mere fabrication. Yet this is not an uncommon sentiment voiced by Western and especially U.S. visitors to Vietnamese museum exhibits that display images from the war, thus questioning the validity and veracity of Vietnamese knowledge and representation. In interviews, Vietnamese photojournalists readily identified the central role that photography played in transmitting news from the front lines in an effort to denounce the war and spread information to national and international audiences, as well as to produce a visual history for future generations (see also Nguyen 2006: 81–83). They often referred to *tuyen truyen*, loosely translated as propaganda, although the cultural meaning is derived from root words linked to the communication and dissemination of knowledge, rather than *misinformation* as commonly used in contemporary capitalist contexts. Vietnamese reference to *propaganda* is not unlike pre–cold war usage in the West as "a *neutral* term evoking any kind of directed construction of information to achieve certain ends" (Wolfe 2005: 9, emphasis added). According to Michael Schudson, the term *propaganda* first surfaced in the 1920s and was used interchangeably with *publicity* in the emerging field of public relations (1978: 137). The association of propaganda with deception and nondemocratic institutions reflects a more recent Western interpretation. In Vietnam the term retains more positive, humanist connotations linked to democratic knowledge transmission and education of the masses, not unlike other socialist models of news production. As Thomas Wolfe has argued in his work on Soviet journalism, "The socialist worldview dictated that the press would be characterized by a particular pedagogical orientation" and not be driven by market interests (2005: 6–7).

The idea that socialist and capitalist news production are fundamentally incompatible glosses over similarities and points of convergence in both practice and principle. For example, most journalists, regardless of the ideological frameworks in which they work, are concerned with the mimetic reproduction of observable "fact" and the production of journalistic "truth" (Peterson 2001: 202).[4] Photojournalists, in particular, often express a belief in the objective and discernible reality embodied in photographic representation — what Reid has called "eyewitness authenticity" in the context of Soviet photographic practices in the 1960s (1994: 33, but see Sontag 1990). Moreover, all journalists, whether located in a socialist or market-based system, operate under certain institutional constraints against which they struggle to bring "facts" to the public. Mark Allen Peterson argues that U.S. journalists are often represented as cogs in the machine, whereas journalists project an image of themselves as free agents (2001: 201). Similarly, in interviews, Vietnamese photojournalists emphasized their creative agency and choice of subject matter, although they were removed from the later stages of image selection and news production. This is not to deny the ideological use of news and images of the war, although I do not see this as unique to the Vietnamese context. Rather, I would like to disentangle ideology from socialist media only, to also recognize analogous constraints and ideological factors at work in the commercial press.

Contrary to popular beliefs that an adversarial press in the United States was instrumental in changing public opinion and augmenting opposition to the Vietnam War, research has shown that journalists, particularly in the early years of the conflict, were largely supportive of U.S. actions and committed to the anti-communist cause (Hallin 1986; Wyatt 1993).[5] Correspondents uncritical of the war and Cold War ideologies often produced news reports steeped with anti-communist rhetoric, despite a commitment to the tenets of "objective journalism."[6] In the early 1960s, for example, front-page stories in the *New York Times* included expressions such as "Red advance," "Communist menace," "Communist threat," and "Communist aggression" (Hallin 1986: 53–54). After relations between the media and the military became strained late in the war (see Hammond 1998), many reporters still toed the official line despite taking a more critical and cynical stance, and they continued to represent "the enemy" as "the dark picture of evil" (Hallin 1986: 150). In short, U.S. press coverage of the war was anything but "fair and balanced" and presented readers with a hegemonic, U.S.-centric perspective that did little to promote opposing and more complex understandings of the conflict.

The Vietnamese press also exhibited a particular bent in its coverage, namely, that the war was a defensive action against U.S. imperial expansion. A content analysis of newspapers from northern Vietnam published during the war revealed a sustained emphasis on narratives of victory and progress on the battlefront, as well as in the fields of technological, agricultural, and scientific development.[7] Not unlike the U.S. military's reliance on (inflated) body counts as a measure of progress toward victory (Gibson 1986: 112–14), in Vietnam a similar approach characterized the headlines. For example, the January 4, 1972, edition of *Nhan Dan* [The People], the newspaper of the Communist Party, summarized the comprehensive victories of the liberation forces in southern Vietnam during 1971. The four-page daily ran with a banner headline, "Heroic Troops and Civilians in the South — Blazing and Total Victory," with bullet point sub-headings arranged to validate this claim: "Close to 250,000 enemy troops exterminated (including 20,000 U.S. troops and vassals); thousands of officers and puppet troops captured"; "1,800 airplanes shot down and destroyed; close to 8,000 vehicles and 650 large weapons destroyed." Front-page statistics also provided a running tally of the numbers of U.S. aircraft shot down during bombing raids over northern provinces and U.S. "enemy pilots" captured or killed while carrying out their "crimes" and "acts of aggression." Insofar as dominant social discourses and political paradigms shaped both Vietnamese and U.S. news production during the war, the presumed distinction between socialist ideological journalism and capitalist objective journalism breaks down.

Although both U.S. and Vietnamese news coverage of the war tended to emphasize victory over defeat, and progress rather than setbacks, the kinds of images used to tell these stories differed considerably. Images of Vietnamese suffering in the international press exposed the shocking violence of the war, but in so doing, they also conveyed to viewers very specific relations of power suggestive of U.S. strength, control, technological superiority, and the possibility of victory. Photographs in the Vietnamese press, on the other hand, provided a broader picture of the war effort by focusing more attention on process rather than events and their violent outcomes. Rather than adopt death, destruction and victimization as a dominant visual theme, war photographers also showed people as active and determined agents involved in production, training, preparation, and defense (Schwenkel 2008: 52–54). Front-page photographs published in *Hai Phong City* newspaper in 1972, for example, showed villagers (often women) raising pigs, transplanting rice, working in factories, and constructing ships — activities seen as integral to the revolution and the anti-U.S. resistance ("everything for the front"). War coverage also included photographs of villagers (again often women) engaged in weapons training and other militia exercises, including posing with anti-artillery units "ready to defend the skies." Images of devastation and death from B-52 attacks were kept to a minimum (only one image of a corpse was published in 1972), although Hanoi-based newspapers with wider circulation (i.e., *Nhan Dan*) covered bomb destruction more extensively, such as the December 22, 1972, bombing of Hanoi's Bach Mai Hospital.

Political and ideological interests undoubtedly motivated news production and its emphasis on victorious achievements and collective acts of solidarity. News could spread information as well as maintain or even raise morale. Yet, in interviews, war photographers also expressed other factors involved in their decisions to focus on the ordinary and routine and not just exceptional events. Some pointed out that they had indeed recorded violence with their cameras, but such images required a specific context of viewing not typically accorded to newspapers, but "War Crimes Exhibition Houses" — spaces in urban areas that displayed photographs of atrocities with the intent to denounce the war and fuel the resistance. Most explained that their work represented a diversity of experiences in war, of which death was but one aspect. One man felt that photographing those killed (and repeatedly looking at the image) was an act of disrespect. And yet others identified a different relationship to the war and to the meanings invested in its representation. Several photographers commented on the attraction to casualties in the Western press, which was mapped onto a specific relational positioning. A director at the Photographic Arts Association in Hanoi explained:

> Each side had a different psychology, a different way of thinking about the war and photographing it, each with a different goal. The United States invaded Vietnam so journalists on that side only saw and photographed death. On the Vietnamese side, our goal was liberation and defense of the country, so we photographed life. Yes, many people died, but we had to remain optimistic. How could the other side be optimistic when they had invaded this country?

This quote shows how journalists working with U.S. media institutions, regardless of their nationality or political persuasion, were not considered neutral, outside, autonomous observers, but were thought to be complicit in the "invasion" of Vietnam insofar as they operated within the larger structure of the war and its machinations.

As the photographer suggested, Western photojournalists produced their own truths shaped by the dominant convictions, mechanisms, and institutions in which they worked. This reflects a radically different understanding of the role of journalism in Vietnam as engaged in (and not detached from) a politics of location. Kevin Latham has shown in the case of China how notions of truth and objectivity are also central to the production of socialist news, though in this context such terms refer to the transmission of "real" social facts and "objective" material realities, rather than balanced "impartial reporting" (2000: 639–42). Attentive to positionality, Vietnamese photographers pointed to the situatedness of journalistic knowledge: they participated in the revolution as "cultural soldiers" and provided accurate views of the resistance; and likewise, Western photographers accompanied U.S. troops and produced their own images of the objective world.

Moreover, unlike in the West, socialist journalism advocated objective truth not through the separation of subject from object but through integration. A key task of journalists, Lenin maintained, was to connect to the masses and to bridge the state and the people (Wolfe 2005: 25; see also Boyer 2005: 125). In

1918, Lenin called upon journalists to work in conjunction with the people and to be more observant of the ways a new socialist society was being constructed. He encouraged reporters to position themselves "closer to life" and to pay more attention to "that everyday side of intra-factory, intra-village, intra-regimental life, to how the new is being built" (quoted in Wolfe 2005: 25–26). In other words, Lenin promoted an *ethnographic* approach to socialist news production that deviated from previous journalist methodologies. In his speeches, Ho Chi Minh echoed a similar sentiment and called on journalists to serve the people, embed themselves in the social context, and work closely in the shared struggle for revolutionary victory (Tran 1996: 110). In the following sections, I examine the stories of two "embedded" photographers who heeded this call.

Photographers as Ethnographers: The Case of Duc

On a humid, sunny afternoon in December, 2004, I knocked on Duc's office door in a museum in Ho Chi Minh City where he works restoring old photographs.[8] Duc and I had met in 2000 at the opening of a transnational war photography exhibit that had marked the 25th anniversary of the liberation of Saigon.[9] Duc, a slight man with graying hair and a warm smile, greeted me at the door with a handful of photography books. We walked to the museum café, sat down on red, plastic chairs, ordered bottled water, and began the interview. Duc first handed me several documents from Vietnamese and U.S. media sources, including one of his images published on the front page of the *New York Times* in 2000.[10] "This should tell you everything you need to know about me," he declared, seeming to suggest that the interview, which had just begun, had already finished. I quickly pulled out a book of his photographs. Duc smiled, pleased to see that I was already familiar with his work.

During the war, Duc had worked as a photographer for the National Liberation Front (NLF), 60 kilometers northwest of Saigon in the district of Cu Chi, famous for its extensive underground tunnel networks. He first began to pursue an interest in photography at the age of 10, and in the early 1950s, he began working with the anticolonial resistance, making false identity cards. In 1960, with the establishment of the NLF, Duc resettled in Cu Chi and began taking photographs for the Front, which were also forwarded to Hanoi for circulation in Vietnamese and international (namely, socialist) presses. After U.S. marines landed in Da Nang in 1965, Duc descended to live underground in the tunnels with NLF forces, where he continued to process and print his images.

At the outset of our conversation, Duc clarified his position in relation to other roles revolutionaries had assumed. "I was not with the [northern] army; I was not a guerrilla. I was a photographer for the NLF. I was not armed; my camera was my weapon. The NLF provided me with everything I needed: cameras, film, and processing equipment."[11] One of the benefits of his close proximity to the large urban area of Saigon was that Duc was never in short supply of film, as NLF contacts in the city kept him well stocked. "I had more film than the photographers from the northern area. I took over 10,000 photographs, and today I have some 3,000 preserved." Duc's emphasis on the management and control of his images reflected a larger discourse of choice and free agency that peppered his speech. He chose his career path and subject matter to photograph. He made two sets of each printed image, one for the Front and one for himself, and he kept his negatives. He also kept track of whether the images had been published in newspapers. Contrary to common Western representations and imaginaries of photographers from the "other side," Duc framed his experiences with news production in relation to his professional agency (choice of career and image subject) and his artistic rights to produce and control his work (keeping a set of images and negatives), as well as to possess knowledge of its use and circulation.

During the interview, Duc tended to shift the conversation away from himself to the people he photographed for 15 years in their villages and in the tunnels. His goal, he said, had been to record the crimes and devastation of war and the daily lives and activities of the guerrilla fighters. Duc's keen attention to the everyday routine in the face of violence and destruction gives his work a unique historical and ethnographic dimension, and demonstrates his role as a cultural producer immersed in the social worlds of people who were his photographic subjects. Like an ethnographer, Duc presented himself as deeply involved in and connected to "his" community: "I did not just live there and take photographs; I also helped dig the tunnels. Everybody took part in this, including me. I could not live there without contributing. So I dug tunnels, collected food — anything to help." Through this long-term immersion and participation in village networks, Duc produced an ethnographic-photographic record of the war from which the viewer gleans detailed and intimate insights into its multiple and often contradictory experiences. At one point Duc handed me a photograph entitled "Happiness," which has found wide circulation in Vietnam, showing a young couple with an infant relaxing in a hammock strung across the inside of a gutted U.S. tank. "War is not only about fighting battles," he told me. "There are also quiet times. My photographs show the many sides to life in war," including leisure, education, and entertainment. Indeed Duc's images often captured moments of diversion that were overshadowed by the war, such as performances in the tunnels, children singing to drown out the sound of exploding bombs, and people swimming in a bomb crater "pool."

Duc was most animated when talking about the ingenuity and resourcefulness of Cu Chi fighters. He invited me to accompany him through one of the museum exhibits on guerrilla weaponry, illustrated with many of his photographs. Pointing to the images, he explained how fighters used dead U.S. bombs to manufacture mines and weapons. "It was very dangerous work!" he exclaimed as he gestured toward a photograph of a woman using her hand to scoop gunpowder from unexploded ordnance into a woven basket. Other works in the exhibit showed gutted U.S. tanks used as a hideout for NLF forces or dismantled for scrap metal and beams in underground tunnels. Children were also represented in the images: if not at school learning, then whittling bamboo into sharp spikes for use in "tiger traps." Men and women, young and old, were shown engaged in various acts of tunnel construction, agricultural production, or the rebuilding of destroyed villages and homes. At one point Duc identified a man in one of the photographs and commented that he was still alive. "Do you often go back to Cu Chi?" I asked. He smiled and replied: "All the time — my house is close to there," thus suggesting the long-term social relationships that developed in the field and continue to exist between photojournalist and subject, a topic to which I now turn.

Return to the Battlefield: The Case of Nhan

I met with Nhan at his house in central Hanoi on a muggy summer morning in July 2006. His wife greeted me at the door and brought me to a room where he was waiting with photography books and videos. On one wall was a large portrait of Nhan as a young war photographer, below which hung a weathered camera and an antiquated wooden rifle. Nhan invited me to sit down at a low lacquered table, offered me some tea, and motioned toward the objects that had seized my gaze: "That weapon is from my time in the northern mountains during the resistance war against the French. It was there in 1949 that I began teaching myself photography." In 1954, after the defeat of the French, Nhan returned to Hanoi and worked as a photographer at the newspaper *Tien Phong* [Vanguard], where he remained until his retirement in 1993. During the war, Nhan traveled widely for the newspaper, photographing youth volunteers, militia forces, and self-defense squads in various provinces north of the Ben Hai River, which temporarily divided Vietnam. He carried an East German camera that now hangs on the wall, and in contrast to Duc, he described his Russian and East German film supplies as "extremely limited." In 1968 Nhan went south to Quang Binh province to live with villagers in an underground tunnel system built as shelter from constant U.S. bomb attacks. It was these memories of Vinh Linh that Nam chose to speak about most.

Like Duc, Nhan preferred to talk about the people he photographed and resided with — how they managed to survive the daily grind of war and violence, how they maintained their courage and determination, how they remained optimistic as they carried out their lives underground. He told me: "When I think of the war, the most precious memories for me are of the people." Thirty years later, Nam has returned to Vinh Linh twice to find the people in his photographs, once in 1999 and again in 2005. Both of these visits have been filmed, the former for *National Geographic* and the latter for VTV (Vietnam Television).[12] "After a long separation, returning to see the people I photographed during the war has been very special and moving for me," Nhan said as he inserted the 2005 video, *Tro ve Vinh Linh* [Return to Vinh Linh], into the DVD machine and hit play.

The video shows Nhan meticulously tracking down various people in his photographs. Miraculously, most are still alive, although it is clear they have led hard lives and many appear quite destitute. As the video played, Nhan excitedly recalled each reunion story, flipping through a book of his photographs as each new scene unfolded. Nhan was particularly enthusiastic about his reunion with female performers whom he photographed as they sang in the tunnels, a famous image that he took by igniting gunpowder removed from a bullet to produce a flash. A re-creation of this scene in the video first shows the young women singing underground during the war, then cuts to their current lives, followed by a scene where the women reposition themselves in the tunnel, now preserved as a tourist attraction, to sing the same melody once again. "They didn't forget the words after all these years," Nhan marveled. His mood became somber with the subsequent story of a woman he had photographed as a young guerrilla proudly posing with her rifle. In the documentary she sees Nhan for the first time in 30 years and begins to cry. She is not well, and her life has been full of hardships, Nhan told me as his eyes welled up with tears. The contrast between the healthy, energetic young adult with a bright smile in wartime and the sickly, impoverished, and prematurely aged woman today was striking and depressing. "This reunion was so emotional, so very moving," Nhan said softly. "It meant so much to me to go back. During the war, life had been extremely difficult. I wanted to return and see the people I photographed in a better time." His voice trailed off. I made an attempt to ask Nhan the extent to which capitalist economic reforms had or had not improved the lives of villagers, but he remained too transfixed by the moment to answer.[13]

Conclusion

In the *National Geographic* documentary *Vietnam's Unseen War*, a legendary war photographer, on a quest to locate photojournalists from the "other side," reflects on the meaning of the war for him as a 20-year old photographer in Saigon in the 1960s: adventure, fun and games, girlfriends, a "wild party."[14] His then detached stance is unsettling, and his carefree attitude becomes all the more disturbing when juxtaposed with the four, now elderly, Vietnamese photographers he visits, all but one of whom break down on film while recollecting the war and the tragedies they witnessed. For these men, war photography was not contingent upon anonymous corpses imbued with professional news value but upon the dynamic lives of individual people — photographic subjects and historical agents — with whom the photographers endured suffering and shared their hopes and visions of an independent Vietnam.

Susan Sontag has argued that the camera, as a tool of objectification, "annihilates moral boundaries and social inhibitions, freeing the photographer from any responsibility toward the people photographed" (1990: 41). This observation assumes a universal framework of Western objectivity that prescribes, indeed requires, a disconnected stance as exhibited by the foreign correspondent in his early years as war photographer in Vietnam. The cases presented here show how Vietnamese photographers defied many of the conventions of Western objective journalism when they immersed themselves in "the field." They engaged in involved rather than impartial photographic practices that blurred the lines between news, social commentary and visual ethnography, and in so doing, they humanized their photographic subjects, ascribing value and meaning to their lives and struggles with the camera, rather than objectifying and morally violating them as Sontag charges.

Sontag's observation nonetheless raises important ethical and moral questions concerning the dehumanizing tendencies of photographic acts that turn terror and violence into spectacle for commodification and consumption (Kleinman and Kleinman 1997; Taylor 1998). Vietnamese war photographers to a certain extent held themselves to a higher ethical standard than their Western counterparts, as evident in the photojournalist's statement that it is not respectful to photograph and repeatedly look at an image of death. Such words, as well as the historical memories, ethnographic-like practices, and human interconnections presented in this chapter serve to unsettle common representations of socialist journalists as lacking in free choice, agency, integrity, and humanity — misconceptions that work to normalize and deflect a critical public eye away from undemocratic and morally questionable journalistic methodologies and representational practices in the "free" press of the West.

Notes

1. See, e.g., the 2004 political cartoon "Abu Ghraib Nam" by Dennis Draughon, which juxtaposes the iconic hooded figure from Abu Ghraib with the iconic napalmed

body of Phan Thi Kim Phuc as she runs naked toward the photographer (Hariman and Lucaites 2007: 202).

2. See, e.g., Hoskins 2004 and Hagopian 2006.

3. For an exception, see Schwenkel 2008. In this chapter I use "Vietnamese" news production to refer to the two press agencies on the revolutionary side of the war: the Liberation News Agency (the press arm of the National Liberation Front in southern Vietnam) and the Vietnam News Agency based in Hanoi.

4. Such similarities are clearly demonstrated in Latham's 2000 comparative study of journalism in mainland China and Hong Kong.

5. Compare with Hagopian 2006: 216–19 and Hariman and Lucaites 2007: 188–203 on the ways Vietnam War photography stirred social consciousness and mobilized political subjectivities.

6. On the practice of objective journalism in the United States, see Tuchman 1972; Schudson 1978: 3–11, 144–59; Peterson 2001; and Pedelty 1995: 169–90.

7. I examined coverage of the war in two national newspapers, *Nhan Dan* [The People] and *Lao Dong* [Labor], and one regional paper from Hai Phong City.

8. All names are pseudonyms.

9. The exhibit, "Requiem — The Vietnam Collection," displayed the works of 135 photojournalists from 11 nations killed in the French and U.S. wars in Vietnam. See Schwenkel 2008 for an analysis of the event.

10. Since the late 1990s, collaborative projects between Western and Vietnamese photojournalists have brought much attention in the United States to photographs from the "other side." See Faas and Page 1997; Page 2002; and the documentary *National Geographic: Vietnam's Unseen War.*

11. Duc is making reference here to Ho Chi Minh's often-cited words that journalists were cultural soldiers of the revolution whose weapons consisted of pencils, paper, and cameras (Ho 2004: 243; Nguyen 2006: 76). Outside a socialist revolutionary context, see Milton 1984 on the camera as a weapon of intimidation and retribution during the Holocaust.

12. Nhan first returned in 1999 with a renowned *Life* and *Time* war photographer who, in *Vietnam's Unseen War,* explores his own return to Vietnam to find photographers on the "other side." In 2004 Nhan revisited Vinh Linh with his son, also a photojournalist, with the intention of locating additional people from his photographs. The success of this television documentary spurred a "before and after the liberation" program about Nhan's surviving subjects in other provinces. On the return of Vietnamese cameramen to villages where they filmed during the war, see Claude Grunspan's video *Gao Rang* [Grilled rice]. See Dietmar Ratsch and Arek Gielnik's *Eislimonade für Hong Li* [Iced lemonade for Hong Li] on the return to Hanoi of celebrated East German photographer Thomas Billhardt to reunite with people in his images taken during and after the war.

13. It is not an uncommon observation that those who fought and sacrificed the most for the revolution, namely, the rural poor, have gained the least in postwar independence. In the film *Gao Rang* [Grilled rice], one veteran war filmmaker who returns to a village in Quang Binh province where he lived and filmed during the war expresses his reluctance to record the postwar lives of his former cinematic subjects on account of the village's abject poverty.

14. See also Herr 1977.

6

Empowerment through Local News Making

Studying the Media/Public Interface in India

URSULA RAO

This chapter engages with local news-making practices of vernacular news-papers in India and focuses on the impact of publication strategies on local public culture.[1] The desire of vernacular news organs to offer their pages as a platform for the exchange of local information has turned them into a po-litical instrument that is appropriated by citizens for the realization of their own interests. People lobby through the newspaper to gain status as leaders. They engage in ideological debates, struggle for the improvement of the local infrastructure, expose the arrogance of leaders, or search for solutions in caste conflicts or neighborhood fights. By spelling out these dynamics, I introduce news making as an interactive process that is shaped through the coordinated action of journalists and citizens.

I propose to redirect the analytical gaze of academic debates about news by reflecting on the media-related practices (Couldry 2004; Rao 2009a) of less-privileged people. Recent years have seen the proliferation of studies about the changing character of news in market-driven publishing cultures, emphasiz-ing the growing influence of the corporate world on news discourses (Curran 2002; Sparks and Tulloch 2000; Thussu 2007a, 2007b; Tracey 1998). This de-velopment is also evident in India, where journalists are exposed to substan-tial pressure from private corporations. Yet developments are not unified and unidirectional. In India the growing profitability of newspapers has turned the vernacular press into an instrument of power beyond an elite space. I follow the bottom-up strategy of local news making to draw attention to a much-neglected aspect of journalistic practices: the integration of the urban population into the process of news making, as one dimension of the media/public interface.

My discussion of local news making leads me to reconsider the notion of public sphere, and I critically engage with Habermas's separation between a bourgeois public sphere and a public sphere created by mass media. Pushing beyond this idealized dichotomy, I characterize the public as a communicative network, which people build up, maintain, and use in order to secure the attention of the press as a powerful organ that defines and shapes public concerns. This idea of the public as a network also punctuates the typical distinction between production and reception and exposes news making as a process that connects a range of practices and desires.

Indian Media and the Transformation of News Making

My discussion is set against the background of radical economic reforms in the early 1990s that moved the Indian economy from a system of state management to free market practices (Nayar 2001). One consequence was the rapid growth and diversification of the mass media (Butcher 2003; Kohli-Khandekar 2006; Sharma 1998). Newspapers participated in this development. The availability of highly paid advertisements, coupled with radical revisions of business culture, aggressive marketing, growing political interest, increasing literacy rates, and improved technology, made newspapers extremely profitable (Jeffrey 1993, 2000). This changed the financial equation. While government funding contributed substantially to newspapers' income in the pre-liberalization period, now revenue is generated heavily from private corporations (Jeffrey 2000). This has consequences for news content.

Until the 1980s, a dominant news ideology promoted the notion of the press as a political agent. Journalistic ethics emphasized the duty of the press to work in tandem with the political elite to modernize the nation and educate its citizens. To protect media from the vested interests of private advertisers and to ensure "progressive" and "objective" reporting, the government heavily subsidized news printing. This fostered preference for political news and a pro-government bias (Peterson 1996; Raghavan 1994: 142–64). In the emerging neoliberal environment, the desire to appease private advertisers has high priority and often supersedes the will for political conformity (Jeffrey 1993, 2000; Kohli-Khandekar 2006). The consequences are summarized by Thussu (2007a) as an evolving process of "Murdochization." His data from the study of Indian private television news (especially Star News) show a shift toward regularly positive depictions of the private industry and a decline in reporting about the interventions of political institutions. There is extensive reporting about film, media, and sports, a narrow focus on urban themes and culturally proximate events. Thussu also diagnoses an almost complete absence of international news. These developments find their equivalent in the press, especially the English-language press, with the *Times of India* as the recognized leader of a thematic and stylistic shift (Sahay 2006) toward infotainment (Rao 2008, 2010).

What remains absent in an analysis focused on proprietors' strategies is the significance of readers beyond their representation in surveys and ratings. This perspective is needed in any analysis of vernacular newspapers; pleasing the local reader is a tactical choice. Vernacular newspapers cater in particular to the lower middle classes and regional and rural populations. Their main recipe for expanding readership — which can then be sold to advertisers — is to provide residents with valuable information about their locality, the district, and the state. The formula to go local has proven to be extremely successful and has delivered exponential growth, so that today vernacular newspapers outnumber English-language papers. Jeffrey (2000) calls the triumph of the vernacular press a "Newspaper Revolution," which is justified considering their enormous political impact. Regional newspapers have contributed substantially to the transformation of the political landscape, poignantly summarized by Pande (2006) as "English for the Elite and Hindi for the Power Elite." Recent developments have produced new powerful and influential political elites with strong regional ties whose political projects increasingly challenge national powers. The engagement of journalists with regional leaders has made vernacular newspapers major players in this process (Rajagopal 1998, 2001).

In this discussion, I move further down the social hierarchy to analyze the news-making activities of local citizens who take advantage of and feed the regionalization of vernacular newspapers. I demonstrate how ambitious personalities and aggrieved citizens mimic political techniques of self-promotion by entertaining media connections and working through the press. Reflecting on the way citizens bring their agency to bear on the news discourse, I redirect the analytical gaze. The participation of people with limited social, economic, or political capital has received little attention in the recent debates about media developments in India (an exception is Ninan 2007). The desires, ambitions, and predicaments of the less privileged find expression in a particular local medium that persists as a reminder of the multiple social positions from which people experience contemporary society.

I do not claim that local voices inhabit a position of resistance to global capitalism. The news activities of citizens do not add up to a coherent set of expressions or a unified social movement. Nor is the investment of "small people" into publicity necessarily aligned with a fight for social justice, equality, or emancipation. We have an abundance of concerns, and the range is dazzling. People invoke ideological struggles, undertake power contests, share individual grievances, and publicize personal ambitions. Only occasionally do these voices join in a focused debate about common political concerns or social interests. More often than not, we are confronted with a cacophony of voices. While they do not create a rational public debate as envisioned by liberal ideologies of the press, they are an important social force. The availability of news space and the willingness of citizens to exploit publicity has facilitated the making of news networks as an alternative avenue for mobilizing support when other strategies of empowerment fail. They provoke the political. They are also a reminder of ruptures and predicaments that persist in real lives, and hence they produce a significant contrast to the flawless images of affluence and consumerism promoted in advertiser-driven content (Cayla 2008; Juluri 2003; Moorti 2004; Munshi 2004; Rajagopal 1998).

My argument about the power of local news proceeds in three steps. I begin by introducing the open-door policy of Hindi-language newspapers that facilitates the influx of citizens' concerns into the news discourse. Next, I spell out two case studies that demonstrate the role of news strategies in local power contests. In the last section I develop the idea of public as network. I critique the prevalent interpretation of the public sphere as a space dominated by elite versions of society and conclude about the nature of the citizen-press interface in a particular market niche.

Local Reporting and the Open-Door Policy

Like all Indian cities, Lucknow has experienced rapid growth of local news making since the 1990s. Today the leading Hindi newspapers in the city, *Dainik Jagaran* and *Hindustan,* devote more than half of their publication to local news, which is equal to about eight pages. In order to fill this space, Hindi newspapers have adopted an open-door policy: they encourage citizens to communicate with the newspaper. The influx of urban concerns, opinions, hardships, and desires passes through three channels: press releases, extensive networks of stringers, and a personalized style of reporting.

Press releases: Hindi newspapers discard press releases only if they show some kind of extreme bias; otherwise, all are printed, usually with very little editing. Twenty percent of all news items (not news space) in the local pages are lifted from press releases written by local citizens or organizations. The city editor of the *Dainik Jagaran* told me: "We try to print all press notes, even if we have to shorten them. The content is theirs; the words are ours" (March 27, 2002).

News networks: Hindi newspapers have divided the city into neighborhoods and communities (such as religious communities, ethnic minorities) and assigned a stringer to each of these groups and places.[2] Their number fluctuates between 30 and 50 stringers in the city of Lucknow for one newspaper. Stringers keep the newspaper office informed about local events, may write articles, and can be contacted when citizens report about occurrences or conditions in their neighborhood. They fulfill the task of mediating between the local community and the newspaper. This turns them into key members of a network that produces publicity. Stringers advertise their connection to the newspaper, since it gives them status and power and ensures that people will come to them with their grievances and stories (see also Ståhlberg 2002).

Policy of naming: Reporters are instructed to name people irrespective of whether they were actually seeking publicity or not. This instruction follows directly from the assumption that people like to read about themselves in the newspaper and that they also buy the newspaper because they want to collect clippings. Besides producing long lists of participants of functions, celebrations, or protest marches, we also find articles that enumerate opinions. *Hindustan* has introduced a daily column that consists of a random survey of 8 to 10 people. They are polled on "themes of the day," and their opinions are printed along with their pictures. The same format is used when controversies arise that mobilize activity in the civil society. Reporters gather the opinions of numerous people and quote them in the newspaper, producing long, often redundant lists of statements.

The requirement of journalists/newspapers to sell a comprehensive picture of local life meets the desire of urban citizens for publicity. The ready availability of news space has encouraged city dwellers to develop what I call a "news culture" (Rao 2010). By this I mean the willingness of a wide range of people to use newspapers as instruments of power through which they acquire social mobility, do business, work through the bureaucracy, or make themselves known to the public.

In the following section I spell out instances of mediated power contests. I focus on a leadership competition during a public fight to prevent the shooting of a feature film and explain the role of newspapers during an intra-caste fight.

News as Strategic Resource

When the Canadian filmmaker Deepa Mehta came to India in 2000 to shoot the film *Water* on the banks of the sacred river Ganges, she encountered protests.[3] Opposition was voiced by local activists who saw the film about the plight of widows in 1930s Banaras as an assault on the dignity of Indian women. Enemies of the film aligned with political forces representing Hindu fundamentalist positions. Their engagement mediated a national debate that reenacted a typical divide in the Indian political landscape. On the one side were activists who advocate the reshaping of India along the ideals of Brahmanical Hinduism. They strongly object to negative depictions of Hindu traditions, since they see Hinduism as a benevolent force that gives identity to the Indian nation. On the other side were feminists and liberals struggling for the maintenance of a secular India that accommodates many traditions, cultivates free speech, and strives toward social equality.

Newspapers became an instrument for rekindling a debate about the fundamental character of the Indian nation. Journalists were solicited by local activists who used the occasion as an opportunity to foster media relations and become famous. While newspapers reported about innumerable protest activities, observations in Banaras revealed that activities in the public arena were limited. Protests were highly localized and had few participants. Most residents of Banaras only followed the controversy in the newspapers, where every expression of protest was covered in minute detail. Journalists published innumerable press releases. They reported from a mushrooming number of miniature press conferences, staged suicide threats, and small protest marches. I questioned journalists about the striking gap between the sparse activity in public places and the excessive reporting that painted the image of a city in turmoil. Their answers showed a high degree of disillusionment with what journalists thought to be a publicity stunt of a select few: A correspondent for the *Hindustan Times* said, "They all meet at Papu's tea stall at Assi Ghat [the place where the shooting was supposed to take place], where they *make* all the news!" (March 8, 2000). The correspondent from *Times of India* remembers there was no need to leave his office, since all the "news" came to him: "During the peak of the protest we got daily press releases from the KSRSS [Organization for the Defense of the Culture of Kashi]. So there was no need to contact them" (March 8, 2000). Competition for coverage and demands from the state office forced journalists to report everything in detail. Flooding journalists with press releases and monopolizing their time by made-for-media events (Pedelty 1995: 120–23) thus proved a perfect strategy for promoting the culturalist project of Hindu nationalism.

However, there was no simple causal connection between what became an amassing of Hindu nationalist voices in the media and the aim to prevent shooting in Banaras. The media event was *not* an orchestrated happening, choreographed by a hidden mastermind to Hinduize India. The proliferation of anti-*Water* activities (as well as pro-*Water* activities) was rather a corollary of an ongoing competition for public recognition in the urban environment. A range of publicity-seeking local citizens grabbed the opportunity to get their names onto the news pages, thereby advertising their "social engagement" and gaining recognition for their organizations. Such activity was intended to pay off in terms of fame, status, and the faint hope for long-term success in a recognized political institution.

In the front line of the protest was Kaushal Kishor Mishra, president of the Organization for the Defense of the Culture of Kashi (Kashi Sanskriti Raksha Sangharsh Samiti, or KSRSS). He entered the controversy relatively late, when he got hold of the script. At that moment he saw himself in a position to "prove" the anti-Hindu bias of the film, which, he claims, triggered a change in journalists' attitude toward the movement. When he realized there was potential for success, Mishra grabbed the opportunity and struggled to make the KSRSS the coordinator of protest activities by creating as much press presence as possible. He thereby advertised his ability as leader in a "clash of civilizations" — he explicitly quoted Samuel Huntington (1996) during our interview (March 8, 2000). More concretely, he wished to ride to power on the wave of this controversy by proving his popularity in front of decision-making bodies of the Indian People's Party (Bharatiya Janata Party, or BJP), the parliamentary wing of the Hindu nationalist movement.[4]

Mishra was not alone. The media reported statements from local representatives of a wide range of Hindu nationalist organizations.[5] There was communication from all locally elected members of parliament, many ex-members of parliament, ex-ministers, ex-presidents, and other public figures.[6] Their activities were not coordinated, but rather the result of an emerging competition that inspired ambitious local personalities to attract public attention. The growing crescendo of voices became a media event that fed into a well-established stereotypical image of Banaras as a conservative place, where a deeply religious population provides an ideal breeding ground for political projects that promote Hinduism as superior fundament for the Indian nation. We were confronted with the picture of a city in turmoil, which clearly impressed the politicians. During a press conference, the responsible chief minister, Ram Prakash Gupta, accepted media "truth" and stated that he would leave things in the "hands of the people of Banaras" (press conference on February 7, 2002; see also the press coverage on February 8, 2002). Through a rhetorical twist, journalists' reporting about the competitive public activities of a wide range of (self-declared) leaders turned into "the voice of the people," an important step toward sealing the fate of the project.

Not all local news gets such prominent attention. In fact, the sheer quantity of local news would usually prevent singular incidents from being widely recognized. My second case shows that this may not be a disadvantage when newspapers are used to gain an edge in local fights. I am taking the example of an intra-caste conflict among members of the Khatik caste in the city of Bhopal.[7] Here newspapers were used in an ongoing struggle between the leaders of two factions of well-off, educated men, who competed for domination in a caste group composed mostly of poor and illiterate people.

The main locus of this competition in Bhopal is the caste-owned Kali Temple, an institution with a significant income and also an important center for Khatik social activities.[8] Shiv Narayan Singh Bagware, an influential leader in the Khatik caste, had managed to manipulate the history of the Kali Temple at a decisive juncture in the 1970s and made himself life-president of the temple trust. Keen to take over this position, Bagware's opponents continually pressured him to set up the trust as a democratic institution and to hold regular elections. Tired of the constant challenges to his position, Bagware escalated the conflict in 1996. In a letter to all members of the numerous temple committees, he asked everyone to account for the money they had received to undertake temple work. After they failed to submit receipts, Bagware dissolved all temple committees and removed the officeholders from their posts by letter, thereby emphasizing his claim to supreme leadership.

Local Khatiks were furious and reacted by calling a meeting of the traditional caste body, the *panchayat,* an assembly of all male Khatiks. In Bagware's absence, the panchayat removed him from his post as temple president and set a deadline of two weeks by which he would have to submit all temple documents to them. Bagware, of course, did not comply. This triggered the panchayat to send a press release to the local news team of the Hindi newspaper *Dainik Bhaskar* on July 1. An article appeared on July 2, announcing that Bagware had been removed from the presidency of the trust. Bagware immediately went to the *patel* (the traditional head of the panchayat) and demanded a refutation. Since the patel himself had little stake in the fight, he signed a second press release now written by Bagware. It informed the press that Bagware was still in office. The "news" was published by *Dainik Bhaskar* on July 4. However, Bagware's opponents would not admit defeat. They met again, reorganized the trust on their own accounts, and published the list of new members of the "trust" (which, of course, had no legal sanction) in *Dainik Bhaskar* and *Nav Bharat* on August 23. But Bagware refused to step down, and the news campaign ended.

Next, opponents used violence to pursue their goal. However, my argument here is not about the trajectory of a leadership fight. Rather, I want to draw attention to the hope that people invest in news. By publishing articles, they wanted to draw on the power of the newspaper to transform relationships. At that level there is a similarity between this and the anti-*Water* case. In both instances social agents used newspapers as catalysts to bring into motion a social process that was intended to create new leaders. Mishra approached the press because he wanted to become an official party representative. Similarly, members of the panchayat hoped for a formal position in the temple trust.[9]

There is power in the news. This assumption guides local actors when they appropriate newspapers in their fights for recognition and status. Being quoted in a newspaper multiplies visibility *and* importance, simply because the statement or topic is being trumpeted through journalistic processes of selection. I call this multiplication of importance through mass mediation the "performative power" of news, referring to Austin's famous formulation and Bourdieu's and Butler's sociological interpretations of it (Rao 2010).

Bourdieu (1990) investigates the social conditions that make performative acts successful. He draws attention to the symbolic capital accumulated in recognized positions, which empowers speakers to successfully complete performative acts. This power is mediated through the existence of a socially shared and generally accepted social "knowledge" of positions and their powers. Butler (1997) critiques this approach as being too static and extends the argument by drawing attention to the uncertainties inherent in performative acts. As quotations they may reenact previously successful performative acts, or they may provoke unexpected results and the formation of new authorizing contexts and thus invite shifts in meaning and structure. Common to both arguments is the insistence on the need for strategies of authorization to make performative acts effective.

The newspaper provides such a context of authorization. In modern democracies the press is supposed to report political events and social developments truthfully and thus control those in power, reflect the state of being in society, and allow citizens to understand and act in a complex world. This globally shared notion of the press translates into the assumption that newspapers give important and correct information about matters of public interest. In reverse, this also means that those who are mentioned in the newspaper must be important and their activities must be of wide social relevance. Thus being mentioned in the paper accelerates importance. The issue here is not only about circulation but about the authority the newspaper lends to a speaker or actor.

This character of the press — which is effectively used by powerful people across the globe — is appropriated by resource poor people in India. The exponential growth of local news making has allowed large numbers of unauthorized speakers (e.g., people who do not have a political office or an administrative post) to cash in on the symbolic capital of the press. They become public speakers but not necessarily as representatives of acknowledged institutions or major organizations in civil society. Their fame may be based solely on the dissemination of their name through the press, which then can be used as a tool in the battle for institutionalized positions.

Mishra, together with a number of other political activists, fueled a controversy by targeting reporters. Journalists gave credit to these voices because they proved — once more — that Hindu nationalism is a force to be reckoned with, as a national ideal or as a threat of violence. As a result, the newspapers created many new (apparent) leaders and confirmed the image of Banaras as a stronghold of the Hindu nationalist movement. It can be believed, it had to be believed, because as an authorized speaker, the press creates the very reality it proclaims. Through extensive coverage, all newspapers produced daily proof that this issue was of major importance. The hype was an effect of a mutual process of authorization, through the press and a wide range of (self-declared) leaders and their "leader-centered organizations" (Mines 1996).

The history of public recognition was much different in the intra-caste conflict. Here we find only three small articles somewhere on the local pages, which would have escaped most people's attention and produced little resonance in the urban community — and which journalists published not because the content was exciting but because the texts helped to fill space. The articles were directed at and could be understood only by a small group of insiders. Yet going public was a strategy. In a situation in which members of the panchayat were unable to push through their claims internally, they approached the press to insert power into their demands. They used the newspaper as an intermediate agent, hoping that the declaration of change in an official medium would lead to the desired transformation.

Although the rivals have not succeeded so far, their action was not in vain. Clippings of the articles are circulated among those who are unfamiliar with intra-caste relations to "prove" membership and positions. As a curious anthropologist I was among those who triggered the production of such "proof." My inquiries about the structures of the caste energized people from all factions to tell their story and present their evidence. It was after long months of fieldwork, when I had managed to work through several layers of narrations, letters, press releases, and articles, that I discovered the many contradictory readings of the history of the Kali Temple that are tied to the political rivalries in the Khatik caste. Newspapers as a source can be expected to gain credibility with time, considering that at some point they turn into historical documents.[10] Thus, when the conflict is retold years later, each side can verify its own version of the truth with news clippings. When the details have been forgotten or cannot be recovered from the depths of history, it is conceivable that something that was not successful in 1996 may suddenly become real. The rivals may finally become what they never were — spokesmen of the temple — even if only as an imaginary memory building on a written "fact."

I have analyzed both cases from the perspective of a leadership competition. Tied to this competition are social concerns, concerns that people desire to insert into the public discourse under their leadership. In the first case there is the worry about the future of Indian society under perceived threats of globalization and secularization. The second case regards the future of caste in urban India. Bagware determinately fights for the creation of a modern caste identity that will communicate a positive sense of belonging to former untouchables (Rao 2002). There are other issues for which people turn to the newspaper as an organ for intensifying their message and strengthening their authority. Any random reading of the local pages proves the wide range of issues carried into the public. Take as an example the local pages of *Hindustan* on April 3, 2002. On that day the paper announced in 10 articles that in Gomti Nagar (a suburb of Lucknow) people feared for their trees, that in Ohm Puri (a suburb of Lucknow) protesters worried about the fate of an old wall, that three organizations (State Youth Industry Trade Association, Lucknow Merchants Association, and City Bus Owners Association) reported mistreatment by the tax department, that teachers (Middle Vocational Teachers Association) and junior engineers had mobilized against irregularities in their employment status, that the police carried out highhanded actions, and that there were unacceptable hikes in electricity rates.

The logic that drives the publication of these issues follows directly from the dynamic described above. By publicizing their concerns in the newspaper, people try to force others to notice their grievances and suggestions. People insert authority into their claims and intensify their demands by getting them recognized and authorized by an official public organ. The outcome of such activity is, of course, contingent. Publishing is one of the possible strategies adapted to press for change. When I asked journalists about the efficiency of publishing grievances, most remained uncommitted. They did not have the time to worry about consequences, but certainly believed that it was important to continue to write, tell, and denounce, hoping that it would make a difference.

> People feel happy if someone listens to their problems. They have already given up the hope that anyone will really help them, so even this much, publishing their grievances, is a lot for them. These people don't say, "The leader does not listen." They say, "The leader is not available to us! He does not see us!" We believe that we have to *hammer it in,* in order to be effective. Even if one out of ten cases gets solved, we are happy. (city editor, *Dainik Jagaran* March 9, 2002)

The expansion of local news making and the open-door policy of editorial teams has opened up the press as a resource to a wide range of people who invest in press relations as a ray of hope, a desire for communication, a road for populist politics, or a strategy for the manipulation of leadership issues. This conclusion caused me to rethink the concept of public sphere that is created through the press. In the next section I will argue that communication between urban dwellers and Hindi-medium journalists—writing for local pages—constitutes a particular aspect of how the public is created through the print media in contemporary India.

Public Channels for Communications

With *The Structural Transformation of the Public Sphere,* Habermas provided a foundational text about the way the political enters the public. Based on an analysis of European social history, he distinguished three successive phases in the development of a public sphere: feudal Europe, bourgeois public sphere, and mass media society. In the feudal state, Habermas asserts, symbols and performances of power were the means by which political leaders created and played out their authority before the people. This, he continues, started to change slowly in the thirteenth century. The emergence of a new class of globally active traders and successful industrialists resulted in the development of a horizontal net of economic relations, the creation of public institutions like the coffeehouse, the salon, and circles of scientific exchange, and the formation of the press, which fermented the emergence of a politically oriented bourgeois public sphere. Habermas characterized this public sphere as a space of debate maintained by private people with the aim of creating a public opinion that criticizes and controls political power and rationalizes it. He argued that the development of an independent press played an important role in this process, since newspapers served as a means of articulating opinion and circulating it within a larger community. He describes the press as a "mediator" and "intensifier" of public opinion in the bourgeois public sphere (1989: 285; 2001: 105).

Habermas identifies another significant change in the structure of the public sphere, beginning in the nineteenth century and gaining momentum in the twentieth. With the loss of exclusivity and coherence, this sphere has become an arena for the realization of private interests. Habermas complains that the press now serves only powerful people and no longer represents the interests of ordinary readers. He speaks of a "re-feudalization" (Habermas 2001: 106) of the pubic sphere in contemporary society. By this he means that public communication no longer serves as a platform for debate among informed citizens, but rather as a medium for (mis)information that aims to influence readers in such a way that this creates advantages for those who hold power. Mass-mediated communication, Habermas asserts, has regained its symbolic character, insofar as it circulates signs of power rather than inviting debate.

Habermas has been criticized for overstating the difference between the various forms of the public sphere, as well as for his clear-cut distinction between the state and civil society. Objections have also been raised to his concept of rational debate, his idea of media-manipulated masses, and his singular emphasis on the role of the media, which ignores other forms of social communication such as gatherings, festivals, or rituals (see, e.g., Dahlgren and Sparks 1991: 5–6;

Hartley 1996; Jeffrey 2000: 11–19; Kaur 2001: 25–26). One consequence of such criticism, then, is a call for more detailed studies of the concrete ways in which particular forms of publics are created and maintained through the practices of social actors and groups, as well as of how they become relevant in the larger political contexts of a nation-state and the global setting.

Following this suggestion I have analyzed the intersection between journalists and civil society by looking at the way urban citizens enter newspapers. This approach blurs the boundaries between production and reception. It shows how the activities of journalists and readers are entangled and how news discourse is influenced by concerned citizens and their power games. The local pages of vernacular newspapers are sites for the amassing of local voices, evoking the city as a patchwork of interests, views, and activities. The detailed accounts from even the most remote areas in the city leave the unfamiliar reader dizzy and caught in a confusing plurality of information. There are stories that follow recurrent themes, collected by beat reporters. Yet on most days this does not create coherent debates. The reader is left with the suspicion that there are few common concerns, except maybe the chronic unhappiness of people about the way that state institutions function. Yet there are also moments of intense debate, e.g., as when the shooting of *Water* caused a national debate on desirable limits to the freedom of artistic expression. Here newspapers' coverage opened up a field for public reasoning that integrated a wide range of literate people.

Summing up the argument, we find that newspapers in India provide opportunities to introduce opinions, grievances, and ambitions as a means of negotiating personal interests or facilitating social transformation. They are appropriated as (1) an instrument of individuals introducing a personal problem to the public, (2) a medium for the expression of a collective outcry against the state, its institutions, and representatives, or (3) a means of promoting social unrest. However, while I conclude that Hindi newspapers create a forum for the practice of democracy and a place to exert pressure on the powerful, too, this is not always liberating or progressive, as the case of anti-*Water* protests clearly shows. In that case, newspapers promoted, more than anything else, the spread of a xenophobic and intolerant movement.

The public that is created here differs from Habermas's two ideal types of the bourgeois public and the mass media–influenced public. Habermas idealizes the public sphere of the bourgeois as a zone for public reasoning that is virtually free of vested interests. It is a shell separated from the world of power in which rational debate leads to an unmasking of political power, described by Habermas as a forum purely for the exchange of views (*Meinungspflege*).

The case study of the *Water* controversy has shown most clearly that newspapers are indeed media for the negotiation of matters of public interest by the members of civil society. Yet at no point was participation free of power struggles. It could not have been, considering that at stake was the character of the public sphere itself, as well as the position of involved individuals within this setting. The movement developed into a conflict between those who believed in a plural and open society that could accommodate contradictory morals and social visions, and a neotraditionalist version of a unified Hindu nation. Besides these general, highly political questions, there were private ambitions that motivated people to enter the public sphere. Actors sought a political career, public recognition, support for a party, or economic advantages.

In this sense the newspaper opened up a space much closer to Habermas's description of the public sphere in times of mass media. Here it appears as a space for pushing private interests by using the authority of the media as a means of persuasion. The actors Habermas has in mind are public relations managers of leading companies and dominant political players, who manufacture made-for-media events in order to push their concerns into the media. It leads to a situation in which those who monopolize private capital and political power stabilize their dominant position through the manipulation of public organs.

The Indian example confronts us with the fact that "small people" (Guha 1982, 1996) have appropriated media strategies stereotypically ascribed to spin doctors acting at the behest of the big and powerful. They are successful in a media landscape that invests more and more in local news. During the *Water* controversy, Hindu nationalists monopolized journalists' time through "manufactured events" in order to promote their viewpoints, advertise their engagement, and build a public career. Similarly, Bagware's opponents introduced their problem to the public through an event that was tailor-made for the newspaper, namely, the election of new officeholders.

Emphasizing the ways that subalterns appropriate news, I do not indulge in a naïve celebration of a new equality. Habermas's disillusionment with the mass media in industrialized societies is not fully out of place.[11] A whole range of studies on journalism in Western countries confirm the elite bias of newspapers, proving that it is those with significant amounts of money, power, and status who dominate newspaper content (Fishman 1980; Goldenberg 1975; Golding and Elliott 1979; Hall et al. 1978; Schudson 2003; Tuchman 1978). In India the influence of the political and economic elite is obvious and all-pervasive, a theme I have dealt with in detail elsewhere (Rao 2010). However, it would be false to assume that the possibility of public reasoning in the press is exhausted by the powerful intervention of dominant actors. At least in the Indian case we find that the desire of newspapers to increase sales by appealing to local citizens has given resource-poor people an official instrument that can help them lobby their causes, advertise their engagement, and spread their ideas and ideologies.

The character of local reporting in Hindi newspapers transforms urban citizens from readers to potential subjects and even writers of news texts.

In order to secure media attention, people utilize the channels provided by the open-door policies of newspapers, by learning to write press releases and by investing in media relations. When I started my fieldwork, I was surprised and then perturbed to find that almost every man I met claimed to be a journalist. It took time to understand what the term *journalist* meant here. In most cases it did not mean that people were fully employed journalists of prestigious newspapers with a large circulation. They could be freelancers or representatives of small local newspapers. I also met editors-cum-publishers-cum-reporters of self-produced newspapers (sometimes of not more than 100 or 1,000 copies), stringers, occasional writers, former journalists with good connections, and regular writers of letters to the editor. They live in the city and establish connections with many citizens. Together they form a hierarchy of people with media connections who open channels for communication through which urban concerns reach the newspaper. These networks constitute an interactive sphere between the media and the consuming public, in which urban themes are discovered, negotiated, and weighted.

Focusing on the encounter between journalists and local citizens, I offer a radically different interpretation of the public than is found in the more common text-based studies (Imhof and Schulz 1996; Neidhardt 1994; Szyszka 1999). There is extensive debate about a reacting audience as forming a public by consuming and processing messages that have been channeled through the media. I propose to shift the focus away from audience research to an investigation of the press/public interface (see also Alasuutari 1999). By doing this I have drawn attention to the intervention of readers and its relevance for the local news discourse. Positioning themselves in a media network and circulating information relevant to their personal lives, urban citizens create a field of social activity that blurs the boundary between writers and consumers. This field offers the symbolic capital of the press for appropriation by resource poor people. The imaginary, the promise, and the experience of power through participation in the media draw people into this field, which constitutes a public characterized by labyrinthine channels of communication. They are activated not for an interest-free debate about best governance but for an advantage-seeking engagement in a public battle about political delivery, leadership, national ideals, and social morals. This practice conflates sets of social activities, which range from institutionalized politics and administration to local conflicts and domestic concerns. The public that is constituted here is not situated in-between, "mediating state and society" (Habermas 2001). It is Realpolitik and as such constitutive for power relations and social images of the political.

Notes

1. I conducted fieldwork in Lucknow for 10 months in the years 1999–2000 and 2002. My cases are taken from the leading Hindi newspapers, *Dainik Jagaran, Hindustan,* and *Dainik Bhaskar.* There is additional material from Bhopal collected during a study on temple politics between 1995 and 1999 (Rao 2003).

2. Stringers usually follow another profession: they could be shopkeepers or local businessmen. Their job is to keep the newspaper office informed about all occurrences in their territory. In return some receive a small monthly salary. More often they are not paid at all. The incentive to become a stringer is usually the desire for a connection to a newspaper that will boost importance and can be used to negotiate deals.

3. After struggling for three months in Banaras, Deepa Mehta gave up the idea of producing the film in India. She later shot it in Sri Lanka without any publicity. It opened the Toronto film festival in 2005. The film is part of a trilogy and a sequel to *Fire* and *Earth.*

4. Today Mishra is vice president of the Uttar Pradesh BJP (Intellectual Cell), and he continues to create arguments about the need to protect Hindu culture in the press.

5. I here refer to the coverage of the Lucknow editions of *Hindustan Times, Times of India, Pioneer, Hindustan, Dainik Jagaran,* and *Amar Ujala* between January 30 and February 9, 2000. Newspapers quoted the Bajrang Dal, the VHP, the RSS, and the Shiv Sena. We learned about small local committees like the City Progress Committee, Sanskar Bharti, the Kashi Scholars Association, the National Hero Abdul Hamid Foundation, and the Banaras Hindu University Teachers Association.

6. There were, of course, also people who spoke in favor of Deepa Mehta, the range of actors being as diverse as in the case of the anti-*Water* voices.

7. Traditionally Khatiks were meat and vegetable sellers. They are counted among the group of former "untouchables," and today they have status as members of a scheduled caste.

8. For more details, see Rao 2002 and 2003.

9. See Rajagopal 2001 for a similar interpretation of the Ayodhya conflict.

10. See also Gupta's ironical suggestion: "Treated with benign neglect by students of contemporary life, they [news articles] mysteriously metamorphize into invaluable 'field data' once they have yellowed around the edges and fallen apart at the creases. And yet it is not entirely clear by what alchemy time turns the 'secondary' data of the anthropologist into the 'primary' data of the historian" (Gupta 1995: 385).

11. Habermas shared this pessimism with other scholars from the Frankfurt School (see, e.g., Horkheimer and Adorno 1998).

Mount Chance, Montserrat, and the Media

Global British Journalism under Local Fire

JONATHAN SKINNER

Daily, we, the regular readers, flick our eyes over the directing signs.
Without conscious awareness, we find our way around the familiar
territory of our newspaper. — Michael Billig, *Banal Nationalism*

In 1995, Mount Chance, Montserrat, a hilltop on a quiet and remote British
territory in the Eastern Caribbean, unexpectedly erupted, resulting in the devastation of two-thirds of the island and the mass out-migration of two-thirds
of its population of British Overseas Territory citizens. Because of the island's
British status, the story was covered prominently in British newspapers — both
the popular tabloids and the "quality" broadsheets. In this chapter, I assess the
coverage of the Montserrat volcano crisis (1995 to present) by the British print
media, concentrating on 1997. My aim is to show that this news production is
politically inflected and nationalistic and that the scenario is symptomatic of
our modern or late-modern fast-paced world. The volcano coverage provides us
with a set of texts within the "symbolic system" of news writing, highlighting
the semiotic and intertextual nature of the news in a postliterate and postmodern world (Peterson 2005; see also Bird and Dardenne 1988). I suggest these
points through context and content analyses of the coverage, concentrating on
what I refer to as the "golden elephants" gaffe of 1997. My goal is to show how a
close, long-term reading of news content can shed light on the way news frames
and constructs meaning in culturally specific ways. My focus is not on individual news accounts as such but on how "the story" of Montserrat evolved.

This study is based on my own longitudinal study of life on the island before,
during, and after the volcano crisis (1994–1995, 2000, 2005) and my work with
travel writers visiting the island (Skinner 2008a). Besides following travel writers while they were visiting Montserrat and tracking their story production, I
have built up an extensive archive of all of the UK coverage and the key U.S.
coverage of the volcano crisis from 1994 to present. This archive, developed over
the last 14 years, contains some 430 articles and items from British papers; 64

articles and items from U.S. papers; three feature pieces in international magazines such as the *National Geographic;* four hours of British television news
items and programs; several thousand internet newsgroup messages (see Skinner 2008b); and a collection of videos and newspaper clippings from Montserrat. This archive's inception develops from American geographer Susan Laffey's
original 250 reports from North American sources before 1990 (see Laffey 1995).
Indeed, I myself have been on several occasions the subject of the news and
travel writing media (radio, television and newspaper), such as in this extract
from the Scottish news media:

STUDENT RECALLS VOLCANO ISLAND ORDEAL

A St. Andrews University post-graduate student yesterday gave an account of his last few days on the Caribbean island of Montserrat, which
for some time has been under threat from a volcanic eruption — and, more
recently, from a hurricane.

Jonathan Skinner (25) described his ordeal as "pretty frightening."

He is now back in St. Andrews, where he is completing his studies in
social anthropology. (*Courier and Advertiser,* September 6: 4)

The island of Montserrat is a 39-square-mile island in the Caribbean with a
population of 10,000. It has a history of natural catastrophes, with the ongoing
volcanic eruption from 1995 following the 1989 hurricane Hugo, which destroyed 98 percent of all buildings on the island. It is a British island where — like
Puerto Rico — there is a strong emigration culture (Philpott 1973). Montserrat
has been a British colony since the 1630s and has a plantation history of both
English and Irish settlement (Skinner 2004; Fergus 1992, 1994; Messenger 1975).[1]
The resilient culture of the indigenous Montserratians has been tested almost
to breaking point since July 1995, when Chances Peak suddenly began erupting. Within a month, two-thirds of the population (6,000) had been evacuated
to the north of the island to live in temporary accommodations. By August 23,
1995, 5,000 people had left Montserrat, and the capital where I had been living
and working was evacuated at night. The events unfolding on the island were
covered by the global media, in particular the British newspapers, which sent
their foreign correspondents to the island.

Michael Billig's *Banal Nationalism* suggests that we are daily bombarded by
the rhetorics and semiotics of nationalism in outlets such as newspapers which
typically divide content into home (domestic) and foreign (international) news,
while placing much more emphasis on the former. With two-thirds of the UK
population reading a newspaper at least three times a week (Jowell, Heath, and
Curtice 1994), this extensive form of rhetorical signposting percolates through
much of the UK population. Billig's thesis is that this is a "banal," everyday way

in which nationalism is expressed. It is even reiterated by the national and international borders at the top of section pages in our daily newspapers. A reader of any UK broadsheet will find signposts to "Home News" and "Overseas News" sections in the *Times;* "News" and "Foreign News" in the *Daily Telegraph;* and a tripartite news division in the *Independent* and the *Guardian* between "Home News," "European News," and "International News" (Billig 2005: 118). The divisions are less marked and the foreign news is less well covered in the more sensationalist popular tabloids such as the *Daily Star,* the *Daily Mirror,* and the *Sun* and in the regional newspapers or regionally edited "nationals."

A "news apartheid" (Billig 2005: 119) — between "us" and "them," the "local" and "the foreign," the familiar and the exotic — has become part of our everyday experience, with divisions reiterated and reconfirmed through other media such as national and independent television and radio.[2] Social scientists, including anthropologists, have become increasingly interested in the study of such phenomena and the role of the media (Askew and Wilk 2002; Ginsburg, Abu-Lughod, and Larkin 2002; Rothenbuhler and Coman 2005) in sustaining them: the "promises" and "profanities" (Coman and Rothenbuhler 2005; Hobart 2005); the technologies and modes of organization and means of production (Born 2005; Miller and Horst 2006); the encoding and decoding of their contents (Beeman 1987; Esch 1999; Moeller 1999; Lutz and Collins 1993; Dominy 1993); and the relationship between media, state, and nation (Anderson 1983; Holy 1996; Postill 2006) and indigenous peoples (Ginsburg 2002). Furthermore, anthropologists are increasingly making use of the media as cultural resources. Ladislav Holy (1996: 14), for instance, made significant use of newspapers to complement his ethnography of Czech identity, arguing that such mass media have now become "the main means of communication of shared cultural meanings." Newspaper articles and editorials are thus of valid interest to anthropologists, a position different from Herzfeld's warning in the 1980s that these texts are deficient objective accounts of reality "pitched to the lowest common denominator" (Herzfeld 1982: 647). Today, anthropologists may read news accounts not merely for the "facts" they might convey but perhaps also for the way that such accounts construct reality, as Bird suggests in this volume.

Thus the study of news as (cultural) narrative is by no means poor man's ethnography. As Leach (1984), Darnton (1984), Bird (2005b), and Bird and Dardenne (1988) point out, the reading of a text can give us glimpses into the unmentionable: the "con"-text (Hobart 1999a), the author's projections (Laffey 1995), the unsaid (Tyler 1978), the "avenues of meaning" (Barthes 1990) between and inside the lines. It is therefore important to consider the texts and stories themselves as well as the production of and audience for news. The news narratives of Montserrat found in an era of late-modernity media are UK national narratives in the sense that the news performs a distinctive "audience function" — with particular politico-cultural patterns, ideologies, and agendas.[3] This chapter offers a case study that reconstructs a news event as it unfolded over some time, with a particular emphasis on UK newspaper coverage. This case study also allows us to engage with Harvey's (1990) thesis of "space-time compression" in a capitalist system, although, in contrast to Harvey, I argue that this compression evinced in these national and international pages does not lead to a dissolution of social and spatial coordinates — a "disembeddedness" of identity for Giddens (1991).

Montserrat in the British News

The volcano emergency developed from July 1995 and featured internationally in all forms of media. It became a front-page global news topic in 1995 and 1997 with unexpected eruptions, and coverage rumbled along in the UK throughout these years with the political ramifications of good governance in the British colonies taking the lead. Initially, headline stories such as those in the *Times* grabbed readers' interest by exploiting the spatial connection between Montserrat and the UK: "Tourists on Alert to Flee Volcano Island" ran one headline, expressing national concern for the 150 tourists and British expatriates still remaining on the island rather than the 10,000 Montserratians living with the volcanic eruptions (Jones 1995). In other words, if a story featured British-based subjects, then it was considered newsworthy, but not if it was about British Overseas Territory citizens. By August 1995, UK defense correspondents were also covering the Montserrat story as the ships HMS *Southampton* and HMS *Westminster* were stationed off Montserrat to provide support for the "voluntary evacuation" of the island, with Royal Marines also helping British scientists and the Montserrat Defense Force:

> A total evacuation of the southern end of Montserrat island was ordered before dawn yesterday after two Royal Marines peered into the crater of the rumbling volcano threatening to erupt over the tiny British dependency in the Caribbean. (Laurence 1995)

Again, coverage of the volcano story is at a tangent, in that the papers ran stories for their assumed readers about the island and its volcanic eruptions only when they had direct consequences on British subjects and UK foreign policy. Yet, despite the colonial link between the two geographical "spaces," the stories all appeared in the international sections of the newspapers.

A typical feature of coverage of major natural catastrophes is what Heringman has described as an "alien agency" that leads the writer "to register nature's otherness, an otherness that not only refuses domestication but also problematizes representation itself" (2003: 97). The metaphors of description and literal containment and understanding of a catastrophe range from the convulsions of the maternal womb (101, 116) to the dynamic (foreboding, ominous, ravenous, malevolent, specter) and the religious (sublime) on this "tear-drop-shaped island" (Davison 1997a). On Montserrat, the metaphor used is "Fire on the Mountain," an old slave song used by the *Guardian's* Caribbean journalist Polly Pattullo as the title of her book about the volcano (2000). In all of these descriptions and characterizations of catastrophes, the otherness of the catastrophe comes from its unimaginable scale and its "incongruity with human purposes" (Heringman 2003: 118). The Montserrat volcano is understood — is made sense of — through an "eruption narrative" style of writing that brings aesthetics to geology (2003: 124), juxtaposes physical danger with domestication, and struggles with the comprehension and representation of such phenomena. Thus Pattullo (2000: 5) translates the volcano growth statistics of 65 million cubic meters between 1995 and 1997 into "the equivalent of a bonfire piled with 65 million sacks of coal," or the equivalent of two or three refrigerators every second of at least the first two years of the eruption, as one scientist told me (Skinner 2007). In these examples, the magnitude of the eruption is expressed in metaphor and phenomenological terms rather than the quantitative. This is because we think "dramatically," as Dowie (1980) notes. We struggle with this form of cognition such that we often resort to the "nature" label; this label is suggestive of the awesome and sublime, but can also be ontologically stabilizing as it objectifies and alienates (Beer 1998).

When Robert Alstead (1995: 16) first cautiously arrived on Montserrat in November 1995 at the start of the crisis, he titled and subtitled an article in the weekend supplement of *Scotland on Sunday* as follows:

Ready to Rock?
The Caribbean island of Montserrat has a place in pop history — but its volcano is rumbling ominously. Robert Alstead waits and quakes.

With this lead-in for the reader, the article opens with an exemplification of Beer and Heringman's points:

It is pure moonscape. Thick grey volcanic ash is all around. Where a luxuriant rainforest once grew is now a barren waste of dusty stalks and trunks. What foliage the hurricanes have left is caked in ash. The small lake looks stagnant, and the ground is like putty. There is not a living thing to be seen or heard. On the top of the 3,000 ft. Chances Peak, the Soufriere Hills volcano of Montserrat has done its worst.

For his Scottish readership, Alstead compares the Montserrat landscape with a lunarscape that they might imagine from media images. The flora, struggling to survive, have been "caked" in ash by the death-bringing volcano. For the journalist, Chances Peak is ominous because it has obliterated the customary human and animal signs and sounds expected on a British Caribbean island. The absence of markers disturbs Alstead. He was there, the reporting journalist, hearing the rumbles of the volcano, joining the pressured wait of the islanders, but not recognizing it as a living force despite its destructive agency; later on into the crisis, the volcano was nicknamed "the Beast" by locals.

The following year, the volcano continued to grow, with scientists quoted in the news predicting an increased severity in the eruptions:

> "We are not expecting a catastrophic event that will be the end of everything," said Simon Young, the British geologist monitoring the ferocious rumblings in the Soufriere Hills that have forced the evacuation of swathes of this former island paradise.
>
> "But there is going to be quite a major lateral blast that could lead to a vertical explosion. We might not get any warning whatsoever," Young said. (Allen-Mills 1996: 17)

Allen-Mills was writing from New York for the World News pages of the *Sunday Times* back in the UK. Over the past year, one might say that there had been a shift in the language used to describe the volcano's activity from "ominous" to "ferocious" rumblings. The warnings continued, and the islanders remained in a state of evacuation and eruption preparedness. This was later characterized as "living with the unexpected" by the German academic Anja Possekel (1999). Here, too, we get an indication that the paradise island has been spoiled, turning into a different sort of "natural" island: volcano island.

The *National Geographic:* A Different Narrative

In 1993, Lutz and Collins published *Reading "National Geographic,"* a comprehensive semiotic and cultural analysis of the famous American magazine that sells 40 million copies a month, deriving its income from subscription rather than advertising. It is known by its readers colloquially as "America's Lens on the World." With such a large readership — generally middle-class, affluent, and influential in the United States — the *National Geographic* arguably has a role in shaping public perceptions and national policies. Lutz and Collins investigated its institutional development from a gathering of government geographers in 1888 into an "All-American" brand. They followed the editorial processes, analyzed over 600 published photographs, and interviewed both readers of and writers for the *National Geographic.* They did not, however, have the option of following a story out in the field as I have on Montserrat, or of analyzing material that they were familiar with as anthropologists. According to Lutz and Collins (1993: 116):

> *National Geographic* presents a special view of the "people out there." This view — a world of happy, classless people outside history but evolving into it, edged with exoticism and sexuality, but knowable to some degree as individuals — is both distinctive in comparison with other mass media representations and continuous with some prevailing cultural norms.

National Geographic is known for its reliance on photographs which typically romanticized children, portrayed people as though they were without history, and exoticized, idealized, naturalized, and sexualized their subjects (1993: 89) in a seemingly straightforward style of representation. This is all bundled in a respectable "conservative humanism" (back cover). It belongs to the "peek-a-boo world of novelty and entertainment," according to Jonathan Benthall (1993: 203), one which attracts our attentions and sympathies before moving on before "compassion fatigue" (Moeller 1999) sets in.

The coverage of Montserrat illustrates *National Geographic*'s approach, written and photographed from a very different stance from that taken by the British media. For Britain, the events on the island were culturally closer and relevant, affecting people who were British subjects. And for UK journalists, the story quickly became a partisan political opportunity, as we shall see. But for *National Geographic,* it became an uplifting story of survival in the face of catastrophe. "Montserrat: Under the Volcano" is one of *National Geographic*'s special articles in the July 1997 edition, written by senior staff member A. R. Williams with photographs by Vincent Musi. Together, they constructed a visual and textual essay about living with the Montserrat "menace." Typical of coverage of many disasters, the cause of troubles is animated and made into a living, breathing troublemaker. This volcano, like other natural catastrophes, was given agency, and the images of it are imbued with emotional efficacy. These are ways in which the writers and editors bring the reader into the piece. The cover shot, for example, spills across two pages: a black boy swimming in a turquoise swimming pool with villas in the midground and the volcano in the background, puffs of cloud turning a dark gray. There is a caption to the visual imagery leading the reader into the longer piece (Williams 1997: 59): "Ash spewing from Soufriere Hills doesn't deter Ian Osborne from a swim at his family's hotel in Old Towne. For two years eruptions have bedeviled this tiny Caribbean island, yet residents are determined to keep their idyllic life afloat." There follows an account of recent volcanic eruptions and how they have affected the lives of local Montserratians. The accounts are first-person interviews deliberately full of hyperbole.

Williams portrays the Montserratians as "under siege" from a "huffing and puffing" volcano, "mesmerizingly powerful" (1997: 66, 75) with "white lace beakers" trimming the debris of pyroclastic rock and mud flows. The writer constructs a dramatic tale of faith in adversity, of coping by adapting — church pews for beds, classrooms for hospital wards in the north of the island. This account of Montserratian resourcefulness and laughter on a "charming, beleaguered island" (1997: 75) contrasts with the more politicized UK newspaper accounts of the volcano crisis. This is Lutz and Collins's romantic and conservative humanism. From my position as an ethnographer of the community, the narrative jars. Where Williams juxtaposes the power and beauty of nature with the resilience of the human spirit, I see the devastation of the paths I've walked along during my various periods of fieldwork. In the comments about the ash, my mouth grows dry and I can taste it in my mouth again. When I see the capital, Plymouth, under the volcano, I am thinking of the scientists' other reports, and I am looking for the house where I used to live. When I read about the difficulties of cooking in the shelters, I am thinking of the separated families, the child rape cases, and the inadequacies of shelters provided by the British in which Montserratians had to live for several years, many of them in shipping containers. I saw the photo of a child swimming under the volcano not as a portrayal of relaxation and coming to terms with the unexpected but as an image of vulnerability and foreboding with the grand vista making the islanders and their trauma seem inconsequential.

July 1997 was the month that saw the first direct fatalities caused by the volcano (Skinner 2000: 172). When the July edition of the *National Geographic* went to press, violent eruptions were spilling down the flanks of Chances Peak into villages such as Trants, Harris, and Streatham. Molten mud flowing at 100 mph incinerated some 23 Montserratians who were tending their crops and animals in these danger zones. By August 1997, Plymouth was blanketed — or "swaddled," to use *National Geographic* language — in the same debris. The capital became a modern-day Pompeii, providing news services with images at a remove from the *National Geographic*'s portrait of the island and offering yet another possible narrative.

The Golden Elephants Gaffe: A Political Opportunity

UK press coverage of the Montserrat volcano crisis peaked at the time of the 1997 eruption for political as well as environmental reasons, and it featured the fast-paced zigzag of political action and reaction events between the UK and Montserrat. On May 1, 1997, Tony Blair's New Labour government came to power in the UK, inheriting the remaining British Dependent Territories (since relabeled British Overseas Territories), including Hong Kong (which would be returned to China on July 1) and Montserrat. The ongoing volcano crisis would test New Labour's foreign policy and principles of democratic good governance. The day after being sworn in, Blair appointed Robin Cook MP as Secretary of State for Foreign and Commonwealth Affairs (Foreign and Commonwealth Office) with responsibility to lead a mission to promote the national interests of the United Kingdom and to contribute to a strong world community. Among other appointments in his new government, Blair named Clare Short MP to head a new ministry, the Department for International Development (DFID), an expansion of the Overseas Development Administration (ODA) which has on several occasions been managed as a part of the Foreign and Commonwealth Office (Burnell 1991: 3–4). In this role, Short had a deputy to assist her, George Foulkes MP, Parliamentary Undersecretary of State for International Development. Their mission was to promote policies for sustainable development and the elimination of poverty. Short and Foulkes also managed Britain's program of assistance to developing countries.

New Labour was faced with an escalating political and environmental problem on the island of Montserrat. By April 1996, Plymouth had been permanently evacuated, but a year later, the status quo on the island shifted again. On June 27, 1997, three days before the handover of Hong Kong and two months into Tony Blair's administration, a series of violent eruptions caused vast pyroclastic flows of super-heated gas, rock, and ash to flow down the side of Mount Chance, the main mountain on the island. It swept into several villages still inhabited by Montserratians who had refused to abandon their land and animals.

With 23 fatalities, the first "direct" victims of the eruption, Montserrat shot to the front page of most international newspapers, particularly in Britain, where the news stories were seen to have especial political, environmental, and defense implications. In response to the circumstances, on the day of the Hong Kong handover, Baroness Symons (a junior foreign office minister) visited Montserrat, making £6.8 million available as emergency aid. (From 1995 to 1997, the assistance program for Montserrat was handled by the ODA's Emergency Aid Department.) Some of this money was spent putting more than 1,000 Montserratians into temporary accommodations in the north of the island, using churches, schools, and prefabricated structures. The following month the British press reported food shortages among the remaining 4,000 Montserratians and rape in their shelters (Rhodes 1997). This was one of the few entirely Montserratian subject–based reports from the island. Frank Savage, the governor of Montserrat, was quoted as telling the government that if the population fell below 4,000, the island would become unsustainable (Loudon 1997). To dispel the rumors flying around Montserrat, many inadvertently set into play by George Foulkes, Symons reasserted Britain's commitment to the island: "Britain is determined to sustain this place," she told the *Guardian* (Black 1997). Thus began a series of exchanges between the UK and Montserrat. These interactions are more than a convergence of space and time. They are what the geographer David Harvey (1990) refers to as "space-time compression" in a capitalist era. Indeed, they approximate Paul Virilio's "speed space" of modern society, one founded on the logic of speed and where "man is present . . . in time," "a new other time" of electronic communication rather than physical presence (Virilio and Armitage 2001: 71).

In the first week of August 1997, while Blair was on vacation with his family, Montserrat's Chief Minister, Bertrand Osborne, flew to London to hold talks with the Foreign Secretary (Binyon 1997), the decision being that face-to-face negotiations were the preferred diplomatic route for concessions. Unfortunately, as soon as he arrived, eruptions spread to his former capital, Plymouth, destroying it in a shower of ash and fire. Robin Cook met with Osborne before his sudden return to reassure him about the security of Montserrat, and Claire Short publicized the fact that Britain was to give £41 million in emergency aid (Owen and Adams 1997). In mid-August, when Osborne had returned to Montserrat, the British government offered to pay the transport and temporary accommodation costs of people fleeing Montserrat, with free flights to neighboring islands and a handout of £2,400 per person. During Parliamentary press briefings in London, Short admitted that this was far less than Montserratians had been requesting, but in defense of her position she reported that the usual work permit regulations for visiting the UK had been waived for 1,400 Montserratians and that they would also receive social security benefits (Marshall 1997). In response to this, on August 20, Montserratians on-island were reported protesting against this relocation package by rioting and demanding consistent information about the volcano (Adams 1997). Once more on the defensive, Short made the unfortunate point that "money doesn't grow on trees" in a broadcast from London carried live on Montserrat radio and reported in the UK news on August 23 (P. Harris 1997). She also made the untimely slip of referring to the problem as the result of an "earthquake" and not a volcanic eruption (Sapsted 1997a).

Short was speaking to a Montserrat in turmoil. The Chief Minister of Montserrat had resigned on August 21, due to island residents' loss of confidence in his governance. Osborne was replaced by firebrand local lawyer David Brandt. That weekend, in an interview with the *Observer*, Clare Short made her now infamous remark that Montserratians would be "wanting golden elephants next," while she rejected Montserratian demands for an increase in their relocation package:

They say 10,000, double, treble, and then think of a number. It will be golden elephants next. They have got to stop this game. It is bad governance. It's hysterical scaremongering, which is whipping people up. (Hibbs 1997a)

Short's comment worsened relations between the UK and Montserrat and was seen as poor handling of the daily "tit-for-tat" exchanges between the colony and the metropole. David Brandt, the new Chief Minister of Montserrat, was quick to seize upon Short's slip on August 25, describing the relocation package as a fool's choice between "misery and the unknown" (Hibbs 1997a). By briefing UK foreign correspondents on Montserrat face-to-face, Brandt was also able to state that Britain's "wait and see" aid freeze gave the "impression" that it was a plot to make the islanders suffer, so that they would eventually all leave the island (Hibbs 1997b; Abrams and Davison 1997). Brandt knew full well that his words would be carried the next day in the UK news media. Indeed, his politics was a reaction to the UK news media reports from the previous day. The newspapers had a field day of reporting, all under graphic images of the volcano. On Monday, August 25, they reported the events: "Short Calls for an End to Row over Aid for Volcano Island" (Sapsted 1997b); "Snub by Short Widens Rift with Volcano Island" ran the front page of the *Times* (Pierce 1997). By August 26, New Labour had clearly lost the news spin of this "speed-time" cycle between Britain and Montserrat. Short had become the "government's brazen elephant" herself, according to the *Times* ("Our Island Story," August 25: 19). New Labour bounced back that Tuesday by announcing that the Foreign Secretary, Robin Cook, was to take over the Montserrat problem personally and that a new government committee was to be set up to oversee aid and development on Montserrat. The committee was composed of Short's DFID, the Home Office, Foreign Office, Ministry of Defense, Treasury, and Bank of England (Abrams and Davison 1997). This development at the end of a charged month of media exchanges was interpreted as Short being "relieved of her responsibility" (Abrams and Davison 1997). She was being "snubbed" (Hibbs and Sapsted 1997). Two days later, the front-page headline of a conservative broadsheet, the *Daily Telegraph* (Johnston 1997), reported statements made by Robin Cook from a tour of Kuala Lumpur about his plan for an immediate six-month review of the status of the Dependent Territories that would provide a "custom-made solution for each one" and that, Cook hinted, could include the restoration of citizenship rights. It was clear that the goal was to bury the tensions between Montserrat and Britain and to stem the stream of negative reporting. Cook made this commanding statement about the Caribbean island from Asia in an attempt to take charge of the escalating political discontent on Montserrat and the daily negative press that his party was getting in the UK. His announcement was perceived to signify the success of the rioting and political news strategies from Montserrat.

The UK newspapers continued to focus on the snub for Short: "Short Shrift" ran the August 27 editorial in the *Daily Telegraph* (see also "Short Rejects Visit to Island," *Herald,* August 25: 8; "Britain — Beyond the Montserrat Relief Scandal," November 17), and the *Daily Mail,* a paper of similar political persuasion, eagerly added that Cook had made the implied rebuke with his comment that Short was currently "working at home" (Hughes 1997). A cartoon image was widely published (Bill 1997) that depicted Claire Short as the angry, erupting face of the Montserrat volcano. Tony Blair returned from his vacation at the end of August, and one of his spokesmen was quoted in the unsympathetic *Daily Telegraph* with the following dismissal: "He is remaining on the big picture. He believes that is what matters; that we are delivering on our pledges. Some of the issues that have preoccupied the press in the last week or two are far less important than that" (Shrimsley 1997).

New Labour sought control of this August newspaper story by burying it as what is known as a "rotting-month story" born out of the "silly season" when Parliament and the Law Courts are out of session and the newspapers are desperate to latch onto any possible story. This fallow news period is a well-known international phenomenon: "rotting-month story" in Sweden (*Rötmånadshistoria*) and Finland (*Mätäkuun juttu*), "summer newshole" in Germany (*Sommerloch*), and "cucumber time" (*Komkommertijd*) in Holland, Norway, and Israel. This time of news drought (*nyhetstorka* in Sweden, *la morte-saison* in France) is also a dangerous time when stories can be picked up and allowed to run out of control.

But the story was kept alive by the UK press: "Clare Short is the Cabinet's own volcano, an 'old Labour' firebrand who for years has smouldered under the constraints imposed by Tony Blair's modern Labour machine," continued Jon Hibbs (1997a), the *Daily Telegraph*'s political correspondent. But Short was not the only politician to cause a political gaffe. The week before, Foulkes had misrepresented a scientific report when he issued a press report in which he said that the volcano had great capacity to go cataclysmic, a hazard which cannot be taken to be negligible, when in fact the report had made it clear that the chances of a "cataclysmic-intensive eruption" were close to zero ("Minister 'Blundered on Volcano Alert,'" *Daily Mail,* August 26: 2; Dalton 1997). By this time, both sides were playing to the crowds on Montserrat and the newspaper readers in Great Britain. Brandt, on Montserrat, persisted with a request that Short visit the island to see conditions for herself. Short rejected such hostile invitations, claiming to have a full diary, which the *Times* eagerly refuted ("Our Island

Story," August 25: 19). Short then became the target of the government's own spin doctors with Whitehall briefings against her. Over the weekend of August 31, the *Independent* leaned a sympathetic ear to Short's own spin by reporting her position at length. "Whitehall Out to Destroy Me, Says Clare Short" ran the front cover of the *Independent on Sunday* (Castle 1997a), and inside, the rather crudely titled "Who Dumped on Clare and Why?" (Castle 1997b). Her response to her loss of support in the government — echoing Osborne's loss of the people's confidence on Montserrat — was to attack the "vile and dishonest government spin doctors" as well as the Foreign Office, which had turned her into the "whipping girl," a clear attempt to destroy her Department for International Development (Castle 1997a). "Too busy to visit Montserrat," Short did send Foulkes, her deputy, to Montserrat that weekend, the start of September 1997, with the proviso that there would be no reopening of the voluntary repatriation package negotiations ("Foulkes to Visit Volcano Island," *Herald,* August 27: 13). While there, Foulkes announced on her behalf that she would visit the island in the immediate future (Penman and Deane 1997). Foulkes also ran his own counterspin in the *Independent* newspaper. Following Davison's (1997b) *Independent* story, which reported that the Montserratians' "colonial rulers had given them diametrically opposed information," Foulkes (1997) wrote a letter of correction to the editor. Unfortunately for him, it was published alongside a lengthy and critical letter from a Montserratian refugee in London, and it appeared under the less-than-exonerating heading "Minister Denies Volcano Island Blunder." On October 15, Short carefully apologized in the House of Commons for her reference to Montserratians, noting that £45 million was to be allocated to Montserrat in aid money (Today in Parliament, BBC Radio Four, October 15).

Clearly, Short's and Foulkes's gaffes, and the spins and counterspins and briefings against her, were bad news for New Labour but good press for the journalists working in the competitive and partisan UK media environment. Forthright and perhaps a little undiplomatic, Short's handling of the press was far more damaging to her work than the less widely reported handling of development on Montserrat by her department (see Skinner 2003). The zig and the zag of actions and reactions, I suggest, are a feature of globalization and compression in this postmodern speed-space era. Newspaper stories in the UK are e-mailed to Montserrat; radio interviews in London can be heard live on Montserrat; riots on Montserrat can be seen on the evening news in the UK; politicians can disseminate policy from Asia; and journalists can create and/or use "events" to press their political agendas or continue their witch hunts. In this case study, Montserrat's influence was felt in the UK without a physical presence, as Brandt's politics and the Montserrat riots proved more successful at precipitating reaction than Osborne's failed visit to London. Harvey (1990) suggests that this compression of space and increase in speed arise from the internationalization of capital and the desire for capital accumulation — that time annihilates space. The result is a placelessness, a disconnectedness or disembeddedness — the senselessness and homogeneity of the free market. However, the people on Montserrat, the politicians in the UK, and the journalists who visit Montserrat or stay in the UK are all harnessing the new media technologies for their own ends. They are not passive consumers of mediocrity as Harvey's criticism of the new world would lead us to believe. Moreover, it is ironic that as the Montserratian homeland is literally being destroyed in front of them, they evince a strong placefullness or authentic relationship with the island. The erosion of physical place is thus not echoed or facilitated by the new media technologies used in the exchanges between the UK and Montserrat, nor is the sense of place attenuated by the UK print media: for all the dromological exchanges, Montserratians, journalists, and politicians remain "inside a place," to use Relph's (1976: 49) original understanding of "belonging" (as opposed to the alienation of "outsideness").

Finally, in early September 1997, Short, now branded the "Golden Elephant Lady" by many Montserrat islanders (Davison 1997c), announced a visit to the island before the end of the year (Penman and Deane 1997). This was interpreted by the UK press as an attempt "to heal the rift with . . . volcano island" (Sapsted 1997c). Short never did visit Montserrat, although she did issue a statement of regret for what she said before a House of Commons International Development Committee (Watt 1997). This was to no avail, as the committee ruled that "incompetence" and a lack of joined-up government had created a crisis-management muddle (Hibbs 1997c; see also Skinner 2003). It recommended that Short's department be stripped of responsibility for the island and the islanders.

Journalists and Anthropologists Narrate the "Other"

In her commentary on the news media and the refugee camp, Liisa Malkki (1997: 93) wryly remarks that "when a crisis hits, the journalist arrives just as the anthropologist is leaving." Certainly, when the volcano erupted in July 1997, I left the island, cutting short my period of fieldwork by a month. But Malkki's point is more about how journalism is dictated by "the event" (see also Esch 1999) and that journalists are attracted to the unnatural, to the different, the extraordinary, the unique, the transitory, and the exception to the norm, whereas the anthropologist seeks out the customary, the traditional, the normal. News organizations have a "journalistic calculus" (Benthall 1993: 8) as they calculate investment in a story with the number of deaths, local relevance for their readers, and its geographical distance from the center — in this case, London. In August 1997, a number of foreign correspondents physically returned to Montserrat to update their coverage of island events, which they had been following since 1995. The *Times, Daily Telegraph,* and *Independent* each "invested" correspondents on-island, while other papers had to rely on Reuters and stringers for their news. This is "the CNN effect," as an emergency response is turned into a morality play (Hammock and Charny 1996; see also Skinner 2003), or a social disaster is framed as an affirmation of conservative humanism — as found in the *National Geographic.* In his study of the relationship between Israeli newspaper media coverage and lived experience of politics in Israel, Peterson writes that the news is highly interpretive and carefully packaged for "imagined" consumers. He imbues journalists with "interpretive creativity" as they work a "socially structured practice" (Peterson 2001: 201), *mimetic* in that they operate with the assumption that the object world can be represented, *deictic* in that the news authorizes itself, and *extraordinary* as the news "breaches" commonsense reality for it to become news (208).

Anthropologists and correspondents might share the same physical transnational contact zone, but the anthropologist seeks local normality whereas the correspondent follows a "troubadour" tradition (Hannerz 2002), "parachuting" into disasters and catastrophes as soon as the death tally becomes newsworthy. So, too, they are writing to different audiences (popular and academic; see Hannerz 1998b: 568, 570) and to different work schedules (daily and over the years), and generally from different perspectives (outsider home-centric versus insider "native point of view"). These two "scribes of tribes" (Hannerz 1998b: 569), with their different "ecologies of reporting" (Hannerz 2002: 60), form a different constituency from that of travel writers and travel journalists (Fürsich and Kavoori 2001; Skinner 2008a) with their attention to humor and destination promotion, the latter producing a "discursive imperialism" (Shome 1996). This tribe is also very separate from the Montserrat island indigenous media (*Montserrat News, Montserrat Reporter, Pan-Afrikan Liberator,* local cable TV, and the government/public radio station ZJB Radio Montserrat). If we are to move toward an anthropological understanding of the different worlds of journalism, we need to explore these generic and culturally specific differences more fully. Stories "resonate" in different contexts for different reasons (Ettema 2005), and journalists as "interpretive communities" (Zelizer 1993) should be aware of the narrative conventions in which they work.

Anthropologists should not fear the journalists' intrusions or feel the need to erect theoretical and practical boundaries around their work practices and publications as Dominy (1993) did when photojournalists arrived on assignment at her New Zealand field site. For her (1993: 324, 327, 330; see also Pratt 1986), anthropology is what journalism is not: anthropology is reflexive, connotative, analytic, and a part of what it studies; journalism is detached, descriptive, and premised on the notion of factual representations and an homogeneous reading. Certainly there is a strong temporality about the newspaper pieces that have also been designed to catch the eye and to capture an event, either visually with hints and silhouettes of a former life (the boy in the swimming pool, the moonscape, the cartoon) or through staccato-dramatic headlines: "Island of the Damned" (Hillmore 1997) and "Short Shrift" (*Daily Telegraph*, August 27: 19). They are also national and nationalistic in their newspaper outreach, in their political and sometimes neocolonial ideologies and assumptions about their readership. Yet journalistic and ethnographic writing do share processes of encoding and decoding, be they in different reading communities if not writing communities. Both are translated and displaced texts written about a place and people for another. By carefully studying the unfolding narratives of journalism as it operates in different cultural contexts, we will surely learn not only how journalism varies but also how its various forms may both resemble and differ from ethnography.

Notes

1. Montserrat was settled by the British and Irish, who established a slave plantation society, a society dictated by the sugar, cotton, and lime plantation owners who continued to control the island until the middle of the twentieth century. In the twentieth century, the island's main source of revenue was its people leaving for North America or the UK and sending back remittance payments.

2. Channels range from British Broadcasting Corporation (BBC) to Independent Television (ITV), satellite TV (Sky and now Virgin), the expanding freeview market (More 4, ITV3, BBC4), and national and independent radio (BBC Radio channels 1–5, Virgin Radio).

3. Here I am making use of Foucault's (1988) "author-function" concept first developed in the context of literature.

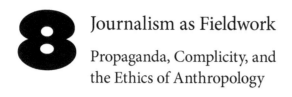

8 Journalism as Fieldwork

Propaganda, Complicity, and
the Ethics of Anthropology

JENNIFER HASTY

Although some would be reluctant to admit it, anthropologists and journalists have a great deal in common. Comparing certain genres from each field—say, a sophisticated form of human interest journalism and an empirically oriented, humanistic ethnography—it can be difficult to draw a hard-and-fast line between the two. Anthropologists and journalists are both inspired to discover and write about the sociocultural world, and both are governed by the professional, methodological, and discursive conventions of their disciplines. Journalism and anthropology are both highly professionalized, transnational regimes of knowledge production, both based on multisited, interpersonal engagement with a social imaginary "out there" beyond the office, both aiming at strategic representation of that world to an imagined audience of readers.

As most anthropologists would be quick to point out, however, these methodological similarities obscure more fundamental differences in discursive motivations and narrative tropes. Anthropology and journalism were constructed in radically different contexts for nearly opposite purposes, journalism as the handmaiden of economic and political modernity and anthropology as the guardian of cultural nonmodernity, often propagating a romantic antimodernity. The two professions developed distinctive practices of method, ethics, and politics, combined in discursive regimes, each situated in a particular sociocultural niche of production, discipline, and circulation. For an anthropologist, dabbling in the realm of journalism means not only negotiating the cultural, historical, and linguistic forces of a particular locality but also becoming subject to a completely different regime of knowledge production, one that inevitably poses contradictions with respect to the contemporary conventions of anthropological fieldwork and ethnography.

Despite this intriguing relationship, the burgeoning field of media anthropology has oddly neglected journalism, focusing instead on film, television, radio, and photography, as Elizabeth Bird discusses in the introduction to this volume. Even as the print media have provided the platform for populist struggles all over the world, journalism has maintained a taint of elitism and Western modernity for anthropologists, and the practices of news media have somehow come to seem less popular and communal than watching soap operas and movies.

However, I suspect that the comparative neglect of journalism in the explosion of interest of media anthropology has deeper roots, traceable to the very heart of our discipline, the critically interrogated seat of anthropological desire. For an anthropologist schooled in controversies over the politics of ethnographic representation, there is something profoundly uncomfortable about the practices of news media, something vaguely reflective of our own discursive practices, more purely politicized but also more politically compromised than anthropology. It's not just that journalism is theoretically naive or conceptually banal; it's also dirtier. Its motives are more apparent, and its instrumentalities are more obvious. But is anthropology really so ethically and political pure by comparison? Maybe what has made journalism so unpopular among anthropologists is a kind of disavowal of anthropology's own dirtiness, a distanciation from its own practical involvement in the murky institutions of power, be it academic, state, or corporate. Beyond the denunciations of colonialism, authoritarianism, bureaucracy, and corporate domination that have animated the discipline since its inception, anthropologists are just as immersed in the dubious obscurities of power and interest as journalists are, perhaps even more so. Illuminating and disrupting anthropology's strategic disavowal of power is the potentially radical possibility of the anthropology of journalism.

Bird (2005a) has discussed the challenges of anthropological perspectives and methods for the practice of journalism. Here, I want to reverse the terms of her illuminating discussion by exploring how journalistic practices may disrupt and undermine anthropological notions of fieldwork, political engagement, and professional ethics, particularly when anthropologists work as journalists "in the field." While journalism may seem a very specialized form of fieldwork, the forms of sociality and writing involved in journalistic fieldwork expose and accentuate contradictions in professional norms and practices common to all anthropological research.

Oppositional Purity and the Pragmatics of Implication: The Ideologies of Anthropology and Journalism

When I first went to Ghana for predissertation research in 1995, I had a notion that something important was happening in African news media, and I wanted to be part of it. As authoritarian regimes throughout Africa were giving way to the forces of democracy, journalists were at the forefront of a "renaissance" of political renewal. Although my first inclination was to head for Nigeria, where journalists were marching in the streets to protest the arrest of dissident author and environmental activist Ken Saro-Wiwa, I decided to stay in Ghana, a much safer place for scholars and journalists alike.

But safety wasn't my only concern. Heavily influenced by Althusser, Foucault, and Bourdieu, I believed the key to understanding the dynamics of authoritarian repression and popular resistance in contemporary Africa lay in getting beyond the ideological rhetoric, moving deeper to study everyday practices in this contentious sphere of political change. And while my own political orientation propelled me in the direction of oppositional politics, I sensed that the whole story could not be told without practical immersion on both sides of that dynamic. In Ghana, not only could I interview journalists and editors from all shades of the political spectrum, but I was also welcome to work as a journalist for both state and private newspapers without any restrictions (Hasty 2005, 2001).

I have wondered how my work might have been different if I had gone to Nigeria. Certainly it would have been animated by the visionary ideals of the oppositional press in those days, brought into sharp focus by the risk and danger of journalism in the Abacha years. Working on behalf of that project, I might have stuck closer to my own familiar political ideals and maintained a more comfortable sense of political and professional coherence. But in the political crucible of Abacha's Nigeria, I would never have been able to alternate freely between state and oppositional journalism as I did in Ghana. I would have been forced to pick a side, and I would have picked the opposition.

In Ghana, I was free *not* to choose, or rather, I was free to choose one and then the other with a kind of political license granted only to a novice foreigner. In terms of expression, this meant I was not free at all but always under a self-imposed directive to set aside my own political convictions in the interest of ethnographic immersion in the political positionality of the newspaper I was working for. And that positionality was constantly changing: I worked first for an oppositional newspaper, then a state newspaper, then another oppositional one, and so on, totaling six news organizations by the end of my fieldwork in 2004. Positioning and repositioning as a strategy of ethnographic balance, my own methodology forced me to speak and write on behalf of a wide variety of political projects, some near and dear and some quite antithetical to my own ideals.

Although I held my ground as best I could, throwing more energy into some assignments than others, these experiences challenged the singular purity of my political identity and forced me to contemplate the professional ethics of this kind of hands-on fieldwork in the political sphere. At best, I felt ambivalent and insincere; at worst, I felt like a traitor or a spy. And beyond my own identity issues, immersion in practical realities on both sides of the dynamic brought into question the purity of any political project, be it the transcendent idealism of resistance against the oppressive monolith of the state or the developmental nationalism of the state against the regressive and irresponsible power mongering of the opposition. As any fieldwork in the quotidian pragmatics of power is bound to discover, both narratives are complicated by tactics of representation, conspiracy, intimidation, prestation, and sociality, all common to politics everywhere. Moving from one assignment to the next, I found it increasingly difficult to assimilate the directive of ethnographic "balance" with my own sense of integrity and desire for political purity, the firm political commitments that drew me into this kind of work shifting continuously under my feet.

Because anthropologists have so often conducted long-term, intensive fieldwork among marginalized groups in non-Western contexts, anthropology as a discipline is animated by a commitment to the welfare of those groups against the forces of state and global domination. Reading the work of Eric Wolf or Laura Nader as undergraduates, many of us felt drawn to the discipline of anthropology (over the other social sciences) out of deep-seated commitments to the politics of opposition. The periodic "crises" in anthropological theory and practice have been largely motivated by an enduring desire among anthropologists to steer clear of the taint of oppressive power (colonial, imperial, state, global), setting a theoretical or methodological course congruent with the original identity of anthropology as the disciplinary refuge for the study of marginalized and disempowered peoples.

Why is this purist form of oppositionality so deeply and continually desired by anthropology, and what are its conditions of sustainability as a raison d'être of the discipline? In a provocative article for *Current Anthropology*, Kulick (2006) described the anthropological drive to identify with vulnerable peoples as a form of masochism. In the Freudian lens, anthropologists experience a profound sense of guilt from their own original identification with power and privilege. Spectacles of poverty and oppression elsewhere confirm this sense of protected favoritism while arousing and intensifying the guilt associated with it. Desiring both to maintain that power (if not enhance it) and to purge the guilt (or at least hold it at bay), anthropologists transfer a desire to resist the arbitrary order of favor and punishment, projecting their redemptive Oedipal desires onto the oppressed other. In this sense, anthropologists are looking to identify with a resistance that they feel unable or unwilling to perform themselves. Whoever "the father" is in this scenario (the state, transnational corporations, professional elites, your actual father), anthropology provides a way of sidestepping the Oedipal dynamic by channeling the desire to confront these forms of power into a desire to engage with and write about alternative theaters of resistance. In the drive to identify with subordinated and suffering others, anthropologists may strategically develop strong bonds of cooperation and friendship with them, while refusing and renouncing forms of engagement with state and corporate power that might complicate the heroic narrative of resistance in favor of a more subtle and complex analysis of struggle.

The emergence of the subfield of media anthropology is a lesson in the centrality of the masochistic narrative to the discipline of anthropology and its function as a gatekeeper to disciplinary legitimacy. In the years since Spitulnik announced that "there is as yet no anthropology of mass media" (1993: 293), the proliferation of undergraduate and graduate courses, edited volumes and course readers, conference panels, and award-winning ethnographies demonstrates the robust development of the subfield. How did the study of media gain legitimacy in anthropology? The answer lies in the integration of the oppositional, masochistic narrative of mainstream anthropology with the methodology of intensive, long-term fieldwork.

Before the study of media was recognized as potentially anthropological, the most dynamic and integrated anthropological scholarship on media took the form of "indigenous media," the appropriation of media technologies by "Fourth World" peoples in their struggles for human rights and cultural survival (Spitulnik 1993). The work of Terence Turner is exemplary (1990, 1992); he reveals how the Kayapo deployed media technologies in their fight to protect their land, obtain fair remuneration for mining rights, and create solidarity with other indigenous groups in the Brazilian rainforest. Ginsberg's exploration of aboriginal media broadcasting in Australia (1991, 1993) exhibits similar themes. While other anthropologists, such as Lutz and Collins (1993), were examining orientalist and primitivist forms of representation in Western media, scholars of indigenous media were grounding their work in the distinctive methodology of the discipline — long-term, intensive, even dangerous — reinforcing the masochistic narrative of their projects.

The work of Turner, Ginsberg, and other scholars of indigenous media is profoundly important and admirable. My discussion of the masochistic narrative embedded in such work should be taken not as criticism but as recognition of the key role of this distinctive form of oppositionality in the founding of a new subfield within anthropology. Anthropologists did venture into the realm of media before the emergence of indigenous media, but those excursions did not result in the embrace of media as a legitimate anthropological field. For instance, Powdermaker's (1950) work on Hollywood in the 1940s, influenced by the Frankfurt school, took a stridently oppositional stance to the Hollywood "culture industry." Yet she did not locate marginalized producers or audiences in struggle against the corporate power of Hollywood, and her work was regarded as an anomalous curiosity rather than the harbinger of a new subfield. In contrast, the scholars of indigenous media took up the perspectives and projects of peoples engaged in struggles against power, making it possible to break an ethnographic path into the territory of media studies. Without indigenous media, the study of media might never have gained disciplinary legitimation, and media anthropology as a subfield might never have emerged.

Building on this scholarship, anthropologists have expanded into broader realms of media production and consumption, while maintaining strategic elements of the discipline's oppositional narrative. In particular, scholarship on national media forms has foregrounded the subject-position of marginalized groups, particularly women (e.g., Abu-Lughod 2004; Mankekar 1999).

While media anthropology has incorporated the disciplinary preoccupation with the perspectives of the subaltern, ethnographic approaches to journalism are potentially more disturbing to disciplinary sensibilities. At first glance, anthropologists and journalists may seem to share an idealistic commitment to strategic forms of discursive representation that champion the voiceless against the abuses of power. Just as many anthropologists express a commitment to global ideals of social justice, many journalists are passionately inspired by universal ideals of free expression, government accountability, and the public interest (Belsey and Chadwick 1992; Kovach and Rosenstiel 2007; Richards 2005) . With its own origins and contemporary practices situated both inside and outside the state, however, journalism is animated by a more contradictory relation to power (as mouthpiece of government policy, as independent "Fourth Estate," as "watchdog" of the people's interest, as public relations) than the pure oppositionality of anthropology. While contemporary journalists often profess a vocational commitment to "the public" over government, business, or other forms of power, the performance of pure opposition to power is a psychological luxury largely denied to journalists employed in news media organizations. Freelancers for the periodical press might be able to route their own resistant desires onto the subjects they write about in feature articles. But the imperatives of daily production compel journalists who write news stories for daily newspapers to routinely interact with business and government elites in the generation and construction of news (Herman and Chomsky 1988; Keeble 2001: 33). While anthropologists are free to renounce power in their identification with oppressed peoples, journalists must strategically engage with elite sources in powerful positions in order to gain access to information and interviews, no matter what the story or their own personal or political sympathies (Reese 1997).

This does not mean that journalism, compared with anthropology, is more sophisticated in its depictions of power. Certainly the journalistic imperative to cooperate with elites contributes to an overall tendency of American newspapers to represent the perspectives and interests of authority, particularly economic and political authority. The point is simply that journalism and anthropology both profess to represent the voiceless, yet the everyday practicalities of journalism interfere with the elaboration of a masochistic relationship to the object of discourse. Engaging routinely with the powerful, some journalists may be positioned as privileged, protected favorites, but the majority are treated as pesky subordinates, sometimes necessary, possibly useful, but just as often a dangerous nuisance. Working their way into the world of the powerful, privileged journalists may identify wholeheartedly with elite perspectives and interests; however, the ideology of "balance" compels most journalists to cultivate a variety of sources representing a range of social perspectives, particularly those that challenge the interests of elites. Positioned in necessarily ambivalent relationships with government and corporate elites, negotiating tricky situations among contradictory interests, journalists are less likely to identify originally and exclusively with power and may therefore be less likely to feel the sting of guilt of this identification. And those favorites who do identify with power are likely to justify this as a necessary part of being an informed and capable political "insider" — just part of the job. With little guilt or resistance to transfer, newspaper journalists are less inspired than anthropologists to locate and celebrate forms of resistance to state and corporate power.

So what happens when an anthropologist takes on the role of journalist in the context of fieldwork? While I have reservations about the implicit generalization of Kulick's argument, I can say that undergraduate and graduate work in anthropology prepared me socially, morally, and intellectually to engineer a passionately idealistic (and perhaps even guilt-ridden) masochistic relation somewhere outside my own privileged country — that is, I wanted my fieldwork to accomplish something good for some disadvantaged group somewhere. Thwarted in an initial attempt to get to a dangerous and difficult theater of resistance, I capitulated to circumstance and settled on a less-perilous context, somewhat satisfied that journalists for the private press in Ghana were indeed waging a noble campaign for democracy and free expression, and that I could struggle along with them. But it was that journalistic compulsion for "balance," along with a theoretical grounding in critical theory and cultural studies, that disrupted the masochistic fieldwork formation, compelling me to move beyond politically compatible contexts to seek out internships with newspapers more invested in state and corporate power and to cultivate relationships with journalists whose professional vocation violated my own idea of the nobility of resistance. And my work for both state and oppositional newspapers taught me the journalistic expediency of developing congenial and cooperative relationships with state officials and business elites, in addition to more subaltern connections to environmental activists and civil society NGOs. Although my graduate training (in the 1990s) was rigorous and challenging, the ethnographies and anthropological theory I read in graduate courses were frankly not much help in following through with these methodological imperatives.

In the Field: The Ethics of Rapport and Complicity

In the first week of my internship at an investigative newspaper, the *Ghanaian Chronicle,* the news editor came to me with an assignment. "We have heard that the ruling party wants to run the First Lady for president in the upcoming elections, since the president himself has reached his term limit. But no one in the ruling party will talk to us, since we are an opposition paper. We want you to go to party headquarters and talk to the general secretary of the party, asking him about the First Lady."

"And you think they will talk to me?"

"You must say to them that you have hard evidence that they are planning to run the First Lady."

"Do we have evidence?"

"No, we don't, but since you are a white lady and an American, they will be shaking in their shoes if you make such an allegation! They will be shocked into making a response!" He beamed, quite pleased with the plan. "The editor himself wants you for this assignment."

"Well," I said, stalling as the implications of this began to play out in my imagination. "I'm working on a story right now, but I'll get back to you when I'm finished."

As a complete neophyte at the newspaper, I was in no position to refuse an assignment, particularly one hatched by the editor-in-chief and relayed so enthusiastically by the news editor. However, I was profoundly uncomfortable with the idea of such a calculated scheme based on racial intimidation and baldfaced lying. The ethnography I had read in preparation for fieldwork suggested that anthropologists should blend in with the community of study, setting aside their own preferences in order to understand and participate in the community's everyday practices. Only through such nonjudgmental participant-observation can the anthropologist come to understand the underlying logic of norms and values that shape the practices and perspectives of local peoples.

Journalists at the *Ghanaian Chronicle* are notorious for their creative and controversial forms of investigative journalism, involving subterfuge, impersonation, document theft, secret recording of private conversations, and even tip-offs to the police or military. I was certainly eager to know how and why these techniques were crafted in the politicized environment of independent journalism in Ghana, but I was not prepared to risk my visa, my integrity, and my local reputation as a researcher-journalist by deploying them myself. After our conversation, I strategically avoided any opportunity for further discussion with the news editor for over a week. I turned in my stories and pretended to be very busy. Perhaps he assumed I was working on the story, surmised that I was reluctant to do it, or forgot the whole thing. In any case, I avoided the topic and thereby refused the assignment, protecting my sense of journalistic ethics and fair play. However, as an anthropologist, I had an unsettling feeling that my refusal signified something more in this fieldwork context, a refusal of imbrication — and implication — in this community of journalists.

Anthropologists most often define fieldwork as a kind of intensive, long-term immersion in another culture. The narrative trope of fieldwork is so common that it has become a kind of symbolic "key scenario" for anthropologists, expressing the masochistic credential of the profession. Ortner (1973) describes key scenarios as compelling narratives that exemplify and idealize the norms and values of a cultural group, stories that "formulate appropriate goals and suggest effective action for achieving them . . . in other words, key cultural strategies" (1342). As the fieldwork narrative often goes, one is initially ignored or rejected by the locals, who may suspect the anthropologist is a representative of some political or corporate interest (Starn 1999). Slowly or serendipitously, as the case may be, the anthropologist capitalizes on some aperture in social relations and begins to build trust (Geertz 1973). If successful, the anthropologist is eventually ushered into a process of enculturation which mirrors that of a growing child (Clark 1994), first treated like a naive youngster, given limited information and access, then gradually earning access to deeper cultural knowledge and responsibility. Ultimately (often through some climactic episode involving embarrassment or near-catastrophe), the anthropologist is finally accepted into the community and treated as a capable adult (Lee 1969). This process is often described as the achievement of productive ethnographic rapport, an achievement that precedes and undergirds the kind of intense engagement required for ethnographically "thick" description (Geertz 1973).

Probing the notion of rapport, Marcus remarks that "many fieldwork stories of achieving rapport are in some way entangled with acts of complicity" (1997: 87). Reading Geertz's famous narrative of achieving rapport in "Deep Play: Notes on the Balinese Cockfight," Marcus points out that Geertz achieved the elusive prize by joining villagers as they ran from a police raid on a cockfight. While rapport indicates a kind of easygoing congeniality based on trust, the notion of complicity goes much further, describing mutual involvement in a project or agenda (such as illegal cockfighting, in particular, or evading the disciplinary reach of the state, more generally). In the fieldwork context, the project or agenda is defined by the people the anthropologist is studying (and *not* by the anthropologist, the police, or other outsiders). The anthropologist becomes an insider by positioning, as an accomplice, against other outsiders. Although Marcus refers to complicity as the "evil twin" of rapport, this commitment to local peoples against outside forces is generally considered a good thing in anthropology. The American Anthropological Association has enshrined a version of complicity in its very definition of ethical and responsible conduct.

Anthropological researchers have primary ethical obligations to the people, species, and materials they study and to the people with whom they work. These obligations can supersede the goal of seeking new knowledge and can lead to decisions not to undertake or to discontinue a research project when the primary obligation conflicts with other responsibilities, such as those owed to sponsors or clients. Regarding the nature of these obligations to the people, the AAA specifies that anthropologists should respect their well-being, "avoid harm or wrong," and, in a more demanding final note, "consult actively with the affected individuals or group(s), with the goal of establishing a working relationship that can be beneficial to all parties involved." While not a direct incitement to complicity in local agendas, these regulations certainly encourage the anthropologist to prioritize the betterment of host communities. This requirement is based on the logic of reciprocity: as anthropologists obtain knowledge and material culture from the communities studied, they should return something valuable to those communities. "They should recognize their debt to the societies in which they work and their obligations to reciprocate with the people studied in appropriate ways."

The broader discussion of anthropological ethics supports the notion that anthropologists should actively collaborate with subaltern communities against power. For example, Jacobs (1987) presents a case study of an anthropologist who, during fieldwork, saw a murder committed outside her window one night. Subsequently, in an effort to "reduce blood feuds," the police arrived on the scene to arrest those involved in the murder. Under questioning, Jacobs denied knowledge of the murder and hid the section of her field notes describing what she had witnessed. Case studies presented by Jacobs (1987), Cassell (1987), and Rynkiewich and Spradley (1981) overwhelmingly depict the anthropologist in complicity with local communities. Wax explains how the renunciation of state and corporate power was a historical reaction against the complicity of anthropologists in colonial, imperial, and counterinsurgency projects, particularly anthropologists working as consultants for federal agencies, military intelligence, and private foundations (Wax 1987).

These widely accepted notions of rapport and complicity highlight the importance of "embedding" ethics into the discourse practices of fieldwork (Meskell and Pels 2005). However, the professional discourse of ethics in fieldwork, in keeping with the discipline's mainstream masochistic ethos, relies on a set of assumptions regarding method, actors, and context, assumptions that often no longer hold in the present conditions of anthropological fieldwork. Particularly for anthropologists studying journalism, the exhortations to responsible complicity articulated by the AAA Code are not so much faulty as incomplete and unhelpful in the most ethically challenging situations.

The anthropological notion of rapport (and hence complicity) was originally situated in a *mise-en-scène* of geographically bounded and temporally continuous fieldwork in remote, face-to-face communities. In that context, certain positionalities and power relations were largely taken for granted: the anthropologist, mobile and well educated, came from a wealthy and powerful (if alienating and unjust) home culture to work among less mobile, less wealthy, and less powerful peoples. The tendency to "study down" (as Laura Nader put it) not only distinguished anthropology from other social sciences but was also a necessary component of the emerging ethos of suffering and resistance. Although many anthropologists have taken up Nader's call to "study up" (1972), the identification with marginalized peoples is so deeply assumed that the imperative to work directly on behalf of the host community is ethically beyond question in the AAA Code.

But what if the "host community" is a nuclear weapons plant (Gusterson 1996), a neo-fascist political organization (Holmes 2003), or a violent youth militia (Hoffman 2005)? In some sense, whether "studying up" or "studying down," the ethos of oppositionality remains the same so long as figures of power are strategically cast as villainous characters in a narrative of domination, oppression, and resistance. The dominant ethos is disturbed, however, when anthropological engagement with representatives of power complicates the narrative of subaltern resistance by situating the agendas of elites both structurally and historically and revealing unexpected forms of idealism, ambivalence, and internal struggle. The implications of this kind of project for the trope of fieldwork are complex, as anthropologists attempt to immerse themselves in the communities of the powerful and develop working relationships. While some anthropologists focus their projects on elites, many more find themselves engaging with representatives of power while pursuing projects examining global and national issues such as environmentalism, human rights, and war. Are mutual trust and reciprocity appropriate in the context of state and corporate elites? A professional discourse of ethics that champions the renunciation of those forms of engagement in favor of pure complicity with the oppressed is not particularly helpful in such situations. As anthropologists examine spectacles of power and the agents of violence, the notion of rapport has become increasingly problematic and seems to be dropping out of ethnographic accounts (Marcus 2006).

The question of positionality between anthropologists and their communities of study is further confounded by the juxtaposition of a young, inexperienced anthropologist in a field of experienced, professional journalists. An anthropologist studying journalism in a non-Western context is likely to be studying people who may seem to be less mobile, less educated, and less powerful than he or she is. In the local context, however, journalists are strategic actors in networks of power and opposition, with friends in high places. Their experience gives them confidence in their professionalism, and many have had opportunities to travel to conferences, professional meetings, and training courses all over the world. Working as a neophyte at a non-Western media organization, the anthropologist may find it difficult to assimilate the authority of well-networked journalists into the hierarchal notion of Western privilege and local vulnerability.

The question of positionality is not easy at the local level either. An anthropologist groping for a way to describe journalists as sociopolitical actors is faced with a profoundly murky field of characters and relationships, defying the heroic narratives of subaltern struggle "from below" against elite forces of power "from above." Are journalists elites or subalterns? As highly literate, discursive producers with privileged access to the political field, they may seem to be elites. However, most journalists are poorly paid and lack the social and intellectual capital of local elites, which tends to subordinate them in everyday interactions with representatives of power. While many journalists resent this, they must rely on those subordinating relationships for tips, information, and commentary. Does this negotiation indicate resistance or capitulation to power? Moreover, journalism is everywhere a dual force of conservative ideology and progressive social change; often both conservative and progressive elements are at work in the same newspaper, even in a single article. In the course of fieldwork on journalism, then, an anthropologist will likely face situations that defy easy classification.

In an effort to study timely and relevant issues, anthropologists increasingly work on projects that require them not just to "study up" or "study down" but to transcend the dubious clarity of this distinction. Contemporary anthropologists must do both, moving from position to position in methodologies that disrupt the assumptions of fieldwork and professional ethics. Often there is no singular host community but rather several, possibly antagonistic, groups vying for representation. Challenges to the traditional *mise-en-scène* of anthropological fieldwork point to the increasingly mobile and episodic nature of anthropological study, calling for multisited methodologies that break with the assumptions of previous generations (Marcus 1998). While Gupta and Ferguson (1997a), in their spatialized optic, welcome the emergence of multisited approaches, the imperatives of contemporary fieldwork frequently demand more than switching or alternating locations. Because each "location" is a unique sociocultural context, the fieldworker cannot assume a singular positionality (as more or less powerful, as critic or advocate, as friend or antagonist) in each context. Switching locations means switching positions while orchestrating a different set of social relations, desires, and obligations in each context.

Here lies the most profound challenge to the ethical sensibilities of anthropologists. If anthropological rapport requires ethical complicity, how can an anthropologist achieve rapport and maintain ethical relationships with multiple groups whose agendas may be completely at odds with one another?

On the Beat: The Ethics of Intimacy and Betrayal

The ethical dilemmas of engaging power and negotiating a multiplicity of contradictory influences are challenges faced by professional journalists every day. While not conducting fieldwork in the anthropological sense, most journalists, particularly beat reporters, do develop long-term relationships based on trust and rapport with a variety of key sources. Journalists working under deadlines rely on these carefully cultivated relationships to generate a reliable stream of tips and information. In the *Washington Monthly,* journalist J. Anthony Lukas describes a common situation for beat reporters.

> In the early sixties, when I was the city hall reporter for the *Sun* in Baltimore, all local news ran on the back page. Each morning an assistant city editor would scrawl "city" on column one of the back page dummy and "state" on column eight, signifying that, absent some typhoon or tidal wave, the state house reporter and I were responsible for supplying the day's two major stories.
>
> This meant that, at all costs, we had to cultivate our sources in hopes that a steady stream of zoning board appointments and updates on the tax rate would feed that voracious back page. And that meant that betrayal was the very last impulse we could afford to indulge. For in the rococo corridors of city hall a reputation for betrayal was a sure guarantee that the supply of news would dry up — and with it our professional aspirations.
>
> No, the premium was on keeping those channels of information open, even at the cost of unseemly coziness with our sources. (Lukas 1990: 3)

Just as anthropologists are drawn into reciprocal complicity in the field, journalists become involved in a set of reciprocal obligations to these sources.

Brandie Bartelt, a reporter for the Lusk, Wyoming, *Herald,* explained, "Without some kind of source development, information dries up. Maybe it's a friendly gesture, or an amicable lunch. Maybe it's holding off on a negative story, or failing to aggressively pursue a tip" (Cuillier 2007: 16). In return, journalists are often compelled to provide anonymity, withhold information, submit stories to sources before publication, and observe a shifting boundary delineating "on the record" from "off the record" commentary (as defined by sources, not journalists). While many journalists resist unreasonable demands, most engage in ongoing negotiations, agreeing to some requests but rejecting others, always calculating the risk to the relationship and the value of future stories.

Journalists are governed not by one code of ethics but by many, including ethical statements by the Society of Professional Journalists (SPJ), the American Society of Newspaper Editors (ASNE), the Associated Press Managing Editors (APME), and the various publications that employ journalists. These codes explicitly address the propriety of relations between journalists and sources, particularly the obligation for journalists to protect the identities of sources who provide information under guarantee of anonymity. Most codes discourage journalists from making such guarantees, however, arguing that the public interest is better served when the source is transparent. Much of the discourse on journalistic ethics revolves around this issue of protecting sources. From the perspective of anthropology (particularly in the age of IRBs), anonymity is rather a minimal guarantee, a mere first gesture in a volley of reciprocal relations. Beyond this fundamental commitment of anonymity, however, journalists are prohibited to venture, at least by the explicit professional standards. Rather, journalists are exhorted to remain "free from obligations" to sources, avoiding problematic implications of intimacy such as undue influence and conflict of interest (quoted from the APME Statement of Ethical Principles). The *New York Times* ethical handbook states, "Staff members may see sources informally over a meal or drinks, but they must keep in mind the difference between legitimate business and personal friendship." *New York Times* investigative reporter Duff Wilson echoes this rule: "You really have to separate friends from sources. You don't make friends" (Cuillier 2007: 18). The professional ideology of "social responsibility theory," the most popular ethical rationale for contemporary journalism, summons journalists to uphold a transcendent public good, working toward the free flow of timely and relevant information crucial to the maintenance of an informed citizenry in a democratic society (Iggers 1998: 67; Richards 2005: 8). As Eric Nalder, Pulitzer Prize–winning investigative reporter for the *Seattle Post-Intelligencer,* puts it, "Reporters should be looking out for citizens, not their sources" (Cuillier 2007: 18).

Unlike anthropology, the ethical codes of journalism do not assume a *mise-en-scène* involving a privileged writer engaged with subaltern sources (although this can be the case, depending on the journalist and the story). Rather, the codes suggest a more common tableau, involving an ambitious, truth-seeking reporter attempting to engage more privileged agents of power. While anthropologists worry about exploiting the people they study, journalists are more concerned with being exploited by their sources, getting co-opted into the factional struggles of the political and corporate spheres. The anthropological perspective imputes a kind of moral purity to informants; journalists are more cynical about the self-interested motives of their sources.

Regardless of the prohibitions, journalists cannot avoid establishing fairly durable relationships that resemble friendship. "No matter what journalism professors or editors say, reporters are going to get too close to their sources," says media ethics scholar Virginia Whitehouse (Cuillier 2007: 20). These relationships do influence their research and writing in direct and indirect ways. Although less common, some journalists admit to forms of physical intimacy with sources, particularly in the interest of getting a good story. The *New York Times* fired reporter Laura Foreman from her position at the Washington bureau after discovering her long-term romantic relationship with Pennsylvania state senator Henry Cianfrani, source and subject of many stories for the *Philadelphia Inquirer,* her previous employer (Goodwin 1983: 109). Former *Chicago Daily News* reporter Jay McMullen was quoted in *Esquire* on the strategic nature of his intimate relations and his professional justification:

> I've screwed girls who worked at city hall for years. All those goddamn bluenoses who think you get stories from press conferences — hell, there was a day when I could roll over in bed in the morning and scoop the Tribune. Anybody who wouldn't screw a dame for a story is disloyal to the paper. (Goodwin 1983: 111)

McMullen's bravado obscures what must have been complicated liaisons nurtured with at least the semblance of mutual trust. (Or else why would his "dames" have revealed anything to him?) His cynical dismissal of that complexity seems calculated to deny any potential conflict of interest created by sleeping with sources, particularly given his assertion of loyalty to his newspaper. But the very value of these entangling relations with sources lies in the sense of complicity, whether sham or genuine, which provides a foundation for the most productive reporter-source relationships. Reporters can elicit the most useful forms of cooperation when they cultivate a feeling of mutuality based on an intersecting set of interests, a sense of being ultimately "on the same side." In a roundtable discussion on "Reporters' Relationships with Sources," journalist Alison Grant described the relations of complicity that she developed with police on a crime story.

Perhaps this is a simple idea, but one way to get to closely held information yet not compromise yourself is to demonstrate your usefulness to the people that you want to have as sources. My relationship with the two detectives [in Beachwood, a suburb of Cleveland] was symbiotic. Over the course of the year, it became more and more the case the detectives and I appeared to be working toward the same end. At times we did trade information. (Frantz, Tofani, and Rashbaum 1999: 11)

While journalists may allow themselves to be seduced into such relations of intimacy, they may also be seduced back to vocational ideals and professional demands when they return to the office to write. Journalists may pretend there is no conflict of interest in their complicitous relationships with sources, but ultimately journalists and sources are not "working toward the same end." Journalists are regularly compelled to write hard-hitting, negative stories that expose their sources to public criticism, thus betraying the sense of trust so carefully cultivated. In a famous case from the 1980s, reporter Joe McGinniss pursued research for a book on alleged murderer Jeffrey MacDonald by cultivating a warm friendship with him. Even after McGinniss became convinced of MacDonald's guilt, he continued to express his support for MacDonald, maintaining the relationship just long enough to finish his research and publish his damning exposé. In her book on the McGinniss-MacDonald case, Janet Malcolm writes, "Every journalist who is not too stupid or too full of himself to notice what is going on knows that what he does is morally indefensible. He is a kind of confidence man, preying on people's vanity, ignorance, or loneliness, gaining their trust and betraying them without remorse" (Malcolm 1990: 1).

Thus while ethical codes are prohibitive, working journalists have not reached consensus about the ethics of intimacy, trust, and complicity with sources. Many openly disagree with the official ethical standards, while others point to the practical impossibility of following them to the letter. While rocked by the occasional ethical scandal involving anthropologists who engage in spying or medical experimentation on subaltern communities (Fluehr-Lobban 2003; Horowitz 1967; Stocking 1968: 273; Jorgensen and Wolf 1970), anthropologists are less liable to admit to the ethical dilemmas operating in the most mundane aspects of contemporary fieldwork. Such fieldwork, like journalism, situates researchers in bewildering fields in which distinctions between power and resistance, self-interest and public ideals, even guilt and innocence, are far from clear and even likely to change during research. While a contentious discussion among journalists regarding the ethics of reporter-source relationships still continues, anthropologists have largely fallen silent about the ethical impurities embedded in contemporary fieldwork that challenge cherished ideals.

FRANK DISCUSSIONS of the problematic of complicity and betrayal in the practice of journalism may arouse feelings of disgust and disavowal among anthropologists. The murky ethics of reporter-source relationships — and the uncomfortable resemblance to fieldwork relationships — may go some way toward explaining why journalism has remained marginal to the anthropology of media over the past two decades. Yet despite the endurance of an idealistic ethos of subaltern advocacy and resistance, the contemporary conditions of fieldwork bring anthropologists into increasingly ambiguous realms; the ethical and methodological dilemmas faced by anthropologists increasingly resemble those so publicly discussed by journalists. Anthropologists who practice journalism (either "in the field" or "at home") cannot disavow their problematic relationships to power and divided loyalties to multiple local agendas. Negotiating such difficulties is crucial to the anthropological project of understanding the cultural production of news media and its role in larger sociopolitical processes. Working through these contradictions, the anthropology of journalism may lead the way toward a more honest and up-to-date articulation of methodological pragmatics and professional ethics for all anthropologists.

PART TWO

NEWS PRACTICES IN EVERYDAY LIFE

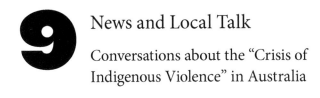

9 News and Local Talk

Conversations about the "Crisis of
Indigenous Violence" in Australia

KERRY McCALLUM

The "problem" of violence and disadvantage in Australian Indigenous communities is one of the most culturally resonant but fiercely contested of all issues confronting Australian news audiences. News media reporting reflects the intractable nature of Indigenous policymaking, and the sharp policy shifts that characterize the governance of Indigenous affairs in Australia (Altman and Hinkson 2007). In this chapter, I argue that the complex set of issues surrounding violence in Indigenous communities represents an important site of public opinion in both media discourse and the conversations held by social groups in their local settings — what I conceptualize as "local talk" (McCallum 2005). I argue that fine-grained analyses of talk in local conversational terrains can illustrate the complex relationships between mediated portrayals and conversational narratives expressed within the social group. Understanding local talk sheds light on the complex nature of the processes of public opinion at play in discourse about this area of Australian Indigenous policy.

The nature of Indigenous affairs policy and reporting was highlighted in June 2007, following the highly publicized release of a report titled "Little Children Are Sacred," which graphically documented child sexual abuse in Indigenous communities in the Northern Territory of Australia (Anderson and Wild 2007). In the context of a federal election campaign, Prime Minister John Howard used the report to justify imposing an "emergency intervention" in remote Indigenous communities (Howard and Brough 2007). This radical incursion into the lives of Indigenous community members involved mandatory child health checks, changes to land-ownership laws, welfare and employment programs, and increased policing and health services. The extensive media coverage that surrounded the policy announcement posed difficult questions for those seeking to understand public discourse about Indigenous issues in a "mediatized" world (Cottle 2004b). Australia's 400,000 Indigenous people live in some of the poorest communities worldwide, often remote from essential services and with health and lifestyle outcomes far below those of other Australians (NACCHO 2003). Despite this, the events of June 2007 starkly reinforced that comments by journalists and political leaders about Indigenous issues are almost universally negative and that they typically focus blame on individuals and generally despair of improvement. In Australia, Indigenous issues are rarely reported outside a narrow frame of public crisis or risk (Mickler 1998; Jakubowicz et al. 1994; S. Cohen 1980; Critcher 2003).

But how do news audiences understand the reporting of our most controversial public policy issue? This chapter draws on an ongoing project designed to better understand mediated discussion of Indigenous politics and to understand how people in their local networks talk about the issues that are the subject of government policy and media interest (McCallum 2005, 2007, 2008; Blood, Tulloch, and Enders 2000). I first mapped the reporting of the words *Indigenous* and *violence* from 2000 through 2006.[1] My analysis of news reporting illustrated that far from being a dominant issue on the news agenda, Indigenous issues were relatively uncommon, except for occasional sharp spikes in reporting of dramatic, alarmist, or shocking events concerning violence in Indigenous communities or the violent behavior of Indigenous leaders. By mapping the flow of news reporting and analyzing dominant and contested news frames, I was able to contextualize my study of everyday conversations — or local talk — about these and related Indigenous issues.

This chapter examines how the members of existing social groups construct, negotiate, and dispute the meanings of issues of violence and deviance in Indigenous communities through local-level dialogue. My study of conversations about Indigenous issues within social groups is informed by the traditions of audience ethnography, emphasizing the recording and analyzing of talk as a valuable source of data for learning how groups and individuals understand and negotiate public issues (Lull 1980; Morley 1992; Tulloch and Lupton 2003). I drew closely on Gamson's 1992 model of "peer conversations" to investigate the meaning that social groups attribute to Indigenous policy issues (see also Augoustinos, Tuffin, and Rapley 1999).

My fieldwork entailed recording, in participants' local settings, more than 50 conversations with groups and individuals about a wide range of Indigenous issues. Using qualitative grounded theory techniques to analyze the data, it was established that participants spoke about Indigenous issues using four main narrative themes and 12 distinct narratives (see table 9.1). This study explored not only the content of participants' discussion but also the processes at play in the expression of public opinion at the local level. When participants talked about violence or crime in Indigenous communities, they localized this talk and understood it using the broad narrative theme of Responsibility. Groups

TABLE 9.1. Narratives of Indigenous Issues in Local Talk

Talk of Identity	Talk of History	Talk of Racism	Talk of Responsibility
Nationalist	Imperialist	Reverse racism	Individual responsibility
Unity	Progress	Racist Others	Social justice
Self-determination	Struggle	Systemic racism	Indigenous rights

and individuals relayed locally shared myths and experiences to explain their understanding of mediated issues that were often remote from their everyday experience. They used mediated representations of remote Indigenous communities as conversational resources and frequently displayed a deep reflexivity (Grbich 2004) about public opinion processes and the development of Indigenous policy.

By examining the way news about Indigenous issues is framed in the Australian media, and by conducting fine-grained analyses of how they are understood in local talk, I draw conclusions that can inform understandings of the wider contexts of journalism practice. Such analyses are essential if we are to develop a better understanding of the relationships between the content of media texts and dialogue regarding such complex social issues as violence in Indigenous Australian communities. Both facets are essential for understanding the wider concept of public opinion about Indigenous issues in Australia.

Theorizing Public Opinion as Polling, Text, or "Local Talk"

The concept of public opinion is a highly contested phenomenon that nevertheless remains fundamental to the study of both communication and politics, and it is particularly useful for reading discourse about Indigenous issues in Australia. Herbst (1998) and Entman and Herbst (2001) theorized that public opinion was a social construction that could be variously understood as the numerical outcome of commercial or scholarly opinion surveys, analyses of media content, mobilized or effective opinion, and local talk in social networks.

Herbst argued that over time the aggregation of individual opinion, through the technology of polling, had come to represent the dominant way of understanding public opinion in the social sciences. Politicians use polls not only to understand community opinion but also to manipulate and justify changes to government policy (Goot 1996; Mills 1999). Likewise, journalists are reliant on opinion polls as a way of reading public opinion and as a source of news production (Lewis 2001; Blood and Lee 1997). Habermas (1989), Herbst (1993), and Splichal (1999) have traced the historical and social conditions that enabled polling to become the hegemonic methodology for researching public opinion and the criticisms that have plagued the method virtually since its inception (see, e.g., Blumer 1948; Ginsberg 1986; Bourdieu 1979). Many in the social sciences have since abandoned aggregated individual opinion altogether as a way of understanding public opinion. Carey argued that the media has severed itself from the public, making public opinion relevant only to the media and elites. He attacked the role of the media in the formation of public opinion, saying, "Public opinion no longer refers to opinions being expressed in public and recorded by the press. Public opinion is formed in the press and modelled by the public opinion industry and the apparatus of polling" (Carey 1995: 392).

Key (1961) argued that public opinion has become merely effective opinion, a shared image of the likely response that elite actors see themselves forced to take into account. Hartley and McKee shifted this argument even further, arguing that the media are no longer a secondary institution, reporting more or less accurately on events that originate or occur elsewhere. Media are primary and central institutions of politics and of idea formation; they are the locus of the public sphere (Hartley and McKee 2000: 4). While acknowledging that framed media content is an integral element of public opinion, I do not share the assumption that the media have taken the place of the public sphere. Rather, my approach accords with Gamson (1992) and Gamson and Modigliani (1989), who saw the content of media discourse as a system of meaning independent of talk in social networks. Media discourse nevertheless provides an important conversational resource and is "a central part of the reality in which people negotiate meaning about political issues" (Gamson 1992: 27).

Conceptualizing public opinion as local talk has been largely ignored in contemporary theorizations of public opinion, but has a long tradition in public opinion theory (Dewey 1946; Gamson 1992, 1996; Peters 1995; Delli Carpini and Williams 1996; Tulloch and Lupton 2003). Early conceptions assumed that public opinion was inherent in conversations about political issues. For example, Gabriel Tarde (quoted in Katz 2006: 265) drew a direct line between news and talk when he said that "if people did not talk . . . it would be futile to publish newspapers . . . they would exercise no durable or profound influence; they would be like a vibrating string without a sounding board."

Ferdinand Tönnies's 1920s critical theory "gave preference to the complex processes in culture and society over their institutionalized forms in politics and the state" (Splichal 1999: 108; see also Tönnies 1971). More recently, Herbst (1998: 104) found that political journalists used conversations in their local social networks to help them better understand the competing narratives in public issues, to interpret the results of opinion polls, and to understand the depth of community feeling about particular issues. Salmon and Glasser's major survey of contemporary public opinion theory concluded that "we know all too little about the extent of political talk in contemporary society and the conditions that nourish it" (1995: xxx). To that end, an important part of my project was to examine the particularized, contested nature of local talk about Indigenous issues, in order to better understand this crucial aspect of Australian public debate.

News Media Representations of Indigenous Issues in Australia

In the Australian context, Indigenous affairs have played a critical role in national political discourse, and in so doing they have challenged the values and practices of journalism. Media scholars have analyzed the role and practice of journalists who report on Indigenous issues, as well as examining the content of such news. Most commonly they have argued that mediated portrayals of Indigenous issues are a form of racist discourse (e.g., Cottle 2000a; Jakubowicz et al. 1994). Meadows (2001) examined depictions of Indigenous people and issues in the national news media, particularly television, concluding that portrayals reinforced the dominant ideology of non-Indigenous racial superiority (see also Hall 1995).

Beyond analyses of news media representation based on race and ideology, several studies have illustrated that journalists frame Indigenous issues in routine and predictable ways. Drawing on Reese's (2001: 11) definition, news frames are understood to be the "organising principles that are socially shared and persistent over time, that work symbolically to meaningfully structure the social world" (see also Miller and Reichert 2003; Altheide 1997; Gamson 1992). News frame analyses emphasize how social issues are contested in public discourse, enabling journalists to draw on several competing frames in their discussion of an issue. Jakubowicz et al. (1994) found that Indigenous people were portrayed as a *threat to the existing order* and a *source of conflict*. At the same time, news media portrayed them as *authentic Australians,* available for *cultural appropriation* and a *source of pride* for all Australians (see also Meadows 2001). Mickler (1998) found that talk radio perpetuated a myth that Indigenous Australians were *privileged* compared with "mainstream" Australians. Brough (1999) found that Indigenous health was portrayed concurrently as *individual failure* and as *Australia's shame.* Meanwhile, Indigenous Australians were also represented as *victims* of the failure of the Australian welfare state. Bell (1997) also identified that non-Indigenous Australians were portrayed in the news media as simultaneously *racist* and *tolerant.*

There have been a number of attempts to address the failure of Australian journalism to adequately engage with the multiple possibilities available to them in the reporting of Indigenous policy issues (Plater 1992; Australian Press Council 2001; Sheridan Burns and McKee 1999). Despite such interventions at the professional and tertiary levels, Ewart interviewed regional journalists to find that they were largely uninterested and unreflexive about the impact of their journalistic practices on local race relations. She said that "addressing the conflicts between ideologies and practices in the newsroom is an issue that needs to be taken up by journalism educators" (Ewart 1997: 115).

These periodic recommendations by scholars of Indigenous media representation, and the ongoing resistance to them by some media practitioners, suggest that the reporting of Indigenous issues in Australia remains problematic. The education of journalists to report less narrowly and more sensitively regarding issues of race is resisted in the face of news values of conflict that dominate the reporting of Indigenous issues. I argue that studying locally contextualized knowledge of news about Indigenous issues might provide a key to understanding and improving journalism practice. Researching local talk to learn about the broader public discussion of Indigenous issues adds a new layer of complexity to this already problematic issue for journalism education and practice, but studying talk may also help journalists to better understand the impacts of their reporting about Indigenous issues on all members of their audience.

Newspaper Reporting of Violence in Remote Indigenous Communities, 2000–2006

In order to contextualize the conversations I recorded about Indigenous issues within the news environment, I mapped the volume and patterns of reporting of the terms *Indigenous* and *violence* in six Australian newspapers between 2000 and 2006. This exercise supported earlier findings that while violence and disadvantage are problems in many remote Indigenous communities, they are not reported as ongoing, newsworthy issues by the Australian media. The reporting of Indigenous violence and substance abuse was not consistent across newspaper genre, location, or time. While for some regional newspapers, Indigenous violence and crime were a major and ongoing source of news (see chart 9.1), city tabloid newspapers—including Australia's largest selling paper, the Melbourne *Herald-Sun*—reported only occasionally on Indigenous issues. Reporting was reduced in most newspapers to periodic episodes or "moral panics" of alcohol or other drug abuse, violence, and sexual abuse in remote Indigenous communities (Mickler 1998: 19; S. Cohen 1980; Critcher 2003; Iyengar 1991). The daily "quality" broadsheets, the *Sydney Morning Herald* and the Melbourne *Age,* published in Australia's two most populous cities, reported Indigenous issues as ongoing and salient for their audiences, but were more likely to frame

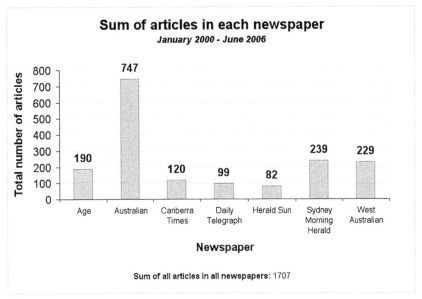

Chart 9.1

these issues in the context of national policy debates or concerning Indigenous leadership and governance.

The national broadsheet, the *Australian,* focused most heavily on the topic of Indigenous crime and violence. Between 2000 and 2006, the *Australian* reported 747 stories about Aboriginal violence and over 550 items mentioning Indigenous people and alcohol. The *Australian,* it can be argued, set the news agenda and established a number of episodic crises over six years (see chart 9.2). During 2001, following highly publicized rape allegations against the head of the Aboriginal and Torres Strait Islander Commission (ATSIC), the *Australian* conducted a campaign to publicize issues of substance abuse, violence, and sexual misconduct in Indigenous communities. The newspaper argued that both media and governments had ignored these issues and abrogated responsibility for resolving them. *Australian* journalist Rosemary Neill (2002: 84) said that fear of being labeled "racist" had stifled public discussion, and she called for breaking the taboo that had prevented governments from developing policies to stop deviant behavior in Indigenous communities (cf. Goodall 1993; Jakubowicz et al. 1994; Meadows 2001). Such mediated "crises" were commonly reported without reference to their historical, social, or economic context (NACCHO 2003: 594), relying on the news values of conflict and frames of threat and individual weakness. Each story centered on the deviant behavior of a small number of individuals, but each time the event was framed to represent a larger crisis in Indigenous Australia. Each story was characterized by calls on

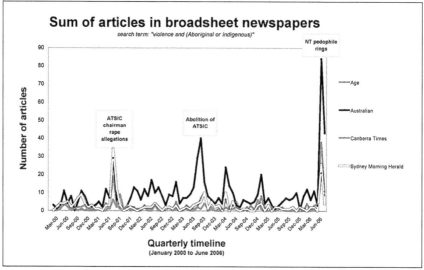

Chart 9.2

governments to resolve the issue. Finally, each story disappeared from the news agenda almost as quickly as it appeared.

Not every newspaper relied on news values of conflict and frames of individual failure; occasionally, alternative news frames were identified. Since 2000, the *Canberra Times* had been most likely to report on stories from the perspective of Indigenous disadvantage. Brough (1999) found that Indigenous health and substance misuse had been portrayed through frames of *Australia's shame* and Indigenous people as victims of the failure of the Australian welfare state. The *Canberra Times* reporting exemplifies the way in which the media draws on competing frames of *blame* and *shame* when representing Indigenous issues.

The reporting of violent and deviant behavior in Australian Indigenous communities has become a routine feature of our media landscape, if also a shocking one. I argue that the persistent representation of Indigenous violence and substance abuse in the mainstream news media has contributed to a discourse of risk and crisis dominating public discussion of Indigenous issues.

Studying Local Talk about Indigenous Issues

Understanding journalistic practice and media portrayals is important for mapping the contours of public debate, but such analyses are limited for fully elaborating public opinion about complex social issues. I needed to analyze the ways in which Australian news audiences constructed Indigenous issues when allowed to explore them in their own conversational terrains. To study local talk about Indigenous issues, I developed a qualitative fieldwork project using ethnographic methods (McCallum 2005). Ethnography has been used to learn about local knowledge (Geertz 1983) and has been adapted to study acts of communication (Saville-Troike 1982: 137). My study drew on the tradition of ethnographic audience studies (Lull 1980; Morley 1992; G. Turner 1993), which generally involves field-based research and the methods of participant observation, qualitative interviews, and thick description of the content of participants' conversations. I did not, however, conduct a full ethnographic study, as I did not immerse myself for long periods in each research site or take on the role of "cultural interpreter." Nor did I conduct a "reception study" of media texts (cf. Morley 1992).

The study aimed to capture "everyday" conversations about a range of topical issues relating to Indigenous peoples and politics. A total of 116 people from Australia's most populous state, New South Wales (NSW), participated in 37 individual interviews and 13 group interviews in 2001–2002.[2] Participants were selected to represent a range of sociocultural factors including age, gender, location, and ethnicity. While both Indigenous and non-Indigenous people were interviewed, most participants were non-Indigenous Australians. A combination of long, semi-structured individual and group interviews enabled me to capture the textured and detailed understandings of Indigenous issues from the perspectives of the participants involved (J. Smith 1995; Barbour and Kitzinger 1999). This methodology drew closely on the earlier work of Gamson (1992) about how people in social networks "talked politics" and with the methodology used by Herbst (1998) to examine how political journalists, activists, and staff understood the concept of public opinion. Interviews took place in natural settings and were informed by a semi-structured interview protocol. Individual interviews followed a life history approach, whereby participants were asked to speak about their own backgrounds and experiences of Indigenous issues, before commenting on a series of "cues" in the form of newspaper articles about contemporary Indigenous issues. Group interviews allowed the group to describe their background and shared experiences, with groups encouraged to emphasize collective experiences and memories, as well as competing positions about a range of Indigenous issues. It is important to note that the style of the interviews allowed groups and individuals to frame the conversations in their own terms, rather than merely responding to questions and cues selected by the interviewer.

Grounded theory methods were utilized in the analysis of the interview material and to identify themes within the talk (Glaser and Strauss 1967; Strauss and Corbin 1990, 1997; Charmaz 1995). This process of inductive qualitative analysis, in which data gathering, coding, and analysis occur simultaneously and the literature review is delayed, meant that findings were grounded in empirical data and theory was built in concert with the relevant academic literature. Interviews were recorded and transcribed, but initial analyses were drawn from observation and thick description of the interviews and repeated listening to recorded conversations.

Responsibility Narratives in Local Talk

Using grounded theory analysis, I coded participants' dialogue in order to develop a matrix illustrating the nature of local talk about contemporary Indigenous issues. This approach enabled me to identify three broad narrative themes and 12 relatively discrete narratives used in the conversations. In local-level dialogue, Indigenous issues were discussed through the themes of Identity, History, Racism, and Responsibility (see table 9.1). The threads of each narrative could be traced through conversational exemplars from participants' conversations.

Talk of Responsibility was one of four broad narratives that participants used to explain their understanding of Indigenous issues. Responsibility narratives underscored many participants' conversations about local experiences and guided their reading of issues in the media. I identified conflicting Responsibility narratives in the participants' talk. The dominant narrative of *Individual Responsibility* argued that Indigenous Australians were subject to the same rights and responsibilities as non-Indigenous Australians. Participants using this narrative argued that many Indigenous people did not follow the established societal rules but were nevertheless rewarded with "special privileges" based on their race. This dominant narrative contrasted starkly with the marginalized narrative of *Self-determination,* which looked to Indigenous community control and empowerment as a solution to issues of disadvantage and powerlessness. A third narrative of *Social Justice* argued that Indigenous disadvantage was the result of historical racial discrimination, and therefore it was the responsibility of the whole community to make reparations for past policies. Narratives of *Individual Responsibility, Social Justice,* and *Indigenous Rights* were each used in participants' conversations to make sense of issues surrounding violence in remote Indigenous communities.

Difficult Conversations about Unspeakable Issues

Detailed analyses of conversations in local terrains can illustrate the complex relationships between mediated portrayals and conversational narratives expressed within the interactive dynamic context of the social group (Delli Carpini and Williams 1994: 787). The following excerpts of conversations recorded for this project address issues of Indigenous disadvantage, crime, and substance abuse. While crime and violence in remote Indigenous communities were not highly salient issues in most conversations, mediated portrayals of these issues provided a backdrop for talk about racial conflict in local communities — a highly salient and controversial issue for many.

Participants drew most heavily on the narrative of *Individual Responsibility* to express their understanding. Stories about experience of crime and violence in local communities and references to mediated portrayals of Indigenous "bad behavior" were used to reinforce the narrative that each person is individually and equally responsible for his or her own behavior and its consequences. These stories reinforced the *Individual Responsibility* narrative, denying rights based on race or culture and looking to the responsibility of each individual to follow the rules of the society. In the following monologue, Mick employed the familiar and accessible framework of the *Individual Responsibility* narrative to illustrate how "Indigenous people do not follow the rules."[3]

> Down here, like in Sydney, in the Redfern area, they give themselves a bad name. Eveleigh Street, it was a terrible Housing Commission street anyway. But to see on the news where the police go in, and people are just throwing rocks at police, and taxi drivers driving past, and these young kids, 9, 10, 11, 12, Aboriginal kids, just roaming the streets, creating havoc and rioting, doesn't do a good cause for themselves. Where's the parent? The parents don't seem to give a hoot about them, and they think it's their right to speak out. There's other ways to speak out. (Mick, middle-aged, Canberra)

Mick did not base his story on his personal experience of Indigenous people in his local community. He adopted the routine framing of Sydney's "Redfern Aborigines" by national current affairs television, illustrating how talk about Indigenous crime was often fueled by mediated representations of Indigenous issues.[4]

While participants used media images as evidence of their concern about the behavior of Indigenous people, they also simultaneously commented that the media acted as a silencing mechanism, so that discussion of these problems remained taboo. Participants drawing on the *Individual Responsibility* narrative were likely to call for greater public discussion of local crime and violence.

> There's not much in the local paper. They say it's covered over pretty well. If you talk to someone who works at the hospital, they'll tell you about the rapes and all that, but that doesn't hit the media. (Elizabeth, older, Western NSW)

> We need to talk about it [Indigenous crime] and while we've got domestic violence as a crime, it doesn't get the same publicity as drunk driving. . . . It really needs personal responsibility . . . social and personal responsibility. (Ron, middle-aged, Western NSW)

By contrast, some other participants used a *Social Justice* narrative of Responsibility to narrate their stories of Indigenous crime. They emphasized that Indigenous disadvantage was a consequence of historical injustice and argued that the responsibility for alleviating that disadvantage rested with the whole society.

Few participants in this study had any firsthand experience with remote Indigenous communities. Some had visited central Australia as tourists and observed the living conditions in some Indigenous communities, and one had worked as a doctor in regional Australia. These people expressed feelings of shock and guilt that people were living like that in "our" country. These firsthand experiences had encouraged a commitment to seeing living conditions improved. Doris, below, linked her reaction to her first experience of remote Indigenous communities with that of a former prime minister.

> I had never dreamt that people lived like that, let alone in Australia. I'm sure that experience [of traveling to Central Australia] had the same impact on me that it had on [former prime minister] Malcolm Fraser. He came back from Central Australia and said, "Something has to be done." I'm sure it was hidden from the community. (Doris, older, Canberra)

Like Doris, Tracey related her growing knowledge of Indigenous disadvantage to personal experiences, acknowledging the impact of European settlement on traditional Indigenous society through the introduction of alcohol.

> I was just horrified and shocked to see those camps and the disadvantage in Alice Springs. I thought I was in another world. It was just an absolute tragedy, and I walked away feeling that these people don't have a chance. There's just no hope. Nobody's going to employ them without meaning in their life. There's no way. . . . I can see why they sat on the banks of the river, because there's just nothing. . . . I didn't know what the solution was, but I didn't blame them or their community. I totally blamed white people. And alcohol's such an issue. It's a really significant part of it. (Tracey, middle-aged, Canberra)

These two participants were more likely to engage with media framing of Indigenous people as *victims*, drawing on a *Social Justice* narrative to argue that it is the responsibility of the whole society to address these problems. Another group explained their understanding of the risk and conflict that they associated with Indigenous Australia. A group of women discussed a local "riot" that was remembered as part of local oral history.

> Clare: A few years ago, there was the riots up the street. Do you remember that, on New Year's Eve? And there was a huge meeting in town, and

they tried to keep the media out. There were cameras, I don't know, WIN TV, but they kept the cameras out, which I thought was good, because everything gets blown out of proportion and whatever. But there were people who stood up and said they were scared. I would have been scared had I been down the street.

Sharon: Did you see it afterwards?

Clare: Yeah.

Sharon: They said it looked like a war zone.

Moira: They had a war out on the lake [the former Aboriginal mission] when I was teaching out there, and the women told me to stay away, and I stayed away for two months. One place was petrol-bombed, and the police would not come, and it was like they were too frightened. All they had to do was station a road block.

Bernie: There's only one road out.

Gabby: They're not allowed to. They have to have a federal officer that's brought down from [the city]. They're not allowed to enter the mission.

Moira: But that's wrong for the protection of the people in mission.

(Group interview, middle-aged, Far South Coast, NSW)

These women told their story using a *Social Justice* narrative, arguing that it remained the whole community's responsibility to protect each member. They talked candidly about what they perceived to be the failure of community institutions such as schools, the police, the criminal justice system, and the media to adequately address the complex issues that have led to such an emphasis on racial conflict. The former Aboriginal "mission" was used as an example of a site where both Indigenous and local non-Indigenous residents were not granted the protection that was the entitlement of each Australian citizen. Through their dialogue, this group also articulated the vulnerable position of both the local Indigenous community and their own small town in relation to wider policy and media interests. This is a position rarely portrayed by journalists, whose reporting tends to blame individual members rather than societal failure when reporting on conditions in remote Indigenous communities. Clare's group also illustrated reflexivity about the processes of public opinion by expressing the collective opinion that while their "riot" had been locally significant, wider publicity would distort the local experience and hamper its resolution. They displayed reflexivity about the role of the media in inflaming and stereotyping such events and the way the local community "managed" the media at the time.

Those who worked in the delivery of health, justice, or education services to Indigenous communities typically had a complex understanding of community responsibility. They were more likely to be deeply and personally involved in Indigenous causes and to draw on an *Indigenous Rights* narrative when talking about particular issues. They commonly argued that poor standards of health, housing, and education could be attributed to past treatment of Indigenous people, particularly the legacy of dispossession of land. Unlike the majority of participants, who readily engaged with the media's depiction of Indigenous people as "problematic," those who used an *Indigenous Rights* narrative were more likely to take an oppositional reading of the media's portrayal of Indigenous disadvantage or crime.

> Our local newspaper leaves a lot to be desired in respect to relations with Aboriginal people. It's only got a few pages of news. The stuff that they do at times inflames the division in race relations in this town.... If they print a story of crime, it's blazing across the front page. (Wesley, middle-aged, Western NSW)

> I just get so sick of what I see in the media. Newspapers, television, even *Lateline* the other night had something on domestic violence in Aboriginal communities. It's just blaming the victim. There's never any talk that the government has stripped funding for domestic violence prevention. The media's on the same side as Prime Minister John Howard. (Kate, middle-aged, Canberra)

Wesley and Kate illustrate that on the subject of Indigenous crime, participants were able to draw on alternative readings of the dominant media frame in their conversations. They translated narrow media frames to fit their chosen conversational narratives — in this case the *Indigenous Rights* narrative blaming a systemic failure for Indigenous disadvantage.

Conclusions: Conversational Narratives and Mediated Crises

In this chapter I have examined public opinion on Indigenous issues from the perspective that "media discourse and public opinion are treated as two parallel systems of constructing meaning" (Gamson and Modigliani 1989: 1). By analyzing news media portrayals through frame analysis and local talk through narrative analysis, a story emerges that can help explain the relationships between these two epistemologically distinct systems, both central to the formation and expression of public opinion.

My analysis of news reporting of Indigenous issues provided valuable baseline data to critique the construction of Indigenous people as problematic. Analysis of the quantity of reporting of these issues in the Australian press showed that stories of Indigenous crime and violence have featured intermittently but dramatically on the public agenda over the past six years. Indigenous issues are framed in routine and predicable ways and are often played out as classic "moral panics" that at times impact significantly on public policymaking.

While textual analyses are limited in their ability to fully explain public opinion about Indigenous issues, understanding such mediated discourses is important for the analysis of local talk. The treatment of stories about Indigenous crime and violence in the national media resonated in particular ways with the conversations of participants in this study. Journalistic framing of Indigenous people as a societal risk or contagion accords in many ways with the *Individual Responsibility* narrative used in local talk. Participants using the *Individual Responsibility* narrative drew on images of crime and violence in their local communities to narrate their view that Indigenous Australians deserved no special consideration for their behavior, based on race or historical factors. The "talking-up" and breaking of taboos about these issues through episodic, sensationalist news frames that blame individuals does not appear to have produced a better understanding in many local terrains of the issues facing remote Indigenous communities. Some participants, however, drew on an oppositional *Social Justice* or *Indigenous Rights* narrative to challenge the dominant framing of these issues and to explain their understanding of these public issues.

The media did not always share the same priorities as those expressed by the participants in this study. Some issues that were highly salient locally were less prominent in news media discussion. Groups noted that local newspapers did not want to talk about local race relations but merely fell back on the narrow frames of Indigenous crime or violence in remote Indigenous communities. Conversely, violence in remote Indigenous communities was rarely discussed in local talk, but localized and understood through more tangible issues. Participants were able to translate the media's narrow and often sensationalist framing of Indigenous issues to fit with their preferred conversational narrative and their own regional setting. Individuals and groups engaged with societal discourses and were able to demonstrate detailed understandings of complex public issues using locally produced meanings. Indigenous issues were understood intertextually when conversations drew on both local experiences and mediated events to explain their understanding of particular stories (Langton 1993; Tulloch and Lupton 2003). In their talk, participants used media coverage as one of several conversational resources, along with local myths, stereotypes, collective memories, and experiential knowledge to retell the story (Gamson 1992). They also negotiated, contested, and challenged those images.

At times, local talk about Indigenous issues illustrated a critical understanding of public opinion processes. Using the methodology of peer conversations, I was able to gain valuable insights about how members of the public understood the role of the media, political elites, and their own roles in the public discussion of Indigenous issues. Some participants were reflexive about the media's role in both talking up and censoring talk of Indigenous disadvantage and Indigenous behavior. While some adopted journalists' narrow framing of Indigenous issues to support their use of the *Individual Responsibility* narrative, others challenged that framing and looked to systemic failures in Indigenous policymaking to understand the issues.

While cynicism was expressed in local talk about newsmaking processes and political agendas, participants attributed to both journalists and political leaders a great deal of responsibility for managing public debates. Media and elites were understood to construct public discussion of Indigenous issues, but participants did not always subscribe to narrow mediated frames. It was understood that Indigenous issues were complex and not easily resolved, but participants identified that the way they were portrayed in the media was not productive. Many younger Australians called for more open and honest debate about racial division in their community. Despite the differences noted between local talk and media representations of Indigenous issues, I must conclude that news reporting and local talk share many of the same broader sociocultural values. There was an overall tendency to narrate Indigenous people as problematic and as a source of risk to the community in both talk and media representation.

The study of local talk provides valuable data to explain why some stories and not others are recognized and attended to by media audiences. It can help explain why journalists slip so readily back into stereotypical and simplistic construction of Indigenous people and their relationship with the wider Australian society. Studying talk can help journalists better understand the impacts of their reporting about Indigenous issues on all members of their audience by analyzing, in some depth, the "commonsense" or "everyday" understandings of mediated Indigenous issues held by non-Indigenous audiences. This research offers a salient reminder of the need for journalists to engage with communities about complex but important social issues. The challenge for those who "publicize" Indigenous issues, such as journalists, politicians, and scholars, is to address the multiple narratives that exist in local talk, thereby entering into a public conversation with their audiences (Carey 1993).

Notes

An earlier version of this chapter was presented (with R. Warwick Blood, University of Canberra) to the International Communication Association Conference, San Francisco, May 24–29, 2007. The project builds on McCallum's 2005 doctoral thesis, "Local Talk as a Construction of Public Opinion on Indigenous Issues in Australia," and the Media and Indigenous Policy project funded through a University of Canberra (UC)

Early Career Researcher Grant and the UC News Research Group. The author is particularly grateful to two research assistants, Stephanie Lyons and Georgie Benecke, for their assistance, and to Professor Blood for comments on an earlier version of this chapter.

1. I use the proper noun *Indigenous* to refer to Australians of Aboriginal and Torres Straits' Islander origin, rather than the term *Aboriginal,* which is more common in everyday talk. This reflects a change in terminology by the Australian Bureau of Statistics since the 2001 census.

2. Approval for the project was granted by the University of Canberra Committee for Human Ethics on October 18, 2001.

3. Participants' names have been changed to protect their identity.

4. Redfern is an inner-city suburb of Sydney and the site of an Indigenous housing project. The suburb is undergoing urban "renewal" and is routinely framed as the site of racial unrest.

10 Getting the News in New Delhi

Newspaper Literacies in an Indian Mediascape

MARK ALLEN PETERSON

I meet Shanker as I am getting off the bus that takes me from my flat in South Delhi to Connaught Place, where he works. He greets me with a "Ram Ram," and we proceed to his shop, where it has been agreed I may interview him. We pause at a newsstand as Shanker considers the large display of newspapers. Apart from the dozen or so foreign papers aimed at the tourists who throng the heart of Delhi, there are more than 40 daily newspapers in the metropolis.[1] Choosing among this abundance of newspapers involves organizing them along a system of gradations that takes into account language, political affiliations, and ties to place. Language distinctions include not only the fundamental differences between English, Hindi, Urdu, and Punjabi but also differences in the registers of those languages. The Sanskritized Hindi of *Nav Bharat Times* is admired by many but rejected by others as pompous and artificial. Newspaper buyers pay attention not only to which political party a newspaper might support but also to whether it is a party mouthpiece, a critical organ in which different factions of the party display their conflicts, or one of many shades in between. Newspapers also invoke locales: for example, *Times of India* publishes editions in six cities, but in each of these cities it is linked to Bombay in the popular imagination, just as *Statesman* is linked to Calcutta, *Hindustan Times* to Delhi, and the *Hindu* to Madras.

Shanker is not trying to make a choice, however; he is waiting for the stand's owner to see him. When he does, they exchange a greeting, and the man hands Shanker his morning copy of *Punjab Kesari*. No money changes hands; later the newsstand owner will send a boy over to get some *paan* or cold drinks from Shanker. Together we hurry to his large steel-and-glass kiosk. Like many of my Indian hosts, Shanker makes a distinction between those newspapers he "takes" and those he merely buys or reads. The newspapers one takes must be chosen carefully because they enter into the texture of daily life. They become identified with you. *Nav Bharat Times* is brought to Shanker's home by a local bicycle delivery man. It is the newspaper that Shanker reads each morning over tea and chapattis before he comes to his shop. The newspaper is conservative and above reproach in its language, so it can be read by Shanker's wife and children. The "chaste" Hindi in which it is written is difficult; it uses the Sanskritized word *pustak* (book), for example, instead of the everyday Hindustani *kitab.* Shanker tells me this will help his children learn proper language and so help them in school.

Even if *Nav Bharat Times*'s editorial stance and style were to change suddenly, Shanker might continue to take it. "Taking" implies a commitment to the newspaper, perhaps even a compulsion. People often inherit the newspaper they take from their family of origin. Indian readers I interviewed were fond of referring to their "habit" of taking certain newspapers. One man who had moved from Calcutta to Delhi to take a job in the dairy industry said that although he also now read the *Hindustan Times,* he could not give up the *Statesman* because it was his habit. An insurance agent jokingly told me "a man would divorce his wife before he would change his newspaper."

The *paan* kiosk is already open when we get there, in the charge of Vijay, Shanker's young nephew, who hurries off to get us *chai.* Shanker always complains of being a poor man, but he does a lively business all day, not only in *paan* but sodas, chocolate bars, and bottled water for the tourists. In the late morning, Padam, who owns the sundries shop behind and to the right of Shanker's stand, comes by and offers Shanker a copy of *Dainik Jagran.* It is not his paper but that of their mutual friend Ram, who will eventually be along to give Shanker Padam's copy of *Jansatta.* The men chat for a bit. They are old friends who trade talk and newspapers in a cycle during the long 14-hour workday. Shanker, Padam, and Ram are occasionally joined by Vikram, who reads the afternoon tabloids. By common agreement, I move from one man to the next, interviewing each in his respective place of work, but also listening to them talk about the news with one another.

I am struck by the degree to which their ways of interpreting news texts involve assumptions about *who* is producing the news and *why.* Again and again, they imagine reasons *why* the newspaper says what it says. Rather than treating the newspaper as a window on the world, these men seem to treat it as a knowledgeable acquaintance — or sometimes a friend — whose understanding of things has to be judged on the basis of one's knowledge of his motives and character. This is why Padam tells me that one's understanding of the news depends on whether or not a newspaper is "sincere."

I have heard this term before from other newspaper readers. Most newspaper readers I have spoken with understand the Indian press to be free from government censorship — in contrast with television news — but this does not mean a newspaper uses its freedom in the public interest. *Sincere* newspapers are trustworthy, but not in the sense of being reliably accurate. Any newspaper may not tell you the complete truth, but sincere newspapers tell the news with an eye to the public good, while other newspapers may lie to you as part of a government plot or to further the interests of their proprietors. Completely insincere papers are contemptuously referred to as *raddi* (wastepaper). The insult is ironic, because all newspapers are *raddi* once their news value is gone. *Raddi* is the material component of the newspaper sold by weight as a recyclable good. To refer to a current newspaper as *raddi* is to imply that it has no news value to begin with.

The Practice(s) of News Consumption

How can we understand this blend of economic, social, and interpretive activities that make up Shanker's news reading practices? For Shanker and his friends, reading the newspaper is not a cognitive act of interpretation; it is not a decoding of a text or an interpellation into a world of discourse. It is a set of practices in which the acts of selecting, buying, interpreting, talking about, and getting rid of the newspaper are all mutually implicated. These men are conscious of the newspaper as one medium among a web of other media. They are aware of differences in kinds of newspapers and in registers of language that index social distinctions. They have an understanding of the news as a construction by political forces of which they believe they have some understanding. Reading the news thus involves a whole complex of knowledges and practices that link the fields of production and consumption, other media genres, the news stories themselves, and the medium as a material object. Understanding what is going on with Shanker, Padam, Vikram, and Ram requires us to go "beyond the audience" (Bird 2003: 1) to look at these men not as consumers of messages but as consumers of newspapers, at once material objects and congeries of messages embedded in a web of social relations. We need to make an effort to understand what they do with these newspapers and with the messages they offer, and how their actions and interpretations are socially productive of them as persons. This requires us to rethink how we engage in the ethnography of news.

Until recently, the ethnography of news was primarily conducted by sociologists who focused on news production (Warner 1971; Epstein 1973; Altheide 1976; Schlesinger 1991; Tuchman 1978; Golding and Elliott 1979; Bantz, McCorkle, and Baade 1980; Fishman 1980; Gans 1979; Gitlin 1983; Soloski 1989). These studies characterized news as "made," "constructed," or "manufactured" and often described newspapers and news programs as "factories" or "machines." Early work in the ethnography of news sought to empirically demonstrate the falseness of the notion that news is "uncovered" or "found," and so undermine the notion that it offers a relatively transparent window on reality. Audiences were methodically ignored in these studies, but implicit in the whole project was the notion that by demonstrating the processes through which stories are constructed, relatively uncritical audiences would be liberated from their misplaced acceptance of news texts.

Criticism arose over the question of audience agency, but the solutions offered tended to focus on how audiences apprehend news content. Although some paid more attention to the contexts of reception than others, most "reception" studies focused on what content people took from the news, what attention they gave to what aspects of the news, or what they remembered after viewing the news. The underlying assumption of nearly all these studies was that news consumption was about the transfer of information from the newspaper to its readers. An important exception, "gratifications" research, paid more attention to the "uses" to which people put news, but was mired in a language of "choices" that reflected an underlying "marketplace" metaphor (Katz and Blumler 1974; Rosengren, Palmgreen, and Wenner 1985). Gratifications studies tend to assume atomistic individual choice-makers, an approach that does not always travel well outside marketplace-oriented fields of consumption to sites like Connaught Place, where the news one reads is partly choice, partly chance, partly the result of one's position in a web of relationships.

More recently, a series of ethnographies of news (Hannerz 2004a; Hasty 2005; Pedelty 1993, 1995, 1997; Peterson 2001; Ståhlberg 2002; Velthuis 2006; Wolfe 1997, 2005) has dramatically opened up the range of models and analytical tropes through which we understand how news is created. This work is part of an explosion of anthropological interest in mass media over the last 15 years (Spitulnik 1993; Dickey 1997; Peterson 2003). Most of this literature can be classed into one of two strands of scholarship: increasingly sophisticated methods of analyzing texts in relation to various dimensions of social and cultural experience (especially using methods drawn from sociolinguistics), and the application of ethnography — in the anthropological sense — to systems of media production and consumption. But while some of the most important work in media anthropology problematizes and retheorizes audiences (Abu-Lughod 2004; Armbrust 1996; Bird 2003; Dickey 1993; Gillespie 1995; Mankekar 1999), most of this work has focused on television and film and has been largely missing from anthropological studies of news.[2] When newspaper consumption *is* touched on, it usually continues to be in terms of how the contexts of "reception" shape the "reading" and hence the "interpretation" of news. While this is certainly an important aspect of news consumption, it assumes the primacy of news content, and it privileges the concept of individual acts of reading. Largely unexamined in all of this is the question of whether "reading" and "reception" are the best possible models for understanding what people are doing personally and socially with news.

An alternative to understanding news consumption as reception is to see the selection, buying, reading, interpreting, talking about, exchanging, and discarding of newspapers as a form of news literacy. This approach draws on a growing literature that views literate practices as emergent in cultural and historical processes and embedded in specific social activities. Instead of "literacy" as a unique practice that produces particular modes of thought and action, contemporary scholars are writing of multiple situated "literacies" (S. Heath 1983; Street 1984, 1993; Besnier 1991; Bloch 1998; Barton, Hamilton, and Ivanic 2000). In the view of the "new" literacy studies (now more than a quarter century old), literacies are understood as sets of social practices associated with different domains of life. Each form of literacy occurs in a social field patterned by social institutions and power relationships; as a result, some literacies are more dominant, visible, and influential than others. This approach recognizes that all written language is located in particular times and places and that literate activity is produced toward particular ends and shaped by broader social practices. Literacy practices are active and oriented toward goals, and they change over time as new ones are acquired through processes of formal and informal learning and sense making (Barton and Hamilton 2000).

In the rest of this chapter, I want to suggest that the activities of Shanker and his friends obtaining, exchanging, reading, and talking about news and newspapers is best understood as a set of literacy practices. Unique in some aspects to these four men, this set of practices nonetheless draws on a broad repertoire of widely distributed cultural practices I have observed throughout New Delhi among news consumers of different classes and educational backgrounds. Through these practices, news becomes productive not merely of information but of persons as news consumers construct themselves as particular kinds of social and national subjects.

Taking the News

Buying a newspaper in New Delhi is not a simple matter of obtaining "the news" as if content could be separated from the vehicle that carries it. Shanker and his friends are confronted with a wide field of newspapers; buying one is an inherently social act that is constitutive of them as persons. Price, language, and availability are not only delimiting factors that help determine the selection of a newspaper; they are also part of what constitutes a particular newspaper's character. These elements combine with the amount and type of advertising, political slant, editorial style, balance of local, national, and foreign news, degree of "spiciness," stories told about the publishers and editors, and other elements to give each newspaper a particular character.

By "character" I refer to the range of meanings associated with a specific newspaper. "Like every plant and animal and person, every newspaper has its *jaati,*" the editor of *Jansatta,* Prabash Joshi, told me in an interview. We are accustomed to translating *jaati* as "caste," but in fact it is a classifying word, a term for describing categories constructed on the basis of perceived similarities and differences, and it can also be translated as class, race, breed, tribe, or genre.[3] Newspaper professionals sometimes refer to this in English as a newspaper's *face:* "Every daily specializes in something or other. This specialization is like its face; it must not and cannot be changed" (Varma 1993: 7). This face is in part a function of its price, in part a function of its use of language, and in part a function of its news and advertising content. Face is also shaped by the stories people tell *about* the newspaper, for in India tales of the heroic stands of editors and the Machiavellian schemes of publishers circulate as part of political gossip. Collectively these elements serve as meta-messages describing a newspaper's character. Each newspaper has its own face, apparently generic yet defined by similarities and differences with other newspapers in the market.

Over in the advertising department of Bennett, Coleman and Company, publishers of the *Times of India, Nav Bharat Times, Sandhya Times,* and a host of magazines, they speak of a newspaper's character in terms of "brands." "Indians have the greatest brand loyalty of anybody in the world," one senior executive assured me. "And newspaper brand loyalty is greater than any other kind." This shift to the language of marketing reminds us that the newspaper's character serves in part as a commodity sign, an image possessing social and cultural value associated with a product such that it extends the meaning of the product beyond its use value (Goldman and Papson 1996). Consumers buy the brand, not the product, because of the ways the character of the brand prefigures the value of the product, but also because they take on some of the character of the products they consume: they talk "about themselves through the medium of the product" (Applbaum 2004: 43). Thus Shanker and his friends take the particular newspapers they do because of that newspaper's character (they do not, after all, know in advance what the content of the paper will be each day); in turn, they partake in some degree of the character of the newspaper, if only to one another.

Shanker's public newspaper, *Punjab Kesari,* was a newcomer, established in Delhi in 1983. In nine years it became the most popular newspaper in the city. Its low-code Hindi is the very opposite of the chaste Hindi of his domestic newspaper. Rife with borrowings from Urdu and English, *Kesari* is unique among Delhi's newspapers for putting its entertainment "magazine" in the front and running hard news behind it. The use of large, full-color photographs on the front page made it hard for Shanker's friend Padam to take it seriously, but all the men agreed that the use of short articles focusing on crime, political controversy, and the entertainment industries made for enjoyable reading. *Kesari* is also known for in-depth magazine style news analyses that run two or three days after an event and not only rely on wire service copy but also lift ideas and information from the higher-prestige newspapers. Shanker didn't see this as a shortcoming but enjoyed having news explained to him rather than simply reported. While he could concentrate on *Nav Bharat Times* in the mornings and evenings at home, *Kesari* was far easier to read in brief snatches on the job. And Shanker enjoys *Kesari*'s political coverage, even when he disagrees with it. His father, who came to Delhi from Punjab, read *Kesari*'s Urdu mother paper, *Hind Samachar,* and *Kesari*'s strongly nationalist, antiterrorist tone appeals to the political sentiments Shanker learned growing up. It is this political stance that makes the paper respectable, he insists. If it is not a serious paper, it is at least a *sincere* paper, honest and committed. In the newspaper's first decade, more than 60 people from the founder and his son to reporters to street vendors were slain by terrorists because of the paper's refusal to abide by reporting directives issued by militants. This character — superficially entertaining but honest, sincere, and courageous underneath — might also serve as a description of the identity to which Shanker aspires. "Always I have a good word for my customers," he said. "But inside, I am thinking about serious issues."[4]

Padam is also seen as a "serious" man by his friends. While the newspaper he takes, *Jansatta,* is regarded by many as the spiciest of the Hindi "quality" press — it tends to adopt an antagonistic and oppositional tone toward authority — Padam says he takes it primarily for its editorials.[5] As a Hindi novelist in Varanasi told me, "The real strength of *Jansatta* lies in its efforts to write intelligently from and for a traditional viewpoint, without apologies." Editor Prabash Joshi insisted on reframing contemporary events from a Hindu ethos. For example, he criticized the government's ready embrace of a Western feminist viewpoint of the 1987 Deorala *sati,* writing, "People who accept this life as the beginning and the end, and see the greatest happiness in their own individual pleasure, will never understand the practice of *sati*" (trans. Tully 1991). Padam cannot read Sanskrit, but he reads popular religious and philosophical books and regards himself as an educated Hindu who seeks to understand modernity through a Hindu ethos. He reads many books, and "he is very intelligent," said Vikram. "He thinks about what these men [editors] say." Like Shanker, Padam takes *Nav Bharat Times* at home. "Padam Bhai takes *Nav Bharat Times* because he is a scholar," joked Shanker (who may also have been working in a backhanded compliment to himself).

Neither Ram nor Vikram took the news as seriously as their older friends, and the newspapers they took reflected this. Ram said he took *Dainik Jagran* for the sports section. Ram, who made his living assisting foreign tourists with the post office, exchanging currency, finding travel deals, or wending through Indian bureaucracies, was one of those guys who can quote you statistics on every major cricket player and footballer in the national clubs. *Jagran* is known throughout northern India for its sports coverage, as well as its use of large photos, short stories, and straightforward Hindi prose. "Even if you don't take *Jagran* for a sports paper, you take it for a sports paper," a reporter for *Jansatta* told me. "*Jagran* writes about politics and about business and about even literature as if it were writing about sports." *Jagran* is a leading newspaper across the Hindi belt, with editions in Agra, Gorakhpur, Jhansi, Kanpur, Lucknow, and Varanasi. Weak on local, urban news, circulation in Delhi is lower than in other cities, but *Jagran* had some success targeting working-class and immigrant communities in Noida and the trans-Yamuna districts

Occasionally the three men were joined by their friend Vikram. Vikram was a tout. He made his living off small commissions from rickshaw wallahs, taxi drivers, travel agents (including Ram), and shopkeepers (including Shanker and Padam) to whom he steered tourists. Vikram did not describe himself as taking a newspaper. A good day was a day when he had no time to read the newspaper because he was engaged with tourists. On a slow day, Vikram's business would slump in the afternoon, and he would buy an "eveninger" like *Sandhya Times* or *Vir Arjun*. These late afternoon newspapers are tabloids on the British model (indeed, Sat Soni, the editor of *Sandhya Times,* told me he learned his craft working for a Welsh tabloid), with large pictures, no stories running more than 400 words, and a focus on crime, entertainment, and sensational news. Frequently he would join the exchange network, offering his eveninger for one of the more substantial papers of his friends. Vikram never spoke about the news in the day I spent with these men, but listened respectfully to their opinions, sometimes inclining his head affirmatively, sometimes shaking his head in disagreement.

Kalman Applbaum points out that goods like these newspapers, which possess "characters," complicate standard anthropological theories of exchange value. Most anthropological concepts of exchange assume that an object's value is determined in the exchange itself "through local forces of uneven power and expressed and negotiated through 'tournaments of value'" (Applbaum 2004: 70). But commodity signs are goods whose meanings partially *precede* the exchange, and these meanings thus enter into the exchange process. Shanker, Vikram, Ram, and Padam solved this problem through their distinction between newspapers they "take" and those they merely "read." Because they exchanged newspapers during the course of the day, all four men have read most of the same newspapers. But the character of the newspaper is understood to reflect only on the initial giver of that newspaper to the exchange network, the one who purchases the newspaper and then offers it to the exchange network. To *read* a newspaper is a social act merely signifying your interest in being informed; to *take* a particular newspaper is to use it as an emblem that says something about who you are in modern New Delhi.

One is thus (in part) defined by the newspaper one takes. A "manifested preference" (Bourdieu 1984: 56) for one particular newspaper — as with preferences in art, food, furnishings, music, or films — is derived from social actors' awareness that they are part of a web of social distinctions whose boundaries are constructed by such tastes. Tastes produce identity largely through processes of distinction; they "are the practical affirmation of an inevitable difference. It is no accident that, when they have to be justified, they are asserted purely negatively, by the refusal of other tastes. In matters of taste, more than anywhere else, all determination is negation, and tastes are perhaps first and foremost distastes" (Bourdieu 1984: 56). Sets of structural continua rooted in mutual negation (e.g., from chaste to vulgar Hindi) thus undergird preferences for one newspaper over another. Yet the penchant for *Punjab Kesari* over *Hindustan* is not freely chosen or discovered but at least partially preordained by class, status, and family background. It is "a virtue made of necessity which continuously transforms necessity into virtue by inducing 'choices' which correspond to the condition of which it is the product."

Bourdieu has been accused, not entirely unjustly, of determinism (Jenkins 1982), but it is certainly true to say of Shanker and his friends that their choices to take *Punjab Kesari, Jansatta,* or *Dainik Jagran* while exhibiting real agency are overdetermined choices, produced by social and economic conditions that rule out many alternatives to produce a "taste for the necessary." Given who they are — their family origins, geographical trajectories, educations, households, and modes of making a living — and the identities they aspire to within their networks of social relations, the number of particular newspapers they can take is significantly limited. What newspapers one takes defines one in certain ways. Within each broad language niche is a multiglossic continuum from low code to high code and between "chaste" and "spicy" content. Positions on these continua link with local language ideologies such that the act of buying and reading materials in a particular code has social consequences. The price of one's paper, its political affiliation, class and geographical associations, the kinds of advertisements it carries — all these serve to place readers in a social field through the act of "taking" a newspaper. These distinctions are obviously connected to wider cultural categories and social differences. They are distinctions that map social stratification in linguistic, political, and economic dimensions. These distinctions are partly coded into the newspapers as part of their brand identities, but they are also constructed by the men through their acts of exchange and their discourses about the newspapers. And their reproduction of these distinctions is oriented toward practical social ends (Bourdieu 1977: 96).

For Shanker and his friends, this web of newspaper exchanges marked social distinctions and enabled sociality. The ritual act of sharing newspapers daily reestablished bonds between these four men. The news content gave them something to talk about from day to day, but the content of what is read and said was less significant than the connection the talk created between the men. Yet even as these practices created sociality, they marked social distinctions. Using their newspaper literacies, Shanker and his friends reestablished on a daily basis their position as middle-class and lower-middle-class shopkeepers, neither rich nor poor, educated but not highly educated, politically knowledgeable (and argumentative) but within the safe, nonradical parameters demarcated by the mainstream press. Through their practices they experience themselves as friends, as citizens, as businessmen, and as Indians.

Telling News Stories

In focusing above on consumption and exchange and on the phatic and status-building aspects of news consumption, I do not want to imply that the content of the news is unimportant. For Shankar and his comrades, news stories are the basis for moral narratives they construct collectively and individually. The stories they tell are *moral* not merely because they evaluate the actions described in the content but because they also seek to understand *why* particular newspapers are telling particular stories by imagining the situations in which news was produced and the intentions of those producing it.

Thus in our conversations about news, Ram suggested that the fatality and injury figures from recent communal riots were being underreported to keep the stories from sparking further riots. Shanker argued that each crisis was reported to divert people's attention from the last, none of them ever being solved. Padam explained that many journalists mean well, but they are at the mercy of their employers, who naturally want newspapers to reflect their own interests.

One possible way to theorize from these stories is to construct a master narrative that accounts for the performances of actual stories in given contexts. For Shanker, Padam, and Ram, this master narrative describes India as an unfinished country whose development is in the hands of powerful people. This narrative is historically rooted in the contradictions of Indian nationalism, which sought to deny British claims of Indian barbarism by acknowledging Western material superiority but contrasting it with an Eastern spiritual authority, defining the national project as the construction of a modern hybrid of both (Chatterjee 1986, 1989). This master narrative was reworked after independence in the light of development narratives (Gupta 1995, 1998) and subsequently reworked in the 1980s and 1990s through discourses of Hindu nationalism, which promoted a core Hindu ethos twinned with a commitment to economic liberalization and globalization (Basu et al. 1993; Hancock 1995). The use of media as a means to imaginatively position one in these narratives has been previously described by Gupta (1995) and Mankekar (1993, 1999).

In a world divided between "big" people who control enormous amounts of social, economic, and political capital and "little" folk who can only hope they do the right thing (Dickey 1993), the press plays an important role. As a bridge between the powerful and the powerless, the press must report on the activities of the government and the wealthy to reveal any negative activities in which they are involved. At the same time, the press is deemed very powerful because it has the power to shape the minds of people. The press must be careful not to abuse its power by reporting things that might adversely affect the proper development of the country — information that might lead to riots, for example. Yet journalists and editors must also be vigilant against newspaper owners, who often will pressure them to slant their news in ways that benefit the powerful but not the common man. Although I was never able to discuss this master narrative with any of these four men, other informants have agreed that it described a general attitude with which they approached news. Such a master narrative, abstracted from many actual instances of discourse, is extremely useful in helping describe coherently the interpretive frames that media consumers bring to their discussions of news.

A current trend in linguistic and semiotic anthropology, however, argues against such abstraction in favor of closer attention to actual instances of performance (Bauman 1986; Briggs 1988; Bauman and Briggs 1990; Briggs and Bauman 1992). This approach asks us to look at how speakers use these kinds of narrative constructions in the immediate and proximate situations of performance to accomplish particular objectives, including that of constructing identities (Bucholtz and Hall 2005). When we look at these men's stories in this light, we find that they draw on this master narrative to construct specific tales that map them into these stories and thus position themselves in the developing nation.

The news narratives spun by Shanker and his friends usually have three actants: the government, the press, and the common man. I am using *actants* here in Greimas's sense of narrative structural roles that are occupied by different actors in actual instances of storytelling (Greimas 1984). An actant is a generic category of character associated with a particular narrative genre, while an actor is the specific version of the type in the individual tale. Thus in one story, the government actant might be played by a bureaucrat, in another tale by the president or prime minister, and in another just by "the government." Talk about the news thus positions speakers in relation to the subject of the news, the newspaper and its related institutions, the government, and Indian publics.

When Ram suggested that the press was understating actual death tolls, he positioned the press and the government together, acting in the pubic inter-est to keep a lid on communal violence. Because he recognized this, he lifted himself out of the norm of publics (who he imagined to be manipulated by these actions), but because he approved of this imagined course of action by the press and government, he positioned himself with them. Shanker cyni-cally positioned himself against both the government and the press, which he described as in collusion to distract public attention from vital civic issues. Important though Ayodhya and its ancillary crises (communal riots, the Cal-cutta and Bombay bombings) were, the obsessive coverage of these issues by the press shifted public scrutiny away from prior crises so that the government was never pressured into actually solving any of India's social problems. Like Ram, Shanker constructed a public manipulated by the press. Unlike Ram, however, Shanker constructed an account in which the manipulation of the public by the press and government was morally reprehensible. In so doing, he positioned himself morally with "the common man." Padam responded to both men by splitting "the press" into two actants, "journalists" (presumably reporters and editors) and "proprietors." He suggested that while journalists try to do the right thing (that is, to use their power over the public responsibly), they are always partly at the mercy of their publishers, whose relationships with the government may be corrupt and self-serving. In so telling the story, Padam positioned himself with the intelligentsia, squeezed between the forces of money and power.

These accounts of news did not merely reflect previously held political posi-tions; they were shaped in part by the relations between the men. Ram's claims reflected his relative conservatism and his conviction that the government and his newspaper in particular act "sincerely." Because of his youth and his sub-ordinate status position in the group, he must defer to the older, more affluent, better-read Shanker's contradiction. Padam resolved the momentary tension between these positions by offering a compromise reading that acknowledged some truth to both positions while restoring the editors he admired to a state of moral rectitude. These versions all derive from and are consistent with the master narrative, but in their specific tellings they express the identity politics of the group members. At the same time these individual tellings also articulate aspects of the men's identities as part of a larger collectivity, that of the Indian nation.

One common feature of the three reader interpretations presented here—and indeed, of most interpretive reading of news I observed in India—is the assumption of some degree of collusion between the press and the government. The nationalist project generates a complex set of relations between press and political institutions. These are reconstructed in different ways by newspaper readers and can create distinctions that key different assumptions within the interpretive frames. Readers may see journalists as cooperating with the government toward ends that are in the best interest of the nation, but could as easily position journalists as in collusion with the government on a project that is not in the best interests of the nation. The press can also be seen as relatively innocent of government control, either being manipulated (which implies that journalists are unaware that they are being used) or coerced (which implies that the government is bringing legal or illegal pressures to bear on the press, usually through the proprietor). These relationships of government-press-reader are the essential material through which interpretations of news are constructed. Newspapers are essentially cultural operators, which, in selecting and representing events as news, makes them resources for the construction of national identities.

Anderson (1983) has emphasized the role that "print capitalism" plays in the making of national identities, both in providing common ritual practices—such as newspaper exchanges, reading rooms, and newspaper deliveries to the home—and the sharing of common content. My account complicates Anderson's model by drawing attention to the ways newspaper rituals become elements in the construction of personal and group identities, but also by suggesting that content and practice intersect in news discussions in ways that enable people to map themselves into positions within the imagined community of the nation. Thus Shanker positioned himself as a critical citizen separate from both the manipulating institutions of power and the manipulated masses. Ram positioned himself with the institutions of power, which he constructed as trustworthy. In talking about the news, these men not only constructed imagined communities but also described the moral universe of those communities and mapped themselves into it accordingly.

THE PARTICULAR PRACTICES I've described for Shanker and his friends are idiosyncratic and unique to their specific spatial and personal relationships. At the same time, because these practices are drawn from a widespread cultural repertoire, they are reflective of more general ways that Indians may consume newspapers and news, getting the news but also using news stories to help shape their public identities. These specific news literacies draw our attention to the wide range of possible discoveries that ethnographies of news consumption may produce once we abandon the nearly ubiquitous assumption that news consumption is primarily about the transmission of content and that contexts of consumption merely affect the nature of reading and interpretation. Instead, I suggest, contexts of consumption constitute social fields in which people engage in narrative and performatory constructions of themselves, reinforce social relations with other actors, negotiate status, engage in economic transactions, and imagine themselves and others as members of broader imagined communities.

Notes

1. In 1992–93, at the time of my fieldwork, the Registrar of Newspapers for India listed some 106 daily newspapers in New Delhi. These figures are skewed, however, since new newspapers are required to register, but no report is required when a newspaper folds. I can vouch for 44 newspapers that I collected during my fieldwork, and some 16 others were described to me. For more on the RNI, see Jeffrey 1994.

2. But see Bird 1992 and 2003 for exceptions.

3. Thus we find such phrases as *maanav jaati* (human race), *gorii jaatiyaa* (white races), *janglii jaatiya* (jungle tribes), *manusya jaati* (mankind), and *hiran kii jaati* (breed of horse).

4. At the time (early spring 1993), the serious issue he said he was thinking about was the destruction of the Babri Masjid in Ayodhya and the subsequent Hindu-Muslim conflicts across India.

5. In 1992–93, *Hindustan, Jansatta,* and *Nav Bharat Times* were the "serious" Hindi newspapers, while *Dainik Jagran, Punjab Kesari,* and *Rashtriya Sahara* represented the major Hindi "popular" press.

11

Personal News and the Price of Public Service

An Ethnographic Window into the Dynamics of Production and Reception in Zambian State Radio

DEBRA SPITULNIK

For many radio listeners in Zambia, the most newsworthy programs on state-owned radio are not *The Main News* or *News on the Hour* but the programs that regularly air messages from listeners in the form of greetings, obituaries, and other personal announcements.[1] With families dispersed across long distances due to labor migration, urbanization, and military service, among other things, radio has been a central means for long-distance interpersonal communication since its introduction in 1938, when Zambia was the British colony of Northern Rhodesia. For decades, programs such as *Forces Greetings, Calling Hospitals and Dispensaries, Zimene Mwatifunsa* (Nyanja language, Yours for the Asking), and *Imbila sha Bulanda* (Bemba language, News of Suffering) have regularly aired messages about births, deaths, marriages, missing persons, and new addresses. As such they have played a critical role in constructing an imagined — and concretely participated in — national community that extends beyond the immediate world of face-to-face encounters.

From the perspective of media studies or communication studies, such radio genres would be classified as falling outside the conventional category of "news." They do not use the standard journalistic genre of the news story. Indeed, they are mainly announcements. Their content is not created by media professionals; rather, it is generated by interested individuals from all walks of life. Their target audiences are not generic or impersonal; they are friends and relatives. None of this is really debatable. However, from the perspective of anthropology, it is less relevant whether the genre of personal radio messages fits or does not fit a certain classification, in an a priori sense. Rather, what matters more for media anthropology is what local actors make of this genre, what they do with it, what its local history and cultural significance are, and how it is placed within a field of other media genres.

This essay examines a particular moment in Zambian history when the broadcast of such personal messages became tangled up in a series of debates about newsworthiness, self-promotion, and state media's responsibilities to the public. In the late 1980s, the state-owned and operated national broadcasting monopoly (ZNBC, Zambia National Broadcasting Corporation) started to shift from a public service broadcasting model to a commercial model. "Making money" began to take precedence over "public service." This reached a crisis point when ZNBC decided to start charging for funeral announcements and other urgent personal news items. What is particularly significant about this crisis and the events surrounding it is how it precipitated some very explicit commentaries on key concepts informing the culture of media production in Zambia: "free news" vs. "paid news," "public service" vs. "commercial service," and "Zambian Humanism" or "socialism" vs. "capitalism." These dynamics continue to inform Zambian state broadcasting to this day, as the ZNBC, like state media in many developing nations, is challenged to integrate what is often a very charged heritage of state paternalism with newer approaches in an increasingly competitive broadcasting environment (cf. Abu-Lughod 2004).

In this chapter, I first explore some of these dimensions of ZNBC production culture. I then turn to the funeral message crisis, considering it a form of media reception in a double sense, as it illuminates both the reception of particular radio programs *and* the reception/evaluation of the broadcasting institution itself. Along the way, I include several extended excerpts from primary data; in some cases, these are blended with ethnographic commentary. The extended pieces serve to further contextualize the story I tell here, and some also provide parallel forms of reception data and analysis that bear on other cultural practices beyond the narrow tale of urgent radio messages. As such they speak to the excess that is real life and deep ethnography, as well as the thoroughly embedded and infinitely expansive nature of people's mediated worlds (see Ginsburg et al. 2002 and Spitulnik forthcoming).

Zambian Broadcasting Culture Shifts Gears

Some are working for ZNBC at 120 miles per hour and others for ZBS at 20 miles per hour. . . . We will make more programs and more money. — Charles Muyamwa, ZNBC program director, speaking to his staff

In April 1988, the government-owned Zambia Broadcasting Services (ZBS) was legally changed to Zambia National Broadcasting Corporation (ZNBC), a profit-making business under the rubric of the nation's largest parastatal holding company.[2] Broadcasting was not privatized by this move, but only placed within a different bureaucratic and economic framework.[3] At the time, ZBS/ZNBC was the nation's sole broadcaster, operating one television station and three radio channels.[4] Broadcasting in Zambia had been a government monopoly since its inception in 1938, during the Northern Rhodesia colonial administration. Essentially the ZBS/ZNBC legal and economic shift did not change these facts. But by an act of Parliament, the new ZNBC was granted powers to establish a revenue account, to invest, to undertake fund-raising activities, and to take out loans, with the ultimate goal being that broadcasting would eventually be able to operate without government subvention.[5] Significantly, this change became etched in the minds of broadcasting staff as "Now that ZNBC is a corporation, we must make money," a phrase repeated over and over again during the time that I conducted field research at the ZNBC headquarters (1988–90).

During the ZBS/ZNBC transition, there was a continuing emphasis on ZNBC as a national public institution, that is, for the Zambian state and its people. But with the move to commercialize broadcasting, a major shift occurred within the institutional culture of ZNBC, namely, a pronounced, almost euphoric embracing of the new ZNBC as a modern professional business. This was manifested in everything from a new corporate logo to speeches about corporate culture and management style.

While commercial advertisements had been an important source of revenue for both radio and television since the 1960s, ZBS had always operated with a philosophy of public service. It was nonprofit, state-run, and for the most part structured around the colonial (and BBC) derived paternalistic authoritarianism, which assumes that broadcasting's role is to build the nation and enlighten society (see MacCabe and Stewart 1986). At the same time, it should be noted that with tight state control over broadcasting, this public service philosophy has functioned in Zambia, as elsewhere on the continent, more as a "distant ideal, not a working reality" (Raboy 1996: 78, quoted in Heath 2001: 91). In this vein, according to Heath (2001: 91), "No African system has achieved public service standards of independence, impartiality, universal access, or special consideration for minorities."

In the broader context, ZNBC's incorporation was part of an acknowledgment of the economic crisis of Zambia's welfare state. Since independence in 1964, nearly all public services — including health care, education, and broadcasting — had been provided free of charge or at extremely low cost. Most basic commodities (such as sugar, cooking oil, and the maize staple, mealie meal) had also been heavily subsidized. Despite these socialistic policies, by the late 1980s Zambians were witnessing, virtually on a daily basis, the dramatic erosion of their standards of living (Ferguson 1999). For example, in 1988, Zambia's annual inflation rate was over 60 percent, and the average cost of living for people at all economic levels was nearly six times that of 1975 (Chiposa 1989). With the state on the verge of economic collapse, the government undertook a far-reaching economic recovery plan to reduce food subsidies, decontrol prices, devalue the national currency, and charge basic fees for health care and other social services. During this period, there was much debate within the Zambian government and among Zambians about the country's ideological orientation: Are we socialists, humanists, or capitalists? What should the nation do for its people? Increasingly, there was a widespread opinion among Zambians that things given free by the government didn't work. At the same time there was the expectation that state paternalism should continue. With the economic shock of increased school fees, health care fees, and prices during an already severe economic crisis, Zambians were reeling.

The new ZNBC was established right in the midst of this dramatic economic restructuring and dire economic shock. It went public on October 1, 1988, when broadcasters began using the new name, the Zambia National Broadcasting Corporation Radio and Television Network, a mouthful that many stumbled over, in place of the previous name, Zambia Broadcasting Services. In addition to the seemingly high-tech term *network*, ZNBC introduced new station identification logos with computer graphics and synthesizer music, newly orchestrated theme songs for the news, and new studio backdrops. For the first time, the country had an early morning weekend television program, *Kwacha Good Morning Zambia*.[6] Modeled after *Good Morning America*, this informal talk show, with a plush living room set and a menu of guests interspersed with news briefs and musical performances, was meant to bring a new sense of ease and prosperity to viewers. The dramatically remodeled nightly TV news also borrowed elements from Western formats: the broadcast was lengthened from 15 to 30 minutes, a second newsreader was added, the visuals for international items were more extensive, and advertisements were inserted at the halfway point. Previously, a single newsreader had appeared before a simple blue backdrop with a modest sign reading, "ZBS News." Now two presenters sat at a long desk with "ZNBC News" written across the front, behind which was a map of the world and the ZNBC company logo. Significantly, the incongruity of ZNBC's plush look and upbeat initiatives with the nation's more dire climate did not go unnoticed by many ZNBC viewers and listeners, as illustrated in the ethnographic vignette below.

A WINDOW INTO RECEPTION
A Parody of the Carefree Post-News Chat
    Jeff, in his late twenties, is one of Zambia's privileged upper class, a University of Zambia graduate, doing postdoctoral studies abroad. On a break back in Zambia, he is talking with a group of friends (myself included)

about how he doesn't like how some television newscasters have adopted a friendlier, less-serious demeanor with the new ZNBC format. Now there is a team of two anchors who take turns reading the news items. At the end of the news, the anchors chat briefly about weekend plans such as relaxing at home or going to parties. Jeff finds one female broadcaster, DK (pseudonym), to be particularly annoying: "DK is just promoting herself. At the end of the news she tries to talk to her co-anchor." Jeff imitates DK's lively voice:

"Well, what are you doing this weekend?"   [DK]
"I'm going to a funeral. What are you doing?"   [co-anchor]
"I'm going to a funeral, too."   [DK]

While Jeff might identify with the leisure activities that broadcasters usually mention, he feels that lighthearted talk is just not appropriate. Instead of acting like a neutral conduit of serious news information, DK is "promoting herself" by taking on a persona and by conveying information about her cheerful and affluent lifestyle. Jeff's response can be seen as a deeper form of social commentary as well: the carefree chat at the end of the news hides the truth about what people are really doing in their off-work hours. They are more likely to be tending to sick relatives or going to funerals and less likely to be going to parties or movies.

While one can read the new ZNBC changes as a straightforward case of media globalization or media imperialism, the reality is more complex. The newly hired ZNBC executives, many of whom hailed from the corporate business world and had extensive international experiences, were eager to leave behind the older (and "less modern") vestiges of ZBS and urged workers to shift gears in attitude, performance, and style, as the above quote from the program director illustrates. A wider world of international sophistication, consumption, and display was indexed by the changes, and as such they functioned as symbolic capital both for the executives bringing about the changes and for the corporation as it signaled its new money-making status. From a cultural history perspective, however, this was not so much a dramatic break in media practices and symbolic associations as it was a continuing association of electronic media with the semiotics of modernity (e.g., excitement, action, and speed), as well as a continuation of Zambia broadcasting's long-standing orientation toward Western standards of media production and evaluation (Spitulnik 1998). This orientation was established through extensive BBC consulting during the colonial period and has been sustained by a host of forces set in motion since that time, including the international training of top media professionals, frequent visits by foreign media consultants, and the everyday consumption habits of many media workers.

As ZNBC embarked on its new mission, its money-making interests began to clash with its historically established relations with both listeners and certain newsmakers. It was as if the conceptual logic of ZNBC had changed almost overnight, with a fresh eye being cast on where charges might be levied. A price could now be put on airtime. The fine, shifting, and often invisible line between intrinsic newsworthiness and giving someone "free" publicity became more subject to discussion and more rigidly construed.

One example of this was ZNBC's decision not to cover traditional annual ceremonies across the country unless they were paid for by the ceremony's organizers. Every year roughly 20 different ethnic groups in Zambia celebrate an annual event observing some aspect of their cultural heritage, for example, a first fruits ceremony, a seasonal migration ceremony, or an event of historic conquest. Radio and television coverage of these ceremonies has always been irregular, and not all 20-odd ceremonies get equal air play, but coverage had previously been free. With ZNBC's shift toward "making money," ethnic groups holding traditional annual ceremonies were likened to interest groups who were publicizing themselves. As one senior executive explained to me, "We should not be giving them publicity free of charge."

A further instance of this logic surfaced when ZNBC defended its decision to air a dramatically shortened version of what had been a lengthy interview with a nonprofit women's development organization. The chairperson of Zambia Association for Research and Development (ZARD) had been interviewed for Television Zambia's current affairs program, *Tonight,* about the upcoming UN International Women's Day and its focus on food security. When *Tonight* aired, however, the interview was cut to 24 seconds. It was the last item in the newsmagazine, and it ended abruptly, as if an editor had added it simply to fill out the rest of the time block, or as if some unanticipated time crunch occurred during real-time transmission. The effect was more jarring because this was the only item on the program dealing with the upcoming Women's Day initiatives. Claiming that this 24-second coverage trivialized the issue of food security, ZARD requested that ZNBC air the full interview. After this was refused at the highest level, ZARD took its complaint to another media outlet and sent a letter to the editor of the state-run *Zambia Daily Mail,* which appeared under the heading "Screen Women's Interview Fully" (March 11, 1989). The letter created an uproar on the top floors of ZNBC headquarters, though perhaps nowhere else. As the head of public relations told me, the furious ZNBC director general handed the matter over to him and demanded that the response to them should be, "If you want to advertise your organization, you should buy airtime."

Increasingly, then, groups and organizations previously considered to be newsmakers were evaluated as self-interested individuals who fell into the category of advertisers. If they did not pay for coverage, it was less likely that their stories and events would reach the airwaves, or so went the argument. Of course, the ruling elites were exempt from this calculus.[7] But it was transferred, for a short time during the late 1980s, to ordinary Zambians who wanted to broadcast their own personal news.

The Funeral Message Debate: A Crisis in Zambian Humanism

On August 1, 1989, ZNBC announced that effective September 1 it would begin charging for "personal call messages." These messages are broadcast in specific programs, in all eight state radio languages: Bemba, English, Kaonde, Lozi, Lunda, Luvale, Nyanja, and Tonga. Most are funeral announcements, giving details of the date and place of death, funeral arrangements, and names of relatives around the country who are requested to attend. On ZNBC Radio 2, in English, the *Personal Call Messages* program occupies prime time, occurring every evening after the *Main News*. The popular Bemba program *Imbila sha Bulanda* (News of Suffering) airs five days a week on ZNBC Radio 1.[8] Messages list family and friends in order of importance, along with the names of their townships, compounds, workplaces, chiefs, and villages. Unlike obituaries in the newspaper, the sender of the message is always cited, usually along with his or her post office box number, phone number, address, and/or place of employment. These messages not only notify those explicitly named but also serve as public announcements of mourning whereby any listener who knows the family is expected to pay condolences. Other messages are about missing persons and seriously ill people.

FROM THE AIRWAVES
Personal Call Messages
[Prerecorded program lead-in] All of us at some time suffer a personal loss or tragedy. A child is missing, a close relative dies, and funeral arrangements have to be made and made known as quickly as possible. In order to lighten the burden of grief in these moments of sorrow, Radio Zambia, in conformity with our philosophy of Humanism, offers its services in the public interest. Messages of an urgent and solemn nature will be broadcast at this time every day.

[Announcer on duty, Dawson Mwendafilumba] And here is the first personal call message for this evening, coming from Mr. Wedson Mumba of house number M144 Kasanda mine in Kabwe. He would like to inform the following relatives and friends: BanaKaele, BanakuluKaune, Bana-Chama, all of Mukwikili village in chief Chinsali; BanaChandalucky of Kapanda village, Chief Mpumba; BanaMalamalemon of Linda compound in Lusaka; Mr. Frederick Mwambi of Chikwanda village in Mpika; and lastly BanaChandalike. The message is that BanakuluChewe, nangu BanaJesnelli, passed away on Tuesday, July 1, 1986, in Ndola Central Hospital. Funeral gathering is taking place at house number 2814 Pamodzi compound in Ndola. All those informed should make an effort of going for burial arrangements as burial arrangements await their arrival.

Another personal call message is from Dawson Shipunga of box 32563 Arrakan Barracks in Lusaka. It is for the information of all relatives and friends and the general public. The message reads as follows: A young lady by the name of Grace Shipunga has been missing from home since June 24, 1986. She is 18 years old, black in complexion, and 1.58 meters in height. If seen, please contact the nearest police station or the elder brother, Mr. Dawson Shipunga of Arrakan Barracks in Lusaka.

And here is another personal call message, from Mr. Neva Ndhjovu of 164 Vuvu Road Bank Houses in Emmasdale Lusaka. For the information of Mr. Christopher Mushilipa Zulu, believed to be in Choma. His wife's maiden name is Senjeni Ndhjovu, and she is from Zimbabwe. The message is that Mr. Neva Ndhjovu from Bulawayo Zimbabwe is stranded and is looking for Mr. Christopher Mushilipa Zulu. Mr. Mushilipa, if you are listening, please phone Mr. Dachani Phiri of Lusaka, telephone number 215837, during business hours.

The other personal call message, that seems to be the last one, is from Kenneth Ntongama of Nakambala Sugar Estate in Mazabuka. For the information of all friends and relatives, the message is that Bamama BaEmma Moyo is seriously sick in Lusaka's University Teaching Hospital. All those people informed should come to Lusaka.

And that's the end of personal call read-outs for today, July 2, 1986. The time on the General Service of Radio Zambia is now 20.47.

During the early days of radio in colonial Zambia, messages of funerals and illnesses were not grouped together into a special program but occurred along with greetings and other announcements. After a major disaster at one of the industrial copper mines in 1970, a decision was made to create distinct programs for "messages of an urgent and solemn nature." In a context where telephone and telegram use is limited by factors of economics, location, and literacy, state radio — open and available to nearly all — became established as a preferred vehicle for urgent personal news.[9] Currently, approximately 25 personal message programs air weekly on Radio Zambia. Each runs about 15 minutes and is usually programmed within the flow of other news and announcement formats. In addition, if there is a short window of empty time between regularly scheduled programs, impromptu readings can also occur, with broadcasters selecting two or three personal messages to bridge a programming gap. The regularly scheduled personal call message programs open with a prerecorded lead-in, in which solemn Christian music plays in the background and a male voice makes a solemn prefatory announcement. The music usually continues as the announcer on duty reads the messages, approximately 17 for each program.

Few people tune in just to listen to personal call programs; rather, they are encountered as listeners tune in for news, popular entertainment programs, or the beginning of their own ethnic language broadcast period. During my field research, such programs and messages were rarely mentioned spontaneously when people talked about their listening habits and preferences.[10] When they were mentioned, people tended to either talk about the informative value of the programs (*batwishibishamo,* they inform us) or the fact that this kind of news was depressing. Still, as an ever-present "small" radio genre, tucked within the flow of other programs, they constitute a significant presence on the Zambian airwaves and are a salient part of the popular imagination, as the following ethnographic vignette illustrates.[11]

A WINDOW INTO RECEPTION
Recycled Media Phrases
One evening about 7 PM Mrs. Kambowe, my neighbor in the Bemba-speaking town of Kasama, returned home from selling buns at the market. I asked her how the day went. Using a version of a Bemba radio program title, she sighed, "Ah mayo, imbila ya bulanda" (Oh, dear, news of suffering). One of the most popular programs on Radio Zambia, *Imbila sha Bulanda* airs nearly every day and serves as a primary vehicle for individuals to send messages announcing illnesses, deaths, and funerals. Here Mrs. Kambowe was using the radio program title to entitle the events of her day. She explained how all the places at the market were filled when she went there at 5:30 AM. She unsuccessfully tried to maneuver for a spot and was forced to return later in the afternoon. Finally she managed to find a place to sell the buns, but the day had been long and exhausting. It was a tale of woe, captioned by a radio program title, but one with a far happier ending.[12]

Shortly after ZNBC's announcement that it would begin charging for the broadcast of these messages, several angry letters to the editor appeared in the state-run daily newspapers. One complained that "it now looks as if we are dumping Humanism because of our ailing economy." The full text of the letter ran as follows:

A WINDOW INTO RECEPTION
Letter to the Editor

Humanism Eroded

Allow me to complain on behalf of those who can't write. Reports that ZNBC will start charging for all funeral and other messages by September this year is worrying. It now looks as if we are dumping Humanism because of our ailing economy. Where will we get direction without our philosophy of Humanism? Zambia is a humanist society, we must not dump all that is good just because we want to raise money. The duty of our leaders is to create conditions under which all men and women will be able to have access to all available opportunities. Alas! They have now dumped us by requesting us to pay for everything. I appeal to the government to intervene in the ZNBC intended move. The free broadcasting of all personal call messages was a "piece of cake" brought about by our independence.

Chingola
August 11, 1989, *Times of Zambia* August 11, 1989: 6

To contextualize and unpack this response, some discussion of the philosophy of Humanism and its role in the Zambian public sphere is in order. Kenneth Kaunda, Zambia's first and longest serving president, publicly introduced his philosophy of Humanism in 1967, and it was adopted as a national philosophy by his ruling party, the United National Independence Party (UNIP), later that year.[13] The doctrines of Humanism served simultaneously as party philosophy, national ideology, guidelines for social morality, and foundations for political administration and economic policy. Up until Kaunda's defeat in October 1991, it was propagated most prominently through pamphlets, speeches, radio programs, and school curriculum.[14] As UNIP was the only legal political party from 1973 to 1990, Zambian Humanism was essentially the only legitimate political philosophy in the country.

From its introduction, Zambian Humanism was presented as the antithesis of Western values. Opposed to what was framed as the Western imperialists' disregard for human dignity and human rights, Zambian Humanism was a codified form of what already existed, according to Kaunda, "at the heart of our traditional culture," the traditional community as a "mutual aid society" (1967: 5).[15] Zambian Humanism thus offered a vision of social morality that was intimately tied to a particular type of economy, one characterized by mutual aid, cooperation, and respect for human relations over material goods. Significantly, one of the primary crimes against Humanism was "the exploitation of man by man," a phrase frequently repeated in government speeches and radio programs. The worst form of exploitation was economic: a violation of the morality of mutual aid by using people for private gain. Since Zambian Humanism was framed as the diametric opposite of the moralities of capitalist nations — materialism, individualism, exploitation, and greed — this inevitably created an ideological time bomb as Zambia started shifting toward a free-market economy in the 1980s. Any attempts at profit making could be read as signs of capitalist exploitation and the erosion of Zambian values. Indeed, this is what stirred the Zambian writer from Chingola to complain that Humanism had been dumped.

The timing of ZNBC's announcement to charge for funeral messages could not have been worse, in terms of both the increased economic strain on the population and the rising death rate. In the first two weeks of July 1989, *all* commodity prices were decontrolled except for that of the maize-based staple food, mealie meal. The prices of cooking oil, sugar, petrol, beer, newspapers, and Coca-Cola shot up dramatically. Protests and looting broke out on the industrial Copperbelt, and the national climate was tense. In early August, junior doctors and other staff went on strike at the main hospital in Zambia's capital of Lusaka, protesting low salaries and poor working conditions. After nine days with no resolution, the workers were fired. Newspapers soon began reporting a rising death toll at the hospital due to shortage of staff, and one ran a front-page photograph of mourners gathering at the hospital mortuary (*Times of Zambia* August 23, 1989).

As the letter from Chingola makes clear, ZNBC's move was analogous to the government's: Humanism and the Zambian people were being *abandoned* because of the need to make money. The ZNBC was exploiting people at the worst possible moment, their time of grief. For this writer, ZNBC's new corporate status did not exempt it from its obligation as a national institution to allow "all men and women" equal access to its services. Instead, the view was that broadcasting (and implicitly the nation) should be held to a principle of being of and for the people. This conceptualization of ZNBC's status is underscored by the fact that during this time, many Zambians understood ZNBC's new name as Zambia National Broadcasting *Cooperation,* not Corporation.[16] This interpretation seemed to be motivated by two factors. First, there was the already widespread currency of the English word *cooperative,* as used in all government-run regional agricultural operations. Second, when the English words *corporation* and *cooperation* are assimilated into Zambian languages or spoken with a Zambian English accent, they sound nearly or completely identical. If understood as a *cooperative,* then the ZNBC would indeed be bound to allow all people "access to all available opportunities." ZNBC's preface to the personal call message programs had been announcing for years just this role of public service "in conformity with our philosophy of Humanism." Now it seemed that commoditizing personal call messages, putting a price on them, amounted to a commoditization of ZNBC's relationship with the public. Reducing social relations to monetary terms was an affront to the national philosophy of Humanism.

While the integrity of Zambian Humanism could be invoked as an issue in this debate, it is critical to note that few Zambians actually believed in its viability or appeal. In fact, throughout Kaunda's administration, Zambian Humanism functioned essentially as a *rhetorical* resource, to be invoked in the name of national identity and state policies. Its lofty and abstract formulations lent a sense of vision and purpose to political pronouncements, but by the late 1980s, party philosophy came under increasing attack as an idealistic rhetoric, which did little to address the harsh realities of people's lives. As such, the well-worn tropes of Zambian Humanism began to be met with great cynicism by most Zambians, sounding especially empty and slightly comical as they continued to be recycled within the context of abundant state ceremonies, propaganda, and display. As David Yumba, a prominent Zambian radio broadcaster, explained to me, the government's plan to teach people about socialism and Humanism was a complete failure: "The leaders themselves were to blame. Instead of socialism, they were practicing capitalism. You find that every leader has a big home and a big farm. People see this and don't believe in socialism."[17]

ZNBC's decision to charge for urgent personal news was challenged in letters to the editor in the state-owned papers and on the very airwaves of Radio Zambia. How this could happen, especially given the sensitivity of the ZNBC executives to any kind of criticism (as evidenced in the ZARD case, above), is a revealing tale of rhetorical maneuvering and personal bravado. In October 1989, on the popular Bemba-language talk show *Kabuusha Taakolelwe Boowa* (The Inquirer Was Not Poisoned by a Mushroom), host David Yumba read a letter in which a radio listener asked, "Do we just like to use the word *Humanism* without practicing it?" Citing the recent announcement about charging for funeral messages, the letter writer complained, "Does decontrol have to touch all areas?" After finishing the letter, Yumba launched into a blistering attack on the writer:

> Don't complain. You never used to say thank you when it was free. Do you complain to the Post and Telecommunications Corporation when they charge you to send telegrams? . . . Don't you know that broadcasting is expensive? . . . And when you go to the market, do the marketeers give things away free? . . . Don't you buy coffins? And when you have them lay out the corpse at the Ambassador Funeral Parlour, is there no charge? (ZNBC Radio 1, October 22, 1989, letter 2. Translated from Bemba)

In his characteristic style of heated hyperbole and social critique, Yumba, one of Bemba radio's best-known and most colorful radio personalities at the time, plays both the voice of reason and the voice of angry exhortation. But notably, as producer of the program, he chose to air the critical letter in the first place. So what is going on here? As a ZNBC employee, Yumba defends the corporation's position that "broadcasting is expensive." He tries to reason with the listener and, by extension, the listening audience. The reasoning is built on two analogies that were used by other defenders of the decision to charge for urgent personal news. First, other things related to funeral preparation are not free. And second, other institutions and individuals charge for their goods and services. Nothing is free, including telegrams, goods at the market, and even electricity. But when viewed in light of Yumba's own off-air criticisms of state politics during research interviews and his frequent practice of using listener letters as vehicles for public critique on this program, the rhetorical maneuvering involved here is complex. In short, Yumba's letter selection and response is a kind of double- or even triple-voicing (Bakhtin 1981: 324). A listener's voice is animated by a producer and is placed in counterpoint to the producer's voice. Simultaneously, the listener's voice can be seen as a veiled form of the producer's opinion.

This subtle slippage across voices and stances is what allows Yumba to use state radio to critique the state. Yumba gives voice to the writer's doubt that the words of politicians are empty, but Yumba violently insults the writer. In particular, the letter writer is likened to an idiot who thinks everything should be free and who is at the same time situated as one of Zambia's wealthiest, able to use the highest status funeral parlor in the country. Ironically, the minute fraction of Lusaka residents who end up at the Ambassador Funeral Parlour are high-ranking government officials whose families do not bear much of the formal funeral costs either. As Yumba's voice rises in a chain of hyperbolic rhetorical questions, the attack on the writer becomes a subtle critique of those very same politicians: those who "just like to use the word *Humanism* without practicing it" are precisely those who lie in state at the prestigious Ambassador Funeral Parlour.

In response to this public outcry, the decision to charge for urgent personal news was revoked. Humanism — or state broadcasting's reputation vis-à-vis the public in an unstable climate — prevailed over incentives to make money. Remarkably, public outcry and thinly veiled critiques by media professionals such as Yumba were not enough to propel the change. The case went to the floor of Parliament. After some debate, the minister of information and broadcasting services was directed to reaffirm the public service mission of ZNBC and run the messages free of charge. The controversy did not end there, however, as broadcasters and some Zambians continued to complain. For example, a tongue-in-cheek letter to the editor of the *Times of Zambia* commended the minister for his move, and then requested that the government

> extend this "humanistic" gesture to other institutions by scrapping all charges on telegrams, telexes, and telephone calls concerning funerals or illnesses. The same should be extended to those travelling for funerals on UBZ buses, trains, and Zambian Airways. Failure to implement Humanism as I have suggested would be unfair to ZNBC, and nobody should blame the corporation for offering poor services to the overdemanding public. (December 20, 1989)

Employing Yumba's strategy of hyperbole, but reversing the theme — everything should be free, including the plane flights taken to attend funerals — this writer alludes to the earlier sentiment that Zambian Humanism is an opportunistically applied rhetoric, used as a cover term for state policies that in the end yield only "poor services."

While space does not allow a detailed postscript to this story, it is important to note that urgent personal news continued to be broadcast free of charge on ZNBC for seven more years. Then in 1996 modest charges were introduced at the rate of 500 Zambian Kwacha (then about five cents) per message. This was a period of widespread economic liberalization and intensified local media competition, particularly between ZNBC and the newly established commercial radio stations. ZNBC's marketing department pushed for the change, and this time there was less resistance. With the rhetoric of Zambian Humanism gone, along with the Kaunda regime, and with pay structures for public services increasingly taking root, the mid-1990s were a more receptive time than the late 1980s. By 2008, the charge had increased to 10,000 Kwacha (about three dollars) per message, which is almost half of what an average family spends on basic daily food costs, but nearly identical to the cost of personal classified ads in the state-run newspaper, the *Daily Mail*.[18]

Conclusion

Joining the other contributions to this volume, my argument here has empha-sized the place and culture-specific values that shape the news and the news-worthy in Zambia. In this case, the symbolic and practical value of urgent per-sonal news on state radio was entangled in a complex field of forces, including a long-standing national philosophy of public service and mutual aid. When this philosophy collided with a crisis in political legitimacy, dramatic economic hardship, and continued human suffering, the value of airtime became as dear and tangible as the personal news it passed on.

While this essay is very much a local story about Zambia and a particularly neoliberal economic moment in Zambian history, it is also a story about glo-balization and frictions in media cultures. The global forces and idioms that impinge on — or that are appropriated by — non-Western media organizations such as the ZNBC are rarely sudden, overnight phenomena. Rather, they are part of a "long conversation" (Comaroff and Comaroff 1991: 17) that dates back to colonial times and that percolates through institutional cultures and every-day lives. Regarding frictions, the case here highlights how cultures of media production are rarely internally consistent in a complete sense. The conflicting directives of ZNBC to make money and serve the public are just one example of this, as is the fact that a broadcaster on state radio can criticize the state by animating the voice of a radio listener.

So, too, in cultures of reception does one find conflicts and incongruencies. For example, there is often a great divide between the intended forms of recep-tion and what people actually do with media discourse, media images, and media messages. Media consumption itself becomes a form of production, as carefree conversation between news presenters is satirically recast to comment on the nation's rising death rate, or as a program title is reanimated to label one's day. "Reception" thus extends beyond moments of immediate media con-sumption to these types of creative reworkings of media. It is also ever present in production, for example, as a national "public" is imagined by broadcasting executives, as producers read letters from listeners, and as one media outlet becomes a vehicle for blasting another. As such, the story of urgent personal messages is part of a larger story that media anthropologists are increasingly addressing: an account about how media work, how people work with media, and how non-Western media outlets navigate the weight of colonial history and contemporary global influences on a daily basis.

Notes

Primary data for this chapter is based on 22 months of media production and media reception research in Zambia (1986 and 1988–90) and archival research at Northwestern University. Zambia fieldwork was supported by grants from the Social Science Research Council, NSF, and Fulbright-Hays, for which I am very grateful.

1. Radio is the most widely consumed mass medium in the country, with state radio reaching approximately two-thirds of the national population. For more on Zambia radio listeners, see Spitulnik 2000. For fuller discussion of the current Zambian media landscape, see Banda 2006. The programs discussed in this chapter still air on Zambian state radio, and on many of the local community radio stations around the country. Their popularity and relevance remain much the same as in previous decades.

2. ZNBC was made part of the Zambia Industrial and Mining Corporation, Ltd. (ZIMCO), a state-owned holding company with over 100 companies which, combined, contributed more than 50 percent of the GDP and one-third of the total national wage employment in the late 1980s. ZIMCO was broken up with the privatization of many of its holdings in the early 1990s. ZNBC remains under state control.

3. The parastatal holding company ZIMCO was government-owned. Furthermore, considerable government control through the Ministry of Information and Broadcasting was written into the parliamentary act that created ZNBC.

4. ZNBC's monopoly over the domestic airwaves ended in 1994, with the legalization of privately owned broadcasting. There are now approximately 20 independent radio stations operating in the country, along with an independent television station and an independent subscription satellite television service provider (Banda 2006).

5. Parliamentary Act no. 16, dated April 19, 1987.

6. *Kwacha* means "dawn" in several Zambian languages. It was one of the key phrases in early nationalist slogans of the 1950s and is the basic unit of Zambian currency.

7. ZNBC news continued to follow the basic formula of treating the state, and particularly the president, as newsworthy, regardless of the actual details of a given event and its impact on other events. See Kasoma 1989 and 1997.

8. A link to a live stream of ZNBC Radio 1 can be found on www.coppernet.zm. Urgent personal news in Bemba can be heard on Sunday mornings at 9:30 AM and on Wednesdays at 8:55–9:00 PM and 9:45–10:00 PM, among other times. A live stream of ZNBC's English-language Radio 2 (formerly the General Service) is not available.

9. In recent years, cell phones have become more prevalent across all sectors of Zambian society, and these are often used for urgent personal messages as well.

10. Significantly, in the country's most extensive national survey of radio listening, personal call message programs are not mentioned at all (Mytton 1974).

11. This is the case in many other African nations as well. For example, in neighboring Zimbabwe, the radio program *Zviziviso* (Death Notices) is ranked as the third most popular (Scannell 2001: 18). The program airs on Zimbabwe Broadcasting Corporation's Radio 2 and receives hundreds of notices each week. In Ghana, many community

radio stations charge for funeral announcements, and this "account[s] for a significant portion of many stations' incomes" (Heath 2001: 97).

12. This example and others like it are discussed further in Spitulnik 1996.

13. See Fortman 1969. Kaunda was one of colonial Zambia's foremost nationalist leaders. He served as president from independence in 1964 until 1991.

14. Zambia's second and third presidents, Frederick Chiluba (1991–2001) and Levy Mwanawasa (2001–2008), abandoned Kaunda's philosophy of Humanism and moved away from state-sponsored socialism with programs of increased privatization.

15. Kaunda's Humanism was greatly modeled after other African intellectuals' concepts of precapitalist "African socialism," most notably that of Tanzania's first president, Julius Nyerere. While "man-centered," Kaunda's Humanism also drew heavily from his Christian background, as the son of a Church of Scotland minister who was also one of the first African Christian missionaries in the Northern Province of Zambia.

16. During my field research, this interpretation was evident from many of the letters that ZNBC received from listeners, as numerous permutations of the institution's name appeared on envelopes, including Zambia National Broadcasting Cooperation, Zambia National Broadcasting Cooperative, Zambia National Broadcasting Cooperation, Zambia National Broadcasting Corporation Net Work, and ZNBC Cooperation.

17. See also Burdette's (1988) analysis of the rhetoric of Zambian Humanism and Ferguson's (2005) discussion of the pervasive critiques during this time of leaders' "selfishness" and "failure to 'feed the people'" (76–77).

18. ZNBC data for this paragraph derive from personal communication with Doris Mulenga, controller of ZNBC Radio, and George Mubanga, former ZNBC senior producer. Cost of living data derive from Jesuit Centre for Theological Reflection, March 2008 press release, "As Cost of Basic Food Continues to Increase, JCTR Asks for a Heightened Expressive, Operative and Evaluative 'Mainstream' Response." Accessed at www.jctr.org.zm/bnb/PrMarch08.html. Document dated April 12, 2008.

12 Gossip and Resistance

Local News Media in Transition: A Case Study from the Alentejo, Portugal

DORLE DRACKLÉ

In southern Portugal, the center of town is an important place. Imagine a Mediterranean town, with whitewashed houses, narrow streets flooded with sunlight, and a central square where the men meet daily, leaning against buildings, exchanging news and gossip. At Odemira, my fieldwork site, this square is aptly named Praça da má lingua (the gossip corner). It has been a traditional place for the dissemination of news, both under the dictatorship and today, and it is a place of gossip and resistance. The title of a local radio program alludes to this; it is also called *Praça da má lingua,* and its host reads announcements from the local administration, interviews politicians, and commemorates or invents local traditions. Indeed, radio has assumed several of the functions of the "gossip corner." These days, blogs (web logs) are also an important public news medium, and they have effectively taken over the function of opposing unwelcome political conditions. In their (partially anonymous) resistance, they constitute a virtual Praça da má lingua that goes beyond the framework of local news, extending into national issues.

In addition to local radio, a monthly newspaper, published first by the Communist Party and now by the Socialist Party, is also at the disposal of the local county administration. Before the revolution left-wing parties had to disseminate their publications illegally, whereas after the revolution it was representatives of the right-right parties who dubbed the official local newspaper the *Pravda* of the Alentejo and attempted to dislodge it from its dominant position.

In this chapter I explore changes in the public sphere in southern Portugal, particularly in the transmission of news. Beginning with the traditional forms of poetry, music, and gossip, I present these changes using the examples of local radio, local newspapers, and internet web logs. Through ethnographic work with journalists and cultural producers, I show how they employ both traditional and modern electronic media to construct their version of the world through news.

Local media are designed mainly to transmit regional news and provide information on subjects important to the producers. They operate in the gray area between gossip and the national media and cannot be studied outside their local context. They have rarely been studied as a media form, and are often not taken seriously by scholars and city dwellers. However, these media lie at the intersection of everyday life and translocal politics, and thus their study can illuminate the way news is created and disseminated.

The media world of the Alentejo is notable for the diverse ways in which news is spread. Nonprofessionals, with a range of motives, have always played a major role in producing local media. Sophisticated specialist knowledge and journalistic experience or training are not required to work at a newspaper, in radio, or on the internet. With its interactive possibilities, the internet is a logical development of everyday media practices that have a centuries-old history in the Alentejo. Although the technology has changed, the wish to report local events and disseminate news produced by and for the middle class has remained the same. In this chapter I introduce individual media and their producers, exploring the history of the media and the struggle for the final word about the conflicts between the powerful and the powerless in this region.

Media Amateurs

The media landscape of the Alentejo comprises many participants operating at different levels. Only a few full-time journalists are employed at newspapers, radio, and television; they work alongside many other people who prepare special programs (for instance, for radio) or are responsible for certain themes, such as sports or other special events. Journalists are also employed by county and municipal public relations departments, but are often not full-time, having responsibilities in other areas, such as culture or sport. Thus they might report news for the newspapers controlled by the local administration while also organizing cultural or sports events.

Alongside professional journalists there are amateurs, including teachers, engineers, secretaries, administrative staff, and so on. They work as journalists after hours and also during regular work hours for the organization, at varying levels of intensity. Many work without payment.

With the explosive growth of blogs, the discussion about journalistic amateurs has become more intense, as internet sites have appeared on which amateurs compete with professionals. Some were able to show that professional journalists sometimes did bad research. Others seized opportunities to spread neglected information or simply to publish opinions. Amateur journalists assumed the important function of making professional journalism more democratic, with the image of David battling Goliath becoming a prominent mythic metaphor (Reynolds 2006). Meanwhile, opponents point out the potential dangers of badly researched or deceptive amateur journalism.

The debate between professionals and amateurs over blogs was hardly the first of its kind; similar ones had occurred much earlier in the history of media. Whenever a new technology has been introduced, discussions about professionalism have invariably ensued, as they did over the introduction of photography (Barthes 2007; Benjamin 2005). As the technology became established in the nineteenth century, criticism arose of amateur photography and its mass diffusion. Bourdieu (2006: 16f.) first presented a reappraisal of such criticism; applying his concept of "habitus," he reinterpreted it as a criticism of class. One social group deprecates the actions of another because of the perception that the other's use of technology and knowledge would not fit its own definition of appropriateness. The discursive conflicts over the value of amateur journalism on the internet bring to mind Bourdieu's reference to the social position of participants in the earlier debate.

In the region of Alentejo, with its diverse media, class plays an important role. Differences of social position are relevant to the history of the media here, revealing great differences in wealth and poverty, power and powerlessness. The media history of the Alentejo is closely linked to the region's political history and reflects regional social conditions, such as the constant resistance and strategies of the powerless to acquire a media voice in political conflicts. And nonprofessionals have always been among the main characters in this story.

Alentejo Media History

The history of southern Portugal is one of oppression and resistance, and the media in the Alentejo have traditionally participated in these political power struggles. The earliest documented reports of news media in Odemira go back to the late nineteenth century. The first local newspapers appeared at this time and are preserved at the Torre do Tombo, the Portuguese national archives, and at the National Library in Lisbon.

To understand the background against which the first newspapers arose, we need a short glimpse of the history of the region, for protest against the structure of ownership and the political situation goes back a long way in the Alentejo. The southern Portuguese province of Alentejo lies below the river Tejo (Alem Téjo) and extends to the southern dividing range that separates the Alentejo from the province of Algarve. The Alentejo has a Mediterranean climate, so its agricultural productivity is limited. Since the Reconquista in the thirteenth century, the land has been divided into large estates (*latifundia*), whose fields were tilled by poor farmworkers. With the middle-class revolution in Portugal in the mid-nineteenth century, the first calls by farmworkers became audible, as they demanded grants of communal land, in order to cultivate gardens and keep animals for their own use. Without these fields, the farmworkers would no longer be able to feed their families. Vast stretches of the *latifundia* lay fallow, and with the beginnings of agrarian capitalism the lives of the workers deteriorated further. The feeling of powerlessness and dependence on landowners was vented in the protests of those who lost their jobs.[1]

Toward the end of the nineteenth century, news of new social movements, particularly of Andalusian anarchism, penetrated to the Alentejo. In the 1880s Andalusia had been the scene of farmworker revolts that had been brutally crushed (Kaplan 1977: 206f.; see also Mintz 1994). Refugees and itinerant laborers from Andalusia spread the news that unjust rule was not a law of nature (Quaresma 1989, 2006). Since most of the rural population were illiterate and could not read newspapers, the task of bringing this news fell to itinerant political agitators. In place of newspapers there flourished a distinctive oral culture, particularly in the Alentejo (Lima 1997: 47ff.). Every village had at least one inhabitant who knew how to rhyme and set the events of the day into verse at celebrations or evenings in the tavern. They were known as *poetas populares*, folk poets. There were also wandering poets, such as the well-known blind bard who went from village to village, spreading news in verse form, reciting stories, and offering folk literature (*literatura de cordel*) for sale at saints' festivals, markets, or on Sundays in front of the church (Braga 1885; Nogueira 2000, 2004). This oral culture of the Alentejo was bound up with a cooperative form of labor; just as today, farm laborers worked in groups of 15 to 20 in the vast fields of the great estates. While they worked, they sang, recited oral literature and *poesia popular,* made rhyming jokes, and discussed the latest events. Gossip functioned as a form of social control.[2]

In his novel *Levantado do chão* (1980), Nobel Laureate José Saramago described this time, based on interviews with farmworkers. The novel describes how farmworkers began to organize themselves, and some learned to read and write and produced pamphlets. The first serious revolts occurred in 1917 when a group of farmworkers in the county of Odemira expropriated the property of big landowners and set up a farming cooperative (Rocha and Labaredas 1982). In accordance with the anarchist motto "The land to those who work it!" the landless now worked the soil under their own direction. After a few weeks, this experiment was brutally brought to an end by the government.

In spite of this bitter disappointment, the idea of the just distribution of property had taken hold and continued to determine the political activities of farmworkers even during the 50 years of the fascist dictatorship. After the 1974 revolution, the anarchist farmworkers' movement was reinvigorated, and again they founded cooperatives, inspired by the same political ideas. During the dictatorship years, news, information, and suppressed reports had been spread by stories told by itinerant laborers and the distribution of pamphlets, often by cadres that had formed around the illegal trade unions and the Communist Party. They roamed the countryside of the Alentejo, depositing pamphlets, party newspapers, and political writings at arranged places where the villagers collected them. All these activities were, of course, illegal and punished severely if discovered. Resistance to the fascist dictatorship was the most important motive for the dissemination of news by the organized farmworkers.

The First Newspapers

In the 1880s the Republican Party of Portugal became journalistically active. This party gathered together all the liberal (that is, antimonarchist) forces that demanded a civil constitution. It was Portugal's first modern, anticlerical political party, working for a separation of church and state and including women who championed the cause of emancipation. The demand for democracy and free elections gained strength against the usual local powers, as writers and artists joined the movement. A typical Republican idea was that the "people" had to be educated by bringing them culture. By "culture," Republicans primarily meant universal formal education (illiteracy was widespread), but also educated pleasures such as theaters, public readings, books, newspapers, and exhibitions. The earliest local newspapers, published by local chapters of the Republican Party, appeared in this decade. They were published even in the remotest regions of the country, like Odemira, where the first Republican weeklies, individual copies of which are preserved at the national archives, were called *Voice of Odemira* (*Voz de Odemira*) of 1893 and the *Odemiran* (*O Odemirense*) of 1897.

These newspapers were tailored to the middle class of the region, addressing the families of big and average landowners who lived in the agrotowns, as well as doctors, teachers, shop owners, and small industrialists. The writers were engaged citizens and members of the Republican Party. The papers contained poems and stories by local and national writers, reports of party activities, news of performances by traveling theater groups, balls, charity organizations, local markets, and farming affairs. And finally, they contained narratives of regional gossip such as when and how members of the upper classes planned to take their summer seaside vacations. The favored resort lay 30 kilometers downstream at the mouth of the Mira River, accessible only by ship. Departures of large households, with servants, children, animals, and provisions for several months, must have been a spectacle (Quaresma 2004: 7–8).

Local newspapers forged a link between subjects of national importance and those being talked about in everyday life. Local grievances were aired, and these early papers already show a trend among the middle class to take up folkloristic elements of the "people," such as harvest customs of the "simple" farmworkers.[3] The few extant copies of these newspapers may be supplemented by several issues of the newspaper *Echo from Mira* (*Ecos do Mira*), which probably appeared between 1914 and 1917.[4] *The Voice from Mira* (*A Voz do Mira*) of 1932 was a local newspaper produced by and for the middle class; because of the advent of the dictatorship and the introduction of censorship, its publication soon ceased.[5]

The best surviving record of these historical newspapers in Odemira is the *Odemirense*, five years (1955–60) of whose back issues have been almost completely preserved in the National Library. The *Odemirense* appeared every two weeks and was the property of the son of a local big landowner, António Joaquim da Silva. Its director and most important amateur journalist was Alberto José de Almeida, son of a businessman and husband of an heiress to a large estate. In 1956, he became president of the Câmara, the county commission of Odemira.[6] His vision of the future was strongly influenced by the modern world and can be discerned in the title design of the newspaper: the name *Odemirense* is flanked on the left by an electric mast whose cables are drawn through the lettering. This vision soon became reality, for the commissioner ensured that electrification came to the county seat in 1960. Under the title *Odemirense* stands the following declaration: "The fortnightly defender of county interests." One hears the implication that the paper defends local interests against encroachments by the national government.

The defense of the local is ambivalent. On the one hand, the *Odemirense* invokes a sense of home and the high value of local culture; at the same time, it knows the county is dependent on investments from the Lisbon government. It admires technical innovations and desires them for the county. On the other hand, national forces are held responsible for developments that fail to materialize. The tenor of the paper suggests that if the county had to rely upon its own financial resources, nothing could happen. Torn between these positions, the amateur journalists espouse *bairrismo*,[7] a parochial praise of home that is accompanied by a rejection of everything outside. This includes the praise of old local traditions that are believed to be documented, references to local history, achievements of the citizens, and the virtues of the local way of life.

We recognize here the proud patriotism of the local elite, which has a strong undertone of nostalgia. Custódio Dimas, a local businessman, quotes more than a page of songs and poems that used to be sung in the *bairros* and that focus on the days of childhood. He invokes the good old days and exclaims, "Odemira sings no more" (*Odemirense* 35, 1956: 2). Along with sadness over what is lost, there is a clear sense that citizens of Odemira feel that their community is inferior to the cities, where everything works better. The paper criticizes the conduct of the local saints' festivals: the procession was insufficiently dignified, the auctioning of donations to the saints was disorderly, the fireworks display was too short, and the local band was unworthy of the occasion and played off-key (*Odemirense* 42, 1956: 5). In short, the provinciality of the county is at issue. Photographs show streets decorated for the festivals.

The defense of the *bairros* also includes criticism of individuals who work against the interests of the community. In full public view, for instance, the paper criticizes Odemira's single baker because he first delivers his bread in the afternoon and even then has really only warmed up the bread from yesterday. Other items are found in every local newspaper: obituaries of illustrious citizens, sports, news, theater and musical events, public readings, interviews with artists, announcements, lost-and-found notices, and business advertisements. The local court publishes its notices and proclamations; the county commission announces which new roads have been opened and which city quarters have been electrified or equipped with sewers and running water.

In addition to *bairrismo,* with its defense of local interests, the *Odemirense* developed a new theme, reminiscent of the Republican newspapers and their sense of a new era dawning: the county of Odemira is moving toward a better future! The hope of modernization, progress, and prosperity accompanied the complaints against abuses that stood in its way. Criticism was directed against both local stagnation and central government inaction — diplomatically, but openly. The *Odemirense* published articles on deficiencies in highways, housing and subsidies for housing construction, local banks, support for agriculture, and general infrastructure.

Through the newspaper, amateur journalists succeeded in forging links to various levels of power in the centralized fascist state, making use of the publication channels that are important to establish the necessary contacts. The component of resistance was addressed as an appeal to local residents who did not want to invest and participate in modernization, as much as to the government, and was often framed in everyday speech, containing aspects of gossip among citizens.

The Newspaper of the County Commission

Following the revolution in 1974, power relations in the Alentejo, and thus those in the county of Odemira, changed significantly. Farmworkers occupied many of the great estates and founded farming cooperatives (Dracklé 1991). Politics changed radically. The Câmara, the county commission, was taken over by the

Communists and remained in their hands for the next 20 years.[8] It was modernized and later staffed with young members who came from professional schools and universities, rather than by the progeny of local elite families practically by right of inheritance. Training and technical expertise were now required to keep abreast of the interests of the county. Thanks to education, the children of the lower social classes, such as children of farmworkers, also received access to higher and secure positions in the administration.

After a couple of years of political upheaval and commotion, the county commission began to attend to its public relations. In other Alentejean counties, administrative proclamations were printed and published, and Odemira began in November 1980 to issue a monthly *Bulletin Municipal*. It served mainly to describe the problems of the county (inadequate sewers, water, electricity, medical services, and roads) and to provide mixed news for the citizens. It was understood as the mouthpiece of the working class, which here meant the farmworkers. The *Bulletin Municipal* was distributed to all the municipalities of the county, but when 10 years later the readership began to decline, the county commission began publishing a more modern periodical. This was the newspaper *Notícias de Odemira,* under the editorship of João Honrado, a writer, activist, and censor for the Communist Party. The county commissioner, Justino Santos, was the publisher. Circulation in the first years of its existence was about 3,000 readers.[9] Production, distribution, and the forwarding of issues to emigrants in Portugal and abroad were undertaken by the county commission. The plan of the newspaper producers was to continue printing the former contents of the *Bulletin* but also to expand its horizon and make it more interesting by establishing selective journalistic accents. The most important device for this was the editorial, with the new paper containing more news and opinions. Politically, it was sworn to the Communist line of the Câmara at this time. The amateur journalists received assistance from professional journalists and photographers of the likewise Communist-oriented weekly *Diário do Alentejo,* which was published in the capital of the district of Beja and financed by several Alentejean county commissions.

The journalistic strategy for the newspaper was carefully weighed. In an interview, João Honrado,[10] the editor-in-chief, described to me his vision of the paper and its amateur journalists: "Look, a privately owned commercial newspaper couldn't exist here. You need three or four professional journalists. Not many people here buy newspapers at all. You have to deliver the product everywhere and look after the subscriptions, and so on. You would have to be a multimillionaire and always throwing money into it, but even that wouldn't help at some point; there are enough examples. It's quite clear to us that we aren't professional journalists, but we see the positive side to this: we can work much more openly and write about concerns that are more important to local residents."

Our conversation finally touched on the difference between cultural anthropologists and journalists. "Take the village Malavado. Why is it called that? We journalists can give a short account of the social and economic history of the name in an article. But scholars write books and can't bother about such details; they simply drop out." And, Honrado went on to say, the journalists of *Notícias de Odemira* could work up marginal histories that happened years ago. Much later the material could serve as a clue worth pursuing for scholars.

In the course of my fieldwork, Honrado and I met frequently at election rallies, public hearings, festivals and agricultural fairs, and at the harbor, where I was recording information about local fishermen suffering under restrictions on the number of fish they could catch. The journalists of *Notícias de Odemira* reported on the purportedly old traditions of fishing on the coast and introduced me to the Communist fishermen. I later wrote an article about EU subsidies and their effect on fishermen in the county (Dracklé 1996). During my meetings with Honrado, we sometimes talked about the different perspectives that led us to eye the publications of the other critically.

With its newspaper, the county commission defended its own policies — not only in the editorials. Naturally, this drew constant complaints from socialist, liberal, and rightist resistance parties, who protested against the squandering of public money for a publication that they called the *Pravda* of the Alentejo. Although it is true that the newspaper's tone was leftist, its contents were strongly reminiscent of the themes of the Republican newspapers and the *Odemirense*: defense of home and protest about the deficient financial and moral support from central government. As before, there were photographs of processions and city quarters decorated for saints' feast days; local folklore and poems rubbed shoulders with recipes for Alentejean dishes. There were stories about the mistakes of the big landowners and their heirs, who still refused to invest in the county economy, just like their fathers, as well as reports about Communist writers and the latest achievements of the Câmara, about sports events and functions for young people.

The newspaper was also used as a mediating power to intervene in the national discussion. In the 1990s there were repeated attacks in national papers by famous journalists who held the Communist county commission responsible for the drastic rise in environmental pollution in the nature park on the Vicentinian coast. In addition to the television appearances of local politicians and of the commissioner himself, the *Notícias de Odemira* regularly published open letters, counterstatements, and resolutions of the Câmara condemning defamatory articles in the national press. In this way the county commission created its own source of power in the local and national public.

The publisher of the *Notícias de Odemira* is now the socialist county commissioner, António Camilo. In the nearly 20 years of its existence, the look of the newspaper has been modernized, but amateur journalists are still mainly responsible for its content, and it still stresses local traditions through poems, stories, and photographs. The editorial remains, but the political tone has grown milder. The harsh resistance against the central government has been moderated; after all, the Socialist Party currently rules in Lisbon. Nevertheless, complaints accompanied by clear demands for support from central government can still be heard.

Radio Práia

An interesting aspect of my fieldwork in the Alentejo was that from the outset I was constantly photographed, filmed, and interviewed by inhabitants, interviewees, and amateur journalists. I had chosen this place because I wanted to study underdevelopment and conflicts over economy, corruption, and bureaucracy in a marginalized region of Europe. Yet I was seeing, for example, a county commissioner who was using a mobile phone in 1991, which was uncommon in Germany at the time. As a postdoctoral researcher with a slender income and little technology, my backwardness in this respect was noted. Further, I was often asked why I as an anthropologist was conducting research in Odemira: were the people here "Indians in a reservation in some jungle" (see also Krauss 1996)? At first I was startled by this question; then it made me reflect on the way in which my own prejudices and fears were intermingled with those of my acquaintances in the region. Who likes being an "Indian"? Who likes being thought of as underdeveloped? Not even postdoctoral researchers who lack the appropriate technological equipment.

On my first day, when I approached the county commissioner to submit my request to carry out studies among his staff, he referred me straightaway to the head of the county office of culture, Deodato Santos. Santos is an artist and writer who has been released from his duties as a teacher to take this post. In the course of a long interview with him about local "culture" and cultural anthropology in general, he invited me to conduct the same interview the next day on local radio. He produced two radio shows that were broadcast weekly on Rádio Praia. One was called *Praça da má lingua*. There he would let his listeners hear how a cultural anthropologist goes about her work. Then, when I began looking for interviewees, potential partners would already be in the know and receive me more openly. This was the way, he said, information was passed on here: through gossip.

The live interview turned into a kind of field research initiation disaster. At first it went smoothly, but in the course of conversation, Santos suddenly turned the tables and began interviewing me. Why had I come here of all places to do research? How had I chosen my subject? What results could I already show? And was I aware that people were saying that an anthropologist studies Indians in reservations and not people here in the Alentejo? I attempted to get out of this as elegantly as I could. In the next days and weeks I learned that all my interviewees had listened to the broadcast; my introduction to the radio audience had proved to be a marvelous door-opener. An artist and poet with whom I met years later could still remember the broadcast exactly. The deeper effect, however, was that I was drawn into the work of the head cultural official of the Câmara and he into mine; we began working for one another, each for the other's view of art and culture. He helped me get started with my "cultural anthropology" project, and I helped him in building up his "cultural" project, and I noticed again that the microphone had changed hands.[11] I had surrendered control of the microphone and thus control over the interpretation of situations, concepts, and narratives. He and I had become almost accomplices, while each pursuing our own cultural project. I became an artist and an amateur journalist while Santos became a cultural anthropologist. Following my interview with him, interviews became a hallmark of his broadcast. He invited guests who could say something about the history of the region — politicians, local historians, artists, craftsmen — and he encouraged them all to talk about the past, their lives, or their work. As in a radio show in the neighboring municipality of Castro Verde, listeners in remote villages and farms could call and tell their stories, play or sing songs, or simply participate in the discussion.[12]

Rádio Praia had begun as a pirate radio station in the late 1980s in the village of Zambujeira do Mar, at a time when pirate stations were springing up throughout the country. The founders of the station were the architect António Camilo (today county commissioner) and three descendants of big landowners, two of whom ran the well-known village discothèque Clube da Praia. The producers had set themselves the goal of countering the local media, dominated by the Communist county commission, with a politically independent radio station that would permit a variety of opinions. The four founders soon put the everyday direction of the broadcasts into the hands of an amateur journalist, the disc jockey at the local discothèque, Luís Martins. In 1988, the government shut down the pirate stations and initiated proceedings to legalize local broadcasters. In 1989 Rádio Praia was able to secure a frequency, and it chose the legal form of a cooperative, for which the five previously mentioned associates were registered as partners. The excitement of producing radio soon cooled down into everyday business. Martins came to journalism from advertising and had to learn his new craft by doing it. The knowledge he had acquired as a DJ helped him in designing the musical form of the broadcasts and dealing with the technical side of things. The four other partners soon retired from the business and did not make further investments in it. Camilo devoted himself to his political career as a candidate of the Socialist Party. Martins, now the boss of three employees, attended to the routine work; he canvassed for advertising, looked after the bureaucratic business and everyday journalism, and solicited funding. Although the local county commission maintained a weekly broadcast at Rádio Praia, it provided the station with no financial assistance, as that would have been against the law. Over the years, Martins negotiated with the commission to be given at least equipment. The commission declined; after all, the candidate for the opposition was one of the owners of the station, and the others were the sons of big landowners. There was already enough money there, it was said, and the Câmara had more urgent business than to support rich men's radio stations. In this way the once-successful Rádio Praia fell into a stagnation from which it never recovered, and it shut down.

Blogs

Blogs have become increasingly important as the site of local discussion in the Alentejo. The most interesting aspect of these blogs is that most, and particularly those which have attained some publicity, were created anonymously. The comments on individual articles are also made anonymously. Blogs thus offer an excellent opportunity for the further development of the long-standing characteristics of local news: gossip and resistance. The internet creates a broader accessibility; many local blogs have even attracted national attention.

One of these blogs, whose subject is the administration of the neighboring district, is notorious for its tough criticism. Opened in June 2003, the blog *Mais Évora* (http://maisevora.blogspot.com) has devoted itself, with much verve and commitment on the part of its anonymous blogger and amateur journalist, "Manoelinho," to passing on information, proposals, and opinions that are "naturally subjective, come from the center of the city, and [circulate] rumors and biting criticism." Like local newspapers, it features photographs of the place, poems, tips on literary and other events, reports on local happenings, and commentary on national politics. Since its beginning, the blog author has composed almost a daily polemic against the local county commissioner of the Socialist Party (PS). In the 2001 local elections in Évora, the Communist Party (PCP) lost power to the PS. The accusations against the new PS county commissioner focus on dubious relations to real estate firms, corrupt dealings with public monies for private advantage, and favoritism in awarding contracts to administration employees — the same sort of accusations that always circulate in the gossip corner of the Praça. On the internet, however, they were supplemented by copies of official and unofficial letters, which sounded so well informed that they seemed to emanate from the center of the administration itself.

In January 2005, the county commissioner submitted a complaint to the Ministry of the Interior against persons unknown on grounds of systematic defamation directed personally against him and, in view of its wealth of information, presumably originating in the Câmara itself. He suspected members of the PCP who belonged to the Câmara staff of continuing the election campaign by other means. On January 26, 2008, a commemorative entry on *Mais Évora* recalled this date and explained the blogger's position: We are not living in ancient Rome where the messenger of bad tidings was killed. The author had no conspiratorial motives in posting the information online; he wrote about the abuses because corruption and nepotism in the administration and politics should be made public.

As it turned out, the Ministry did not pursue the county commissioner's complaint, and as of March 2008 *Mais Évora* continued to publish daily stories documenting his dubious dealings. In Évora the talk is of a blog war between staff members of the county commission that began roughly when the county commissioner's complaint was made public. Since then, angry and defamatory comments are sent in response to Manoelinho's every entry, as the opponents conduct their feud on the internet with unflagging energy. Many people occupy themselves for hours every day with their adversaries and the political debate, employing traditional amateur journalistic methods.

Not all blogs are so lively. Many are built more like a website, adding a piece of news now and then. Most of the regional blogs treat events in their small towns or have fixed themes, such as traditional music and folklore (e.g., José Matos at www.blogfixe.com).What they frequently have in common is their layout and criticism of local politics. Texts are accompanied by photographs or short films about abuses, mixed with cooking recipes, poems, stories about cases of corruption, laments about the times (architectural eyesores, the wildness of the young, the failure of the schools), or concrete complaints about the methods of the police, their entanglement in smuggling (the coast is notorious for drug and cigarette smuggling), and environmental destruction, as described on milfontex.blogspot.com.

Local News Media in Transition

Local media are closer to their audience, closer to the scene of events, closer to the life of the community. Local media in the Alentejo make it possible for many interested nonprofessional journalists to publish their views, broadcast news, express opinions, and take part in the construction of the real and the virtual communities (and their intermediate stages). Similarities can be recognized among the various local media in the Alentejo that run through their entire history. The similarities lie in the forms and contents, even while each medium and historical situation is completely different. In the course of a century, the Alentejo has witnessed the activities of Republican, Fascist, Communist, and Socialist cultural producers. Continuity and change are simultaneous, in the habitus of the media producers and in their products. Every form of expression here is bound up with the wish to put knowledge of local politics and its difficulties into words and to oppose the local administration or the central government and its supposed neglect of the region. Yet this wish to fly one's colors in public is also hedged with caution. The traditional narrative forms in which information is passed permit people to express themselves in the form of gossip and thereby to remain more or less anonymous — in the gossip corner of the city, as the "voice of the people." Through gossip, one can have an effect.

During the dictatorship and in the exciting years after the revolution, many Alentejeans learned it is dangerous to express themselves in public. There is censorship, and the tradition of publishing opinion anonymously did not arise without reason. Although gossip is anonymous, it clearly signals resistance in a place where everybody knows everybody else and power relations among the social classes are particularly marked. Research and objective presentation, as enshrined in the ideal of the professional journalist, is emphasized less when everyone knows the author and can compare the attitudes in his articles to knowledge of his person. When information remains anonymous, one can surmise its origins. As they learn to assess journalistic work in supraregional media, so too Alentejeans have accommodated themselves to censorship — whether it is the censorship of the fascists, censorship exercised by the Stalinist Communist Party apparatus, or the censorship of opinion at the *Praça da má língua*, whose influence penetrates into blogs, radio, and television. And the members of the elites continue to engage in conversations with each other through their activities as amateur journalists.

The democratization of the media in the Alentejo has been extended from the old to the new elites, to the younger generation that was educated after the revolution. In addition to the technological elites, there are now various cultural producers — artists, musicians, and political activists who engage in local media production. They think it is important to communicate their version of the "world" to others and to assert their outlook against resistance. The subtleties of the microlevel reveal a complex tissue of power relations that define the social relations of people to each other, and media are used within these relations to strengthen positions. The study of local media shows us the whole complexity, enmeshment, and disorderliness of life. As yet, there are relatively few anthropological studies of local media; more research on the phenomenon of local amateur journalists will enable us to grasp media not as isolated, independent functions in a society but rather as concrete realities within a personal, historical, and power-related context.

Notes

The information in this article was collected during several periods of fieldwork in Portugal, beginning in 1987. The basic ideas were developed during my tenure as visiting distinguished professor (Hélio and Amélia Pedroso/Luso–American Foundation Endowed Chair in Portuguese Studies) at the University of Massachusetts at Dartmouth in 2007. I would like to thank my colleagues there, particularly Andrea Klimt, for the many interesting discussions during my stay.

1. On the history of the Alentejo, see Dracklé 1991, Krauss 2001, Oliveira Marques 1998, and Saraiva 1993.

2. The arguments presented here are drawn from interviews and participant observation (cf. Dracklé 1991). According to various scholarly studies, the phase of oral literature extends to our own times, if no longer with the same intensity. Illiteracy is still high in the Alentejo, particularly among the older population. On current oral literature, see Lima 1997: 60 and Krauss 1998.

3. At this time the first monographs about customs, rites, and objects of rural life in the Alentejo appeared, written by members of the middle class (e.g., Picão 1983).

4. The Mira is the river flowing through the county of Odemira, transport route for agricultural goods. This changed with the construction of the railway at the beginning of the twentieth century, and by midcentury the first roads were built that enabled transport to Lisbon. *Ecos do Mira* probably ceased publication due to the unstable political situation in Portugal in 1917.

5. In interviews, I learned of the journal *O Idealista,* published by the writer "Adorinha" (the swallow), who was the daughter of one of the big local landowners. No copies of it exist in the libraries and archives. Journals were also published in several smaller communities in the county, for example, the *Journal de Sabóia* in Colos, S. Luis, and Sabóia. Unfortunately, there are also no extant copies.

6. The Portuguese position of president of the Câmara corresponds to the American county commissioner or the German *Landrat* and is the highest ranking official at the county level. Almeida held the position from the fascist period until the revolution in 1974. During my first field trip in the early 1990s, I conducted several interviews with him.

7. *Bairro* means quarter, community, or neighborhood. The theme of *bairrismo* repeatedly came up during my fieldwork ("I don't like *bairrismos,* but . . ."). It is regularly discussed in the features pages of the newspapers and appears repeatedly in literature. Inhabitants of the capital and the national elites, on the other hand, point out the provinciality and exaggerated patriotism of this attitude.

8. The Communist Party of Portugal (PCP) cleaves to the Stalinist party line, from which it has never distanced itself — the only Communist party in Europe that has never done so.

9. The county of Odemira has about 30,000 inhabitants. Today the paper's circulation has doubled to 6,000 readers per issue. *Notícias de Odemira* no longer appears monthly, and it has been transformed from a black-and-white newspaper to one with a colorful format presented on better paper and with more pages.

10. The interview with Honrado took place in November 1991, close to the start of the newspaper's publication. After the change of the political staff of the county commission at the end of the 1990s, the paper was taken over by the socialist leadership of

the commission. The director of the newspaper and county commissioner was now António Camilo of the Socialist Party, who had previously been editor-in-chief and co-founder of Rádio Praia. João Honrado is a writer and activist for the Communist Party. During the fascist period, he was active in the underground and imprisoned for many years.

11. Faye Ginsburg calls this movement the "parallax effect" (1995). Cf. Himpele 2002 on the similar beginning of his fieldwork on Bolivian television.

12. The radio show in Castro Verde is described by Reis (2006).

13 Musical News

Popular Music in Political Movements

MARK PEDELTY

What do audiences get from listening to politicized pop? Does it persuade? Motivate political action? Build community? Inform? I have been working with a team of undergraduate and graduate students to answer those questions, incorporating participant observation, interviews, and quantitative content analysis into a coordinated ethnographic endeavor.

In order to provide a broader context for those local projects, I also administered a survey to political activists around the United States. The results were somewhat surprising. In addition to the expected finding — that music performs an important community-building function — it is clear that music plays an informational role in the political lives of activists. Evidently, the ancient tradition of musical news is not completely dead.

History

Music and news share a common ancestry. The lyrical poems of ancient Greece performed informational functions, both in choral form (Ingalls 1999: 392) and as spoken word. However, the topical songs of ancient Greece mainly provided mythical accounts of events long past. The distance separating audiences and events had collapsed a bit by the medieval period in Europe. Itinerant minstrels sang ballads of battles, leaders, edicts, and natural disasters, in many ways paralleling contemporary journalism in function, if not form. The invention of the printing press did not diminish this tradition. In the fifteenth through seventeenth centuries, printed broadsides assisted balladeers as they continued to deliver the news in song (Stephens 1988: 100). The invention of the newspaper in the seventeenth century and the spread of literacy gradually did away with the balladeers, but it was a process that took centuries.

As late as the twentieth century, Mexican balladeers continued to practice the ancient musical news tradition. As war ravaged the Mexican countryside, cutting off rural villagers from metropolitan news sources, guitarists traveled from town to town singing songs about major battles, generals, presidents, and *Yanqui* interventions. Even during the postrevolutionary period, these *corridos* (literally, "that which is current") served as the "newspaper of the folk" (Redfield 1930: 186). Although they have lost their central news role, these *corridistas* continue to provide critical news commentary in Mexico (Wald 2001).

Why has music served a central journalistic role in so many historical and cultural contexts? First, music is an excellent mnemonic device. Rhyming verse is an effective means of remembering, retelling, and recording events in oral cultures. Therefore, balladeers and *corridistas* were judged in large part by the length of their repertoire and the amount of information they could retain. Musical rhyme also helps audiences remember news details. Labor organizer and musician Joe Hill explains: "A pamphlet, no matter how good, is never read more than once, but a song is learned by heart and repeated over and over; and I maintain that if a person can put a few cold, common sense facts into a song, and dress them up in a cloak of humor to take the dryness off of them, he will succeed in reaching a great number of workers who are too unintelligent or too indifferent to read a pamphlet or an editorial on economic science" (Smith 1984: 19).

Second, one can project his or her voice much further and for a longer period when singing than when simply shouting. Musical news kept the ancestral "news anchor" from becoming hoarse.

Third, musical technology can be relatively simple and is universally understood. Neither a printing press nor literacy is required, just a voice and possibly a lyre, guitar, or drum.

Finally, musical performances attracted larger audiences than would have been possible with spoken word alone. The aesthetic advantages of music were no less important to the balladeers than they are to contemporary TV news broadcasters. The latter still score news stories with any number of musical accompaniments, including temporal and tonal variations of the program's signature song. The modern musical news score is arranged to emphasize the tragic, unsettling, or uplifting nature of a news story, changing with the event and broadcaster's intent.

However, although music still plays a role in news delivery, few would argue that it is a central one. Music is no longer the essential source of news it was in medieval Europe or revolutionary Mexico. Although scholars of contemporary popular music might occasionally mention its informational possibilities, popular music is more often viewed as an ideological narcotic or, in the case of political pop, a community-building tool. Rarely is the informational content or function of popular music taken very seriously.

The Political Functions of Popular Music

Scholars have downplayed the informational elements of political music, instead emphasizing its community-building potential. Ray Pratt argues that by "affectively empowering emotional changes, music promotes establishment of sustaining relations of community and subculture," conditions "that are fundamental to creation of an alternative public realm" (1994: 14).

Reebee Garofalo's analysis of musical "mega-events" holds much in common with Pratt's analysis of political pop. Although he recognizes that large benefit concerts are "no substitute for a political movement," Garofalo sees great potential in the "contested terrain" of popular music: "It is in this fertile arena, with all of its contradictions, that progressive forces must either make their voices heard or risk being relegated to the margins of political struggle" (1992: 35). For both Garofalo and Pratt, music can provide a means to mobilize counter publics and potentially inspire political change.

Mark Mattern places even greater emphasis on community than Pratt and Garofalo. Mattern argues that music can serve as either "social cement or social solvent" (1998: 144), but ultimately he sees music as an essential element for defining communities, both internally and externally. Mattern's main thrust is very much in line with that of Pratt, Garofalo, and most scholars of political pop. Mattern argues, "The communities that musicians have helped to form and sustain provide the social basis for political action that would be difficult or impossible among individuals who are not tied together in this way" (1998: 5).

While many scholars have argued that music serves a community-building function, few have claimed an informational role for popular music. Conversely, music journalists and musicians often make that claim. For example, music journalist Pat Gilbert argues that "the Clash may have woken up Midwest teenagers to the terrible things their government was doing in their name in Nicaragua and El Salvador" (2004: 364). Similarly, Bob Marley argued that "music is like the news" (McCann 1993: 28). In the following sections I will investigate Marley's claim.

Survey Method

A simple five-question survey was administered to labor, peace, environmental, and human rights activists. The goal was to better understand the functions of music in political movements. The main intention was to gain qualitative knowledge via responses to open-ended prompts. However, the results provided some quantitative insights as well. The questions were as follows:

Question 1: How old are you?

Question 2: Has a musician or song ever informed you about a political, social, or environmental issue, person, or event that you had not previously heard of?

Question 3: Has listening to a musician or song ever caused you to think or feel differently about an issue?

Question 4: Has a musician or song ever inspired you to act on an issue or provided extra inspiration for actions that you were already taking in regard to an issue?

Question 5: Has listening to live or recorded music with other activists ever enhanced your sense of community and shared purpose?

All five questions were delivered on a single page.

I decided to ask whether music had ever fulfilled the specified function, rather than require a higher threshold of effect (e.g., "Does music inform you?"). The latter construct would imply continual, as opposed to occasional, effect. It is important, first, to establish whether music performs a given role before attempting to measure the depth or duration of that function. The open-ended prompt then allows respondents to provide detailed examples. Those examples provide a wider window into the musical lives of the activists.

A website was created for the survey, along with an explanation of the research project and a statement concerning informed consent. Because of the political nature of the survey, no names or identifying demographic data were solicited other than age. As will be seen, this ethical constraint limited the statistical inferences that could be drawn from the resulting survey data.

A request for participation was placed in 30 public online discussion forums. All of the forums are oriented toward labor, peace, environmental, and human rights activists. Messages were also sent directly to the "contact us" e-mail addresses listed for 86 labor, peace, environmental, and human rights organizations based in the United States. It is not known how many of those solicitations were shared with the organizations' members. In the e-mail, staff members were asked to respond to the survey and, if they deemed it appropriate, to share it with other staff and the general membership. No subsequent solicitations or reminders were sent to the discussion sites and organizations, to minimize the sense of personal invasion and coercion.

Pratt notes that the "conception of political action held by nearly 90 percent of the U.S. population in most studies consists of very individualistic acts, for example, voting in presidential elections for the candidates of one of the two pro-capitalist parties" (1994: 204). I hoped that by sending solicitations to organizations actively engaged in political work, I would create a window into the experiences of citizens whose political action goes much further than an occasional vote. I was also interested in developing knowledge that could assist labor, human rights, peace, and environmental organizations in their recruiting and public outreach activities.

Although the list of national organizations was fairly exhaustive, the voluntary and untraceable nature of the responses means that this is not a truly random sampling of members of labor, peace, environmental, and human rights organizations in the United States. It is, instead, the most exhaustive sampling possible without acquiring complete membership lists, which would be neither possible nor ethical given the subject matter. The responses contain descriptions of political activities, including acts of civil disobedience. It would be unethical to solicit, maintain (however temporarily), or publish demographic data that could connect these fairly detailed responses to the respondents.

As a result, rather than a truly random sample, this is a voluntary sample, limiting the potential for statistical inferences to a larger population. Therefore, no tests of external validity were completed. Instead, the following statistics are mostly descriptive, along with a few measures of internal validity.

Results

The survey site was active from April 18 to August 1, 2007. After removing submissions from respondents under 18 years of age, I collected 139 responses in the following age categories:

Age	Respondents
18–29	33
30–39	22
40–49	21
50–59	31
60–69	21
70–86	11
Total	139

Seventy-two percent answered yes to question 2 (informational influence), 54 percent to question 3 (persuasion), 67 percent to question 4 (motivation), and 72 percent to question 5 (community building).

There was a much greater disparity in the number of examples offered. A response was counted as an example if it included the name of a performer, composer, song title, genre, performance context, or a combination thereof. For example, any of the following would be counted as a single example: Bob Dylan, "Hurricane," Bob Dylan's "Hurricane," and Bob Dylan concert. Respondents

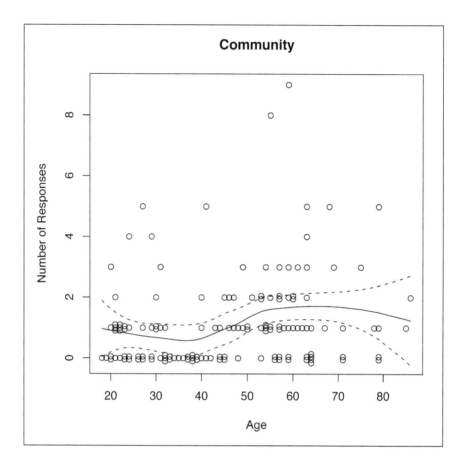

provided 241 examples of informational influence, 123 examples of persuasion, 152 examples of musical motivation, and 160 examples of community building.

Both the qualitative and quantitative data would indicate that the informational function of music might be more important during youth than in the later years. A nonparametric linear regression provides visual illustration.[1] The curved line in each chart represents the mean number of examples. The dotted lines represent confidence bounds. Note the "hump" in the information table for the youngest cohort. Conversely, the youngest cohort is at the low end of the other three response categories.

It would appear that for this sample of activists, the informational role of music is more important for younger respondents. In fact, even the examples offered by older respondents seem to support that conclusion. Most examples offered in response to the information question appear to be drawn from memories of youth rather than recent experience. A few of the answers to question 2:

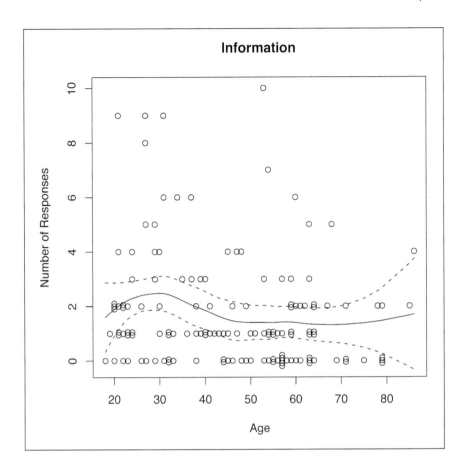

Age 35: "Yes, but mostly when I was really young."

Age 41: "Neil Young, Ohio. Was young and had not heard of Kent State until then."

Age 56: "When I was about 13 years old I heard a rendition of Bob Dylan's song, 'With God on Our Side,' and it helped make me aware of the role religion can play in tribalizing people. I am now an atheist."

Age 71: "Yes, in late childhood or early teens. The Weavers, Pete Seeger, others . . . maltreatment and deportation of migrant workers, aspects of the labor movement, etc."

In other words, an inordinate number of the informational examples from respondents ages 30 to 86 represent musical experiences as adolescents or young adults. Most of the song examples given were first released and, most likely, first experienced when the respondent was a teenager or young adult.

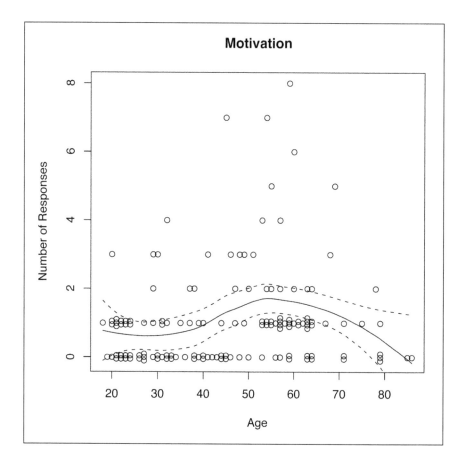

Several respondents explained that hearing about a topic, event, person, or issue in music led them to further exploration:

Age 22, in answer to question 2: "Yes. The first time this happened, I looked up all the books on the CD jacket to Rage Against the Machine's CD and found that my public library didn't carry any of them!"

Age 21, in response to question 3: "Dave Matthews's music inspired me to actually read news about other countries and investigate issues on a deeper level. Their music awakened in me the passion to learn about the world and framed global issues in ways that I could really understand and identify with."

The above respondent also credits Matthews with motivating his or her choice of college majors and careers.

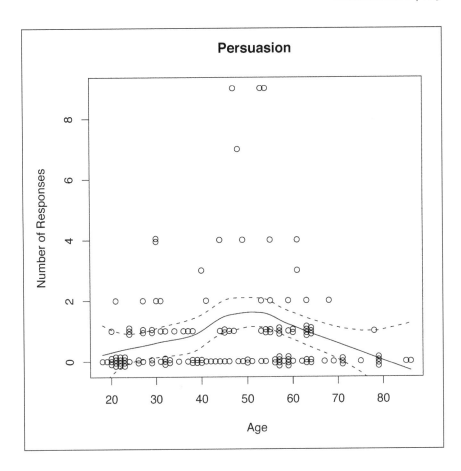

ALTHOUGH QUESTION 2 is the one most directly relevant to the subject of musical news and information, many responses to questions 3, 4, and 5 remain relevant. Questions 3, 4, and 5 take us away from matters of news delivery and consumption (i.e., communicating information) into the realm of production (i.e., motivating action that could potentially result in news events and stories).

There were fewer yes responses and examples listed for question 3 (persuasion) than for any other. Among the affirmative examples:

> Age 29: "'Hurricane' (Bob Dylan) made me reevaluate my stance on the police. That was back in my more GOP obedient days, and the thought that such purposeful misjustice [takes place] led me to at least question the side of authority."
>
> Age 45: "In my struggles to come to terms with the Israel/Palestinian

conflict, the songs of David Rovic HAVE helped me get past my bias for Israel to see that there are TWO PEOPLES' fates at stake. This issue has been the hardest for me to come to terms with, VERY painful. Rovic's songs made Palestinians AS REAL to me as Jews had always been" (caps by respondent).

Age 86: "From an early age I liked military band music, and marches made me feel patriotic. Especially 'The Stars and Stripes Forever' and the national anthem. The Viet Nam era antiwar song 'Where Have All the Flowers Gone?' helped change my opinion of the infallibility of our leaders. 'Blowing in the Wind' made me more aware of human dignity and interdependence."

Many of those who answered no to the persuasion question qualified their responses by explaining that musicians and their songs do not persuade them but instead reinforce their preexisting opinions and political outlooks. As one respondent explained, "They don't change my opinions, but they confirm and intensify them."

The same holds true for motivation. As was true of the persuasion category, there were fewer yes answers in response to the motivation question than in response to the information or community-building questions. Nevertheless, the affirmative responses and examples indicate music can motivate political action. Two examples:

Age 56: "Phil Ochs inspired me to join the Vietnam War protests when I was in college in the late '60s."

Age 57: "'Ohio,' by Crosby, Stills, Nash, and Young inspired me to protest at the Burlington, Iowa, munitions factory after the Kent State riots."

Similarly, a 49-year-old described how seeing Bruce Springsteen in New Orleans after Hurricane Katrina helped strengthen his or her resolve to assist in rebuilding the city.

In question 5, activists were asked whether music had played a community-building role in their lives. A 22-year-old explained that music adds to a group's "sense of shared purpose." Some respondents enthusiastically described their collective musical experiences:

Age 31: "Hell, yeah. It's like being in church, in a way. When you hear truth to power being spoken, it is an incredibly moving, powerful experience, and it helps to be surrounded by others who are feeling it, too."

Age 32: "Maintaining nonviolence in a world so violent is a real challenge, and music helps to create a positive channel for the high emotions that people are feeling as a result of the horrible actions being carried out by factions within the societies of the world."

Others provided more specific examples:

Age 57: "Singing songs of peace together during the protest after Kent State here at the University of Florida was very powerful. To my mind, music is the strongest tool there is for creating community."

One respondent offered critical insight into the difficulties as well as the ultimate goal of musical community building:

Age 20: "I have had conflicting experiences with live music and a sense of community. At some points I do feel like everyone is living in the moment and having fun with 'strangers,' but at other times people are so miserably self-conscious that they cannot break out of their own mind and be in a community."

The above response indicates that the central goal of community music making, like all rituals, is to form a collective body. In turn, the act of forming a collective body makes it possible to attain shared goals.

There were several interesting trends in terms of musical genre, especially in relation to age. Not surprisingly, rock was by far the dominant genre for young activists. Folk was the most cited genre for older activists.

Surprisingly, of the 676 examples given across all four categories combined, only 12 involved classical composers or performers. A single respondent, a 55-year-old, presented all 12. Although significant academic attention has been paid to the political analysis of classical music, especially in cultural studies, classical music in the European tradition would seem to have little relevance to the political lives of these labor, human rights, peace, and environmental activists.

The final set of results relevant to the news question concern performance context and the cited musicians' geographic reach. Whereas musical news was once anonymously penned and sung by relatively unknown local performers in face-to-face contexts, it is now mainly experienced via copyrighted recordings of well-known musicians. Of the 676 examples offered, only 48 mentioned local musicians. Of those 48 examples, most were fairly generic descriptions of participatory events, ranging from impromptu drumming in the street to organized bands and choral groups. Only a handful actually named a local performer. However, it is in some cases difficult to determine if a soloist or band should be considered "local" or an "indy" act with greater geographic reach.[2]

Given that the activists almost exclusively cited acts with national and global reach, it is fair to say that the musical news discourse travels in roughly the same way as other informational discourses, via electronic mass media. Famous acts — those experienced via recordings and large concerts — were dominant in all four question categories, even community building. Conversely, local acts and participatory forms were restricted almost exclusively to the community-building responses, and even there it is mainly a matter of big-name recording artists and participatory events serving the purpose, not local professional musicians.

Discussion

The results show that music functions as a source of information for many activists. The informational function of music is particularly important for young people. Perhaps this is because youth are less exposed to news and other sources of information, particularly alternatives to the mainstream. Therefore, they are more likely to gain first contact with an event, issue, or person through music. Conversely, older activists, having already added alternative information sources to their repertoire, are less likely to hear about an issue through music. Older activists are already exposed to alternative news sources and know how to actively seek such knowledge.

For young activists, in particular, music may be a gateway into political activism. For them, popular music might play a role in sparking political curiosity and serve as an interlocutor into dissident discourse.

Also, it is clear that "activist groups and organizations do not fare well as sources for news production" (de Jong, Shaw, and Stammers 2005: 6). Activist artists and audiences alike may turn to popular music for political expression and discourse due to their lack of representation in mainstream corporate news. To more fully answer those questions, however, would require additional research.

Having established that popular music plays an informational role for these activists, is it warranted to claim that it therefore serves a "journalistic" function in their lives and work? Is topical music a form of journalism? Admittedly, modern pop songs are fairly shallow in terms of informational content, no matter how rich they might be in emotional context and critical commentary. The audience for Peter Gabriel's *Biko*, for example, learns little beyond the basic facts: a man named "Biko" died "in police room 619" one day during the month of "September 1977" in the town of "Port Elizabeth." The journalists' essential "who, what, where, and when" are there, along with some contextual commentary as to "why," as well as a brooding sense that there was a gross miscarriage of justice. However, the typical news story contains more facts and information than even the most detailed topical pop song.

Yet how much news information do audiences really consume and retain? According to Machill, Köhler, and Waldhauser, news consumers retain little from a story beyond its most basic facts (2007). Based on experimental evidence, they argue that a rich narrative structure helps news audiences better retain information. Songs are rich narrative structures, meaning that although they contain less information, the basic facts might be retained comparatively well. Music might, on occasion, function as an effective headline service.

For many people, news itself is little more than a headline service. In fact, it could be argued that consumers of a typical news organ in the United States must often look elsewhere to get meaningful context and information. Most newspapers and television news programs tend to present fairly brief stories oriented to the basic facts of a story rather than deeper context. While musical journalism is sporadic and highly uneven in its news "coverage," in no way approaching news in that regard, it appears that music might occasionally provide seminal information concerning people, places, events, and issues.

Take the case of Steve Van Zandt. He first heard about Steve Biko's death from Gabriel's song "Biko." That resulted in Van Zandt's powerful "Ain't Gonna Play Sun City" Project (Drewett 2007: 44–45). News concerning South African apartheid was spread via music and a network of performers, audiences, and activists throughout the world. While music is not news per se, popular musicians sometimes perform a journalistic role, one that is more akin to both ancient musical news practices and modern news making than is typically acknowledged.

However, the strongest connection between these two narrative forms, news and topical music, is not their relative lack of contextual depth. Instead, the strongest connection is that news and music are both forms of storytelling. The semiotic salience of a news story or song is largely determined by the degree to which the text-in-performance resonates with dominant cultural values and meta-narratives. Often, the more effectively a song or news story resonates with the audience's mythological world, the more widely it will travel. In journalistic lingo, such stories have "legs." Such songs become hits.

By mapping the growth and travel of an urban legend as it was transformed into news — the story of a fictitious "Angel of Death" who was purposely spreading AIDS during the panic-stricken 1980s — Elizabeth Bird demonstrates that " 'big stories,' 'moral panics,' and even tenacious 'little stories' . . . are not created by journalists alone; rather, journalists may also be the brokers for the stories a culture is already telling" (2003: 163). We "tend to think of news and folklore as the opposite of each other; news is factual and verifiable, while legends are false and unverifiable," explains Bird, yet "the line between news and legend is not so clear" (149).

As popular storytelling forms, topical music and news are close kin. Topical songs and news stories alike must capture the mythological imagination of audiences in order to effectively communicate ideas and information. In fact, even if the manifest content of a story lacks veracity, it may resonate as "true" on a deeper, cultural level. Bird shows that to be the case with a factually inaccurate but culturally salient news story. Contests concerning truth are never restricted to assessments of informational accuracy alone, no matter how much journalists might want to believe that to be the case. They are also matters of meaning, debates of interpretation waged within the mythological and ritual parameters of a given cultural moment and community. For any story to become popular, it must strike a chord beyond its denotative or manifest content, a fact that we readily accept with music but often ignore when it comes to news.

As is also true in journalism, the geographic scale of musical storytelling has changed greatly since the days of the itinerant balladeer. Although local news stories are still popular, most outlets for "local news" are owned and distributed by corporations operating on a decidedly non-local scale. Furthermore, local news tends to emphasize "human interest" and crime stories, leading to a relative dearth of coverage of local politics, economic trends, and other matters with more serious human stakes and collective relevance. For those stories, one generally has to look to national and global news sources.

The same seems to be true of local music. If one wants to listen to meaningful topical music, it is much more likely to come from the record store or website than it is to be heard live in the local café or music club. Granted, even within national and globally distributed popular music, political pop is a relatively small subgenre. However, it is becoming extremely rare at the local level. One of the subprojects referenced earlier is exploring the reasons for this through interviews with local musicians. Although a full accounting of the reasons for the relative lack of local political pop is beyond the scope of this chapter, one overwhelming conclusion is that audiences of local live music, and the contexts within which such performances take place, mitigate the potential for political communication. Local performance sites are much too heavily oriented toward fun and consumption for meaningful political communication to take place. Such communication can take place on a personal level, between iPod and listener, or even in a U2, Pearl Jam, or Ani Difranco concert, but it is considered too much of "a downer" in the clubs, fairs, weddings, corporate events, and other sites where most local music is made and financially supported. That is perhaps one reason why local musicians are largely missing from the activists' survey responses. Local musicians recognize the ideological danger and off-putting incongruity of injecting political content into live performances. Similar pressures may be at work in local news. In music this results in safe songs about romance and sexual angst. In local news it results in stories that stay safely within the parameters of permissible discourse, consensus news.

The lack of locals in the activists' survey responses might also be a matter of name recognition. A 53-year-old wrote, "A folk singer named Danny motivated me about a year ago to work harder for forest protection, after a night of listening to him play songs he had written." Similarly, a 57-year-old activist mentioned enjoying the music of "some young guys" at a political event.

In other words, it might be a question of brand-name recall. Marketing students are told that consumers need to hear a product name at least seven times before they will recall it. Local musicians do not receive the constant brand-name reinforcement that national and globally marketed acts do. Therefore, respondents might not be able to recall the name of a performer they have only heard once, even if the information, persuasion, motivation, or sense of community remains. Conversely, if they hear something from a performer they listen to repeatedly, both the information and source might stick with them. However, based on the survey, there is little evidence that local musicians play a significant role in activists' lives and almost no evidence that they serve an informational function.

The community-building responses raise additional questions concerning how music functions within political movements. The answers demonstrate two types of community building: participatory, localized, face-to-face forms, such as those illustrated by Mattern (1998), and the types of large-scale, mass-mediated networks and events discussed by Pratt (1994) and Garofalo (1992). While face-to-face music making and community building continue to exist, mass-mediated forms of community participation appear to be more common among these activists. The political communities, or perhaps "networks," formed by recorded and broadcast music across great distances of time and space may be as, or even more, important than face-to-face music making.

In fact, the two forms of musical experience are often mixed in the responses. Many of the moments described in the community-building responses involved social interactions around recorded music. For example:

Age 37: "I often share CD compilations of political and revolutionary music with my fellow activists. It does build a sense of community, which is really important to sustaining activism. It is hard work done after working paid jobs, so it's important to have that emotional release that music provides."

Age 50: "Sure. Steve Earle fans frequently discuss among ourselves his politics. Even with those who disagree with his politics, they often respond to his issues with thoughtful responses."

Age 60: "Dylan — listened to coming from the awful Democratic convention in '68 Chicago. My colleague and I felt renewed and restored in the face of danger."

Age 64: "Having even recorded music definitely improves the environment and helps to bring us together, as long as it's not too loud and
intrusive to the proceedings or conversation."

Some of the activists view their communitarian musical practices in contradis-
tinction to mainstream musical consumption. One 30-year-old was particularly articulate on the topic:

> I'd like to point out that the way most Americans experience music is
> vastly different than 100 years ago. When we first hear of a band, it's
> usually been heavily marketed by some corporate media conglomerate
> through promotional crap (I used to work for a public radio station), and
> more importantly, it's recorded. The idea that real music, live and un-
> mediated, can exist out on the streets, in public places, has all but been
> destroyed by the corporate monolith, mainly because Americans lead
> private existences rather than public ones. Most folks who attend con-
> certs have already heard the said band a few times, most likely have their
> albums, and know what to expect. This was not true at the turn of the last
> century. To that end, there are still a few good musicians out there that
> eschew T-shirts, bumper stickers, and other promotional advertising in
> favor of live unamplified sound. The best example of this I can give you
> is of an anarchist jug punk band that embraces the format heard in most
> folk songs — sing-alongs. There are no lead singers. Everyone knows the
> lyrics, and they chant them like drunken pirates. They break the barrier
> between spectator and performer. Indeed, they transcend the entire con-
> cept of identity through the consumption of rebellious music.

As the above respondent indicates, participatory music is the ideal among activists, but not necessarily the norm.

Other responses demonstrate that it is not a simple matter of mass-mediated
music experienced individually (privately) vs. live music shared communally
(public):

Age 27: "It is the duty of any citizen in the know to throw some Rage
Against the Machine, Bad Religion, Slayer, whatever, on the good ol'
iPod and take to Washington."

In line with Pratt's analysis, responses like the one above indicate that activists, like many other audiences, create "a kind of cultural free space made of
materials taken from thousands of composers and musicians who contribute
the essential elements of what is propagated by the culture industries" (1994:
14). There is no intrinsic link between message and medium. The mainstream

products of the culture industries form a large part of the symbolic stock that political communities, both Right and Left, use to further their goals.

Such recycling has been going on for a long time. For example, musician and labor organizer Joe Hill (1879–1915) used sacred hymns to deliver his biting political and secular lyrics. Subsequent musicians drew on Joe Hill's name and music, folding it into new popular contexts. Alfred Hayes's 1930 song "I Dreamed I Saw Joe Hill Last Night" has been performed and recorded by Paul Robeson, Joan Baez, Ani Difranco and Utah Phillips, Billy Bragg, and countless others. In other words, political communities are connected across time and space by recordings and live performances.

Such communities are local, national, global, mass-mediated, recorded, and live. As demonstrated in the survey responses, musically mediated communities are experienced in geographic and temporal isolation — via iPods, radios, and televisions — and face-to-face in large groups. However, even the more individuated forms of consumption can be highly social. Although there are temporal and spatial distances between individual listeners, they are conscious of shared musical, emotional, and political interests with those who are listening to the same music elsewhere. They are alone together, consciously networked into a community of interest in spite of temporal and geographic separation.

Although question 2, regarding information, is the most directly connected to journalism, the community-building aspect of music making referred to in question 5 is not without its journalistic elements. Musical communities form networks through which political information is shared. In other words, music provides information (content) and is also part of the cultural mechanics through which communication is made possible (structure).

Not only are musical communities structural conduits for news but they occasionally produce news as well. The ostensible goal of activist communities is to influence the political behavior of other citizens by forming democratic majorities. While that work takes place via direct contact with other citizens, nonprofit and nongovernmental organizations must also find ways to get messages into mainstream mass media in order to achieve success. That is what makes the "movement-media dance," as Todd Gitlin first described it, so important (1980: 17). As Gitlin notes, the necessity of media appeal is what makes the movement-media dance a constant threat to movement cohesion and purpose.

Grabbing the attention of news media requires more than analytical argumentation. Because the Left tends to be either ignored or denigrated by corporate media, it is not easy for labor, human rights, peace, or environmental advocacy organizations to influence mass audiences. For such groups to grab the headlines requires creativity and hard work, including the production of the sorts of spectacular mass rituals that constitute "newsworthy" events in the minds and practices of mainstream journalists. "For better or for worse," notes Garofalo, "we inhabit the society of the spectacle" (1992: 55). Music plays an essential role in such political spectacles, from the most localized land preservation protests to national presidential conventions. In other words, music informs potential activists, serving as news in and of itself, and it is a tool for activists interested in influencing mainstream news coverage indirectly.

Recommendations and Applications

A few suggestions for practical application have arisen from the survey. The first is aimed at movement organizers. The power of popular music should not be underestimated as a potential tool, especially in reaching younger audiences and potential activists. While it is rarely possible to enlist the assistance of pop stars for local events, it is apparent that their music has great currency and can be productively integrated into organizing activities, even in recorded forms.

The survey also reminds us that popular music has a strong age-related bias. Its application within movements should reflect audience tastes in that and other regards. Perhaps the two most common mistakes at political events are (1) musical acts and genres that do not appeal to the audience, especially potential new activists, and perhaps (2) a tendency to overemphasize local acts, such as singer-songwriters. While many of us retain the romantic notion of local performers stirring the masses to action, it does not appear to represent the music that activists actually listen to or how they listen to it.

When integrating local music into events, the more participatory the better. Participatory ensembles like those represented in the HONK! Festival are ideal in this regard (honkfest.org). They take on all comers, regardless of musical talent, and break the barrier between performer and audience. They are an excellent recruiting tool and a means for forming meaningful political communities oriented around music. In addition to big-name acts, participatory performances and ensembles seem to truly excite respondents.

The second suggestion is for organizers to look beyond event-based politics. It is important to recognize that, with or without organizational involvement, political communication is also taking place through widely distributed communication channels and networks. This is as true for music as it is for other forms of political communication. From the individual iPod-wearing activist to groups of friends discussing the latest Steve Earle CD, clearly much of the political life of activists is taking place electronically and in electronically mediated environments (de Donk, Loader, Nixon, and Rucht 2004; de Jong, Shaw, and Stammers 2005). Face-to-face organizing and live spectacle are complemented, and in some cases even replaced, by asynchronous forms of organization and action. Organizers would do well to find ways to integrate music into electronically mediated environments as intentionally and successfully as they have done with live marches, demonstrations, rallies, and protests. The examples listed by these respondents may already be fulfilling that function, serving as a soundtrack for cyberpolitics.

In the words of one respondent, music "has to be good" to fulfill a meaningful purpose. The most effective music appears to be that which is "good" enough to warrant our troubled attention as an audience (Pratt's Bruce Springsteen or Garofalo's Paul Simon) or, conversely, that which gets the entire community directly involved in music making, regardless of how "good" any single participant is musically (Mattern's community examples). Professional popular music is alive and well on the internet. However, participatory music making is still underdeveloped. New performance, recording, and listening technologies are making it possible for people of all talent levels to express themselves musically. Online organizers should consider drawing on the power of both professional and participatory music to enthuse, connect, and mobilize their fellow activists. Despite their constant condemnation of mass-mediated popular culture in the United States, this is something right-wing journalists like Sean Hannity and Glenn Beck have done quite well, linking grassroots organizing with musical, political, and journalistic performances on a national scale. Hannity's "Freedom Concerts" are perhaps a better model than many liberal and left-wing musical mega-events in that they effectively use sustained online networking and an ongoing series of live, local performances to maintain activist networks. Conversely, many liberal and left-wing benefit concerts are one-off events less connected to local and national movements. Of course, there is a great disparity in resources between the Left and the Right, but that is all the more reason to make up the difference with creativity, recognizing that it takes more than information to engage publics. It also takes pleasure, performance, meaning, and a greater sense of purpose. Music is an ideal form of communication in that regard.

The Ethnographic Project and Future Research

The survey detailed here is part of a larger ethnographic project. The other elements of the project involve a talented team of undergraduate and graduate researchers. Together we are interviewing performers and fans, using quantitative content analysis to examine lyrics, and conducting participant observation at political performance sites.

The survey is providing useful context for the other subprojects. However, it does not probe the deeper cultural meanings and functions of music. It takes participant observation to explore the inextricable relationships linking music, meaning, performers, audiences, and politics, none of which can be reduced to simple, measurable variables.

This is also where the anthropological definition of significance (cultural) might be at odds with the statistical definition of the term. For example, although local musicians might not show up in the survey as a significant political force, they are important in context. Martha Nandorfy's experience in Canadian coffeehouses illustrates the point (2003: 174):

> Memories and hopes confronted the young Canadians who attended the peñas with a reality that seemed to belong to some secret society in that it was spoken about only within that community, while those who relied on television and other mainstream media seemingly knew nothing about the concentration camps, the disappeared, the CIA involvement, and general U.S. support for fascism in Chile and elsewhere in the Americas.

Although not significant in a statistical sense, intimate local performances are nevertheless meaningful to their participants. That is despite, or perhaps due to, their unrepresentative nature. As much as I would have liked such local performance contexts to show up in the survey — challenging a priori beliefs is, after all, the point of such methods — they did not. However, that does not mean that local musicians are not important.

Nevertheless, the survey served its intended purpose. It has provided context and also helped us to redirect our local ethnographic work. Whereas we had been mostly approaching the problem of political music as one of local musicians performing for local audiences in local political contexts, we are doing more to incorporate recorded and participatory forms of music. Whereas we had initially been seeking out local spaces where political music is made, we now recognize that no matter how important such venues are to the dedicated participants, they are just one, somewhat marginal, space for political music making.

In fact, the survey may have helped explain why so little music of a political nature is made locally. There is much less of an intersection between "activist" and "local" musical audiences than I had assumed when initiating the project. While there are several local musicians in the Minneapolis area who incorporate political songs into their repertoires, in our interviews most of these performers have expressed frustration that the political element of their performances is lost on the local audience and is often even unwelcome. Only those who work directly in organizational contexts feel that their political music really hits the mark.

Our participant observation work is leading to a similar conclusion. We formed a band and have been performing at local clubs, the types of places where local musicians find employment. Our audiences have expressed interest in our music, but they generally ignore the lyrics. Only in our quieter solo and duo performances do people seem to recognize that there is a political message and respond to it in post-concert conversations. On the local level, it would seem that political music making is most effective as a tonic for the troops, a way of organizing and energizing the most dedicated core of existing political organizations rather than as a form of political discourse with new audiences or even a general activist audience. If the survey is any indication, the latter are doing what most people do, listening to their favorite bands on their iPods and at the occasional headliner's concert, not at the local club or café.

Before conducting this survey, I underestimated the informational potential of recorded popular music, as has most of the academic literature. It was an odd oversight. When Gilbert wrote that the band Clash "may have woken up Midwest teenagers to the terrible things their government was doing in their name in Nicaragua and El Salvador," he could have been talking about my experience as a teenager (2004: 364). Growing up in Iowa, I first learned about Central American intervention through listening to Clash records, or at least I first came to care about it that way. Their music, along with that of Peter Gabriel and a few others, provided hints that there were legitimate points of view outside the narrow frames debated in mainstream news. Among other things, these tunes made me question the basic ideology of American exceptionalism. As a teenager and young adult, through listening to albums like *Sandinista* I came to understand that there were a lot of issues, events, and perspectives missing, downplayed, or narrowly covered in mainstream U.S. news. The Clash and other musicians provided an alternative headline service. Interested in music and new ideas, I sought out other, more complete and contextual sources of information.

I am apparently not unusual in that regard. During my college years, several politically active peers told me how they first heard the story of Steve Biko in Peter Gabriel's tune, Nelson Mandela in the Specials' song, new perspectives on the Nicaraguan revolution in lyrics by the Clash, and so on. Nevertheless, it was not until I was reading the survey responses that I understood just how widespread this phenomenon of musical news is among activists. Those sharing my age cohort cite many of the same artists I have above. So, too, each age range of activists seems to have its seminal musicians, from the older folks who cut their teeth on Woody Guthrie and Pete Seeger, to the youngest respondents who count Rage Against the Machine and Michael Franti among their first sources of alternative information about the world.

Conclusion

There is a strong, often untested assumption that music plays an important role in political movements. This survey is part of a larger project designed to investigate the relationship between music, news, and political movements. Based on the survey results, it appears that music is an important source of information for these labor, environmental, peace, and human rights activists. That is especially true for the younger activists, many of whom first heard about an event or issue in a song. Music can provide essential information about people, issues, and events that are downplayed or even missing from mainstream news.

We entered into this intensive, long-term project in part to answer a basic political question: "Does music matter?" For most of these 139 respondents, the answer is clearly yes. While that is a foregone conclusion in much of the literature, there has been a dearth of systematically derived empirical evidence. The survey results not only demonstrate that music does matter but also provide some indication as to how.

In his song "Waiting for the Great Leap Forward," Billy Bragg sings: "Mixing pop and politics he asks me what the use is / I offer him embarrassment and my usual excuses." Based on the survey results, it would appear that no excuses are required. There are several "uses" for music in political movements. Musicians perform several roles in the lives of peace, human rights, labor, and environmental activists, including an important informational one. In this and other respects, the ancient tradition of musical news continues.

Notes

1. Nonparametric regression completed using loess function of R 2.7.2. See R Development Core Team (2008).

2. All musicians cited by name are presented below, along with the number of respondents who cited each one, in parentheses. The count does not include names inferred from song titles; the musician must be mentioned explicitly by name. It is important to remember that these counts refer to the number of respondents mentioning the musician. In other words, 29 respondents mentioned Bob Dylan at least once, 14 cited Pete Seeger, and so on:

Bob Dylan (29), Pete Seeger (14), Rage Against the Machine (14), John Lennon (13), Phil Ochs (12), Woody Guthrie (11), Bob Marley (9), Neil Young (9), Joan Baez (8), U2 (7), CSNY (6), Peter, Paul, and Mary (6), Beatles (5), Dixie Chicks (5), Country Joe and the Fish (4), David Rovic (4), Green Day (4), Joe Hill (4), Syracuse Community Choir (4), Utah Phillips (4), John Denver (3), John Lennon (3), Judy Collins (3), Midnight Oil (3), Peter Gabriel (3), Propagandhi (3), Tom Lehrer (3), Victor Jara (3), Against All Authority (2), Ani Difranco (2), Arlo Guthrie (2), Ben Harper (2), Billy Joel (2), Bruce Springsteen (2), Charlie King (2), Dead Kennedys (2), Gil Scott-Heron (2), Grateful Dead (2), Holly Near (2), Indigo Girls (2), Joni Mitchell (2), KRS-One (2), Larry Long (2), Manu Chao (2), Melissa Ethridge (2), Michael Franti (2), NOFX (2), Paris (2), Paul Simon (2), Phil Ochs (2), Pink (2), Public Enemy (2), Steve Earle (2), Sting (2), Sweet Honey in the Rock (2), the Clash (2), the Weavers (2), Tom Paxton (2), Tom Waits (2), Tracy Chapman (2), 2 Live Crew, Abilities, Aceyalone, Against Me, Anne Feeney, Anti-Flag, Aztlan Nation, Bach, Bad Religion, Bahamadia, Barry McGuire, BB King, Beastie Boys, Beethoven, Biggie, Billie Holiday, Billy Bragg, Bobby Darin, Body Count, Born Against, Bright Eyes, Bruce Cockburn, Bruce Hornsby and the Range, Buffalo Springfield, Buffy Sainte-Marie, Burning Spear, Café Tacuba, Cat Stevens, Charlie Murphy, Choking Victim, Chris Calloway, Chris Rice, Cisco Houston, Clampdown, Clan Dyken, Colleen Kattau, Cranberries, Dana Lyons, Danny, Dave Matthews, David Bowie, Dead Prez, Doors, Earth Crisis, Ed McCurdy, Eliza Gilkyson, Everlast, Eyedea, Fela, Five Iron Frenzy, Florence Reese, Fred Small, Fugazi, George Harrison, Granary Girls, Groundation, Guardabarranco, Iggy Pop, Immortal Technique, IMO, Inti-Illimani, Jackson Browne, James Brown, JayLive, Jay-Z, Jefferson Airplane, Jimi Hendrix, JoAnna James, John McCutcheon, John Seed, John Trudell, John Fogarty, Jonathan Edwards, Kalib Kweli, Kelly Clarkson, Kim and Reggie Harris, Ladysmith Black Mambazo, Leftover Crack, Leonard Cohen, Lynyrd Skynyrd, Marilyn Manson, Marvin Gaye, Masta Killa of Wu-Tang, Matt Redman, Michael Cooney, Michael Jackson, Michael Joncas, Mimi Fariña, Minor Threat, Mos Def, Natalie Merchant, Neville Brothers, Nickelback, Nine Inch Nails, NWA, Paul Anka, Paul Schwartz, Pennywise, Phillips, Craig, and Dean, Quilapayún, Radiohead, REM, Ricky Skaggs, Romanovsky and Phillips, Sarah Jones, Saul Williams, Simon and Garfunkel, Slackers, Slayer, Steel Pulse, Steve Agrisano, Steve Goodman, Stevie Ray Vaughn, Stevie Wonder, Stiff Little Fingers, Sublime, System of a Down, the Coup, Freedom Singers, Men They Couldn't Hang, Oysterband, Toad the Wet Sprocket, Tupac Shakur, Whitney Houston, and Willie Nelson.

NEWS IN THE ERA OF NEW MEDIA

14 Making (Sense of) News in the Era of Digital Information

DOMINIC BOYER

Anthropological research on news and journalism is relatively recent. The pioneering works — for example, Bird's research on tabloids (1990, 1992) and Pedelty's study of foreign correspondents (1995) — are less than 20 years old, and the more recent expansion of anthropological interest in research with journalists (see, e.g., Boyer 2000, 2005; Hannerz 2004a, 2004b; Hasty 2005; Hernandez-Reguant 2006; Marchetti and Ruellan 2001; Peterson 2001; Ståhlberg 2002) has developed only in the past decade. On the other hand, this periodization is misleading, since a first wave of sociological ethnographies of news and news culture had already appeared in the 1970s (Fishman 1980; Gans 1979; Tuchman 1978; Tunstall 1971). Even if there was a fairly long fallow period between the classic monographs and the more recent work of sociologists of journalism (Boczkowski and de Santos 2007; Deuze 2002; Klinenberg 2005), the sociology of news has been quite lively (Boczkowski 2005; Bourdieu 1996; Schudson 1978, 2003; Zelizer 2004). This richness raises the question as to what specific contribution anthropology can make.

In thinking through this question, it is important to admit that anthropology, in its capacity as a social-scientific mode of analysis and representation, has not yet told us anything startling that other social-scientific research, particularly qualitative sociology, has not. However, the anthropology of news and journalism has helped sharpen and refine a focus on the semiotic and epistemic dimensions of journalism as a professional practice with special attention paid to the cross-cultural features of the contexts, meanings, and activities of journalism. I argue elsewhere (Boyer n.d.) that the core of the craft of social-cultural anthropology is the polylogue between the analytical work of social theory and the representational work of ethnography. Although this polylogue is not anthropology's special province or jurisdiction, I think it is fair to say that it is an important conversation within the social sciences and that, as our specialty, we do it well. In this respect, I expect more conceptually nimble and ethnographically substantive work to emerge from the developing anthropology of journalism, although we should remain aware that we are relative latecomers and that much of what appears vividly immediate to us has also been identified by other social-scientific crafts.

Making Sense of News

The motivating question of this chapter is, to put it bluntly, who or what "makes news" today. This question has a particular historicity in that, even as recently as the 1970s, no one seems to have doubted that journalists were the social agents capable of "making news." The first generation of ethnographies of news making, brilliant books like Tuchman's *Making News* and Fishman's *Manufacturing the News,* were heavily invested, as one can judge from their titles alone, in what we might term a "praxeological" perspective on the skilled ability of journalists to craft, manage, and circulate news messages. Although the early ethnographies were quite aware of the exigencies that wreathed journalistic labor, from financial relations to institutional procedures, to professional expectations, at the center of their narratives the journalist always stood as a productive presence. My point of departure is the increasingly contingent character of praxeological understandings of "making news" today. Journalists report that they are increasingly concerned not only about their capacity to influence the trajectory of the news industry but also about their ability to exercise what they view as the appropriate critical-analytical skills of their vocation in the everyday practice of news journalism itself. In tandem with the conversion to digital information, journalists' sense of praxeological agency has become epistemically reshuffled. To be sure, journalists continue to view themselves as agentive in the practice of journalism, but they also acknowledge a rising sense of exposure and vulnerability to medial forces, forces like the velocity and abundance of information flows, the deprofessionalization of journalism, the fickleness of capital, and so on. It was never certain, but in the contemporary practice of news journalism, praxeology seems more clouded than ever by doubt.

We find a parallel tension within academic media theory as well. The anthropology of media, for example, supports a rich praxeological tradition epitomized in the recent works of Faye Ginsburg (1991, 1993), Terence Turner (1992, 1995, 1997), and their students and collaborators. At the same time, praxeological media anthropology shares space with the "negative dialectical" interventions of anthropology inspired by Heidegger and the Frankfurt School (Heidegger 1977; Horkheimer and Adorno 1994; Mazzarella 2003; Weiner 1997) and now increasingly with the cyberneticist tradition following Bateson (1987) and McLuhan (1964). This latter tradition tends to interpret media less as instruments of human crafts and purposes than as networks of relations (or, in McLuhan's language, "extensions") that have evolved into a more autonomous force matrix, as in Friedrich Kittler's socio-informatic "discourse networks" (1990) or Niklas Luhmann's constructivist vision of autopoetic mass media (2000). Such "mediology" — to borrow from Siegfried Zielinski — is actually best known to mainstream social-cultural anthropology through the unexpected source of (who else?) Foucault. His work on *pouvoir* ("power" or, better yet, "enablement") offers a kind of mediological or, more precisely, cybernetic-informational theory of society and history (e.g., Foucault 1979) that has given no end of irritation to praxeologists across the social sciences and humanities.

So the question of what analytical strategy we should use to make sense of contemporary news and news making seems refreshingly uncertain at this moment (and I should say that this uncertainty is not solely a matter of academic media analytics but also saturates the contemporary social knowledge of news professionals). As a way of triangulating the praxeological-mediological tension that I have encountered in my field research, I turn to a third analytical craft, social phenomenology, and I define two conditions that may help us better understand contemporary news journalism (what I term the "social phenomenology of fast-time practice" and the "harmonization of attentions" in the news industry).

Let me begin with two ethnographic episodes drawn from my earlier field research with former East German news journalists who helped to sensitize me to the changing experiential conditions of news journalism in the wake of digitization in the late 1990s and early 2000s.

Episode 1: Hollowing Critical Attentions

The first encounter occurred at a retreat for public radio journalists near Potsdam in June 1998. The retreat was designed for midcareer journalists to exchange knowledge and hone their skills through training exercises. I had been invited to lecture on East and West German relations in radio journalism, but I was allowed to stay on to participate in the practical seminars during the afternoon. Late in the day, on the sun-bleached patio of the resort hotel where the retreat was taking place, my friend Michael, a former East German journalist who had become the news director of a large regional public broadcaster, stood up to begin his seminar on the practice of news journalism.

He spoke briefly — an introduction to the economy of words in news journalism to which I will return later — giving only his professional background and title. Michael then explained that the best and perhaps only way to understand his job was to try to do it, and he gestured to several large stacks of about 300 news reports he had collected that morning at his office. There was some nervous laughter from the other journalists as Michael divided us into teams of two or three and gave each team 30 minutes to sift one stack and define the five "slam dunk" (his term) stories — the reports that would absolutely have to be picked up for his news program. Emphasizing that each stack was only a fraction of the 2,000 or so *Informationen* (pieces of information) that his department might expect to receive on news agency wires, by phone, fax, and internet in a given day, he chuckled that we shouldn't find the exercise too taxing. In reality, the only person untaxed by this exercise was another news journalist, and while the rest of us fell desperately behind, madly shuffling paper and trying to read and discuss the substance of the reports, Michael and the other news journalist charged ahead. Their practice was always to have one report in each hand, glancing at the headlines of one while raising the other into their field of vision. Then the first report was dropped into the reject pile as a new report was pulled off the stack. Only occasionally did a report find its way into a pile of possibles. In this way, Michael did a rapid rough sort of about 20 to 1, narrowing his stack to a much smaller pile, which he then reread more carefully for content. Michael finished his stack well in advance of the other teams and waited patiently until it was clear that the rest of us had no hope of processing our stacks in the allotted time. Michael then broke the exercise off to give a brief lecture on why he had selected the stories he had. He told us that the key challenge for a news department at a regional broadcaster was finding a way to balance stories of the greatest regional interest alongside important national, international, and local news. The artistry (*Kunst*) of the job came in how one filled up an entire news program with a mosaic of reports that balanced short- and long-term coverage of a wide field of issues in order to allow an audience to become deeply and broadly informed at a variety of scales of civic interest.

Michael outlined a vision of news making in keeping with a Habermasian model of *Öffentlichkeit* (publicity or "the public sphere"; Habermas 1984, 1987, 1989). If every intellectual profession engenders and integrates itself with reference to a domain of expert knowledge, then the jurisdictional locus of expertise for news journalism in the Habermasian model is its guarantee of a transactional continuum of information relatively unimpeded or deformed by governmental or commercial interests. This continuum distills the epistemic transparency required for the effective political and communicative activity of a Habermasian critical and rational public. It bears a Wittgensteinian family likeness with the Anglo-American image of journalism as a fourth estate, denoting a group of intellectuals invested with the professional autonomy, privilege, and responsibility of "speaking truth to power" on behalf of a public. From his own university training, Michael was indeed familiar with the Habermasian ideal and was proud of his efforts to sculpt a space for information flows that was maximally insulated from manipulation by exterior interests. However, after the seminar I asked him whether it wasn't difficult to exercise his own critical-rational skills concerning the criteria of newsworthiness given the intensity of his labor conditions. Michael replied, "Yes, for me now it's largely an intuitive process. I have a sense [*Gefühl*] of what's important and of interest for this audience, the eastern German public [*Publikum*], and that is always in the back of my mind. The process is too intuitive, really, because during my shift I have less time than I would like to think strategically about where to take the news program as a whole. That's something I have to save for after work really, for evaluations or long-range planning meetings." Once I asked Michael whether he or anyone in his news department ever had the chance to generate their own news content through reporting. Sighing and shaking his head, he told me, "That would be great, of course, but it simply isn't possible given what we have to manage here. We don't have the manpower to do that except in the most extraordinary circumstances. Like when our own studios were about to be flooded by the Elbe River. We *could* report on that, of course. But basically our job is to filter and to coordinate the news that comes in, to put together a news program that is appropriate for our regional audience here."

Sitting in his office in Magdeburg some weeks later, Michael returned to the themes of intuitive judgment and the vocation of filtering as he reflected on how the sheer volume of reports had risen demonstrably over the course of his career, especially with the arrival of digital information technology. He explained that in addition to what he viewed as legitimate news feeds, "every local politician wants us to know his latest position on X or Y issue. And it's not just politicians. There is always a small flood of press releases from other organizations and advocacy groups as well. And 99 percent of the time it's just self-promotional crap, not real news. But we have to read it all the same."

What I would underline in Michael's testimony is his discussion of the uneasy entanglement of the critical-rational and intuitive dimensions of evaluating newsworthiness. The qualities of importance and relevance valorized in contemporary news journalism presuppose, as they long have, senses of temporal immediacy, deictic proximity, and mimetic representability that are most easily bundled with the "event-ness" of classic spot news like a fire or a strike. Meanwhile, no less real and significant but perhaps more mediate and open-framed issues (like the future of social welfare or the persistence of gender inequality, for example) are perceived as having at best a contingent event-ness, often requiring the further "supporting event" of expert commentary or the release of a scientific study to warrant entry into a given news cycle. What Michael often lamented to me about his profession was that so much of his time now was occupied filtering, sorting, and selectively elaborating an increasing mountain of incoming information that it left him little time to think carefully through the broader social issues that cut across or contextualized the endless stream of event reports. The shift to digital information has created a new regime of mediated knowledge whose scope, distributed networks of communication, and accelerated temporality have served to challenge the vocational parameters and institutional practices of his professional expertise. In Michael's own terms, digital media has served to *aushöhlen*, to hollow out, his engagement with the news.

Episode 2: Journalistic Distraction and Demoralization

My second encounter took place in Michael's garden four years after the Potsdam retreat. Michael had invited me to lunch along with a mutual friend, Joachim, who several months earlier had quit his job as news director of a different radio station in eastern Germany to become a freelance writer. Joachim explained that he had decided to quit because the current state of news journalism had begun to demoralize him. He said he had always justified his work to himself as helping to stimulate people to think through issues rather than trying to persuade them of something or just bombarding them with uncontextualized "facts." Now, Joachim explained, he simply could no longer stand being an accomplice to a journalism that he saw as increasingly evolving into an infotainment business, and he uttered the word *infotainment* with particular scorn.

Sympathetically, Michael corroborated Joachim's point by telling us about a recent event in his news department that had reminded him of his journalistic work in East Germany before 1989 and of the extent to which political parties could subtly manipulate news journalism in the Western system as well. The campaign for the German chancellorship was heating up during the summer of 2002, and the Christian Democratic candidate, Edmund Stoiber, had just assembled his shadow cabinet, whom he referred to as his *"Kompetenz-team"* (literally, competence team, with dual neutral and positive connotations to the term just as in English).

Michael began, "A few days ago in the campaign coverage, Stoiber held a press conference where he mentioned adding someone to his Kompetenz-team, and without fail all the journalists in the office were suddenly using this term and talking about Stoiber's Kompetenz-team and who else might be added to it. My reaction was 'Kompetenz-team'? Hold on a second. They really had ought to have used the term *Wahlmannschaft* [election team], which is more accurate and neutral. But it's characteristic of the problem that a phrase like that is floated by the parties and then suddenly it becomes part of everyday journalistic language."

Joachim replied, nodding, "The thing is that half the time the journalists don't even realize they are doing it. They are busily doing their business, and they hardly even notice how those in power are manipulating them. It really is more of an unconscious process. Because, on the one hand, you have what I see as a general decline in objectivity in journalism, especially in the last, let's say, five to seven years. And then in public radio you have the entire party system that intersects with this and intensifies it. I think the real problem is that there are no longer any forums in which to discuss the praxis. Given the character of the work nowadays, there is precious little time to think or to talk about what it is that you are doing, so it is very hard to step back from the work and to identify where these sorts of political manipulations are taking place. Something needs to change, and it has to start, in my opinion, with the news agencies because it is the news agencies, the *holy* news agencies, which really dominate news making nowadays. They have *incredible* influence over what is transmitted, but you never get the feeling that they are thinking too closely about what it is that they are doing. What I'm sure they *aren't* doing is spending much time on training the younger journalists. Why? Because it's expensive to commit resources to that kind of work." At the end of his outburst, Joachim sank back into his seat and sighed. "You know, the tipping point was Princess Diana's death. How news media covered that . . ." He shook his head. "I mean, after Diana, it seemed as though any crap from the boulevard was now fit for the news."

Joachim's deep sense of estrangement centered on his feeling that the trajectory of news journalism was sapping the vitality of the public sphere. But equally if not more disturbing to him was the sense that journalists were not even entirely aware of what was happening to them. Joachim complained that the demands of news journalism now leave little time and, worse yet, place little value on critical reflection as to what should be in the news. Like Michael, Joachim had also worked for many years in East German news radio, and he compared the mindlessness of following party directives with the mindlessness of following consumer directives on many occasions. In both situations, Joachim understood the sacrifice of critical reflection and self-analysis as a betrayal of the vocation of news journalism. Despite trying to persuade Joachim to rejoin the profession on this occasion, Michael left his own news directorship a year later in order to manage a more popular talk- and music-oriented program. "It's true," he admitted to me a little sheepishly. "I was feeling a bit burned out on the news."

Analysis: Harmonized Attentions in a Fast-time Context

Taken together, these brief ethnographic encounters gesture toward two interrelated conditions that help us to make better sense of news making today. I will term the first condition *the social phenomenology of fast-time practice* and the second *the harmonized attentions of the contemporary news industry.*

But before schematizing these in more detail, since my ethnographic approach and conceptual language are obviously colored by phenomenology, especially social phenomenology in the tradition of Karl Marx and Alfred Schutz (1970), I should digress briefly to explain this decision: why look at news journalism phenomenologically? It seems to me that a key pressure point in news journalism today is the juncture between intuitive judgment and critical reflection in the evaluative moments when events and issues are gendered "newsworthy" and thus worthy of further circulation. Of course, this juncture has always been present in news journalism. But Michael and Joachim's testimony suggests that it has become more experientially salient and problematic in the digital era in that the sheer volume of information flows and the temporal intensification of evaluating and publicizing information ("feeding the beast," as American journalists sometimes put it) has significantly encroached upon personal and organizational time set aside for critical reflection upon newsworthiness, for pursuing ideas and projects that seem less temporally immediate, and for mentoring younger journalists in the Habermasian/fourth estate ideals. If not quite the instantaneity suggested by the popular label *real-time,* news journalism operates very much in a "fast-time" mode, often unwinding its crucial evaluative principles (principles such as "what is important for people to know" or, more commonly today, "what people want to know") into more individualized, intuitive, and uncoordinated practices. Not unlike Michael's exercise, many decisions about newsworthiness are made by editors quickly, instinctively, with potentially lasting consequences for what stories will enter and be sustained within news cycles. This heightens not only the significance of journalists' intuitions about newsworthiness but also the importance of their attentions — that is, what features they immediately notice in a story, what editors have already decided will constitute the news agenda for that day, what else might be vying for their attention in a given moment. Without belaboring this point, phenomenology is a good strategy for analyzing the social environment of news journalism because it represents the most elaborate engagement of social theory with the relations between attention, intuition, knowledge, and communication in human life. This is especially true in terms of its concern with attention as a mode of knowing that is neither passively empirical nor purely analytical, but rather, in Merleau-Ponty's language, an "active constitution of a new object which makes explicit and articulate what was until then . . . no more than an indeterminate horizon" (1989: 30). To put this in other terms: phenomenology argues that knowledge emerges and is refined through attentional practices. And I would argue that the term *attentional practices* captures much of the essence of news journalism, today and always.

So how might we sketch the social phenomenology of news journalism in the era of digital information? In most of the 15 print, radio, and news organizations where I have done research in Germany, a news editor like Michael was responsible for monitoring incoming news feeds, for running a daily editorial meeting, and for distributing specific stories to journalists for fact-checking, rewriting, or updating. These transactions always moved quickly, often with minimal commentary. Otherwise, journalists sat alone at their computer terminals, typing feverishly, breaking off only for phone calls, meals, brief bathroom breaks, or quick conferrals with colleagues. There simply wasn't a great deal of time for informal conversation about news or anything else. Michael once contrasted the professional intensity and austerity of Western journalism with his experience in East Germany, where news departments were both overstaffed and underemployed. "I find it really striking that one can work next to people for years in this system and know almost nothing about them, not where they were born, not even whether they have children." As a researcher, I quickly learned that my expectations of eavesdropping on extensive arguments over news stories were the fantasies of a craft — ethnography — that is something other than a fast-time intellectual practice. As Michael and Joachim suggested, such debates over newsworthiness were certainly desired, at least by some journalists, but were considered epistemic luxuries and often displaced by the necessity of fast-time consensus, intuition, and efficiency.

Although I found that journalists outside the newsroom were capable of speaking endlessly and eloquently about the ideals and practical challenges of journalism and about the newsworthiness of a range of current events and issues, at the office it was difficult and intrusive to get them to reflect at length about particular stories in the very moments when they were evaluating them. When prompted to reflect after the fact, my interlocutors would typically move past the specific cases-in-point toward more generalized judgments such as, "Oh, that was interesting, but something that wouldn't have had much resonance for our audience," or "We had that one already, and I didn't see anything new in this version." On two occasions when I was more stubborn about why a certain news story was judged resonant or not, I was ultimately told that one simply had to have a "sense" or "feel" for news relevance. (Germans have a lovely expression, *Fingerspitzengefühl*, the sense of one's fingertips, that captures this well in a tactile metaphor.)

In October 2005, I had the opportunity to sit in at the political desk of a small German news agency in Frankfurt during its highest period of activity. It was a busy news day because an *Eilmeldung* (the most urgent class of news bulletin) had come through from their Berlin office in the morning alerting the staff that a grand coalition government was forming under Angela Merkel, thus finally confirming the long-anticipated end of Gerhard Schroeder's chancellorship. Like many offices in Germany and elsewhere, the Frankfurt office was an open-layout archipelago of partial dividers, desks, bookshelves, and terminals, all unobjectionable gray and taupe, disrupted in the political department only by the fragile presence of a drooping ficus tree, which overhung an equally neglected table of daily newspapers and weekly magazines. Many desks were empty, since the office operates around the clock on three shifts. In one corner, the chief editor and assistant chief editor occupied their own private glass-walled offices. As the press conference announcing the new government was taking place, the chief editor stayed in his office, standing in front of his desk watching two monitors displaying German television news and CNN international, occasionally fielding calls from Berlin, and chuckling to himself as each new member of the coalition government was announced. The assistant chief editor also remained in his office throughout the afternoon, focused on filing a story on the legal dispute between the EU and Microsoft, almost completely ignoring the breaking political news. Meanwhile, the coordinating editor (or *Chef vom Dienst*), known in agency journalism as a "slotter," worked feverishly on updates to the main political story line while handing off other stories to two journalists and frequently checking in with a returning reporter whose car was trapped in a traffic jam somewhere near Hannover. Behind him, a large printer continuously disgorged the latest bulletins off the agency wires. Every 15 minutes or so, he swirled around to scan the new stack of bulletins and then transferred them to what the assistant chief editor, Paul, later joked was their "most important workstation," an enormous trashcan half-filled with paper. Besides the muffled sound of the television emerging from the chief editor's office, the soft whine of the printer, the hum of the computer terminals, and the constant clicking of keyboards, the department was starkly silent. Curiously, so it seemed to me, the forming of the new government provoked little obvious interest or dialogue in the political department. The journalists were clearly too engaged with their various tasks to devote time to discussing the potential significance of the unfolding events. When a new writer came on his shift in the late afternoon, he greeted the slotter and said simply, "Well, that's it." Hardly looking up from his monitor, the slotter queried, "Yes?" "He's gone," the journalist continued. "Schroeder?" the slotter asked. His colleague grunted, "Yup," and then the two of them shared a significant glance as the new journalist settled himself down at his monitor.

In a later interview, Paul explained to me how hectic news agency journalism has become: "Recently there has been increased demand from our clients for a greater volume of news production, but our staff has remained much the same. The most intensive time of the day for us is from about 2 PM to 6 PM, especially for the slotters, where you are getting pressure from several different sides at once. On the one hand, there is the "news input" [*Nachrichteninput*] that has to be monitored, and then there are articles coming in from correspondents that have to be edited to send back out. And the correspondents are text-messaging you asking why the latest version of what they just sent you isn't out yet. You have to hand stories off to the writers, decide to whom you should assign each text, and edit what they produce as well. Then a telephone call comes in from a newspaper with a special request for something. But the chief editor has just shown up at your desk asking why we haven't sent out a report on this other theme yet. That's a plurality of simultaneous demands overwhelming [*einstürzen*] the slotter that make the work, subjectively speaking, increasingly stressful."

The focused attention, the economy of language, the fast pace, the heightened importance of intuitions and snap judgments, the informational volume, and the unceasing character of news journalism in a digitally mediated 24/7 news organization all contribute to what I am terming the social phenomenology of "fast-time" news. Sociologist Eric Klinenberg offers the arresting and only partly hyperbolic image of a "news cyclone" for news making in the age of digital media (2005: 54).

I should note that analogous conditions exist even within well-funded and well-staffed online news groups in the United States and other countries. During a recent interview, John, the vice president of the online news division of a major American national newspaper, echoed Michael's concerns about finding the time to step back and reflect. "The 24/7 nature of working over here means that . . . the pressure is less stark but more consistent . . . which can be difficult at times, because I think the one thing that's nice about the newspaper cycle is that you can come in at 10 in the morning and think big thoughts until lunch. Then go have lunch and come back at 2 and think about the paper the next day. We don't really have that big thoughts time as much as we would like because we're always cranking stuff out. It can get really operational over here, and you can spend all day just keeping the site updated." A blogger at John's paper laughed along with the idea that news content was becoming more circular, even homogeneous, under these conditions. "It's true, it's true, we do constantly sit and watch everything else that's going on, and clip and post stuff. I mean, we pay attention to the extent that we can. But just keeping up with what's going on [at other news organizations] is a full-time job itself."

After listening to enough journalists express similar sentiments, after one realizes to what extent news journalists inform themselves about newsworthy events and issues through the medium of other news makers and news organizations, one begins to see the attraction of a cybernetic analysis of contemporary news. The circuits are not really quite so autopoetic or sealed as Luhmann might suggest, but the effects on the character of news are nonetheless significant. It creates an environment within which stories and classes of stories that have previously been gendered newsworthy are far more likely to survive the rapid, intuitive evaluation process characteristic of fast-time practice. It also creates an environment in which stories that are already easily "at hand" (for example, via news agency wires) are more likely to be drawn upon and relied upon. Even as reporting staffs have shrunk demonstrably at many news organizations over the past two decades, office staffs, especially those engaging in online news, have increased substantially. Baisnée and Marchetti (2006) call this the rise of "sedentary journalism" in their recent ethnography of the television broadcaster Euronews, "where technical tools play a dominant role . . . [and] it is mostly news produced outside which is re-processed, with the editors obtaining their raw materials from documents, the written press, dispatches of press agencies. . . . Almost the entire staff only physically leave the editorial offices . . . to eat or to drink coffee or to smoke" (2006: 114).

These observations also point toward what I am calling the "harmonized attentions of the contemporary news industry." This is the emergence of an institutional regime in which news organizations and news journalists are continually observing each other for attentional and evaluative cues as to what is newsworthy. Partly, this new regime can be explained through the standardization of digital information technologies and through the greater organizational interdependency created by mergers within the news industry. Another partial explanation for harmonized attentions is that the social conditions of fast-time journalism reframe the stakes of interorganizational competition. In the era of proliferating news portals and aggregators like Google news, it is increasingly difficult to preserve a proprietary hold on news (especially "breaking" news), so proportionally more energy is now expended at most news organizations on coordinating news feeds rather than on establishing distinct competitive streams.

There are at least three aspects of harmonized attentions that deserve brief discussion. The first is the centrality of news agency journalism to the new institutional regime. In Germany, four major international wire services dominate the news market: Deutsche Presse Agentur, Reuters, AFP, and AP. Together they have increased their total bulletin output by 50 percent since 1989 to a combined average of over 1,500 per day (Wilke 2007). The average length of their texts has increased to over 200 words in the same period. Although each of these organizations identifies itself as global in its mission and maintains hundreds of bureaus around the world, all are headquartered in Western Europe or the United States. Hannerz (2004a) has noted that they tend to follow the priorities and trends of Western news organizations more generally in terms of where they assign correspondents and where they prioritize news coverage. This helps to explain Wu's findings that international news coverage has become strikingly uniform across every continent. According to his study of foreign news stories in 44 countries, 55.2 percent of the stories focused on just 10 countries, 7 of which were European or North American (Wu 2004).

In the United States, the effect of news agency dependency and consolidation upon news journalism is even more striking. With the collapse of UPI, the virtual wire monopoly that the Associated Press now enjoys exercises a considerable influence over what events and issues are made available for public information and political communication on a national basis. On any given day, one can find the same AP-derived international and national news coverage — indeed, often verbatim the same texts — in almost every small or medium-sized newspaper across the United States. This is not entirely unlike the situation in East Germany before 1989, which also had a monopolized central news service albeit for reasons of party ideology rather than market efficiency. The harmonization of accredited political discourse is also not dissimilar. Thus it is perhaps not surprising to find that the satirical and hyperironic engagements of political communication that flourished in late socialism (especially those that satirized through obscene overidentification) are appearing now within late capitalist public culture as well (from *The Yes Men* to *South Park* to *The Colbert Report*).

As Paul hastened to explain to me in a later interview, news agencies are not acting conspiratorially to dominate news production. Rather, their rise has been driven by demand from client organizations to deliver them increasingly finished forms of news in order to reduce their clients' own production costs. As part of an industrywide trend toward prioritizing local news, many news managers justify outsourcing translocal news, arguing either that the audience is not principally interested in such stories or that the expense of generating original news content outweighs its marginal return in a digital market environment.

A second issue is the fast-time tightening of a competitive yet elite field of interdependent organizations and actors (including government agencies, political parties, bloggers, public relations and marketing firms, corporations, advertising firms, lobbying groups, and other news organizations) whose combined efforts to attract the attention of journalists and to deliver desired content into news cycles saturate the social environment of news journalism and congest its access points. The congestion of news access has two consequences that have been widely recognized: (1) by overwhelming news organizations with an abundance of targeted information, it reduces the opportunity for messages originating outside this competitive field to gain access to news cycles, and (2) by hiving off news cycles from a greater variety of worldviews and interests, it creates what some see as radical inconsistencies between the plurality of events (let alone issues) in the world and the limited sphere of news media events. News journalists, I should note, say they are less vulnerable to obvious acts of organizational manipulation like the much-debated video news releases than to cogent persuasion by other media experts as to what issues their clients and audiences care about. This is particularly true in the nascent field of online journalism, where robust metrics and consulting industries have developed to help news media organizations "build their brands" in cyberspace. At one online news organization I recently visited, senior staff mentioned that "viral marketing" efforts to increase brand presence via social networking sites and alliances with bloggers were now demanding surprising amounts of journalists' time and energy.

Congestion and persuasion are closely connected to the third dimension of the new institutional regime: the emergence of a handful of media organizations as what in Germany are known as *Leitmedien* or "lead media" within international and national fields of news journalism. My interlocutors at smaller news organizations in Germany have noted a remarkable tendency to defer to the evaluative decisions made by news agencies and international news giants like the BBC and CNN. "According to that logic," as one German news journalist put it, "if one of the lead media is carrying it, then there must be something to it."

While sitting in his remarkably dim and claustrophobic office in Berlin, Heinrich, a radio news journalist, explained to me that he was concerned about the "pack mentality" of news media but even more concerned about the unquestioned legitimacy of these "lead media" who drive the pack forward. "There are lead media like [the news magazine] *Spiegel* or [the tabloid] *Bild Zeitung*, and you get the sense that when they do something then suddenly there is this pressure in our department . . . that we have to do the same things. And sometimes what's forgotten . . . is that we may well have covered this topic four weeks before, and in a sense it's the lead media who are coming late to it, but that is somehow forgotten and there is a pressure for us to do something again."

The importance of lead media extends even to news agency journalism. Acknowledging a tendency in news media toward what he termed, in English, "self-referentiality," Paul explained to me:

> Foreign coverage is the most independent of this tendency because there the emphasis is on factual events. In Monrovia, if there are people on the street who are shooting at each other, that's an event that we report on regardless of what other media are doing. . . . In the domestic coverage, however, this tendency of self-referentiality is much more influential. We're speaking now

of lead media. [The news magazines] *Spiegel* and *Focus* send out interviews on the weekend and thereby influence very strongly the "agenda-setting" for the upcoming week. For example, whether a debate over pension reforms will spread across Germany without necessarily anything concrete having happened, other than perhaps that some "back-bencher" has seen fit to give an interview. And then all the media react to it, and we, as a news agency, feel then that we have to report it as well.

Lead media, I would argue, should be understood as the logical extension of widespread informational recursion and imitation in news journalism in the digital era. Given what I have described as the social phenomenology of fast-time practice, it is easy to see how another news organization, especially one with a positive professional reputation, is viewed not only as a threatening competitor but also as a kind of mirroring Hegelian-Lacanian Other. The authority and more durably objective character of this leader's news output offers a desirable counterpart to the often harried experience of one's own news-making process and thus, in many instances, they become objects of partial imitation.

There are, of course, other important aspects of fast-time practice and harmonized attentions in news journalism that I do not have space to discuss in the detail they deserve, the most important of which is the impact of both conditions upon the work of reporters, correspondents, and stringers. Since my own research has focused more on the office side (as opposed to the field side) of news journalism, I will simply reference a recent ethnographic account by Velthuis (2006), a Danish sociologist-turned-journalist, of his experience as a correspondent on the World Trade Organization beat. He offers a provocative autobiography of a kind of organizationally dependent journalism that consists largely of waiting in hallways for closed-door sessions to finish, of cultivating good relations with politicians' publicists, of jockeying for sound bites to meet deadlines, and so on. Such organizational beats have long existed in news journalism but have become more the norm in correspondent work since, in the logic of maximizing returns on resource allocation, international editors and managers like to position their correspondents where they are already organizationally guaranteed to receive information organizationally preconceived as newsworthy. In the end, Velthuis expresses concern bordering on dismay with how little he actually learned about the WTO's internal negotiation processes despite having covered them for some time.

THE ETHNOGRAPHIC PURPOSE of this chapter has been relatively straightforward: to explore and to map the range of forces that constitute news today, focusing especially on how journalists are rethinking the parameters and possibilities of their vocation in the wake of digitization. The conceptual purpose of the article invites, however, some further discussion. I am working on a way to bring praxeological, phenomenological, and mediological approaches to understanding media and mediation into a more helpful alignment with one another (see also Boyer 2007). As is likely already apparent, much work in the anthropology and sociology of media (including research on news and journalism) has been strongly influenced by praxeological analytics of production and consumption (see, e.g., Ginsburg, Abu-Lughod, and Larkin 2002; D. Miller 1992). But these analytics have come to share space more recently with the mediological and informatic sensibilities of theorists like Kittler and Luhmann in their emphasis on systematicity, networks, and circulatory modalities of power and reason. In addition to these conceptual approaches and analytical strategies, I suggest in this chapter that a social-phenomenological perspective is very fruitful, especially for studying the specific practical character of news journalism. My argument is not that a social-phenomenological perspective somehow trumps the other two. On the contrary, I would argue that all three offer vital insights into the research problem at hand. What I am hoping to demonstrate is that it makes little sense for us as scholars of media to encamp ourselves around a praxeological, mediological, or phenomenological approach and then, as is all too often the case, to ignore, trivialize, or talk around the other approaches' virtues, creating the kind of conceptual impasse in media studies that I find rather forlorn. The point is not to strive for a conceptual rapprochement that would paper over real and important differences between these analytical perspectives but rather to create the space for more intimate conversations and confrontations between the different analytical strategies to which we are disposed. In this chapter, with its dual interests in digital information and journalistic agency, I mean to provide the ethnographic space for just such conversations and confrontations, moving beyond the limited communications of distant encampments and toward more densely conversant analytical strategies for engaging the massively complicated range of differently scaled forces knotted in all of our field sites.

15 When Common Sense No Longer Holds

The Shifting Locus of News Production in the United States

MARIA D. VESPERI

> [Anne Newport] Royall published the first issue of her Washington, D.C., paper, *Paul Pry*, in 1831. . . . At sixty, she was arrested and found guilty of being a common scold, avoiding the ducking stool only because of her age.
> — Loren Ghiglione 1990: 15

> The Internet has unleashed a type of news that was common in nineteenth-century America — news with a partisan spin.
> — Thomas E. Patterson 2007a: 12

"All the News That's Fit to Print" has emblazoned the front page of the *New York Times* since the 1890s. More than an advertising slogan, "All the News" is a pledge, renewed daily. Like most solemn promises, this one draws meaning through indexical reference to a world of alternate possibilities, a world where the powerful and greedy conspire to hide vital facts from the reading public by omission or by "spinning" events to tilt their significance. As a pledge, the *Times* motto is also performative; it represents the collective activity of reporting, editing, publishing, and, of course, underwriting the news institution as a whole.

An advertising poster from 1896 proclaimed that the *New York Times* was the "model of decent and dignified journalism." The accompanying illustration, timed for the Easter holiday, featured a field of lilies and a white-gowned woman holding a single flower. *Magna est veritas et praevalebit* (Truth is mighty and will prevail) appeared at the bottom for good measure. As Loren Ghiglione explains in *The American Journalist: Paradox of the Press*, "During the white heat of the Yellow Journalism war between the New York *World* and the New York *Journal*, the owners of the New York *Times* chose an ethically pure and 'decent' approach" to presenting the news (1990: 159).

In the United States, readers' expectations about "All the News" are informed today as in the past by commonsense constructions that differentiate general circulation newspapers from magazines and other print media. Mainstream journalists are guided by professional values and standards of practice that resonate with these criteria and thus "make sense." Anthropologists who move beyond content analysis to study the actual production of news are positioned to identify and evaluate the impact of shifts in social, economic, and technological expectations on journalism culture and practice. As a former working journalist who remains connected to the field through the Poynter Institute in St. Petersburg, Florida, I have watched with growing concern as economic and popular support for journalism's traditional focus on public affairs and social issues has slipped away. Cultural categories and their borders are always fluid, of course, but in recent years the definitions of "All," "News," "Fit," and "Print" have begun to shift radically and with accelerating speed. Well-marked boundaries between news, entertainment, and advertising have blurred, not only in broadcast media but also in print; the *Wall Street Journal* has even considered a design that embeds advertising in news stories. As online news aggregators continue to deconstruct traditional categories, journalists are left to wonder whatever happened to their operating assumptions: *All* (adj.) a comprehensive set, gathered objectively and without bias. *News* (noun) current information deemed worthy of public attention. *Fit* (adj.) news presumed to be accurate, fully vetted, free of libel, and presented in accord with a community's aesthetic and moral standards. *Print* (verb) the act of time-stopping "All the Fit News" and framing it as a portable object that can be read, saved, or shared.

The goal of delivering "all the news" informs journalists' behavior as reporters in the field, influences their interpretation of complex events, and enables them to perform discrete tasks among teams of highly specialized workers in hierarchical, high-stakes work environments. The values and practices of journalism constitute a tangible, self-reflexive system that is taught in classrooms, evaluated as job performance, challenged in public forums, and routinely reviewed in court. The cultural constructs that shape journalism into a recognizable career of habits, outlooks, and expectations rest in turn on shared assumptions about how to pluck "news" from the stream of daily events and the need to establish its truth value through a multistage process of crafting, framing, and institutionalized presentation.

Beliefs about common sense and how to make it are fundamental to journalists' traditional understanding of their work. Following discussion of the intersubjective world by Alfred Schutz (1971; see also Michael Jackson 1998 and Clifford Geertz 1983), one might say that the values of news journalism constitute a set of commonsense guidelines for practice. The willingness of reporters, editors, and publishers to persist in the face of widespread public criticism, distrust, and even outright scorn has been buoyed by the conviction that they are doing the right thing, not as celebrity renegades or guerilla freelancers but as team players who operate with the full support of organizations that employ and protect them. Basic questions such as "What is news?" and "What makes someone a journalist?" were rarely examined and remained self-reinforcing throughout most of the twentieth century.

In "Common Sense as a Cultural System," Geertz proposes that the self-reinforcing qualities of commonsense thinking demonstrate "the desire to render the world distinct" (1983: 77). That desire has certainly been at the forefront of traditional news reporting, editing, and layout. Yet the traditional newspaper with its discrete news and feature sections and its reliance on story placement to signal relevance no longer resonates with the commonsense worldview of younger readers, who have largely abandoned the medium (Patterson 2007b). Perhaps most challenging is the way bloggers with no journalism training and no editorial oversight have laid claim to the role of the news reporter, sometimes forcing mainstream journalists to acknowledge them as sources. The title of a 2007 book by attorney Scott Gant summarizes the shift: *We're All Journalists Now: The Transformation of the Press and Reshaping of the Law in the Internet Age.*

In just a decade, a withering of support for print news and the flourishing of internet-based information sources have challenged journalists' own commonsense understanding of their project to its core. Schutz, a phenomenologist, explains that commonsense thought takes place in an "intersubjective world of culture," wherein everyday life is governed by the assumption that individual differences in perspective are overcome by the belief that perceptions are interchangeable — "that if I change places with him so that his 'here' becomes mine, I shall be at the same distance from things and see them with the same typicality" (1971: 10, 12). Schutz pairs this with "congruency of relevance," the idea that others share one's sense of an empirical world. Together these assumptions form a taken-for-granted viewpoint on the everyday that Schutz labels "the general thesis of reciprocal perspectives." He suggests that the thesis of reciprocal perspectives "leads to the apprehension of objects and their aspects actually known by me and potentially known by you as *everyone's* knowledge. Such knowledge is conceived to be *objective* and *anonymous,* i.e., detached from and independent of my and my fellow-man's definition of the situation, our unique biographic circumstances, and the actual and potential purposes at hand" (1971: 12, emphasis added).

The assumption that empirical reality is culturally shared — "independent" of biography and circumstances — gives journalists a frame for action and lends weight and value to their work. Newspapers are published with communities of readers in mind, and in the 1990s some papers began to host focus groups as a way to gauge changes in local worldview. They recognized that a newspaper's "appeal" rests in part on its ability to present an orderly, intelligible accounting of events — to make the strange familiar, as the saying goes. The traditional goal of the ethnographer identified by Geertz in *Works and Lives* describes the task engaged by mainstream journalists as well: "Ethnographers need to convince us . . . not merely that they themselves have truly 'been there,' but . . . that had we been there we should have seen what they saw, felt what they felt, concluded what they concluded" (1988: 16).

The spike in *New York Times* readership after the September 11 attacks was a poignant example. In their moment of confusion, large numbers of readers were eager to follow events through the eyes of a powerful institution with the credentials to "be there" across fire and police lines. In an early 2002 Poynter Institute panel, "Reflection on the Value of News in the Context of September 11," Tom Brokaw, James Carey, and Howell Raines explored the implications of this watershed moment. All three were working in Manhattan at the time: Brokaw as anchor of *NBC Nightly News,* Carey as a scholar and mentor at the Columbia University School of Journalism, and Raines as executive editor of the *New York Times.* All seemed to agree that September 11 sparked an extraordinary — if short-lived — surge of hope and purpose for journalists. (See Zelizer and Allan 2002 for a range of perspectives on this topic.) Carey recalled readers lining up 30 deep to buy the *Times,* signaling a rediscovered confidence in newspapers to inform people about their community. Raines, who took over as *Times* executive editor just weeks before September 11, explained that the newspaper's remarkable "Portraits of Grief" feature "grew out of an organic newsroom process." In the immediate absence of accurate statistics about all the people who died, "a deputy managing editor came up with the idea of doing it the old-fashioned way, one page at a time," he explained. The relentless, cumulative focus on unfulfilled hopes and aspirations under the unified theme of "a life interrupted" conveyed the collective scope of the loss in a way that spoke to all readers.[1]

The Minneapolis–St. Paul *Star-Tribune*'s 2007 coverage of the I-35W bridge collapse provides an interesting comparison. Speaking at the Poynter Institute in early 2008, Deputy Editor for Interactive Media Matt Thompson demonstrated "13 seconds in August," the paper's interactive follow-up to the event (accessed at www.startribune.com/local/12166286.html). Working from an aerial view of the tragedy, *Star-Tribune* reporters identified occupants of 78 of the 84 cars that were visible on the bridge or underwater. Each car was numbered; clicking on a number brought the viewer to text, interviews, audio, and photos. Earlier in the Poynter meeting, Thompson said that journalists were "being tugged in two different directions. . . . We can do better journalism than we were ever able to do . . . but as an industry, we feel adrift." Thompson presented "13 seconds in August" as an online example of what can be done "with the tools that are afforded us."

"Creative De[con]struction"

Ironically, it is their mandate to seek the common denominator that has caused many mainstream journalists to stumble and lose their bearings. While their work has been marked — to varying degrees — by increased attention to diversity and multicultural communities of readers, traditional print journalists still direct themselves to an imagined audience that shares their news culture. So strong is their faith in the importance of news to a democratic citizenry that they persist in already frustrated efforts to attract readers' attention. Some assume that the problem is lack of inclusiveness; thus newspapers offer "less of more" in an ever-self-diluting effort to draw in the young and disaffected with bullet points and news digests. Others try for niche marketing that tells readers of varying ages and backgrounds, "We know who you are and what you want."

Collectively, such efforts fail to acknowledge the impact of postmodern approaches to writing, representation, analysis, and reading itself. All of these approaches problematize and challenge the primacy of commonsense knowledge and "reciprocal perspectives." Top-down, mass-mediated statements about almost any issue are as likely to be labeled hegemonic, and hence rejected, as they are to be embraced as unifying — or even useful. Journalists who work online understand this best, and the youngest are actively exploring its implications. In a 2008 Poynter Institute discussion about the state of the industry and its future, some participants questioned the focus on technology in relation to a notable absence of discussion about content and, well, *writing.* One young online editor replied that narrative form was no longer the issue when it came to attracting readers to a story. Even when stories were not well crafted, readers valued the big picture that emerged through personal accounts.

The Wikimedia Foundation has touched this nerve by providing an instantly popular online platform for collaborative information-building. Readers who open the home page of Wikinews (2007a) and click the last three words of its motto, "The free news source you can write!" are led to detailed tutorials about how to submit and edit news copy: "Welcome all to Wikinews, the free news source written by you! Everything you read here is written by individuals just like yourself. You can edit any article — fix spelling mistakes, punctuation, or grammar, correct mistakes, or further expand the article!" (2007b).

Exclamation points aside, Wikinews policy adheres rather closely to the journalism values of balanced presentation and full, transparent sourcing. Potential contributors are advised right up front: "First and foremost, Wikinews articles are written from a neutral point of view and don't contain opinion or commentary (if you want to tell the world what *you think* about a news item, try blogging)." Click on "neutral point of view" and you find an "absolute and nonnegotiable" policy, with detailed instructions about how to recognize and achieve the goal of unbiased news presentation (2007c). Of course, much critical analysis has been devoted to the dangers inherent in an assumption that "neutrality" can be achieved, and anyone who has actually worked as a reporter or ethnographer has undoubtedly barked a shin on the numerous obstacles between "the event" and individual or collaborative narratives about it. Even the most conservative mainstream news outlets have experimented openly with first-person perspectives and narrative form. Thus it is notable that Wikinews rejects the traditional news-gathering process but uncritically embraces the traditional end product — the so-called neutral or objective story.

In "Creative Destruction: An Exploratory Look at News on the Internet," a 2007 study supported by the Carnegie-Knight Task Force on the Future of Journalism Education, Thomas E. Patterson examines internet news traffic in relation to more traditional news sources. His study confirms the widespread belief that online technology "is redistributing the news audience in ways that [are] threatening some traditional news organizations," particularly newspapers (2007a: 13). Yet he also points out that a single online source will never achieve dominance in the news market. Even as the absolute number of visitors to a site increases, he explains, the site's relative influence is diluted by the proliferation of alternatives: "Like the cosmos, the Internet is expanding" (2007a: 6).

User-generated news sites such as Wikinews and digg.com develop some content through original reporting and some through aggregation of existing stories, which are then reordered and sometimes reedited. Other sites have no original content at all; they simply collect "all the news" that traditional news organizations have already published. Patterson refers to such aggregators as free riders, "competitors that have not borne an equitable share of the production costs" (2007a: 11). Sometimes their appeal is simply convenience; sometimes they offer news content tailored to particular readership niches or even to individual news consumers.

Preference and *personal* are the operative words here. Widely available technology enables music listeners to override the selection of songs on a compact disc in favor of their own compilations; television audiences resist both the content and time sequence of broadcast programming with recording equipment that has become a home standard. News consumers, especially younger ones, are equally impatient with general-content sources that can't be reshaped to fit their interests.

At the other end of the online news spectrum is the aggregator who abandons responsibility for the individual consumer altogether by surrendering authority for both form and content. The website allthenewsthatsfittoprint.net is a striking example of just how far the dismantling and repositioning of news can go. Like Wikipedia or digg.com, this project circumvents the authority of top-down media professionals, but it also pushes the medium of electronic presentation much further by treating headlines, text, and photos as a wellspring of graphic images that can be divorced from narrative form and aggregated in random spatial and temporal sequences. The site's creators describe it best:

> ALL THE NEWS THAT'S FIT TO PRINT uses the daily *New York Times* as its point of departure. It explores the relationship between how the news and the images that accompany headline stories are presented online and in-print. The front page image usually disappears online. The headlines are often different. The lines between what is hard news and what is filler blur. This project uses the headlines and front page images from the print version of the *New York Times* located online, and presents them as a random sequence of image and text. The juxtapositions become wrong, sad, funny, inexplicable, and often to the point. The headline and image are presented in conjunction with the daily paper's image. One is drawn to the initial layout, the language of the headline and to the sensationalism of the image.

Online and "inprint." If this is a typographical error, it is nevertheless telling.

Tearing and repositioning newsprint to create a montage is not a fresh idea; newspapers have long been commandeered for alternative purposes, artistic or otherwise. It is taken for granted that the medium and the message are easily separated. One reads "the" newspaper but also grabs "some" newspaper for tasks far removed from politics and stock prices. Yet transforming news pages seamlessly to communicate new meanings is both novel and disconcerting. When journalists joke that their hard-won copy will be birdcage liner the next day, they allude not only to the ephemeral nature of their accomplishments but also to the reassuring concept that once printed and read, the information has served its purpose. Mistakes can reach across time to haunt a journalist, but for better or worse, most stories remain fixed "for the record."

News Values vs. News Value

Half a century ago, print journalism held sway to the extent that the radically different and potentially disruptive new medium of television was initially adapted to serve its values, not the other way around. Now, desperate to hold younger viewers, broadcast producers mimic the internet by framing news anchors with streaming video and running banners. "The most classic example of an aggressive campaign to bring in younger viewers is the revamped CNN *Headline News*," media consultant Callie Crossley told me in a 2001 interview on television news and images of aging. A former producer with the ABC television newsmagazine *20/20*, Crossley explained that the CNN redesign was a hopeful appeal to a "direct demographic" of younger viewers because "that's what they do on the web" (Vesperi 2001). Younger viewers who follow the news are indeed most likely to watch it on television, a recent study found, but a majority of teens and young adults "find a bit of news here and there and do not make it a routine part of their day" (Patterson 2007b: 3).

As television scrambles to retain viewers who are less and less willing to adapt their schedules to a nightly news hour, some newspapers have attempted to compete with cable news and the internet by adopting a 24-hour news cycle. This can require reporters to post "raw" news to the paper's website, offering updated drafts and corrections as the articles develop. Some journalists thrive in this environment, and most understand it as a survival tactic. Nevertheless, the practice of posting unfinished stories for the public to read strikes hard at journalists' pride in their collective work. The traditional trajectory of a news story begins at the reporter's desk, moves to an editor for review, returns to the writer for corrections or polishing, and ends at the copy desk, where it is edited again. Each review narrows the margin of error and widens the opportunity for a well-crafted narrative. Traditionally, most journalists worked hard to protect against potential errors of style, organization, fact, emphasis, and omission. The real anxiety came from the pitfalls that lurked beyond control — sources who lied, circumstances that changed suddenly, and crucial facts that emerged only after the story was broadcast or printed.

The traditional newsroom was a textbook case of Schutz's "reciprocal perspectives" because most managers came up through the ranks of reporters and editors. One early indicator of the changes to come was a shift in viewpoint from the top down. In the mid-1990s, public policy specialist Marty Linsky interviewed media CEOs to investigate reports of shifting allegiances within and between media companies and concerns about the impact of corporate restructuring on the news business. The result was a bellwether monograph, *The View from the Top: Conversations with 14 People Who Will Be Running Journalism Organizations into the 21st Century*. "On the whole, the moguls do not see themselves primarily as heirs to a legacy of public affairs journalism," Linsky found. "They speak a different professional language than the reporters who work for them" (1997: 11).

In an interview with Geneva Overholser for *American Journalism Review* just one year later, newspaper veteran Harold Evans offered this prediction: "The challenge of the American newspaper is not to stay in business, it is to stay in journalism" (Overholser 1998). Overholser, a journalism educator with wide experience as an editor and columnist, returned to this quote in her 2004 Senate Commerce Committee testimony on media consolidation. It's an important one because news values don't always line up neatly with business values; investigative series and watchdog coverage of public policy at all levels of government are costly offerings that readers of many newspapers can no longer expect to find on a regular basis, if at all.

The shift away from hard news and a concomitant blurring of the line between news and entertainment has been well documented by the Project for Excellence in Journalism (1998, 2004, 2005, 2007). And in "Young People and News," another study for the Carnegie-Knight Task Force, Thomas E. Patterson found that many young people could not distinguish between hard news and what he describes as "stories about disasters, celebrities, and the like," so-called soft news. "Not only were the younger respondents less likely than older respondents to be aware of hard news stories, they were also less likely to correctly identify the factual element of such stories," he writes. "Whereas 50 percent of older adults who claimed awareness of a hard news story correctly identified the factual element, only 39 percent of young adults did so" (2007b: 16).

Respondents across Patterson's sample of 1,800 teenagers, young adults, and older adults reported the heaviest news exposure from television. Surprisingly, the internet represented first exposure to a major story for only 18 percent of the younger age groups. He found only 9 percent of teenagers reporting daily contact with print news pages (2007b: 9). Contrary to the popular assumption that the internet is the medium of choice for young news readers, Patterson notes, "The large fact about teens and young adults is not that they are heavily dependent on new media but that they partake only lightly of news, whatever the source. A shift in sources is occurring, but the larger tide has been the movement away from a daily news habit" (2007b: 21).

That newspapers are substantial and useful as household objects has not detracted traditionally from their commonsense value as sources of information. Indeed, the behaviors connected with handling a newspaper may offer one key to understanding the complex question of why adolescents don't read them. Patterson speculates that the "almost unthinking" morning ritual of retrieving the paper and opening it are central to the formation of such habits. He points to research that indicates "online news exposure is less fixed by time, place, and routine — elements that reinforce, almost define, a habit" (2007b: 22). Patterson concludes:

The Internet cannot be faulted for the decline in news interest among young adults. Other factors, including a weakening of the home as a place where news habits are acquired, underlie this development. Notwithstanding the cartoon father with his nose buried in the paper after a day at work, news exposure in the home was a family affair. The newspaper sections were shared, as was the space around the radio or in front of the television set. Today, media use is largely a solitary affair, a single face staring at the television or computer screen (2007b: 23–24)

As high-turnover devices for individualized information gathering continue to proliferate, the shared medium of the single-copy, home-delivered newspaper has raised ecological questions and drawn scorn among young people for its ungainly nature. Motivated by such concerns and by the cost of newsprint, publishers have invested heavily in redesign and retooling aimed at economizing the size of newspapers. Writing for *Commonwealth* magazine, journalist Dan Kennedy uses Patterson's findings as a platform for a wider discussion of how young people have abandoned the news habit. Kennedy points to observations by Peter Kadzis, executive editor of the New England–based *Phoenix* weeklies. The *Phoenix*'s own studies suggest that "young adults are accustomed to using media that are well designed and easy to use — cell phones, laptops, and iPods. The broadsheet newspaper (though not as broad as it used to be) is seen by this age group as a 19th-century relic, says Kadzis, who presided over a 2007 redesign to make the Phoenix papers more magazine-like in appearance" (Kennedy 2007).

Journalists have yet to fully appreciate another of Patterson's findings. Twenty-eight percent of his teenage respondents who were aware of a top news story reported first contact with it through "another person," the second-largest source after television, at 41 percent, and well above the internet at 18 percent (2007b: 19). Citing his own work on the "vanishing voter" (2005), Patterson notes, "Research studies have found that older adults are more likely than young adults to discuss public affairs, which would lead to the prediction that older respondents would be more likely to obtain news stories through another person. Yet our survey yielded the opposite finding; young adults exposed to a story were three times more likely than older adults (12 percent versus 4 percent) to say they had heard about it from another person. Teen respondents were even more likely to report that another person, rather than direct news exposure, was the story source" (2007b: 16). This finding articulates well with Barnhurst's characterization that young people "act as bricoleurs" in their construction of workable political identities. Looking specifically at a young American's self-reporting about awareness of famine, he observes that "news is but one of many sources (especially entertainment media) they use to make sense of the political world. Understanding an issue comes scattershot, as in the case of the famine essay, from pop songs, TV commercials, documentary films, and—most importantly—personal discussions more than from journalists" (1998: 216).

"Impossible Worlds"

As a member of the Poynter Institute board of trustees, I have the opportunity to audit workshops and seminars with journalists from newspapers and television stations nationwide. At a 2006 Institute seminar, participants were asked to identify challenges faced by newsrooms. The topics were generated through group discussion and then written in bold letters on a flip chart. The result was a striking list of deficits:

Not enough time to do the work
Everyone for himself/herself
Not enough people
Not enough money
People who don't want to change
Learning new stuff while still doing old job
Lack of motivation/reward
No accountability
No follow through
Lack of support from upper management
Fear of the future
People don't see a future for themselves in this
Am I going to have a job?
People who upgrade skills end up doing more work
I'm not gonna like that job
Lack of control

"It is when ordinary expectations fail to hold . . . that the cry of witchcraft goes up," Geertz observes in his discussion of common sense (1983: 79). He explains that attributing anomalous occurrences to sources that are extraordinary, even supernatural, "acts to reassure" by circumventing the need to revise one's notions about how the world works. Journalists—some quite belatedly—have realized that their commonsense knowledge of today's news industry has little predictive value when it comes to envisioning the newsroom of tomorrow. Dangers and deficits are easy to identify, but the way forward is not. Some journalists see the internet as a kind of blind supernatural force, destroying craft and content with the inhuman power and speed of its technology. For others, the internet is just another tool, and the witchcraft stems from ethics — we have them, they don't.

In journalism as in anthropology, however, ethics is a hard sell. Folks in both professions are quick to note *un*ethical behavior, and once the shouting is over, thoughtful discussion can raise the bar. In fact, one could argue that it takes a major scandal to prompt professionwide soul-searching. Even then, the focus is usually on what others did wrong, not on the values, goals, and environments that undergird good and bad practices alike. Flagrantly unethical behavior gets lots of attention, but proactive approaches to ethics just aren't regarded as sexy topics. In the absence of naughty counterexamples, codes and standards are difficult to rally around.

Such guides exist on paper, of course. Professional associations, universities, and news institutions never tire of crafting documents that detail hypothetical do's and don'ts — mostly don'ts. Plans for federally sponsored research in the social sciences are reviewed for the protection of human subjects; the emphasis here is "first, do no harm." Under federal mandate, universities have routinized practice by establishing institutional review boards, adopting versions of the federal standards to guide their own assessment of a scholar's research project. The review process builds "reciprocal perspectives" about how to craft sound research and how to recognize it.

In the newsroom, editors are similarly vigilant about conflict of interest, libel, plagiarism, taking gifts from sources, and other outright ethical breaches among reporters. When reporters flout ethical codes in a spectacular way, their editors are often expected to fire them and then resign themselves. Once again, though, the spotlight is usually trained on what *not* to do. Don't make stuff up. Don't strip quotes of context. Don't take food from the hand you should be biting. In the less well lit areas of routine interviewing and writing, it is easy to tacitly conclude that behavior not earmarked as wrong or debated as questionable is, by default, ethical practice.

And yet, as Yeats so famously wrote, the center no longer holds. If "we're all journalists now," where is the line between professional practice and anyone who can snag a cell phone picture of, say, Saddam Hussein's execution and quickly post it online? From a journalist's point of view, free-riding bloggers and aggregators thrive and multiply by rifling through and appropriating "All the News That's Fit to Print," then transgressing the category of news itself.

In his perceptive discussion of why mixed metaphors are often rejected as undesirable, Dale Pesmen states that "a metaphoric prediction implies an association not only of two terms, but also of two worlds, in what is felt as a sort of promise of union" (1991: 216) Mixed metaphors, he explains, "suggest impossible worlds" (1991: 214).

Kenneth Burke describes metaphor as a kind of perspective, "a device for seeing something *in terms of* something else. It brings out the thisness of a that, or the thatness of a this" (1969: 503, emphasis in original). Following Pesmen, one might say that metaphors work because "this" and "that" are culturally coherent; they offer novel perspectives by reinforcing familiar categories, not by transgressing them. "This notion of coherence governs our judgments of the 'truth,' 'validity,' and 'realism' . . . and distinguishes things we *can* think about from things we find objectionable and/or impossible to think" (Pesmen 1991: 213, emphasis in original). Looked at another way, attempts to police metaphorical boundaries "describe implicitly what worlds we consider possible" (1991: 215). Pesmen suggests that a shift in domain caused by mixing metaphors can initially be perceived "as leaving a set of potentialities behind" (1991: 216) and the sense of loss that accompanies it.

The challenges journalists describe as fear of the future, lack of control, and inadequate resources to get the job done — if there is a job, and whatever it might turn out to be — are symptomatic of rapid shifts in the once-coherent, self-reinforcing domain of news. "And we gazed upon the chimes of freedom flashing," goes the refrain of an old Bob Dylan song. I have heard that line discussed as a striking example of mixed metaphor, and the blend of hope and trepidation it captures could apply as easily to journalists today as to those caught up in the worldview shifts of the 1960s.

Note

1. *Portraits: 9/11/01: The Collected "Portraits of Grief"* has since been published as a collection, with a foreword by Howell Raines (2002).

16 Salon.com and New-Media Professional Journalism Culture

ADRIENNE RUSSELL

The emergence of participatory journalism, journalism which includes readers in the editorial process, has spurred much discussion recently about the ongoing role of professional editors and reporters, as news, like all cultural industries, has been deeply challenged by the proliferation of new media. This new genre of journalism has been spurred in part by the development of web publishing tools and powerful mobile devices, combined with an increasing skepticism about mainstream media, which have prompted readers to become active participants in the creation and dissemination of news. Video and text bloggers, do-it-yourself media activists, and professional journalists are vying for the attention of the public, struggling over the right to define the truth, and attempting to discover which form of news production yields the most viable products.

This chapter explores these changes through an ethnographic study of Salon .com, one of the longest running and most widely trafficked independent journalistic outlets online. According to Scott Rosenberg, one of the site founders, Salon is "old new media" because, since its inception, most of its staff has been culled from the world of traditional journalism, either from mainstream outlets or from journalism schools. The site straddles old and new journalism categories as those categories have been elaborated in much contemporary analysis. Although emerging participatory journalism projects such as Indymedia (www.indymedia.org/en/index.shtml), Ourmedia (www.ourmedia.org/), and Associated Content (www.associatedcontent.com/) seem to be doing away with the need for professional editors and reporters, there are also emerging genres of online news that aim to be nontraditionally professional. The cultural norms and practices that have developed at Salon over the past 12 years are significantly and consciously different from those that have guided magazine and newspaper journalists for decades. Nevertheless, although Salon staffers aim to disrupt the norms of traditional journalism, they are concerned with and constrained by many of the same basic variables that have long defined journalism — economic viability, accuracy, timeliness, quality, and the desire to serve the public interest. By looking closely and more ethnographically at the norms and practices that are emerging in response to these age-old pressures, we can move beyond exaggerations about the death of professional journalism and begin to understand the ways new rules and traditions have evolved and are evolving from within the field.

News and the Culture of Journalism

Related approaches to studying news have developed based on the premise that the best way to understand the field is to look at what news and news work mean within the culture of journalism and the larger cultures within which it exists, rather than attempting to study it from the outside as product or institution. Carey famously calls for a departure from the transmission view of journalism to a ritual view, which understands communication as "a symbolic process whereby reality is produced, maintained, repaired, and transformed" (1989: 23). Drawing on the work of Clifford Geertz, Carey suggests studying communication as culture in order "to understand the meanings that others have placed on experience, to build up the vertical record of what has been said at other times, in other places, and in other ways" (62). Along these same lines, Zelizer (1992) argues that journalism should be considered not only a profession but also an interpretive community, where members are united by a shared discourse and by collective interpretation of key public events. In her analysis of coverage of John F. Kennedy's assassination, she demonstrates the process by which journalists interpreted events in a way that argued for their legitimacy as storytellers. Ettema and Glasser (1998) approach investigative journalism as a form of social and moral inquiry and use interviews with journalists to explore the tensions and contradictions that characterize professional mainstream American journalism. More theoretically, sociologist Bourdieu (2005), in his analysis of what he called the journalistic field, argued that journalistic product is primarily shaped by the ways its members negotiate among themselves. Don't look to the readers, he said. "The essential part of what is presented in [the newspapers] *L'Express* and *Le Nouvel Observateur* is determined by the relationship between *L'Express* and *Le Nouvel Observateur*" (2005: 5).

Journalism scholars, however, have focused their attention almost exclusively on the culture and products of mainstream professional outlets, which now represent only a small and shrinking dimension of contemporary journalism (Zelizer 2004). Dahlgren and Sparks (1991) call this the "metonymic character" of journalism scholarship, that is, the tendency to define journalism based on the study of only a small portion of news products and producers. "Consider the repertoire," writes Zelizer, "of candidates that would not currently merit membership under the narrowed definition of journalism: *A Current Affair,* MTV's *Week in Rock,* internet listservs, Jon Stewart, nakednews.com, reporters for the Weather Channel, and rap music are a few that come to mind" (6). Although scholars are opening their perspective as alternative forms proliferate and increasingly capture public attention, an artificial division remains separating the study of mainstream and alternative journalism forms and is manifest in the way scholars still mostly treat anything but traditional news practices as only tangentially related to news discourse (Russell 2007). As the practices, forms, and technologies for creating and distributing news increase and become more diverse, such journalism scholarship becomes less and less relevant.

The failure to integrate emerging forms of news fully into the study of journalism is reflected in popular characterizations of the news media environment as either doomed or saved by new digital tools. Several recent books have been published that lament the detrimental effects on journalism of emerging technologies and alternative practices, arguing, for example, that the internet is the most recent in a series of information technologies that have worked to break up the mass audience for newspapers (Meyer 2004) and spurred young people to "tune out," creating a generation of the uninformed and thereby threatening "democracy itself" (Mindich 2004). On the other hand, books such as Dan Gillmor's *We the Media* (2004) celebrate new technologies for providing grassroots journalists with the means to challenge the corporate monopoly on journalism, transforming news from lecture into conversation and news consumers into producers. Similarly, recent works on blogging see the emergence of a whole new structure of politics and news driven by personal digital publishing and broadcasting tools and by the networks in which they circulate (see, e.g., Armstrong and Zúniga 2006; Kline et al. 2005; and Reynolds 2006). These exaltations of new journalistic forms and practices are based on often compelling anecdotal evidence but overlook the offline structures and power dynamics reflected in online communication.

My analysis draws on research on journalism undertaken by scholars such as Boczkowski (2005) and Allan (2006), work that avoids either utopian or dystopian discourses by looking at social infrastructures when considering how new technical capabilities may be influencing cultures of producers (and consumers). In 2006, I conducted in-depth interviews with more than 20 Salon writers, editors, and website architects at both the New York office and the San Francisco headquarters, a large portion of the site's relatively small staff. Drawing on these interviews and on the site content,[1] I will examine the approaches taken by the staff toward readership, sourcing, and the vaunted norm of objectivity — three foundational or central components of professional journalism as it has been defined over roughly the past 100 years. Positions toward these key components, I think, have been significantly adapted and in some cases reinvented within the journalistic culture at Salon.

Salon as a Distinctive Form of Journalism

Salon was founded in 1995 by David Talbot — former arts, features, and Sunday magazine editor for the *San Francisco Examiner* — along with a group of *Examiner* journalists. The group received funding from Adobe, Apple, and Hambrecht & Quist. Talbot (2001) describes Salon as an extension of *Image,* the *Examiner*'s Sunday magazine:

> I always thought that, not to be boastful, the work Gary Kamiya and I were doing and the kind of writers we were drawing on here in the Bay Area were of a national caliber. But we didn't get much national attention. The internet, of course, allowed us to show the world what we can do. It was a way to have a national if not international platform. All of these people who were a part of our posse [at the magazine] are now with us, including Scott Rosenberg, who is Salon's managing editor, and Joan Walsh, who is our news editor and was a freelancer at *Image.* Laura Miller, our New York editor, was also a freelancer at *Image.*

Salon also has ties to the *Whole Earth Catalog,* launched in San Francisco in 1968 by Stewart Brand and a group of like-minded artists and thinkers. Brand has argued, like many, that *Whole Earth*–style countercultural ideals regarding decentralization, personalization, and the power of free information shaped the internet and much of the early information age. In the words of Fred Turner, these activist-philosophers — Brand and later Kevin Kelly, Howard Rheingold, John Perry Barlow, and others — turned digital media "into the emblems of their own shared way of living and the evidence of their individual credibility . . . , giving voice to the era's techno-social visions" (Turner 2006: 7). One of these emblems is the Well, one of the oldest and most respected online communities, a combination of the Whole Earth community, computer nerds, intellectuals, hippies, and journalists. The Well was bought by Salon in 1999. Rheingold, whose experiences on the Well inspired his book *Virtual Communities,* wrote of his enthusiasm for the Well-Salon partnership in *Wired* magazine: "I have known Salon staffers Scott Rosenberg and Andrew Leonard as Well regulars. Cliff Figallo, the storied Well manager from the 1980s, and longtime Wellite Mary Elizabeth Williams are in charge of Salon's virtual community. . . . Salon couldn't be much savvier about what works for the Well" (Rheingold 1999).

Salon has always been an interactive site to some degree, but the "salon" concept has always played out separately from the site's editorial content. In addition to the Well, the site supports a reader forum, Table Talk, and a section called Open Letters, where readers comment on articles and blogs posted by Salon writers. Since 1995, Salon has evolved from a biweekly magazine to a daily magazine with emphasis on U.S. politics and culture and with a left-leaning bent. The site is renowned, perhaps, as much for longevity as for its content, riding as it has each wave of the web era and managing despite the odds to poke its head up time and again. As Scott Rosenberg, now vice president of new projects, put it, "Salon's struggle to survive is the stuff of legends." When it went public in 1999, the performance of its stock offering was mediocre. In 2001 Salon launched Salon Premium, a pay-to-view content subscription, which signed more than 130,000 subscribers. Despite the money raised from subscriptions, the company announced in 2002 that it had accumulated $80 million in losses. In 2003 it made an appeal for donations to keep the company running. With the help of donations, an increase in subscriptions, and a resurgence in the online ad market, Salon managed to turn things around and, as of spring 2007, was making small quarterly profits (OTC Bulletin Board 2007). Throughout, Salon has had no difficulty attracting talented journalists and columnists, a feat Talbot ascribes to the increasingly marketing-driven mainstream news environment and its constraints on journalists. "One of the reasons why Salon and other websites have been so successful at attracting talent despite how risky it is — particularly nowadays to go to work for a dotcom — is because journalists were at the end of their ropes. They felt they were completely stifled creatively because newspapers and magazines and television had become so formulaic and marketing-driven" (Talbot 2001). Salon has featured controversial and high-profile columnists, such as Camille Paglia, whose writing on contemporary feminism and academic theory has drawn heated criticism; "politically incorrect" comedian Bill Maher; and torture expert military instructor Malcolm W. Nance. Several of the site's writers teach at New York University's Cultural Reporting and Criticism program, which has turned into a sort of feeder program for Salon. Scott Lamb, graduate and former Salon editor, describes the program as offering a form of highbrow alternative journalism training that combines journalistic skills with the individual writer's voice. It focuses on a broad understanding of contemporary culture and the ability to analyze, criticize, and build an argument. Kerry Lauerman, New York editorial director, contrasts the organizational structure at Salon with those of offline outlets at which he has worked, describing it as a "flat company." Unlike traditional magazines, where editors assign stories, at Salon editors create what Lauerman calls "coverage spots," leaving particular story topic and content up to the writer. "The whole purpose of Salon is to be bottom up," he says.

Salon dramatically entered the mainstream news agenda in 1998 by breaking the story that Henry Hyde, House Judiciary Committee chairman and adamant supporter of impeaching President Bill Clinton for his affair with Monica Lewinsky, had himself conducted a four-year extramarital affair. When asked in 2001 what aspect of Salon he appreciates most, founding editor-in-chief David Talbot responded:

> I think we've broken story after story that the rest of the media refused to break, even when they had the story, because they were scared of the story, or they just didn't think it was appropriate. Conventional media is pretty narrow when it considers what is newsworthy — and worthy of their attention. I could mention a lot of stories; Henry Hyde would be one. I think that was important for the American people to know. I think that had an impact on sort of the impeachment bandwagon that was building for Clinton. I think it slowed it down.

Another founding member of Salon, Douglas Cruickshank, echoed this sentiment when he described Salon as a "conventional newsroom with an unconventional willingness to take on stories that mainstream journalism will not." Perhaps most famously, in 2004, nearly two years after the initial images of detainees emerged from Abu Ghraib in Iraq, Salon obtained and published files and other electronic documents from a leaked report from the U.S. Army's internal investigation of the scandal. According to Jeanne Carstensen, Salon's managing editor:

> The Abu Ghraib package was a journalistic opportunity that comes along very rarely, and it was a perfect marriage of an extremely important journalistic story that had to be told and the right medium to tell it in. It was perfect because creating galleries of those photos on the web was the best way that you could ever hope to present such an archive and we were able to build it in such a way that now exists as the definitive record of the Abu Ghraib scandal.

The Hyde and Abu Ghraib stories form an important part of the collective memory of the Salon staff, notable not only for including material the mainstream media would not publish but also for the editorial reasoning behind the argument for running them. One or both of these stories were mentioned as important moments in Salon's development by all but a few of the Salon staff members I interviewed. In repeated conversations, Salon writers and reporters articulate norms that have emerged in their newsroom as a response not only to new technologies but also to perceived new economic and political realities.

Salon and Readers

Salon caters to a distinct and loyal readership made up of what Rosenberg describes as "educated and intelligent people in both coastal and isolated places."

The latter, he says, become the most avid readers, using Salon to connect with fellow readers across the country. Unlike online news outlets now experimenting with participation by anointing readers as de facto reporters, Salon maintains that good journalism depends on more careful management of reader contributions. So while Salon makes considerable efforts to foster community among its readers, reader discourse largely takes place outside the realm of staff- and freelancer-produced content.

Lauerman says Salon "begins with the assumption that our readers are smart. I remember taking journalism courses as a university student and being told to write for a third grade reading level. . . . At Salon we are not pandering. We're interested and we create content that we think smart readers would want to read." There is admitted tension at Salon between the desire to attract intelligent and vocal readers and having to contend with their opinions. At its inception, the Open Letters section, which allows readers to post comments at the end of each story, for example, drew readers in closer to the content but also spurred disagreement among the staff. According to Lauerman, the motivation for creating Open Letters was to give readers the opportunity to participate in the publication and to harness their intelligence. Instead, he said, in many cases "it just empowered people to say mean things." Indeed, readers often attack writers whose views don't match their own. "Lauren Sandler is a liar (I use the term advisedly)," reads one letter on a piece written by Salon's Life editor. "Her reporting is bogus to the extreme. Salon has zero credibility if they keep her on staff" (Colorado Boy 2006).

Staff ambivalence about this kind of participation is shared by Salon readers. A poll taken around the time Open Letters was launched demonstrated that the overwhelming majority of readers did not want readers "to take over site content." Drawing on his pre-internet news experience, Rosenberg explained, "It's the same as it was at the *San Francisco Examiner,* when any type of change sparked an uproar among readers. Readers always hate change." Salon readers are now given the option of viewing all letters or a pared-down selection tagged "only editors' choices." Salon writers and editors have responded to letters directly for years, a contrast to the barriers that have long existed at traditional outlets. According to Scott Lamb, former Salon editor, "There is intentionally not a big wall between Salon readers and writers and editors."

A general understanding that responsiveness to readers is an integral part of the Salon product butts up against consensus that "editorial shouldn't pay too much attention to reader criticism," as Sandler put it. "The conversations that spin out of Salon stories can be great, but we never let readers shape coverage, ever. We don't cater to readers or advertisers. . . . And that's something that's really different compared to glossies. I've had tons of articles killed [at offline publications] because they just didn't cater to the reader." There is a feeling among the staff that, as the curtain is increasingly pulled back on the digital-era newsroom, journalists can find themselves producing content to please involved reader-subscribers just as easily as they can to please involved corporate bosses.

Indeed, readers have come to expect Salon stories to reflect a certain ideological point of view, and they have often resisted what Rosenberg describes as "Salon's commitment to accuracy" when it goes against the grain. He elaborates on his blog:

> At Salon, we don't make any claims to nonpartisanship but do maintain our own tradition of journalistic pride, and a commitment to fairness and giving the "other side" a say, and a belief in telling the story as you find it, not as your political preferences might dictate it. This has regularly placed us at odds with at least some of the readers who are funding our stories with their subscription dollars. (Rosenberg 2006)

He gives the example of an investigation into 2004 election irregularities by Salon writer Farhad Manjoo, who asserted that Bush's victory wasn't a result of voter fraud. Although the story was well documented and argued, according to Rosenberg, "it wasn't what many of our readers wanted to hear."

> Ever since, Salon has had a steady trickle of disgruntled subscribers cancel on us, citing these stories as a factor. It's never been enough to make any difference to our business, and it certainly won't stop us from doing further reporting on the subject and presenting our findings accurately. But it's disheartening. (Rosenberg 2006)

This awareness of reader preferences is heightened by the fact that Salon staff have access to statistics on traffic to each story. Many of the staff confess that they became obsessed with tracking traffic to their stories when the data first became available, but they say that now that the novelty has worn off they pay less attention. Carstensen, Lauerman, and others say they realize that not everything that should be covered is going to be wildly popular among readers. Yet the availability of such statistics adds layers to editorial discussion. According to Lamb, "The official line from [Executive Editor] Joan Walsh is that, if we think a story is important, we go with it, even if it's not going to get a lot of hits. She doesn't weight things toward the part of the publication that gets the most hits."

Salon journalists speak about readers in remarkably similar terms — as intelligent, opinionated, sometimes invasive, and always as an essential element to the Salon brand. At Salon there is no blurring line between reader and journalist. There is, however, an online dance, a controlled, wary, and constantly evolving interaction. Readers are not viewed as the passive consumers of the past (Carey 1986, 1989; Schudson 1978, 2003) or as the expanded staff of a new-era populist pastiche-style journalism (Gillmor 2004; Rosen 2004).

Salon and Sources

Several Salon journalists describe one of the strengths of Salon stories as born from their frequent use of sources that fall outside the realm of what is considered by more traditional news organizations as bureaucratically credible. Salon has its own distinct set of criteria to determine the desirability of writers and the acceptability of sources. Sandler says that she looks for writers with "a unique voice and something to say. Those sort of writers are what make Salon. That's the sort of writer that I am and as a freelancer I got very tired of seeing my pieces killed or sanitized or stripped of any voice or point of view by editors." Lauerman says, "Sources used to inform Salon stories are broadened by the types of people we choose to write for us." Rather than looking at whether or not a source is authoritative, he says, "we look at whether or not the source will stand up over time, whether he or she is being accurate." Sandler explains that there is a concerted effort not to echo the point of view of the official sources typically used in traditional news stories. "We have a skeptical eye but probably in the opposite way that mainstream media does. We are most skeptical of anything coming from official sources," meaning the government.

This strategy famously went wrong when in 2002 Salon ran a story by Jason Leopold that implicated Bush administration official Thomas White in the Enron scandal. The story turned out to be both plagiarized and unverifiable. The Jason Leopold scandal was mentioned over and over again in interviews with Salon staff members as a sort of cautionary tale about the need to be vigilant about the accuracy of writers and their sources. Soon after the story ran, the *Financial Times* informed Lauerman, the story editor, that a large portion of the story was plagiarized from an article that had appeared in their publication. Then, as Lauerman puts it, "we fell down the rabbit hole." They discovered that they could not authenticate an e-mail that said White was aware of the financial machinations of the division he ran. Salon retracted the story but not before *New York Times* columnist Paul Krugman and several other national news outlets had picked it up, making Leopold's piece and Salon's error a national news story.

To Lauerman, Leopold's enduring popularity on the web despite the widespread coverage of this and subsequent incidents of fraudulent reporting represents a significant problem of some web-based journalism:

Leopold definitely represents the dark side of the web. There are so many positives to the internet and the ways it can equalize the playing field. But on the other hand people cling to places that just validate their worldview and the truth really takes a seat behind that. He could never get published after that scandal at an established news organization. Yet he became this sort of hero for throngs of people online. He capitalizes on the heavily partisan echo chamber aspect of the web.

The Leopold scandal looms large in the history of Salon because its journalists and editors work hard to maintain accuracy, without filtering out the reporters' points of view. Indeed, in opposition to traditional aspirations toward objectivity in reporting, Salon strives to demonstrate that accuracy and opinion can coexist. "Salon is sort of a civilized filter," Lauerman says, and if Salon editors fail to filter out the likes of Leopold, then they have failed to do their job according to the standards they have set for themselves.

The Question of Objectivity

Although Salon has an Opinion section specifically reserved for editorial-style pieces that assert a particular argument, the classification of stories as either news or opinion is often ambiguous. "If it is a reporting-driven piece," Lauerman explains, "even if it has a point of view, we put it in the news. It's an opinion piece if it is clearly a rhetorical argument based on the writer's opinion." A separate opinion section was originally established by a former editor with a background in newspaper journalism who was bothered by mixing the two types of stories. Lauerman thinks the distinction is artificial and unnecessary. "Our readers get the post-impartial or the post-objective thing," he says, echoing a sentiment voiced in many of my interviews with the staff.

Carstensen sees Salon content as more like that of magazines than newspapers. "There is a healthy tension between the enterprise of reporting — trying to tell a full and balanced and fair story — and allowing point of view to come through in reported stories. I don't think the goal here is to be entirely neutral. And rather than pretend that's not there, which is what newspaper stories often do, you can allow that in magazine stories there's a sort of thesis that a writer is testing out and do your best through your skills as a reporter. You also have to sell the reader on your reporting."

This view of objectivity as an outdated concept is articulated in journalist and editor conversations about what they do and also in the work they produce, which combines serious reporting and unabashed engagement with the issues and ideas raised by the reporting. Two weeks after Salon broke the story of

Henry Hyde's affair with Cherie Snodgrass, it ran an editorial explaining the decision to do so. After verifying the story with sources that included Hyde himself, Salon decided to run the story, which came to them on a tip from Norm Sommer, a friend of Snodgrass's ex-husband, who had been trying to "leak" the story for months to various publications, including the *Los Angeles Times,* the *Boston Globe,* and the *Miami Herald.* The editorial's tone reflected the controversial nature of the story and the heated politics of its context:

> Ugly times call for ugly tactics. When a pack of sanctimonious thugs beats you and your country upside the head with a tire-iron, you can withdraw to the sideline and meditate, or you can grab it out of their hands and fight back.
>
> We hope by publishing today's article to bring this entire sordid conflict to a head and expose its utter absurdity. Does the fact that Henry Hyde engaged in an adulterous affair and tried to keep it hidden from his family and constituents mean he is not fit to hold public office? Absolutely not. And the same is true of President Clinton. It's time to put an end to the confusion of the personal and the political, this moralistic furor that has wreaked utter havoc with our system of governance. (Salon 1998)

Scott Rosenberg sees the Hyde story as "a defining moment that made Salon known as a sort of partisan outlet for progressive politics." He says that there is a "push and pull between general contrarian journalism and fairness and balance. While we are clearly identified with certain politics, we are serious journalists."

Salon staff points to its coverage of Abu Ghraib as another example of its post-objective professionalism. The site was leaked photos from an internal U.S. Army investigation. The resulting story and images generated a lot of controversy and drew a lot of readers. The photos spurred editorial discussion about the possibilities the story afforded Salon as a news site that could run hundreds of images without concern for space versus traditional editorial sensibilities that gave the story's editors pause. Jeanne Carstensen remembers the deliberations and how the editors played devil's advocate with themselves:

> I think it took vision on the part of Salon to be able to put that many re-sources into that kind of a project and take the risk of publishing it. We had to think about it long and hard. Some people, of course, feel that it's an insult to our country, to our soldiers, that it's endangering national security. But we believe that the public deserves to know the truth of what was done in our name. We spent a long time researching everything, and to the best of our ability, presenting it without any kind of distortion. That

meant that by the time we really published it, the work we did had a lot of integrity, and we really did not get very much hate mail. I mean, the praise and appreciation far outweighed the criticism.

Both the Hyde and Abu Ghraib stories and the discussion surrounding them illustrate Salon's particular brand of post-objective era journalism where the political value of information is fully acknowledged and exploited. Lauerman says, "At Salon there has always been a perspective that most serious news organizations operate under this phony guise of being objective and being free of any point of view, like robots, bloodless."

Conclusion

Salon has been staking out ground in online journalism for more than a decade. Where it once seemed brash in its bending of traditional norms — flouting objectivity in favor of authenticity, working unofficial sources, encouraging writerly liberties, drawing on reader reaction — it now seems brash for carving out a suddenly more traditional-seeming space, where a certain genre of first-wave online news professionalism is being defended, advanced, and updated, the audience both encouraged to participate and held at bay. The shared understanding among staffers is that Salon offers a viable professional genre of news, that the formula worked out at Salon over the years that newspapers and magazines resisted any real change will prove increasingly a model of the professional journalism of the future. On the one hand, Salon seems to have freed itself from the norms and practices shaped by the "tyranny of authoritative facts" that communication scholars have long suggested tends to serve officialdom and corporate interests (Schiller 1991; Schudson 1978) and also to have moved instinctively, on the foundation laid perhaps by the Whole Earth community, toward the journalistic storytelling model that Carey called for long before the dawn of the world wide web: "The public will begin to reawaken," Carey wrote, "when they are addressed as a conversational partner and are encouraged to join the talk rather than sit passively as spectators before a discussion conducted by experts" (1987: 14).

On the other hand, in an era when news blogs multiply faster than anyone can count, and technologies appear that can exponentially increase "network effects" wherein digitized words and images from every corner of the world and beyond link with each other to tell us the stories of our realities,[2] Salon's evolution in its relationship with its readers — those nonprofessional contributors looking for "excuses to be mean" or to resist change — may prove most significant. Columns such as Salon writer Glen Greenwald's, where a writer with much knowledge in a certain area produces in near real time copious original material based on like-minded reader tips and links, suggest at least one of the ways journalism beat reporting may be evolving to include network era readers and technologies without "catering" to them.

As opportunities have increased for amateur cultural production, news audiences have called into question the procedures and values of professional journalism that have dominated news culture for the past century, increasingly resisting the content and practices of mainstream news by creating alternatives and by using professional journalism products as mere launching points to offer contesting points of view. What is noteworthy about Salon is its position on the threshold: the fact that it offers a measured departure, replacing mass-media era norms and practices with an updated but strongly rooted journalistic culture and fairly distinct standards and practices. The surprising consistency with which the Salon staff, from executive and founding editors to reporters and interns, can articulate the mission and culture of Salon-style news writing is another nod to the transitional nature of contemporary news. Nothing about the Salon approach to news is taken for granted. There is no reliance on any "received knowledge" about what constitutes journalism today. The way Salon has renegotiated and is renegotiating the professional journalism norms and practices developed over the past century is distinct to Salon as an institution and recognized as such. The staff has seemed to internalize those negotiated norms, and the work they produce as a result is Salon-style news rather than what in a recently passed era might have simply been accepted as "news." Seen from this perspective, it seems now that in studying journalism-communication, scholars must approach news outlets and newsroom cultures distinctly, letting preconceptions about generalized journalism culture fall away, including the obsolete but lasting theoretical dichotomy that posits the continuing existence of a "traditional" journalism on one side and a "new-media" journalism on the other. Further, if newsroom cultures are to be seen as especially particular and distinct in this transitional era, where each one is on some advanced level negotiating its culture and product, then it makes sense that an anthropological approach to their study, which begins at direct observation, would be a most productive avenue of inquiry.

Notes

1. All quoted material from Salon staff members is taken from interviews with the author unless otherwise noted.

2. A recent example would be Microsoft's Photosynth software based on Seadragon technology presented at the May 2007 TED (Technology Entertainment Design) conference (www.ted.com/index.php/talks/view/id/129).

Works Cited

Abbott, Andrew. 1993. The Sociology of Work and Occupations. *Annual Review of Sociology* 19: 187–209.

Abrams, Fran, and Phil Davison. 1997. Tempers Rise over Volcano Island. *Independent,* August 26: 6.

Abu-Lughod, Lila. 2000. Locating Ethnography. *Ethnography* 1(2): 261–67.

———. 2004. *Dramas of Nationhood: The Politics of Television in Egypt.* Chicago: University of Chicago.

Adams, David. 1997. Fury as Montserrat Islanders Flee Volcano. *Times,* August 20: 9.

Aday, S., S. Livingston, and M. Hebert. 2005. Embedding the Truth: A Cross-cultural Analysis of Objectivity and Television Coverage of the Iraq War. *Harvard International Journal of Press/Politics* 10(1): 3–21.

Alasuutari, Pertti. 1995. *Researching Culture: Qualitative Methods and Cultural Studies.* London: Sage.

———, ed. 1999. *Rethinking the Media Audience.* London: Sage.

Aldridge, Meryl. 2007. *Understanding the Local Media.* Maidenhead: Open University Press.

Allan, Stuart. 2004. *News Culture.* 2nd ed. Maidenhead: Open University Press.

———. 2006. *Online News.* London: Open University Press.

Allen-Mills, Tony. 1996. Experts Fly to Volcano Island. *Sunday Times,* December 1: 17.

Alstead, Robert. 1995. Ready to Rock? *Scotland on Sunday,* November 5: 16.

Altheide, David. 1976. *Creating Reality.* Beverly Hills: Sage.

———. 1997. The News Media, the Problem Frame, and the Production of Fear. *Sociological Quarterly* 38(4): 647–69.

Altman, John, and Melinda Hinkson, eds. 2007. *Coercive Reconciliation: Stabilise, Normalise, Exit Aboriginal Australia.* Melbourne: Arena Publications.

American Anthropological Association. 1998. *Code of Ethics of the American Anthropological Association.* Accessed at www.aaanet.org/committees/ethics/ethcode .htm.

American Society of Newspaper Editors. 2007. *ASNE Statement of Principles.* Accessed at www.asne.org/kiosk/archive/principl.htm.

Anderson, Benedict. 1983. *Imagined Communities: Reflections on the Origin and Spread of Nationalism.* New York: Verso.

Anderson, Pat, and Rex Wild. 2007. Little Children Are Sacred: Report of the Northern Territory Board of Inquiry into the Protection of Aboriginal Children from Sexual Abuse 2007. Darwin: NT Government.

Appadurai, Arjun. 1990. Disjuncture and Difference in the Global Cultural Economy. *Theory, Culture, and Society* 7: 295–310.

Applbaum, Kalman. 2004. *The Marketing Era: From Professional Practice to Global Positioning.* New York: Routledge.

Armbrust, Walter. 1996. *Mass Culture and Modernization in Egypt.* Cambridge: Cambridge University Press.

Armstrong, Jerome, and Markos Moulitsas Zúniga. 2006. *Crashing the Gate: Netroots, Grassroots, and the Rise of People-Powered Politics.* White River Junction, Vt.: Chelsea Green.

Askew, Kelly, and Richard Wilk, eds. 2002. *The Anthropology of Media: A Reader.* Oxford: Blackwell.

Associated Press. 2006. Chávez Backs Possible Vote to Close Private TV Stations. December 4.

———. 2007. Venezuelans Protest Shutdown of TV Station. *Palm Beach Post,* May 27: 24A.

Associated Press Managing Editors. 2004. *Ethics Code.* Accessed at www.asne.org/index.cfm?ID=388.

Atton, Chris. 2008. Alternative and Citizen Journalism. In *Handbook of Journalism Studies,* ed. K. Wahl-Jorgensen and T. Hanitzsch. Mahwah, N.J.: Lawrence Erlbaum Associates.

Augoustinos, Martha, Keith Tuffin, and Mark Rapley. 1999. Genocide or a Failure to Gel? Racism, History, and Nationalism in Australian Talk. *Discourse and Society* 10(3): 351–78.

Austin, John Langshaw. 1980. *How to Do Things with Words: The William James Lectures Delivered at Harvard University in 1955.* Oxford: Oxford University Press.

Australian Press Council (APC). 2001. *Reporting Guidelines.* Accessed at www.presscouncil.org.au/pcsite/guides/gpr248.html.

Awad, Isabel. 2006. Journalists and Their Sources: Lessons from Anthropology. *Journalism Studies* 7(6): 922–39.

Baisnée, Olivier, and Dominique Marchetti. 2006. The Economy of Just-in-Time Television Newscasting: Journalistic Production and Professional Excellence at Euronews. *Ethnography* 7(1): 99–123.

Bakhtin, Mikhael M. 1981 [1934–35]. Discourse in the Novel. In *The Dialogic Imagination: Four Essays,* ed. M. Holquist. Austin: University of Texas Press.

Banda, Fackson. 2006. *African Media Development Initiative Zambia Report.* London: BBC World Service Trust.

Bantz, Charles, Suzanne McCorkle, and Roberta C. Baade. 1980. The News Factory. *Communication Research* 7(1): 45–68.

Barbour, Rosalind, and Jennifer Kitzinger, eds. 1999. *Developing Focus Group Research.* London: Sage.

Barnhurst, Kevin G. 1998. Politics in the Fine Meshes: Young Citizens, Power, and Media. *Media, Culture & Society* 20(2): 201–18.

Barr, Cameron W. 2002. After 21 Months of Intifada, a Wall Is Born. *Christian Science Monitor,* July 10: A1.

Barthes, Roland. 1981. Theory of the Text. In *Untying the Text: A Post-Structuralist Reader,* ed. Robert Young, 32–47. Boston: Routledge and Kegan Young.

———. 2007. *Die helle Kammer: Bemerkungen zur Photographie.* Frankfurt am Main: Suhrkamp.

Barton, Mary, and David Hamilton. 2000. Literary Practices. In *Situated Litera-*

cies: Reading and Writing in Context, ed. Mary Barton, David Hamilton, and Roz Ivanic. New York: Routledge.

Barton, Mary, David Hamilton, and Roz Ivanic, eds. 2000. *Situated Literacies: Reading and Writing in Context.* New York: Routledge.

Basu, Tapan, Pradip Datta, Sumit Sarkar, Tanika Sarkar, and Sambuddha Sen. 1993. *Khaki Shorts and Saffron Flags: A Critique of the Hindu Right.* New Delhi: Orient Longmans.

Bateson, Gregory. 1987. *Steps to an Ecology of Mind.* Northvale: Jason Aronson.

Bauman, Richard. 1986. *Story, Performance, and Event.* New York: Cambridge University Press.

Bauman, Richard, and Charles Briggs. 1990. Poetics and Performance as Critical Perspectives on Language and Social Life. *Annual Review of Anthropology* 19: 59–88.

Beeman, William. 1987. Anthropology and the Print Media. *Anthropology Today* 3(3): 2–4.

Beer, Gillian. 1998. Has Nature a Future? In *The Third Culture: Literature and Science,* ed. E. Schaffer. Berlin: Walter de Gruyter.

Bell, Phillip. 1997. News Values, Race, and "The Hanson Debate" in Australian Media. *Asia Pacific Media Educator* 2: 38–47.

Belsey, Andrew, and Ruth Chadwick, eds. 1992. *Ethical Issues in Journalism and the Media.* London: Routledge.

Benedict, Ruth. 1946. *The Chrysanthemum and the Sword.* Boston: Houghton Mifflin.

Benjamin, Walter. 2005. Eine kleine Geschichte der Photographie. In *Das Kunstwerk im Zeitalter seiner technischen Reproduzierbarkeit: Drei Studien zur Kunstsoziologie.* Frankfurt am Main: Suhrkamp.

Benthall, Jonathan. 1993. *Disasters, Relief, and the Media.* London: I. B. Taurus.

Besnier, Niko. 1991. Literacy and the Notion of Person on Nukulaelae Attoll. *American Anthropologist* 93(3): 570–87.

Bew, Ros. 2006. The Role of the Freelancer in Local Journalism. In *Local Journalism and Local Media: Making the Local News,* ed. B. Franklin. New York: Routledge.

Bill. 1997. Short Active Volcano Blows Top. Cartoon, *Herald,* August 25: 13.

Billig, Michael. 2005. *Banal Nationalism.* London: Sage.

Binyon, Michael. 1997. London Starts Talks on Volcano Island's Future. *Times,* August 5: A6.

Bird, S. Elizabeth. 1990. Storytelling on the Far Side: Journalism and the Weekly Tabloid. *Critical Studies in Mass Communication* 7(4): 377–89.

———. 1992. *For Enquiring Minds: A Cultural Study of Supermarket Tabloids.* Knoxville: University of Tennessee Press.

———. 1998. News We Can Use: An Audience Perspective on the Tabloidisation of News in the United States. *Javnost: Journal of the European Institute for Communication and Culture* 3: 33–50.

———. 2003. *The Audience in Everyday Life: Living in a Media World.* New York: Routledge.

———. 2005a. The Journalist as Ethnographer? How Anthropology Can Enrich Journalistic Practice. In *Media Anthropology,* ed. Eric Rothenbuhler and Mihai Coman. Beverly Hills: Sage.

———. 2005b. CJ's Revenge: A Case Study of News as Cultural Narrative. In *Media Anthropology*, ed. Eric Rothenbuhler and Mihai Coman. Beverly Hills: Sage.

———. Forthcoming. From Fan Practice to Mediated Moments: The Value of Practice Theory in the Understanding of Media Audiences. In *Theorising Media and Practice*, ed. Birgit Bräuchler and John Postill. New York: Berghahn.

Bird, S. Elizabeth, and Robert W. Dardenne. 1988. Myth, Chronicle, and Story: Exploring the Narrative Qualities of News. In *Media, Myths, and Narratives: Television and the Press*, ed. James W. Carey, 67–86. Beverly Hills: Sage.

———. 2008. Rethinking News and Myth as Storytelling. In *Handbook of Journalism Studies*, ed. K. Wahl-Jorgensen and T. Hanitzsch. Mahwah, N.J.: Lawrence Erlbaum Associates.

Bishara, Amahl. 2006. Local Hands, International News: Palestinian Journalists and the International Media. *Ethnography* 7(1): 19–46.

Black, Ian. 1997. Britain "Stands by" Montserrat. *Guardian*, July 26: 14.

Bloch, Maurice. 1998. *How We Think They Think: Anthropological Approaches to Cognition, Memory, and Literacy*. Boulder, Colo.: Westview.

Blood, R. Warwick, and Paul Lee. 1997. Public Opinion at Risk: An Elaboration of Public Opinion about Pauline Hanson's Agenda. *Australian Journalism Review* 19 (2): 88–103.

Blood, R. Warwick, John Tulloch, and Michael Enders. 2000. Risk Communication and Reflexivity: Conversations about Fear of Crime. *Australian Journal of Communication* 27(3): 15–39.

Blumer, Herbert. 1948. Public Opinion and Public Opinion Polling. *American Sociological Review* 13: 542–55.

Boczkowski, Pablo J. 2005. *Digitizing the News*. Cambridge, Mass.: MIT Press.

Boczkowski, Pablo J., and Martin de Santos. 2007. When More Media Equals Less News: Patterns of Content Homogenization in Argentina's Leading Print and Online Newspapers. *Political Communication* 24(2): 167–80.

Born, Georgina. 2005. *Uncertain Vision: Birt, Dyke, and the Reinvention of the BBC*. New York: Vintage.

Borofsky, Robert. 2005. *Yanomami: The Fierce Controversy and What We Can Learn from It*. Berkeley: University of California Press.

Bourdieu, Pierre. 1977. *Outline of a Theory of Practice*. Cambridge: Cambridge University Press.

———. 1979. Public Opinion Does Not Exist. In *Communication and Class Struggle*, ed. A. Mattelart and S. Siegelaub. New York: International General.

———. 1984. *Distinction: A Social Critique of the Judgment of Taste*. Cambridge, Mass.: Harvard University Press.

———. 1990. *Was heißt Sprechen? Die Ökonomie des sprachlichen Tausches*. Wien: Braumüller.

———. 1991. *Language and Symbolic Power*. Cambridge, Mass.: Harvard University Press.

———. 1996. *On Television*. New York: Free Press.

———. 2005. The Political Field, the Social Science Field, and the Journalistic Field. In *Bourdieu and the Journalistic Field*, ed. R. D. Benson and E. Neveu. Cambridge: Polity Press.

———. 2006. Einleitung. In *Eine Illegitime Kunst: Die Socialen Gebrauchsweisen der Photographie*, ed. P. Bourdieu and L. Boltanskie. Frankfurt: Europäische Verlagsanstalt.

Bowman, Glenn. 2000. Two Deaths of Basem Rishmawi: Identity Constructions and Reconstructions in a Muslim-Christian Palestinian Community. In *Perplexities of Identification: Anthropological Studies in Cultural Differentiation and the Use of Resources,* ed. H. Driessen and T. Otto. Aarhus: Aarhus University Press.

Boyer, Dominic. 2000. On the Sedimentation and Accreditation of Social Knowledges of Difference: Mass Media, Journalism, and the Reproduction of East/West Alterities in Unified Germany. *Cultural Anthropology* 15(4): 459–91.

———. 2001. Yellow Sand of Berlin. *Ethnography* 3: 421–39.

———. 2003. Censorship as a Vocation: The Institutions, Practices, and Cultural Logic of Media Control in the German Democratic Republic. *Comparative Study of Society and History* 45: 511–45.

———. 2005. *Spirit and System: Media, Intellectuals, and the Dialectic in Modern German Culture.* Chicago: University of Chicago Press.

———. 2007. *Understanding Media: A Popular Philosophy.* Chicago: Prickly Paradigm Press.

———. n.d. Anthropology as Social Theory and Ethnography. Manuscript under review.

Braga, Théophilo 1885. *O Povo Português Nos Seus Costumes, Crenças E Tradições.* Lisbon: Publicações Dom Quixote.

Brennen, Bonnie. 1995. Cultural Discourse of Journalists: The Material Conditions of Newsroom Labor. In *Newsworkers: Towards a History of the Rank and File,* ed. H. Hardt and B. Brennen. Minneapolis: University of Minnesota Press.

Briggs, Charles L. 1988. *Competence in Performance: The Creativity of Tradition in Mexicano Verbal Art.* Philadelphia: University of Pennsylvania Press.

———. 2007. Mediating Infanticide: Theorizing Relations between Narrative and Violence. *Cultural Anthropology* 22(3): 315–56.

Briggs, Charles, and Richard Bauman. 1992. Genre, Intertextuality, and Social Power. *Journal of Linguistic Anthropology* 2: 131–72.

Britain — Beyond the Montserrat Relief Scandal — The Remains of a Defunct Empire. 1997. *Class Struggle (Internationalist Communist Union),* October/November. Accessed at www.union-communiste.org/?EN-archd-show-1997-6-446-2296-x .html.

Brough, Mark. 1999. A Lost Cause? Representations of Aboriginal and Torres Strait Islander Health in Australian Newspapers. *Australian Journal of Communication* 26(2): 89–98.

Bucholtz, Mary, and Kira Hall. 2005. Identity and Interaction: A Sociocultural Linguistic Approach. *Discourse Studies* 7(4/5): 585–614.

Burdette, Marcia M. 1988. *Zambia: Between Two Worlds.* Boulder: Westview Press.

Burke, Kenneth. 1969. *A Grammar of Motives.* Berkeley: University of California Press.

Burnell, Peter. 1991. Introduction to *Britain's Overseas Aid since 1979: Between Idealism and Self-Interest,* ed. Peter Burnell and Anuradha Bose. Manchester: Manchester University Press.

Butcher, Melissa. 2003. *Transnational Television, Cultural Identity, and Change: When STAR Came to India.* New Delhi: Sage.

Butler, Judith. 1997. *Excitable Speech: A Politics of the Performative.* New York: Routledge.

Carey, James W. 1986. Why and How. In *Reading the News,* ed. M. Schudson and R. K. Manoff. New York: Pantheon Books.

———. 1987. The Press and Public Discourse. *Center Magazine* 20 (March/April): 4–16.

———. 1989. *Communication as Culture: Essays on Media and Society.* Boston: Unwin Hyman.

———. 1993. The Mass Media and Democracy: Between the Modern and the Postmodern. *Journal of International Affairs* 47(1): 1–12.

———. 1995. The Press, Public Opinion, and Public Discourse. In *Public Opinion and the Communication of Consent,* ed. T. Glasser and C. Salmon. New York: Guilford.

Carey, John M. 2003. The Reelection Debate in Latin America. *Latin American Politics and Society* 45(1): 119–33.

Cassell, Joan. 1987. *Cases and Comments* (Special Publication Number 23). American Anthropological Association. Accessed at www.aaanet.org/committees/ethics/ch4 .htm.

Castañeda, Jorge G. 2006. Latin America's Left Turn. *Foreign Affairs,* 28–43.

Castle, Stephen. 1997a. Whitehall Out to Destroy Me, Says Clare Short. *Independent on Sunday,* August 31: 1.

———. 1997b. Who Dumped on Clare and Why? *Independent on Sunday,* August 31: 13.

Cayla, Julien. 2008. Following the Endorser's Shadow: Shah Rukh Khan and the Creation of the Cosmopolitan Indian Male. *Advertising & Society Review* 9(2). Accessed at http://muse.jhu.edu/journals/advertising_and_society_review/ v009/9.2.cayla01.html.

Charmaz, Kathy. 1995. Grounded Theory. In *Rethinking Methods in Psychology,* ed. J. A. Smith, R. Harré, and L. van Langenhove. London: Sage.

Chatterjee, Partha. 1986. *National Thought and the Colonized World.* London: Zed.

———. 1989. Colonialism, Nationalism, and Colonized Women: The Contest in India. *American Ethnologist* 16(4): 622–33.

Chávez, Hugo. 2001. Aló Presidente. Broadcast address, December 17.

———. 2004. Aló Presidente. Broadcast address, February 1.

Chiposa, S. 1989. Shock Kwacha Move Sparks Confusion. *African Business* 133: 17–19.

Clark, David, Brian Breger, Tim Page, and Penny Trams. 2002. *Vietnam's Unseen War Pictures from the Other Side.* Washington, D.C.: National Geographic Video.

Clark, Garcia. 1994. *Onions Are My Husband: Survival and Accumulation by West African Market Women.* Chicago: University of Chicago Press.

Cohen, Akiba A., Mark R. Levy, Itzhak Roeh, and Michael Gurevitch. 1996. *Global Newsrooms, Local Audiences: A Study of the Eurovision News Exchange.* London: John Libbey.

Cohen, Richard. 2002. Build a Fence. *Washington Post,* April 16: A19.

Cohen, Stanley. 1980. *Folk Devils and Moral Panics: The Creation of Mods and Rockers.* 2nd ed. Oxford: Morten Robertson.

Colorado Boy. 2006. Letters. Accessed at http://letters.salon.com/news/feature/2006/11/08/mr_biggs/view/?show=all.

Coman, Mihai, and Eric Rothenbuhler. 2005. The Promise of Media Anthropology. In *Media Anthropology*, ed. Eric Rothenbuhler and Mihai Coman. London: Sage.

Comaroff, Jean, and John L. Comaroff. 1991. *Of Revelation and Revolution*, vol. 1, *Christianity, Colonialism, and Consciousness in South Africa*. Chicago: University of Chicago Press.

Conti, Joseph A., and Moira O'Neil. 2007. Studying Power: Qualitative Methods and the Global Elite. *Qualitative Research* 7(1): 63–82.

Cook, Catherine, Adam Hanieh, and Adah Kay. 2004. *Stolen Youth: The Politics of Israel's Detention of Palestinian Children*. London: Sterling Press.

Cotter, Colleen. 2001. Discourse and Media. In *The Handbook of Discourse Analysis*, ed. D. Schiffrin, D. Tannen, and H. E. Hamilton. Oxford: Blackwell.

Cottle, Simon. 2000a. Media Research and Ethnic Minorities: Mapping the Field. In *Ethnic Minorities and the Media: Changing Cultural Boundaries*, ed. Simon Cottle. Buckingham: Blackwell.

———. 2000b. New(s) Times: Towards a "Second Wave" of News Ethnography. *Communications* 25(1): 19–41.

———, ed. 2003. *Media Organization and Production*. London: Sage.

———. 2004a. Producing Nature(s): On the Changing Production Ecology of Natural History TV. *Media, Culture & Society* 26(1): 91–101.

———. 2004b. *The Racist Murder of Stephen Lawrence: Media Performance and Public Transformation*. Westport: Praeger.

———. 2007. Ethnography and News Production: Past Findings, New Developments. *Sociology Compass* 1(1): 1–16.

Cottle, Simon, and Mark Ashton. 1998. *From BBC Newsroom to BBC Newscentre: Changing Technology and Journalist Practices*. Bath: Bath Spa University College.

Couldry, Nick. 2004. Theorising Media as Practice. *Social Semiotics* 14(2): 115–32.

Covington, Dennis. (1996). *Salvation on Sand Mountain: Snake-Handling and Redemption in Southern Appalachia*. London: Penguin.

Critcher, Chas. 2003. *Moral Panics and the Media*. Maidenhead: Open University Press.

Cuillier, David. 2007. Getting to the Source: Developing Reporter-Source Relationships without Becoming Chums. *Quill*, April 1: 16–22.

Curran, James. 2002. *Media and Power*. London: Routledge.

Curran, James, and Myung-Jin Park. 2000. *De-Westernizing Media Studies*. New York: Routledge.

Dahlgren, Peter, and Colin Sparks, eds. 1991. *Communication and Citizenship: Journalism and the Public Sphere in the New Media Age*. London: Routledge.

———. *Journalism and Popular Culture*. London: Sage.

Dalton, Alastair. 1997. "Cataclysmic" Eruption Alert Spurs Montserrat Evacuation. *Scotsman*, August 19: 9.

Dao, James. 2002. Redefining an Idea as Old as Civilization Itself. *New York Times*, April 21: 14.

Davidson, Lawrence. 2001. *America's Palestine: Popular and Official Perceptions from Balfour to Israeli Statehood*. Gainesville: University Press of Florida.

Davison, Phil. 1997a. Echoes of Pompeii on Stricken Isle. *Independent,* August 30: 12.
——. 1997b. Thanks, Britain, for This Tent and Stinking Latrine. *Independent on Sunday,* August 24: 12.
——. 1997c. Volcano Isle Gets Building Plan and Short Visit. *Independent,* September 3: 11.
de Donk, Wim van, Brian Loader, Paul Nixon, and Dieter Rucht. 2004. *Cyberprotest: New Media, Citizens, and Social Movements.* New York: Routledge.
de Jong, Wilma, Martin Shaw, and Neil Stammers. 2005. *Global Activism, Global Media.* Ann Arbor: Pluto Press.
Delli Carpini, Michael, and Bruce Williams. 1994. Methods, Metaphors, and Media Research: The Uses of Television in Political Conversation. *Communication Research* 21(6): 782–812.
——. 1996. Constructing Public Opinion: The Uses of Fictional and Non-fictional Television in Conversations about the Environment. In *The Psychology of Political Communication,* ed. Ann Crigler. Ann Arbor: University of Michigan Press.
Deuze, Mark. 2002. *Journalists in the Netherlands.* Amsterdam: Aksant.
——. 2007. *Media Work.* London: Polity Press.
Dewey, John. 1946. *The Public and Its Problems.* Chicago: Gateway.
Dickey, Sarah. 1993. *Cinema and the Urban Poor in South India.* Cambridge: Cambridge University Press.
——. 1997. Anthropology and Its Contributions to Studies of Mass Media. *International Social Sciences Journal* 154: 413–27.
Dimitrova, D. V., and J. Strömbäck. 2005. Mission Accomplished? Framing of the Iraq War in the Elite Newspapers in Sweden and the United States. *International Communication Gazette* 67(5): 399–417.
Dominy, Michele. 1993. Photojournalism, Anthropology, and Ethnographic Authority. *Cultural Anthropology* 8(3): 317–37.
Dowie, J. 1980. Bounds and Biases. In *Risk and Rationality,* ed. C. Wooldridge, N. Draper, and T. Hunter. Milton Keynes: Open University.
Dracklé, Dorle. 1991. *Macht und Ohnmacht: Der Kampf um die Agrarreform im Alentejo. Eine diskursanalytische Untersuchung zur Strukturierung von Machtbeziehungen am Beispiel einer südportugiesischen Agrarkooperative.* Göttingen: Edition Re.
——. 1996. Europäische Bürokraten und Fisch: Feldforschung in Südportugal. In *Ethnologie Europas,* ed. D. Dracklé and W. Kokot. Berlin: Dietrich Reimer.
Drewett, Michael. 2007. The Eyes of the World Are Watching Now: The Political Effectiveness of "Biko" by Peter Gabriel. *Popular Music and Society* 30(1): 39–51.
Drummond, Lee. 1996. *American Dreamtime: A Cultural Analysis of Popular Movies and Their Implications for Humanity.* Lanham, Md.: Littlefield, Adams.
Edwards, D. B. 1994. Afghanistan, Ethnography, and the New World Order. *Cultural Anthropology* 9(3): 345–60.
Edwards, Elizabeth, ed. 1992. *Anthropology and Photography, 1860–1920.* New Haven, Conn.: Yale University Press.
Ellner, Steve. 1996. Political Party Factionalism and Democracy in Venezuela. *Latin American Perspectives* 23(3): 87–109.

———. 2001. The Radical Potential of Chavismo in Venezuela: The First Year and a Half in Power. *Latin American Perspectives* 28(5): 5–32.

Entman, Robert, and Susan Herbst. 2001. Reframing Public Opinion as We Know It. In *Mediated Politics: Communication in the Future of Democracy,* ed. W. L. Bennett and R. Entman. Cambridge: Cambridge University Press.

Epstein, Edward J. 1973. *News from Nowhere: Television and the News.* New York: Random House.

Esch, Deborah. 1999. *In the Event: Reading Journalism, Reading Theory.* Stanford, Calif.: Stanford University Press.

Ettema, James S. 2005. Crafting Cultural Resonance: Imaginative Power in Everyday Journalism. *Journalism* 6(5): 131–52.

Ettema, James S., and Theodore L. Glasser. 1998. *Custodians of Conscience.* New York: Columbia University Press.

Ewart, Jacqui. 1997. The Scabsuckers: Regional Journalists' Representation of Indigenous Australians. *Asia Pacific Media Educator* 3: 108–17.

Faas, Horst, and Tim Page, eds. 1997. *Requiem: By the Photographers Who Died in Vietnam and Indochina.* New York: Random House.

Fabian, Johannes. 1983. *Time and the Other: How Anthropology Makes Its Object.* New York: Columbia University Press.

Farrell, Stephen. 2005. Today's Joseph and Mary Would Face 15 Checkpoints. *Times,* December 23.

Feld, Steven. 1996. Pygmy POP: A Genealogy of Schizophonic Mimesis. *Yearbook for Traditional Music* 28: 1–35.

Feldman, Ilana. 2007. Difficult Distinctions: Refugee Law, Humanitarian Practice, and Political Identification in Gaza. *Cultural Anthropology* 22(1): 129–69.

Fergus, Howard. 1992. *Montserrat: Emerald Isle of the Caribbean.* Basingstoke: Macmillan Press.

———. 1994. *Montserrat: History of a Caribbean Colony.* Basingstoke: Macmillan Press.

Ferguson, James. 1999. *Expectations of Modernity: Myths and Meanings of Urban Life on the Ambian Copperbelt.* Berkeley: University of California Press.

———. 2005. *Global Shadows: Africa in the Neoliberal World Order.* Durham, N.C.: Duke University Press.

Fishman, Mark. 1980. *Manufacturing the News.* Austin: University of Texas Press.

Fluehr-Lobban, Carolyn. 2003. Darkness in El Dorado: Research Ethics, Then and Now. In *Ethics and the Profession of Anthropology: Dialogue for Ethically Conscious Practice,* ed. Carolyn Fluehr-Lobban. Walnut Creek, Calif.: AltaMira Press.

Forde, Eamonn. 2003. Journalists with a Difference: Producing Music Journalism. In *Media Organization and Production,* ed. Simon Cottle. New York: Sage.

Fortman, B., ed. 1969. *After Mulungushi: The Economics of Zambian Humanism.* Nairobi: East African Publishing House.

Foucault, Michel. 1979. *Discipline and Punish.* New York: Pantheon.

———. 1988. What Is an Author? In *Modern Criticism and Theory: A Reader,* ed. D. Lodge. London: Longman.

Foulkes, George. 1997. Letter to the Editor. *Independent,* August 26: 12.

Franklin, Bob, ed. 2006. *Local Journalism and Local Media: Making the Local the Local News.* London: Routledge.

Frantz, Doug, Loretta Tofani, and William Rashbaum. 1999. Reporters' Relationships with Sources. *Nieman Reports* 53(3): 10–13.

Fürsich, Elfrieda, and Anandam Kavoori. 2001. Mapping a Critical Framework for the Study of Travel Journalism. *International Journal of Cultural Studies* 4(2): 149–71.

Gamson, William. 1992. *Talking Politics.* Cambridge: Cambridge University Press.

———. 1996. Media Discourse as a Framing Resource. In *The Psychology of Political Communication,* ed. Ann Crigler. Ann Arbor: University of Michigan Press.

Gamson, William, and André Modigliani. 1989. Media Discourse and Public Opinion on Nuclear Power: A Constructionist Approach. *American Journal of Sociology* 95: 1–37.

Gans, Herbert J. 1979. *Deciding What's News: A Study of CBS Evening News, NBC Nightly News, Newsweek, and Time.* New York: Pantheon.

Gant, Scott. 2007. *We're All Journalists Now: The Transformation of the Press and Reshaping of the Law in the Internet Age.* New York: Free Press.

Garofalo, Reebee, ed. 1992. *Rockin' the Boat: Mass Music and Mass Movements.* Boston: South End Press.

Garrido, Alberto. 2007. La ofensiva de Hugo Cháves. *El Universal,* January 14: 1–6.

Geertz, Clifford. 1973. *The Interpretation of Cultures.* New York: Basic Books.

———. 1983. *Local Knowledge: Further Essays in Interpretive Anthropology.* New York: Basic.

———. 1988. *Works and Lives: The Anthropologist as Author.* Stanford, Calif.: Stanford University Press.

Ghiglione, Loren. 1990. *The American Journalist: Paradox of the Press.* Washington, D.C.: Library of Congress.

Gibson, James William. 1986. *The Perfect War: Technowar in Vietnam.* Boston: Atlantic Monthly Press.

Giddens, Anthony. 1991. *Modernity and Self-Identity: Self and Society in Late-Modernity.* Cambridge: Polity Press.

Gilbert, Pat. 2004. *Passion Is a Fashion: The Real Story of the Clash.* Cambridge, Mass.: Da Capo Press.

Gillespie, Marie. 1995. *Television, Ethnicity, and Cultural Change.* London: Routledge.

Gillmor, Dan. 2004. *We the Media: Grassroots Journalism by the People, for the People.* Beijing: O'Reilly Media.

Ginsberg, Benjamin. 1986. *The Captive Public: How Mass Opinion Promotes State Power.* New York: Basic.

Ginsburg, Faye. 1991. Indigenous Media: Faustian Contract or Global Village? *Cultural Anthropology* 6(1): 92–112.

———. 1993. Aboriginal Media and the Australian Imaginary. *Public Culture* 5(3): 557–78.

———. 1995. The Parallax Effect: The Impact of Aboriginal Media on Ethnographic Film. *Visual Anthropology Review* 11(2): 64–76.

———. 2002. Screen Memories: Resignifying the Traditional in Indigenous Media.

In *Media Worlds,* ed. Faye Ginsburg, Lila Abu-Lughod, and Brian Larkin. Berkeley: University of California Press.

Ginsburg, Faye, Lila Abu-Lughod, and Brian Larkin, eds. 2002. *Media Worlds: Anthropology on New Terrain.* Berkeley: University of California Press.

Gitlin, Todd. 1980. *The Whole World Is Watching: Mass Media in the Making and Unmaking of the New Left.* Berkeley: University of California Press.

———. 1983. *Inside Prime Time.* New York: Pantheon.

Glaser, Barney, and Anselm Strauss. 1967. *The Discovery of Grounded Theory.* Chicago: Aldine.

Goldenberg, E. 1975. *Making the Papers: The Access of Resource-Poor Groups to the Metropolitan Press.* Lexington, Mass.: D. C. Heath.

Golding, Peter, and Philip Elliott. 1979. *Making the News.* London: Longman.

———. 1999. Making the News (excerpt). In *News: A Reader,* ed. H. Tumber. Oxford: Oxford University Press.

Goldman, Robert, and Stephen Papson. 1996. *Sign Wars: The Cluttered Landscapes of Advertising.* New York: Guilford Press.

Goodall, Heather. 1993. Constructing a Riot: Television News and Aborigines. *Media International Australia* 68: 70–77.

Goodman, Jane. 2005. *Berber Culture on the World Stage: From Village to Video.* Bloomington: Indiana University Press.

Goodman, Nelson. 1978. *Ways of Worldmaking.* Hassocks: Harvester Press.

Goodwin, H. Eugene. 1983. *Groping for Ethics in Journalism.* Ames: Iowa State Press.

Goot, Murray. 1996–97. The Perils of Polling and the Popularity of Pauline. *Current Affairs Bulletin,* December 1996–January 1997: 8–14.

Gott, Richard. 2005. *Hugo Chávez and the Bolivarian Revolution.* London: Verso.

Grbich, Carol. 2004. *New Approaches in Social Research.* Thousand Oaks: Sage.

Greenberg, Joel. 2005. Wall Casts Shadow on Arabs in Bethlehem. *Chicago Tribune,* December 21.

Greimas, Algirdas Julien. 1984. *Structural Semantics.* Trans. R. Schleifer, D. McDowell, and A. Velie. Lincoln: University of Nebraska Press.

Grioni, Raul, and Donatella Iacobeli. 2004. *Venezuela's Diario Vea: A New Way to Do Journalism,* June 25. Accessed at www.venezuelanalysis.com/articles.php?artno=1206.

Grunspan, Claude. 2000. *Gao rang* [Grilled rice]. Brooklyn: First Run/Icarus Films.

Guha, Ranajit, ed. 1982. *Subaltern Studies I: Writings on South Asian History and Society.* Delhi: Oxford University Press.

———. 1996. The Small Voice of History. In *Subaltern Studies IX: Writings on South Asian History and Society,* ed. S. Amin and D. Chakrabarty. Delhi: Oxford University Press.

Gupta, Akhil. 1995. Blurred Boundaries: The Discourse of Corruption, the Culture of Politics, and the Imagined State. *American Ethnologist* 222: 375–402.

———. 1998. *Postcolonial Developments: Agriculture in the Making of Modern India.* Durham, N.C.: Duke University Press.

Gupta, Akhil, and James Ferguson. 1997a. Discipline and Practice: "The Field" as Site, Method, and Location in Anthropology. In *Anthropological Locations: Boundar-*

ies and Grounds of a Field Science, ed. Akhil Gupta and James Ferguson. Berkeley: University of California Press.

———, eds. 1997b. *Culture, Power, Place: Explorations in Critical Anthropology.* Durham, N.C.: Duke University Press.

Gürsel, Zeynep. 2006. Reflecting on Daguerreotypes in the Digital Age. *English Language Notes* 44(2): 169–74.

Gusterson, Hugh. 1996. *Nuclear Rites: A Weapons Laboratory at the End of the Cold War.* Berkeley: University of California Press.

Habermas, Jürgen. 1984. *The Theory of Communicative Action I: Reason and the Rationalization of Society.* Boston: Beacon Press.

———. 1987. *The Theory of Communicative Action II: Lifeworld and System, a Critique of Functionalist Reason.* Boston: Beacon Press.

———. 1989. *The Structural Transformation of the Public Sphere.* Trans. Thomas Burger and Frederick Lawrence. Cambridge, Mass.: MIT Press.

———. 2001. The Public Sphere: An Encyclopedia Article. In *Media and Cultural Studies: Keywords,* ed. Meenakshi Gigi Durham and Douglas M. Keller. Oxford: Blackwell.

Hacking, Ian. 1999. Making Up People. In *The Science Studies Reader,* ed. M. Biagioli. New York: Routledge.

———. 2000. *The Social Construction of What?* Cambridge, Mass.: Harvard University Press.

Hagopian, Patrick. 2006. Vietnam War Photography as a Locus of Memory. In *Locating Memory: Photographic Acts,* ed. A. Kuhn and K. E. McAllister, 201–22. New York: Berghahn Books.

Hall, Stuart. 1985. Signification, Representation, Ideology: Althusser and the Post-Structuralist Debates. *Critical Studies in Mass Communication* 2(2): 91–114.

———. 1995. The Whites of Their Eyes: Racist Ideologies and the Media. In *Gender, Race and Class in Media,* ed. G. Dines and J. M. Humez. Thousand Oaks: Sage.

Hall, Stuart, Chas Critcher, Tony Jefferson, John Clarke, and Brian Roberts. 1978. *Policing the Crisis: Mugging, the State, and Law and Order.* New York: Palgrave Macmillan.

Hallin, Daniel C. 1986. *The "Uncensored War": The Media and Vietnam.* Berkeley: University of California Press.

Hammock, John, and Joel Charny. 1996. Emergency Response as Morality Play: The Media, the Relief Agencies, and the Need for Capacity Building. In *From Massacres to Genocide: The Media, Public Policy, and Humanitarian Crises,* ed. Robert Rotberg and Thomas Weiss. Washington, D.C.: Brookings Institution.

Hammond, William M. 1998. *Reporting Vietnam: Media and Military at War.* Lawrence: University Press of Kansas.

Hancock, Mary. 1995. Hindi Culture for an Indian Nation: Gender, Politics, and Elite Identity in Urban South India. *American Ethnologist* 22(4): 907–26.

Hannerz, Ulf. 1986. Theory in Anthropology: Small Is Beautiful? The Problem of Complex Cultures. *Comparative Studies in Society and History* 28(1): 362–67.

———. 1998a. Other Transnationals: Perspectives Gained from Studying Sideways. *Paideuma* 44: 109–23.

———. 1998b. Reporting from Jerusalem. *Cultural Anthropology* 13(4): 548–74.

———. 2001. Journalists, Anthropologists, and the Cosmopolitan Imagination. Paper delivered at American Anthropological Association conference, Washington, D.C.

———. 2002. Among the Foreign Correspondents: Reflections on Anthropological Styles and Audiences. *Ethnos* 67(1): 57–74.

———. 2004a. *Foreign News: Exploring the World of Foreign Correspondents.* Chicago: University of Chicago Press.

———, ed. 2004b. *Antropologi/Journalistik: Om sätt att beskriva världen.* Lund: Studentlitteratur.

Hariman, Robert, and John Louis Lucaites. 2007. *No Caption Needed: Iconic Photograph, Public Culture, and Liberal Democracy.* Chicago: University of Chicago Press.

Harries, Gemma, and Karin Wahl-Jorgensen. 2007. The Culture of Arts Journalists: Elitists, Saviors, or Manic Depressives? *Journalism* 8(6): 619–39.

Harris, John. 2005. Marooned: Bethlehem. *Guardian,* November 5.

Harris, Paul. 1997. Montserrat Returns to Calm after Street Riots. *Scotsman,* August 23.

Harrison, Jackie. 2000. *Terrestrial TV News in Britain: The Culture of Production.* Manchester: Manchester University Press.

Hartley, John. 1996. *Popular Reality: Journalism, Modernity, Popular Culture.* London: Arnold.

Hartley, John, and Alan McKee. 2000. *The Indigenous Public Sphere: The Reporting and Reception of Aboriginal Issues in the Australian Media.* Oxford: Oxford University Press.

Harvey, David. 1990. *The Condition of Postmodernity: An Enquiry into the Origins of Cultural Change.* Cambridge, Mass.: Blackwell.

Hasty, Jennifer. 2001. From Culture of Silence to Culture of Contest: Hegemony, Legitimacy, and the Press in Ghana. *Journal of Cultural Studies* 3(2): 348–59.

———. 2005. *The Press and Political Culture in Ghana.* Bloomington: Indiana University Press.

Heath, Carla W. 2001. Regional Radio: A Response by the Ghana Broadcasting Corporation to Democratization and Competition. *Canadian Journal of Communication* 26: 89–106.

Heath, Shirley Brice. 1983. *Ways with Words.* Cambridge: Cambridge University Press.

Heidegger, Martin. 1977. *The Question Concerning Technology and Other Essays.* New York: Harper.

Hellinger, Daniel. 2003. Political Overview: The Breakdown of Puntofijismo and the Rise of Chavismo. In *Venezuelan Politics in the Chávez Era,* ed. S. Ellner and D. Hellinger. Boulder, Colo.: Lynne Rienner.

Henry, N. 2007. *American Carnival: Journalism under Siege in an Age of New Media.* Berkeley: University of California Press.

Herbst, Susan. 1993. *Numbered Voices: How Opinion Polling Has Shaped American Politics.* Chicago: University of Chicago Press.

———. 1998. *Reading Public Opinion: How Political Actors View the Democratic Process.* Chicago: University of Chicago Press.

Heringman, Noah. 2003. The Style of Natural Catastrophes. *Huntington Library Quarterly* 66(1/2): 97–133.

Herman, Edward S., and Noam Chomsky. 1988. *Manufacturing Consent: The Political Economy of the Mass Media.* New York: Pantheon.

Hernández, Alberto Jordan. 2005. Sin Censura Nació la Prensa. *El Universal,* October 25.

Hernandez-Reguant, Ariana. 2006. Radio Taino and the Cuban Quest for Identi . . . Qué? In *Cultural Agency in the Americas,* ed. D. Sommer. Durham, N.C.: Duke University Press.

Herr, Michael. 1977. *Dispatches.* New York: Alfred A. Knopf.

Herzfeld, Michael. 1982. The Etymology of Excuses: Aspects of Rhetorical Performance in Greece. *American Ethnologist* 9(4): 644–63.

Hess, Stephen. 2001. The Culture of Foreign Correspondence. In *Media Occupations and Professions,* ed. J. Tunstall. Oxford: Oxford University Press.

Hibbs, John. 1997a. Short Calls for an End to Row over Aid for Volcano Island. *Daily Telegraph,* August 25: 18.

———. 1997b. Montserrat Aid Delay "Was Plot to Clear Island." *Daily Telegraph,* October 29: 11.

———. 1997c. MPs Attack Muddle over Aid to Montserrat. *Daily Telegraph,* November 28: 6.

Hibbs, John, and David Sapsted. 1997. Cook Snubs Short with Whitehall Team for Montserrat. *Times,* August 26: 1.

Hillmore, Peter. 1997. Island of the Damned. *Observer,* August 24: 16.

Himpele, Jeff D. 2002. Arrival Scenes: Complicity and Media Ethnography in the Bolivian Public Sphere. In *Media Worlds,* ed. Faye Ginsburg, Lila Abu-Lughod, and Brian Larkin. Berkeley: University of California Press.

Ho Chi Minh. 2004. *Ve Bao Chi* [On journalism]. Hanoi: Chinh Tri Quoc Gia.

Hobart, Mark. 1999a. As They Like It: Overinterpretation and Hyporeality in Bali. In *The Problem of Context,* ed. Roy Dilley. Oxford: Berghahn Books.

———. 1999b. After Anthropology? A View from Too Near. Paper read at the Anthropology Department Seminar, School of Oriental and African Studies, University of London.

———. 2005. The Profanity of the Media. In *Media Anthropology,* ed. Eric Rothenbuhler and Mihai Coman. London: Sage.

Hoffman, Daniel. 2005. Violent Events as Narrative Blocs: The Disarmament at Bo, Sierra Leone. *Anthropological Quarterly* 78(2): 329–54.

Hoffman, Katherine. 2002. Moving and Dwelling: Building the Moroccan Ashelhi Homeland. *American Ethnologist* 29(4): 928–62.

Holmes, Douglas R. 2003. *Integral Europe: Fast-Capitalism, Multiculturalism, Neo-fascism.* Princeton, N.J.: Princeton University Press.

Holy, Ladislav. 1996. *The Little Czech and the Great Czech Nation.* Cambridge: Cambridge University Press.

Horkheimer, Max, and Theodor Adorno. 1994. *The Dialectic of Enlightenment.* New York: Continuum.

———. 1998. *Dialektik der Aufklärung.* Frankfurt: Fischer.

Horowitz, Irving. 1967. *The Rise and Fall of Project Camelot: Studies in the Relationship between Social Science and Practical Politics*. Cambridge, Mass.: MIT Press.

Hoskins, Andrew. 2004. *Televising War: From Vietnam to Iraq*. New York: Continuum.

Howard, John. and Mal Brough. 2007. Joint press conference with the Hon. Mal Brough, Minister for Families, Community Services, and Indigenous Affairs Canberra. Interview transcript, June 21. Accessed at http://pandora.nla.gov.au/pan/10052/20070823-1732/www.pm.gov.au/media/Interviw/2007/Interview24380.html.

Høyer, Svennik. 2003. Newspapers without Journalists. *Journalism Studies* 4(4): 451–63.

Hughes, David. 1997. The Humbling of Clare Short. *Daily Mail,* August 26: 2.

Huntington, Samuel P. 1996. *The Clash of Civilizations and the Remaking of World Order*. New York: Simon and Schuster.

Iggers, Jeremy. 1998. *Good News, Bad News: Journalism Ethics and the Public Interest*. Boulder, Colo.: Westview Press.

Imhof, Kiurt, and Peter Schultz, eds. 1996. *Politisches Raisonnement in der Informationsgesellschaft*. Zürich: Seismo.

Ingalls, Wayne B. 1999. Traditional Greek Choruses and the Education of Girls. *History of Education* 28(4): 371–93.

International Crisis Group (ICG). 2007. *Venezuela: Hugo Chávez's Revolution*. February 22. Latin America Report no. 19. Accessed at www.unhcr.org/refworld/docid/45f012032.html.

Iyengar, Shanto. 1991. *Is Anyone Responsible? How Television Frames Political Issues*. Chicago: University of Chicago Press.

Jackson, Michael. 1998. *Minima Ethnographica: Intersubjectivity and the Anthropological Project*. Chicago: University of Chicago Press.

Jacobs, Sue-Ellen. 1987. *Cases and Solutions* (Special Publication no. 23). American Anthropological Association. Accessed at www.aaanet.org/committees/ethics/ch3.htm.

Jakubowicz, Andrew, Heather Goodall, Jeanne Martin, Tony Mitchell, Lois Randall, and Kalinga Seneviratne. 1994. *Racism, Ethnicity, and the Media*. Sydney: Allen and Unwin.

Jeffrey, Robin. 1993. Indian-Language Newspapers and Why They Grow. *Economic and Political Weekly* 28: 2004–11.

———. 1994. Monitoring Newspapers and Understanding the State: India, 1948–1993. *Asian Survey* 34(9): 748–63.

———. 2000. *India's Newspaper Revolution: Capitalism, Politics, and the Indian-Language Press, 1977–1999*. New York: St. Martin's.

Jenkins, R. 1982. Pierre Bourdieu and the Reproduction of Determinism. *Sociology* 16(2): 270–81.

Johnson, Richard. 1986. What Is Cultural Studies Anyway? *Social Text* 16(4): 38–80.

Johnston, Phil. 1997. Cook Orders Review of Territories. *Daily Telegraph,* August 28: 1.

Jones, Tim. 1995. Tourists on Alert to Flee Volcano Island. *Times,* August 9: 1.

Jorgensen, Joseph, and Eric Wolf. 1970. Anthropology on the Warpath in Thailand. *New York Review of Books* 15(9): 26–35.

Journalism Training Forum. 2002. *Journalists at Work: Their Views on Training, Recruitment, and Conditions.* London: NTO/Skillset.

Jowell, R., A. Heath, and J. Curtice, eds. 1994. *Labour's Last Chance?* Aldershot: Dartmouth.

Juluri, Vamsee. 2003. *Becoming a Global Audience: Longing and Belonging in Indian Music Television.* New York: Peter Lang.

Kaniss, Phyllis. 1991. *Making Local News.* Chicago: University of Chicago Press.

Kaplan, Temma. 1977. *Anarchists of Andalusia, 1868–1903.* Princeton, N.J.: Princeton University Press.

Kasoma, Francis P. 1989. *Hierarchical Newsplay: Africa's Emerging Journalistic Ritual.* Mimeograph. Lusaka: University of Zambia.

———. 1997. Communication and Press Freedom in Zambia. In *Press Freedom and Communication in Africa,* ed. Festus Eribo and William Jong-Ebot. Trenton, N.J.: Africa World Press.

Katz, Elihu. 2006. Rediscovering Gabriel Tarde. *Political Communication* 23(3): 263–70.

Katz, Elihu, and Jay Blumler, eds. 1974. *The Uses of Mass Communications.* Beverly Hills: Sage.

Kaufman, Asher. 2001. Phoenicianism: The Formation of an Identity in Lebanon in 1920. *Middle Eastern Studies* 37(1): 173–94.

Kaunda, Kenneth D. 1967. Humanism in Zambia and a Guide to Its Implementation, Part 1. Lusaka: Zambia Information Services.

Kaur, Raminder. 2001. Rethinking the Public Sphere: The Ganpati Festival and Media Competitions in Mumbai. *South Asia Research* 211: 23–50.

Keeble, Richard. 2001. *Ethics for Journalists.* London: Routledge.

Kennedy, Dan. 2007. Plugged In, Tuned Out: Young Americans Are Embracing New Media but Failing to Develop an Appetite for News. *CommonWealth,* Fall.

Kent, Robert B. 2006. *Latin America: Regions and People.* New York: Guilford Press.

Key, Valdimer Orlando. 1961. *Public Opinion and American Democracy.* New York: Knopf.

Khalidi, Rashid. 1987. The Palestinians Twenty Years After. *Middle East Report* (146): 6–14.

Khalili, Laleh. 2007. *Heroes and Martyrs of Palestine: The Politics of National Commemoration.* Cambridge: Cambridge University Press.

Kinney, Katherine. 2000. *Friendly Fire: American Images of the Vietnam War.* New York: Oxford University Press.

Kitch, C. 2000. "A News of Feeling as Well as Fact": Mourning and Memorial in American Newsmagazines. *Journalism: Theory, Practice, and Criticism* 1(2): 175–95.

———. 2003. "Mourning in America": Ritual, Redemption, and Recovery in News Narrative after September 11. *Journalism Studies* 4(2): 213–24.

Kittler, Friedrich A. 1990. *Discourse Networks 1800/1900.* Stanford, Calif.: Stanford University Press.

Kleinman, Arthur, and Joan Kleinman. 1997. The Appeal of Experience; the Dismay of Images: Cultural Appropriations of Suffering in Our Times. In *Social Suffering,* ed. Arthur Kleinman, Veena Das, and Margaret Lock. Berkeley: University of California Press.

Kline, David, Dan Burstein, Arne J. De Keijzer, and Paul Berger, eds. 2005. *Blog! How the Newest Media Revolution Is Changing Politics, Business, and Culture.* New York: CDS Books.

Klinenberg, Eric. 2005. Convergence: News Production in a Digital Age. *Annals of the American Academy of Political and Social Science* 597: 48–64.

Kohli-Khandekar, Vanita. 2006. *The Indian Media Business.* 2nd ed. New Delhi: Response Books.

Kosnick, Kira. 2004. "Speaking in One's Own Voice": Representational Strategies of Alevi Turkish Migrants on Open-Access Television in Berlin. *Journal of Ethnic and Migration Studies* 30(5): 979–94.

Kottak, Conrad P. 1990. *Prime-Time Society: An Anthropological Analysis of Television and Culture.* Belmont, Calif.: Wadsworth.

Kovach, Bill, and Tom Rosenstiel. 2007. *The Elements of Journalism: What Newspeople Should Know and the Public Should Expect.* New York: Three Rivers Press.

Krauss, Werner. 1996. "Wir Sind Nicht die Indianer Europas": Feldforschung, Regionale Identität, und Ökologischer Diskurs am Beispiel eines Landschaftsschutzgebietes im Südwesten Portugals. In *Ethnologie Europas: Grenzen, Konflikte, Identitäten,* ed. D. Dracklé and W. Kokot. Berlin: Reimer.

———. 1998. Poetas do Sudoeste. In *OBSERVA: "Etnografia do Sudoeste."* Lisbon: ISCTE.

———. 2001. *"Hängt die Grünen!" Umweltkonflikte, Ökologischer Diskurs und Nachhaltige Entwicklung.* Berlin: Diedrich Reimer.

Kulick, Don. 2006. Theory in Furs: Masochist Anthropology. *Current Anthropology* 47(6): 933–52.

Laffey, Susan. 1995. Representing Paradise: Euro-American Desires and Cultural Understandings in Touristic Images of Montserrat, West Indies. M.A. thesis, University of Texas, Austin.

Langton, Marcia. 1993. "Well, I Heard It on the Radio and I Saw It on the Television": An Essay for the Australian Film Commission on the Politics and Aesthetics of Filmmaking by and about Aboriginal People and Things. North Sydney: Australian Film Commission.

Latham, Kevin. 2000. Nothing but the Truth: News Media, Power, and Hegemony in South China. *China Quarterly* 163: 633–54.

Laurence, Charles. 1995. Island Fears Rise after Marines Scale Volcano. *Daily Telegraph,* September 24: 15.

Leach, E. 1984. Glimpses of the Unmentionable in the History of British Social Anthropology. *Annual Review of Anthropology* 13: 1–23.

Lee, Richard. 1969. Eating Christmas in the Kalahari. *Natural History,* December 22: 60–63.

Lemoine, Maurice. 2002. *Venezuela's Press Power: How Hate Media Incited the Coup against the President.* Le Monde diplomatique, August. Accessed at http://mondediplo.com/2002/08/10venezuela.

Lewis, Justin. 2001. *Constructing Public Opinion: How Political Elites Do What They Like and Why We Seem to Go Along with It.* New York: Columbia University Press.

Lilibeth da Corte, Maria. 2006. No Habrá Nueva Concesión Para Ese Canal Golpista RCTV. *El Universal,* December 29.

Lima, Paulo. 1997. Artistas da Fala a Sul do Tejo. In *Artes da Fala,* ed. J. Freitas Branco and P. Lima. Oeiras: Celta Editora.

Linsky, Marty. 1997. *The View from the Top: Conversations with 14 People Who Will Be Running Journalism Organizations into the 21st Century.* St. Petersburg, Fla.: Poynter Institute for Media Studies.

Lippard, Lucy, ed. 1992. *Partial Recall.* New York: New Press.

Loudon, Andy. 1997. Deserted in the Volcano's Shadow of Death. *Daily Mail,* July 2: 23.

Lounsbury, Michael, and William N. Kaghan. 2001. Organizations, Occupations, and the Structuration of Work. In *Research in the Sociology of Work 10,* ed. S. Vallas. Amsterdam: JAI.

Luhmann, Niklas. 2000. *The Reality of Mass Media.* Stanford, Calif.: Stanford University Press.

Lukas, J. Anthony. 1990. The Journalist: A Source's Captive or Betrayer? *Washington Monthly,* 22(4): 44–49.

Lule, James. 2001. *Eternal Stories: The Mythological Role of Journalism.* New York: Guilford.

Lull, James. 1980. The Social Uses of Television. *Human Communication Research* 6: 197–209.

Lutz, Catherine A., and Jane L. Collins. 1993. *Reading "National Geographic."* Chicago: University of Chicago Press.

Lybarger, Loren D. 2002. *Between Sacred and Secular: Religion, Generations, and Collective Memory among Muslim and Christian Palestinians in the Post-Oslo Period.* Chicago: University of Chicago Press.

MacCabe, C., and O. Stewart, eds. 1986. *The BBC and Public Service Broadcasting.* Manchester: Manchester University Press.

Machill, Marcel, Sebastian Köhler, and Markus Waldhauser. 2007. The Use of Narrative Structures in Television News. *European Journal of Communication* 22(2): 185–205.

Madianou, Mirca. 2005. *Mediating the Nation.* London: UCL Press.

Malcolm, Janet. 1990. *The Journalist and the Murderer.* New York: Knopf.

Malkki, Liisa H. 1997. News and Culture: Transitory Phenomena and the Fieldwork Tradition. In *Anthropological Locations: Boundaries and Grounds of a Field Science,* ed. Akhil Gupta and James Ferguson. Berkeley: University of California Press.

Mankekar, Purnima. 1993. National Texts and Gendered Lives: An Ethnography of Television Viewers in a North Indian City. *American Ethnologist* 20(3): 543–63.

———. 1999. *Screening Culture, Viewing Politics: An Ethnography of Television, Womanhood, and Nation in Postcolonial India.* Durham, N.C.: Duke University Press.

Manzella, Joseph, and Leon Yacher. 2005. The Kyrgyz Republic's Liminal Media: Assessing a Journalistic Rite of Passage. *Journalism Studies* 6(4): 431–43.

Marchetti, Dominique, and Denis Ruellan. 2001. *Devenir Journalistes: Sociologie de L'entrée dans le Marché du Travail.* Paris: Documentation française.

Marcus, George E. 1995. Ethnography in/of the World System: The Emergence of Multi-Sited Ethnography. *Annual Review of Anthropology* 24: 95–117.

———. 1997. The Uses of Complicity in the Changing Mise-En-Scène of Anthropological Fieldwork. *Representations* 59 (Summer): 85–108.

———. 1998. Ethnography in/of the World System: The Emergence of Multi-Sited Ethnography. In *Ethnography through Thick and Thin,* ed. G. E. Marcus. Princeton, N.J.: Princeton University Press.

———. 2006. Where Have All the Tales of Fieldwork Gone? *Ethnos* 71(1): 113–22.

Marshall, Andy. 1997. Row over Montserrat Aid Package. *Independent,* August 22: 12.

Martin, Vivian. 2008. Attending the News: A Grounded Theory about a Daily Regimen. *Journalism: Theory, Practice, and Criticism* 9(1): 76–94.

Matos, José. 2008. Accessed at www.blogfixe.com/?w=josematos.

Mattern, Mark. 1998. *Acting in Concert: Music, Community, and Political Action.* New Brunswick, N.J.: Rutgers University Press.

Matthews, Julian. 2003. Cultures of Production: The Making of Children's News. In *Media Organization and Production,* ed. Simon Cottle. New York: Sage.

Mazzarella, William. 2003. *Shoveling Smoke: Advertising and Globalization in Contemporary India.* Durham, N.C.: Duke University Press.

McAlister, Melani. 2001. *Epic Encounters: Culture, Media, and U.S. Interests in the Middle East, 1945–2000.* Berkeley: University of California Press.

McCallum, Kerry. 2005. Local Talk as a Construction of Public Opinion on Indigenous Issues in Australia. PhD diss., University of Canberra.

———. 2007. *Public Opinion about Indigenous Issues in Australia: Local Talk and Journalistic Practice.* Australian Journalism Monographs. Gold Coast, QLD: Griffith University.

———. 2008. Indigenous Violence as a "Mediated Public Crisis." In *Communication, Civics, Industry: Proceedings of ANZCA2007,* ed. John Tebbutt. Melbourne: Australian New Zealand Communication Association and La Trobe University.

McCann, Ian. 1993. *Bob Marley: In His Own Words.* New York: Music Sales Corporation.

McChesney, Robert. 1999. *Rich Media, Poor Democracy: Communication Politics in Dubious Times.* New York: New Press.

McLuhan, Marshall. 1964. *Understanding Media: The Extensions of Man.* New York: McGraw-Hill.

Meadows, Michael. 2001. *Voices in the Wilderness: Images of Aboriginal People in the Australian Media.* Westport: Greenwood.

Merleau-Ponty, Maurice. 1989. *Phenomenology of Perception.* New York: Routledge.

Meskell, Lynn, and Peter Pels. 2005. *Embedding Ethics.* New York: Berg.

Messenger, John. 1975. Montserrat: The Most Distinctively Irish Settlement in the New World. *Ethnicity* 2: 281–303.

Meyer, Phillip. 2004. *The Vanishing Newspaper: Saving Journalism in the Information Age.* Columbia: University of Missouri Press.

Michaels, Eric, Marcia Langton, and Dick Hebdige. 1994. *Bad Aboriginal Art: Tradition, Media, and Technological Horizons.* Minneapolis: University of Minnesota Press.

Mickler, Steve. 1998. *The Myth of Privilege: Aboriginal Status, Media Visions, Public Ideas*. South Fremantle: Fremantle Arts Centre Press.

Miller, Daniel. 1992. The Young and the Restless in Trinidad: A Case of the Local and the Global in Mass Consumption. In *Consuming Technologies: Media and Information in Domestic Spaces*, ed. R. Silverstone and E. Hirsch. New York: Routledge.

Miller, Daniel, and Heather Horst. 2006. *The Cell Phone: An Anthropology of Communication*. Oxford: Berg.

Miller, M. Mark, and Bonnie Reichert. 2003. The Spiral of Opportunity and Frame Resonance: Mapping the Issue Cycle in News and Public Discourse. In *Framing Public Life*, ed. S. Reese, O. Gandy, and A. E. Grant. Mahway: Lawrence Erlbaum.

Mills, Stephen. 1999. Polling, Politics, and the Press, 1941–1996. In *Print, Politics, and Popular Culture*, ed. A. Curthoys and J. Schultz. Brisbane: Queensland University Press.

Milton, Sybil. 1984. The Camera as Weapon: Documentary Photography and the Holocaust. *Simon Wiesenthal Center Annual* 1: 45–68.

Mindich, David T. Z. 2004. *Tuned Out: Why Americans under 40 Don't Follow the News*. New York: Oxford University Press.

Mines, Matthison. 1996. *Public Faces, Private Voices: Community and Individuality in South India*. Delhi: Oxford University Press.

Minneapolis Star-Tribune. 2007. Thirteen Seconds in August. Accessed at www.startribune.com/local/12166286.html.

Mintz, Jerome R. 1994. *The Anarchists of Casas Viejas*. Bloomington: Indiana University Press.

Mitchell, W. J. T. 1994. *Picture Theory: Essays on Verbal and Visual Representation*. Chicago: University of Chicago Press.

Mitnick, Joshua. 2005. Christmas behind Israel's Wall. *Christian Science Monitor*, December 22: 6.

Moeller, Susan. 1999. *Compassion Fatigue: How the Media Sell Disease, Famine, War, and Death*. London: Routledge.

Moleiro, Alonso. 2007. No tengo claro si el socialismo chavista será democrático. *El Nacional*, January 21: A1–A2.

Moorti, Sujata. 2004. Fashioning a Cosmopolitan Tamil Identity: Game Shows, Commodities, and Cultural Identity. *Media, Culture & Society* 26(4): 549–67.

Morley, David. 1992. *Television, Audiences, and Cultural Studies*. London: Routledge.

Morris, Harvey. 2005. Isolated Bethlehem Struggles for Its Survival. *Financial Times*, December 24: 5.

Munshi, Shoma. 2004. A Perfect 10 — "Modern and Indian": Representations of the Body in Beauty Pageants and the Visual Media in Contemporary India. In *Confronting the Body*, ed. J. H. Mills and S. Sen. London: Anthem.

Mytton, Graham. 1974. *Listening, Looking, and Learning: Report on a National Mass Media Audience Survey in Zambia (1970–73)*. Lusaka: Institute for African Studies, University of Zambia.

Nader, Laura. 1972. Up the Anthropologist — Perspectives Gained from Studying Up. In *Reinventing Anthropology*, ed. Dell Hymes. New York: Pantheon.

Nandorfy, Martha. 2003. The Right to Live in Peace: Freedom and Social Justice in the Songs of Violeta Parra and Victor Jara. In *Rebel Musics: Human Rights, Resistant Sounds, and the Politics of Music Making,* ed. D. Fischlin and A. Heble. Montréal: Black Rose Books.

National Aboriginal Community Controlled Health Organisation (NACCHO). 2003. Substance Misuse. In *Aboriginal Primary Health Care,* ed. S. Couzos and R. Murray. Oxford: Oxford University Press.

National Geographic: Vietnam's Unseen War. National Geographic Video, 2002.

Nayar, Baldev Raj. 2001. *Globalization and Nationalism: The Changing Balance in India's Economic Policy, 1950–2000.* Delhi: Sage.

Neidhardt, F., ed. 1994. *Offentlichkeit, Offentliche Meinung, Soziale Bewegungen.* Opladen: Westdeutscher Verlag.

Neill, Rosemary. 2002. *White Out: How Politics Is Killing Black Australia.* Sydney: Allen and Unwin.

Nerone, John, and Kevin G. Barnhurst. 2003. U.S. Newspaper Types, the Newsroom, and the Division of Labor, 1750–2000. *Journalism Studies* 4(4): 435–49.

Neuhouser, Kevin. 1992. Democratic Stability in Venezuela: Elite Consensus or Class Compromise? *American Sociological Review* 57(1): 117–35.

Nguyen Tien Mao. 2006. *Co So Ly Luan Anh Bao Chi* [Theoretical foundation of photojournalism]. Hanoi: Thong Tan.

Ninan, Sevanti. 2007. *Headlines from the Heartland.* New Delhi: Sage.

Nogueira, Carlos de. 2000. *Literatura oral em verso: A poesia em Baião.* Vila Nova e Gaia: Estratégias Criativas.

———. 2004. *O essencial sobre a literatura de cordel portuguesa.* Lisbon: Imprensa Nacional — Casa da Moeda.

Obenzinger, Hilton. 1999. *American Palestine: Melville, Twain, and the Holy Land Mania.* Princeton, N.J.: Princeton University Press.

Oliveira Marques, António H. R. de. 1998. *História de Portugal,* vol. 3, *Das Revolucões aos Nossos Dias.* Lisbon: Editorial Presença.

Open Bethlehem. 2005. Launch Speeches. Accessed at http://openbethlehem.org/index.php?option=com_content&task=view&id=61.

Ortner, Sherry. 1973. On Key Symbols. *American Anthropologist* 75: 1338–46.

OTC Bulletin Board. 2007. Salon Media Group Inc. SLNM. Accessed at www.otcbb.com/asp/Info_Center.asp?symbol=SLNM.

Overholser, Geneva. 1998. Editor Inc. *American Journalism Review,* December: 48–64.

Owen, Geoff, and David Adams. 1997. Cook Pledges Aid to Volcano Island. *Times,* August 6: 11.

Page, Tim. 2002. *Another Vietnam: Pictures of the War from the Other Side.* Washington, D.C.: National Geographic Press.

Palestinian Central Bureau of Statistics. 2007. Poverty in the Palestinian Territory, 2006: Main Findings Report. Ramallah: PCBS.

Palriwala, Rajni. 2005. Fieldwork in a Post-Colonial Anthropology: Experience and the Comparative. *Social Anthropology* 13(2): 151–70.

Pande, M. 2006. English for the Elite: Hindi for the Power Elite. In *Making News,* ed. U. Sahay. New Delhi: Oxford University Press.

Patterson, Thomas E. 2005. *Young Voters and the 2004 Election.* Boston: Harvard University.

——. 2007a. Creative Destruction: An Exploratory Look at News on the Internet. A report from the Joan Shorenstein Center on the Press, Politics, and Public Policy, Harvard University.

——. 2007b. Young People and News. A report from the Joan Shorenstein Center on the Press, Politics, and Public Policy, Harvard University.

Pattullo, Polly. 2000. *Fire from the Mountain: The Tragedy of Montserrat and the Betrayal of Its People.* London: Constable.

Pedelty, Mark. 1993. News Photography and Indigenous People: An "Encounter" in Guatemala. *Visual Anthropology* 6(3): 285–301.

——. 1995. *War Stories: The Culture of Foreign Correspondents.* New York: Routledge.

——. 1997. The Marginal Majority: Women War Correspondents in the Salvadoran Press Corps Association. *Critical Studies in Mass Communication* 14(1): 49–76.

Peñaloza, Pedro Pablo. 2007. Chávez Anuncia Que Está en Campaña por la Reelección. *El Universal,* January 14: 1–4.

Penman, John, and John Deane. 1997. Montserrat Aid Effort Steps Up as Short Does U-Turn on Visit. *Scotsman,* September 3: 12.

Pesmen, Dale. 1991. Reasonable and Unreasonable Worlds: Some Expectations of Coherence of Culture Implied by the Prohibition of Mixed Metaphors. In *Beyond Metaphor: The Theory of Tropes in Anthropology,* ed. J. Fernandez. Stanford, Calif.: Stanford University Press.

Peters, John Durham. 1995. Historical Tensions in the Concept of Public Opinion. In *Public Opinion and the Communication of Consent,* ed. T. Glasser and C. Salmon. New York: Guilford.

Peterson, Mark A. 1996. Writing the Indian Story: Press, Politics, and Symbolic Power in India. PhD diss., Brown University.

——. 2001. Getting to the Story: Unwriteable Discourse and Interpretive Practice in American Journalism. *Anthropological Quarterly* 74(4): 201–11.

——. 2003. *Anthropology and Mass Communication.* New York: Berghahn.

——. 2005. Performing Media: Toward an Ethnography of Intertextuality. In *Media Anthropology,* ed. Eric Rothenbuhler and Mihai Coman. London: Sage.

——. 2007. Making Global News: "Freedom of Speech" and "Muslim Rage" in U.S. Journalism. *Contemporary Islam* 1: 247–64.

Philo, Greg. (2008). Active Audiences and the Construction of Public Knowledge. *Journalism Studies* 9(4): 535–44.

Philpott, Stuart. 1973. *West Indian Migration: The Montserrat Case.* London: Athlone Press.

Picão, José da Silva. 1983. *Através dos campos: Usos e costumes agrícolo-alentejanos.* Lisbon: Publicações Dom Quixote (1903).

Pierce, Andrew. 1997. Snub by Short Widens Rift with Volcano Island. *Times,* August 25: 1.

Pinney, Christopher, and Nicolas Peterson, eds. 2003. *Photography's Other Histories.* Durham, N.C.: Duke University Press.

Plater, Diana. 1992. Guidelines to Reporting Aboriginal Affairs. In *Signposts: A Guide for Journalists,* ed. K. Eggerking and D. Plater. Sydney: Centre for Independent Journalism.

Possekel, Anja. 1999. *Living with the Unexpected: Linking Disaster Recovery to Sustainable Development on Montserrat.* London: Springer.

Postill, John. 2006. *Media and Nation Building: How the Iban Became Malaysian.* Oxford: Berghahn Books.

Postill, John, and Birgit Bräuchler, eds. Forthcoming. *Theorising Media and Practice.* Oxford: Berghahn.

Powdermaker, Hortense. 1950. *Hollywood, the Dream Factory.* Boston: Little, Brown.

Pratt, Mary Louise. 1986. Fieldwork in Common Places. In *Writing Culture: The Poetics and Politics of Ethnography,* ed. James Clifford and George E. Marcus. Berkeley: University of California Press.

Pratt, Ray. 1994. *Rhythm and Resistance: The Political Uses of American Popular Music.* Washington, D.C.: Smithsonian Institution Press.

Prieto, Alfredo. 2004. Current Paths and Challenges for a Christian Publishing House in Cuba. *Transforming Anthropology* 12(1/2): 68–74.

Project for Excellence in Journalism. 1998. *Changing Definitions of News: A Look at the Mainstream Press over 20 Years.* Washington, D.C.: Project for Excellence in Journalism.

———. 2004. *The State of the News Media 2004: An Annual Report on American Journalism.* Accessed at www.stateofthemedia.com/2004/.

———. 2005. *The State of the News Media 2005: An Annual Report on American Journalism.* Accessed at www.stateofthemedia.org/2005/.

———. 2007. *The State of the News Media 2007: An Annual Report on American Journalism.* Accessed at www.stateofthenewsmedia.org/2007/index.asp.

Quaresma, António Martins. 1989. *Odemira: Subsidios para uma monographia.* Odemira: Câmara Municipal de Odemira.

———. 2004. *O turismo no litoral alentejano — do início aos anos 60 do século XX. O Exemplo de Milfontes.* Accessed at www.milfontes.com/E-book/Historia_do_Turismo_Milfontes.pdf.

———. 2006. *Odemira: 750 anos de história. Estudos a documentos.* Odemira: Câmara Municipal de Odemira.

R Development Core Team. 2008. *R: A Language and Environment for Statistical Computing.* Statistical assistance and code by Aaron Rendahl. Vienna: R Foundation for Statistical Computing. Accessed at http://cran.r-project.org/doc/manuals/refman.pdf.

Rabinowitz, Dan. 2001. Natives with Jackets and Degrees: Othering, Objectifiction, and the Role of Palestinians in the Co-existence Field in Israel. *Social Anthropology* 9(1): 65–80.

Raboy, Marc, ed. 1996. *Public Broadcasting for the Twenty-first Century.* Luton, Bedfordshire: John Libbey Media.

Raghavan, G. N. S. 994. *The Press in India: A New History.* Delhi: Gyan.

Raines, Howell. 2002. Foreword. In *Portraits 9/11/01: The Collected "Portraits of Grief" from the "New York Times."* New York: Times Books/Henry Holt.

Rajagopal, Arjun. 1998. Advertising, Politics, and the Sentimental Education of the Indian Consumer. *Visual Anthropology Review* 14(2): 14–31.

———. 2001. *Politics after Television: Hindu Nationalism and the Changing of Indian Public.* New York: Cambridge University Press.

Rao, Ursula. 2002. Assessing the Past in Search for a Future: The Changing of Caste and the Writing of Caste History in Contemporary Urban India. In *A Place in the World: New Local Historiographies from Africa and South Asia,* ed. A. Harneit-Sievers. Leiden: Brill.

———. 2003. *Negotiating the Divine: Temple Religion and Temple Politics in Contemporary Urban India.* Delhi: Manohar.

———. 2008. Writing Infotainment: Commercialisation and the Emergence of a New Style of Political Reporting. In *Proceedings of the Seventeenth Biennial Conference of the ASAA.* Accessed at www.arts.Monash.edu.au/Mai/asaa/ursularao.pdf.

———. 2010. *News as Culture: Journalistic Practices and the Remaking of Indian Leadership Traditions.* Oxford: Berghahn.

Ratsch, Dietmar, and Arek Gielnik. 2000. *Eislimonade für Hong Li* [Iced lemonade for Hong Li]. Berlin: Progress Film-Verleih.

Ravi, N. 2005. Looking beyond Flawed Journalism: How National Interests, Patriotism, and Cultural Values Shaped the Coverage of the Iraq War. *Harvard International Journal of Press/Politics* 10(1): 45–62.

Redfield, Robert. 1930. *Tepoztlan, a Mexican Village: A Study of Folk Life.* Chicago: University of Chicago Press.

Reese, Steven D. 1997. The News Paradigm and the Ideology of Objectivity: A Socialist at the *Wall Street Journal.* In *Social Meanings of News: A Text Reader,* ed. D. Berkowitz. London: Sage.

———. 2001. Prologue: Framing Public Life: A Bridging Model for Media Research. In *Framing Public Life,* ed. S. Reese, O. Gandy, and A. E. Grant. Mahwah: Lawrence Erlbaum.

Reid, Susan Emily. 1994. Photography in the Thaw. *Art Journal* 53(2): 33–39.

Reis, Filipe Marcelo Correia de Brito. 2006. Communidades Radiofónicas: Um estudo etnográfico sobre a radiodifusão local em Portugal. Department of Anthropology, Instituto Superior de Ciências do Trabalho e da Empresa, Lisbon.

Relph, Edward. 1976. *Place and Placelessness.* London: Pion.

Reynolds, Glenn. 2006. *An Army of Davids: How Markets and Technology Empower Ordinary People to Beat Big Media, Big Government, and Other Goliaths.* Nashville, Tenn.: Thomas Nelson.

Rheingold, H. 1999. As the Well Turns. *Wired* 7(7).

Rhodes, Tom. 1997. Rescuers Fear Final Blow of Island Volcano. *Times,* July 1: 17.

Richards, Ian. 2005. *Quagmires and Quandaries: Exploring Journalism Ethics.* Sydney: University of New South Wales Press.

Richardson, John E. 2008. Language and Journalism. *Journalism Studies* 9(2): 152–60.

Roberts, Kenneth M. 2003. Social Correlates of Party System Demise and Populous Resurgence in Venezuela. *Latin American Politics and Society* 45(3): 35–57.

Rocha, Francisco Canais, and Maria Rosalina Labaredas. 1982. *Os trabalhadores rurais do alentejo e o sidonismo: Occupações de terras no vale de Santiago.* Lisbon: Edições um de Outobro.

Rofel, Lisa. 1992. Eating Out of One Big Pot. In *Workers' Expressions: Beyond Accommodation and Resistance,* ed. John Calagione, Doris Francis, and Daniel Nugent. Albany: SUNY Press.

Romero, Simón. 2007. Chávez's Move against Critic Highlights Shift in Media. *New York Times,* May 27.

Rosen, Jay. 2004. *Top Ten Ideas of '04: News Turns from a Lecture to a Conversation* 2004. Accessed at http://journalism.nyu.edu/pubzone/weblogs/pressthink/2004/12/29/tp04_lctr.html.

Rosenberg, Scott. 2006. Newassignment.net: New-model Journalism. Accessed at www.wordyard.com/2006/07/25/newassignment/.

Rosengren, Karl Erik, Philip Palmgreen, and Lawrence A. Wenner, eds. 1985. *Media Gratifications Research: Current Perspectives.* Beverly Hills: Sage.

Rothenbuhler, Eric, and Mihai Coman, eds. 2005. *Media Anthropology.* London: Sage.

Russell, Adrienne. 2007. Digital Communication Networks and the Journalistic Field. *Critical Studies in Media Communication* 24(4): 285–302.

Rynkiewich, Michael, and James Spradley. 1981. *Ethics and Anthropology: Dilemmas in Fieldwork.* Malabar, Fla.: Robert E. Krieger.

Sahay, Uday, ed. 2006. *Making News: Handbook of the Media in Contemporary India.* New Delhi: Oxford University Press.

Sahlins, Marshall. 1981. *Historical Myth and Mythical Realities.* Ann Arbor: University of Michigan Press.

———. 1983. Other Times, Other Customs: The Anthropology of History. *American Anthropologist,* n.s., 85(3): 517–44.

Sal-Ari, Andrés. 2007. Carta de un trabajador despedido del diario VEA (January 28). Accessed at www.aporrea.org/trabajadores/a2996.html.

Salmon, Charles, and Theodore Glasser, eds. 1995. *Public Opinion and the Communication of Consent.* New York: Guilford.

Salon. 1998. Why We Ran the Henry Hyde Story. Accessed at www.salon.com/news/1998/09/16newsc.html.

Sanchez-Aranda, Jose J., and Carlos Barrera. 2003. The Birth of Modern Newsrooms in the Spanish Press. *Journalism Studies* 4(4): 489–500.

Sapsted, David. 1997a. Governor Appeals for Calm after Volcano Isle Riot. *Daily Telegraph,* August 23: 14.

———. 1997b. Britain "Is Forcing Choice between Misery and Unknown." *Daily Telegraph,* August 25: 18.

———. 1997c. Short Aims to Heal Rift with Visit to Volcano Island. *Daily Telegraph,* September 3: 14.

Saraiva, José H. de. 1993. *Historia de Portugal.* Lisbon: Publicações Europa-America.

Saramago, José. 1980. *Levantado do chão.* Lisbon: Caminho.

Saville-Troike, Muriel. 1982. *The Ethnography of Communication: An Introduction.* Oxford: Blackwell.

Scannell, Paddy. 2001. Music, Radio, and the Record Business in Zimbabwe Today. *Popular Music* 1: 13–27.

Schiller, Herbert I. 1991. Not Yet the Post-Imperialist Era. *Critical Studies in Mass Communication* 8: 13–28.

Schlesinger, Philip. 1991. *Putting "Reality" Together.* London: Methuen, 1978.

Schroder, Kim Christian. 2007. Media Discourse Analysis: Researching Cultural Meanings from Inception to Reception. *Textual Cultures* 2(2): 77–99, 165.

Schudson, Michael. 1978. *Discovering the News: A Social History of American Newspapers.* New York: Basic Books.

———. 2003. *The Sociology of News.* New York: Norton.

Schutz, Alfred. 1970. In *On Phenomenology and Social Relations: Selected Writings,* ed. H. R. Wagner. Chicago: University of Chicago Press.

Schwenkel, Christina. 2008. Exhibiting War, Reconciling Pasts: Journalistic Modes of Representation and Transnational Commemoration in Contemporary Vietnam. *Journal of Vietnamese Studies* 3(1): 36–77.

Seymour-Ure, Colin. 1968. *The Press, Politics, and the Public.* London: Methuen.

Shankman, Paul. (2001). Requiem for a Controversy: Whatever Happened to Margaret Mead? *Skeptic* 9(1): 48–53.

Sharma, Andrew. 1998. India and Its Media: Commercialization, Liberalization, and Democratization. In *Global Media Economics,* ed. A. B. Albarran and S. M. Chan-Olmsted. Ames: Iowa State University Press.

Shepherd, Naomi. 1987. *The Zealous Intruders: The Western Rediscovery of Palestine.* San Francisco: Harper and Row.

Sheridan Burns, Lynette, and Alan McKee. 1999. Reporting on Indigenous Issues: Some Practical Suggestions for Journalists. *Australian Journalism Review* 21(2): 103–16.

Shome, Raka. 1996. Postcolonial Interventions in the Rhetorical Canon: An "Other" View. *Communications Theory* 6(1): 40–59.

Shrimsley, Robert. 1997. Look at the Big Picture, Blair Urges Ministers. *Daily Telegraph,* August 27: 4.

Siebert, Fred S., Theodore Peterson, and Wilbur Schramm. 1963. *Four Theories of the Press.* Urbana: University of Illinois Press.

Silverstein, Michael. 1996. The Secret Life of Texts. In *Natural Histories of Discourse,* ed. M. Silverstein and G. Urban. Chicago: University of Chicago.

———. 2002. The Kabyle Myth: Colonization and the Production of Ethnicity. In *From the Margins: Historical Anthropology and Its Futures,* ed. B. K. Axel. Durham, N.C.: Duke University Press.

Skinner, Jonathan. 2000. The Eruption of Chances Peak, Montserrat, and the Narrative Containment of Risk. In *Risk Revisited,* ed. P. Caplan. London: Pluto Press.

———. 2003. Anti-social "Social Development"? The DFID Approach and the "Indigenous" of Montserrat. In *Negotiated Development: Power and Identity in Development,* ed. J. Pottier, A. Bicker, and P. Sillitoe. London: Pluto Press.

———. 2004. *Before the Volcano: Reverberations of Identity on Montserrat.* Kingston, Jamaica: Arawak.

———. 2007. From the Precolonial to the Virtual: The Scope and Scape of Land, Land Use, and Land Loss on Montserrat. In *Land and Development,* ed. J. Besson and J. Momsen. London: Macmillan.

———. 2008a. Glimpses into the Unmentionable: Montserrat, Tourism, and Anthropological Readings of "Subordinate Exotic" and "Comic Exotic" Travel Writing. *Studies in Travel Writing* 12(2): 167–91.

———. 2008b. At the Electronic Evergreen: A Computer-Mediated Ethnography of a Newsgroup from Montserrat and Afar. In *Electronic Tribes: The Virtual Worlds of Geeks, Gamers, Shamans, and Scammers,* ed. Tyrone L. Adams and Stephen A. Smith, 124–40. Austin: University of Texas Press.

Smith, Gibbs. 1984. *Joe Hill.* Salt Lake City: Peregrine Smith Books.

Smith, Jonathon A. 1995. Semi-Structured Interviewing and Qualitative Analysis. In *Rethinking Methods in Psychology,* ed. J. A. Smith, R. Harré, and L. Van Langenhove. London: Sage.

Smith, Vicki. 2001. Ethnographies of Work and the Work of Ethnographers. In *Handbook of Ethnography,* ed. P. Atkinson, S. Delamont, J. Lofland, and L. Lofland. London: Sage.

Society of Professional Journalists. *Code of Ethics.* Available from www.spj.org/ethicscode.asp.

Soloski, John. 1989. News Reporting and Professionalism: Some Constraints on the Reporting of News. *Media, Culture & Society* 11: 207–28.

———. 1999. News Reporting and Professionalism: Some Constraints on the Reporting of the News. In *News: A Reader,* ed. H. Tumber. Oxford: Oxford University Press.

Sontag, Susan. 1990. *On Photography.* Reprint of 1977 ed. New York: Anchor Books.

Sparks, Colin, and John Tulloch, eds. 2000. *Tabloid Tales: Global Debates over Media Standards.* Lanham, Md.: Rowman & Littlefield.

Spitulnik, Debra. 1993. Anthropology and Mass Media. *Annual Review of Anthropology* 22: 293–315.

———. 1996. The Social Circulation of Media Discourse and the Mediation of Communities. *Journal of Linguistic Anthropology* 6(2): 161–87.

———. 1998. Mediated Modernities: Encounters with the Electronic in Zambia. *Visual Anthropology Review* 14(2): 63–84.

———. 2000. Documenting Radio Culture as Lived Experience: Reception Studies and the Mobile Machine in Zambia. In *African Broadcast Cultures: Radio in Transition,* ed. R. Fardon and G. Furniss. Oxford: James Currey.

———. Forthcoming. Thick Context, Deep Epistemology: A Meditation on Wide-Angle Lenses on Media, Knowledge Production, and the Concept of Culture. In *Theorising Media and Practice,* ed. Birgit Bräuchler and John Postill. New York: Berghahn.

Splichal, Slavko. 1999. *Public Opinion: Developments and Controversies in the Twentieth Century.* Lanham, Md.: Rowman and Littlefield.

Ståhlberg, Per. 2002. *Lucknow Daily: How a Hindi Newspaper Constructs Society.* Stockholm: Almqvist and Wiksell.

Starn, Orin. 1999. *Nightwatch: The Politics of Protest in the Andes.* Durham, N.C.: Duke University Press.

Stephens, Mitchell. 1988. *A History of News: From the Drum to the Satellite.* New York: Viking.

Stocking, George W. 1968. *Race, Culture, and Evolution: Essays in the History of Anthropology.* New York: Free Press.

Stoler, Ann L. 2002. *Carnal Knowledge and Imperial Power: Race and the Intimate in Colonial Rule.* Berkeley: University of California Press.

Strauss, Anselm, and Juliet Corbin. 1990. *Basics of Qualitative Research: Grounded Theory Procedures and Techniques.* Newbury Park: Sage.

———, eds. 1997. *Grounded Theory in Practice.* Thousand Oaks: Sage.

Street, Brian. 1984. *Literacy in Theory and Practice.* New York: Cambridge University Press.

———, ed. 1993. *Cross-Cultural Perspectives on Literacy.* New York: Cambridge University Press.

Szyszka, Per, ed. 1999. *Öffentlichkeit. Diskurs Zu Einem Schlüsselbegriff Der Organisationskommunikation.* Opladen: Westdeutscher Verlag.

Talbot, David. 2001. Interview with Salon.com's David Talbot. Accessed at www.journalismjobs.com/interview_talbot.cfm.

Taylor, John. 1998. *Body Horror: Photojournalism, Catastrophe, and War.* New York: New York University Press.

Thussu, Daya Krishan. 2007a. The "Murdochization" of News? The Case of Star TV in India. *Media, Culture & Society* 29(4): 593–611.

———. 2007b. *News as Entertainment. The Rise of Global Infotainment.* London: Sage.

Tierney, Patrick. 2000. *Darkness in El Dorado: How Scientists and Journalists Devastated the Amazon.* New York: Norton.

Tönnies, Ferdinand. 1971. The Power and Value of Public Opinion. In *Ferdinand Tönnies on Sociology: Pure, Applied, and Empirical,* ed. Werner J. Cahnman and Rudolf Herberle. Chicago: University of Chicago Press.

Tracey, Michael. 1977. *The Production of Political Television.* London: Routledge & Kegan Paul.

———. 1998. *The Decline and Fall of Public Service Broadcasting.* Oxford: Oxford University Press.

Tran, Duong. 1996. Chu Tich Ho Chi Minh voi Nhiep Anh va Doi Ngu Cac Nha Nhiep Anh [President Ho Chi Minh on photography and photographers]. In *Nhiep Anh ve Chien Tranh Cach Mang* [Photography of revolutionary war]. Hanoi: Vietnam News Agency.

Trinkunas, Harold A. 2002. The Crisis in Venezuelan Civil-Military Relations: From Punto Fijo to the Fifth Republic. *Latin American Research Review* 37(1): 41–76.

Tro ve Vinh Linh [Return to Vinh Linh]. 2005. Television documentary. Hanoi: Vietnam.

Trouillot, Michel. 1991. Anthropology and the Savage Slot: The Poetics and Politics of Otherness. In *Recapturing Anthropology: Working in the Present,* ed. R. Fox. Santa Fe: School of American Research.

Tuchman, Gaye. 1972. Objectivity as Strategic Ritual: An Examination of Newsmen's Notions of Objectivity. *American Journal of Sociology* 77(4): 660–79.

———. 1973. Making News by Doing Work: Routinizing the Unexpected. *American Journal of Sociology* 79(1): 110–31.

———. 1978. *Making News: A Study in the Construction of Reality.* New York: Free Press.

Tulloch, John, and Deborah Lupton. 2003. *Risk and Everyday Life.* London: Sage.

Tully, Mark. 1991. *No Full Stops in India.* New Delhi: Penguin.

Tunstall, Jeremy. 1971. *Journalists at Work: Specialist Correspondents: Their News Organizations, News Sources, and Competitor-Colleagues.* London: Constable.

———. 2001. Introduction to *Media Occupations and Professions,* ed. J. Tunstall. Oxford: Oxford University Press.

Turner, Fred. 2006. *From Counterculture to Cyberculture: Stewart Brand, the Whole Earth Network, and the Rise of Digital Utopianism.* Chicago: University of Chicago Press.

Turner, Graeme. 1993. The Active Audience: Reception Traditions. In *The Media in Australia: Industries, Texts, Audiences,* ed. S. Cunningham and G. Turner. Sydney: Allen and Unwin.

Turner, Terence. 1990. Visual Media, Cultural Politics, and Anthropological Practice: Some Implications of Recent Uses of Film and Video among the Kayapo of Brazil. *Communication and Visual Anthropology Review,* Spring: 8–13.

———. 1992. Defiant Images: The Kayapo Appropriation of Video. *Anthropology Today* 8(6): 5–16.

———. 1995. Representation, Collaboration, and Mediation in Contemporary Ethnographic and Indigenous Media. *Visual Anthropology Review* 11(2): 102–6.

———. 1997. Comment on J. Weiner, "Televisualist Anthropology." *Current Anthropology* 38(2): 226–29.

Turner, Victor. 1969. *The Ritual Process: Structure and Anti-Structure.* Chicago: Aldine.

Tyler, Stephen. 1978. *The Said and the Unsaid: Mind, Meaning, and Culture.* New York: Academic Press.

Valencia Ramírez, Cristóbal. 2006. Venezuela in the Eye of the Hurricane: Landing an Analysis of the Bolivarian Revolution. *Journal of Latin American Anthropology* 11(1): 173–86.

Varma, Adarsh Kumar. 1993. *Advanced Journalism.* New Delhi: Har-Anand.

Velthuis, Olav. 2006. Inside a World of Spin: Four Days at the World Trade Organization. *Ethnography* 7(1): 125–50.

Vesperi, Maria D. 2001. Broadcast News: Attitudes toward Featuring Elders and Responding to an Aging Audience. *Generations* 25(3): 31–33.

Virilio, Paul, and John Armitage. 2001. SPEED-SPACE: Interview with Chris Decron. In *Virilio Live: Selected Interviews,* ed. John Armitage. London: Sage.

Volkmer, Ingrid. 1999. *News in the Global Sphere: A Study of CNN and Its Impact on Global Communication.* Luton: University of Luton Press.

Wahl-Jorgensen, Karin. 2007. *Journalists and the Public: Newsroom Culture, Letters to the Editor, and Democracy.* Creskill, N.J.: Hampton Press.

Wahl-Jorgensen, Karin, and Bernadette Cole. 2006. Media and the Right to Communicate in Sierra Leone. *Media Development,* no. 4: 29–33.

Wahl-Jorgensen, Karin, and Bob Franklin. 2008. Journalism Research in the UK: From Isolated Efforts to an Established Discipline. In *Global Journalism Research,* ed. M. Loffelholz and D. Weaver. New York: Blackwell.

Wald, Elijah. 2001. *Narcocorrido: A Journey into the Music of Drugs, Guns, and Guerillas.* New York: Rayo.

Warner, Malcolm. 1971. Organisational Context and Control of Policy in the Television Newsroom: A Participant Observation Study. *British Journal of Sociology* 22.

Watt, Nicholas. 1997. Apologetic Short Reveals Her Frustration over Montserrat. *Times,* October 15.

Wax, Murray. 1987. *Some Issues and Sources on Ethics in Anthropology.* Special Publication no. 23. American Anthropological Association. Available from www.aaanet .org/committees/ethics/ch1.htm.

Weiner, James. 1997. Televisualist Anthropology: Representation, Aesthetics, Politics. *Current Anthropology* 38(2): 197–236.

Wikinews. 2007a. http://en.wikinews.org/wiki/Main_Page.

———. 2007b. http://en.wikinews.org/wiki/Wikinews:Wikinews_needs_you%21.

———. 2007c. http://en.wikinews.org/wiki/Wikinews:Neutral_point_of_view.

Wilke, Jürgen. 2003. The History and Culture of the Newsroom in Germany. *Journalism Studies* 4(4): 465–77.

———. 2007. Das Nachrichtenangebot der Nachrichtenagenturen im Vergleich. *Publizistik* 52(3): 329–54.

Williams, A. 1997. Montserrat: Under the Volcano. *National Geographic* 192(1): 58–75.

Wittel, Andreas. 2000. Ethnography on the Move: From Field to Net to Internet. *Forum: Qualitative Social Research* 1(1): 1–9.

Wolcott, Harry F. 1999. *Ethnography: A Way of Seeing.* Walnut Creek, Calif.: Alta-Mira Press.

Wolfe, Thomas C. 1997. The Most Visible Hand: Russian Journalism and Media-Context. In *Cultural Producers in Perilous States: Editing Events, Documenting Change,* ed. G. E. Marcus. Chicago: University of Chicago Press.

———. 2005. *Governing Soviet Journalism: The Press and the Socialist Person after Stalin.* Bloomington: Indiana University Press.

Wu, H. Denis. 2004. The World's Windows to the World: An Overview of 44 Nations' International News Coverage. In *International News in the 21st Century,* ed. C. Paterson and A. Sreberny. Eastleigh: John Libbey.

Wyatt, Clarence R. 1993. *Paper Soldiers: The American Press and the Vietnam War.* Chicago: University of Chicago Press.

Zelizer, Barbie. 1992. *Covering the Body: The Kennedy Assassination, the Media, and the Shaping of Collective Memory.* Chicago: University of Chicago Press.

———. 1993. Journalists as Interpretive Communities. *Critical Studies in Mass Communication* 10: 219–37.

———. 2004. *Taking Journalism Seriously: News and the Academy.* New York: Sage.

Zelizer, Barbie, and Stuart Allan, eds. 2002. *Journalism after September 11.* New York: Routledge.

Contributors

S. Elizabeth Bird is Professor of Anthropology at the University of South Florida, where she studies the role of the media and popular culture in everyday life. Her books include *For Enquiring Minds: A Cultural Study of Supermarket Tabloids; Dressing in Feathers: The Construction of the Indian in American Popular Culture;* and *The Audience in Everyday Life: Living in a Media World.*

Amahl Bishara is an assistant professor in the Department of Anthropology at Tufts University. She is completing a manuscript on the production of U.S. news in the West Bank. She has published on this topic in *Cultural Anthropology* and *Ethnography.*

Dominic Boyer teaches anthropology and social theory at Rice University. He has done ethnographic fieldwork with German news journalists since 1996 and now studies online news journalism in the United States. He has published *Spirit and System: Media, Intellectuals, and the Dialectic in Modern German Culture* and *Understanding Media: A Popular Philosophy.*

Dorle Dracklé is Professor of Social Anthropology at the University of Bremen, Germany, and editor of the journal *Social Anthropology/Anthropologie Sociale.* She has published various articles and books on media anthropology, media and migration, eGovernment and diversity, elite, culture, economy, and the European Union.

Zeynep Devrim Gürsel is a postdoctoral fellow in the Michigan Society of Fellows and assistant professor of anthropology at the University of Michigan. She approaches media as a site in which anthropologists can investigate the central role of the imagination in the production of knowledge, culture, and identity.

Jennifer Hasty is a visiting scholar at the African Studies Center, University of Pennsylvania. For her ethnography, *The Press and Political Culture in Ghana,* she worked as a journalist for six news organizations, including both state-owned and independent newspapers. She has published articles on corruption, media, and the state.

Joseph C. Manzella is Professor of Anthropology at Southern Connecticut State University. He has published on news media cultures in the United States, Indonesia, Kyrgyzstan, and South Africa. Before entering academia in 1988, he was a journalist for 16 years, most of that time with the *Hartford Courant.*

Kerry McCallum is Senior Lecturer in Communication at the University of Canberra, Australia. Her research focuses on the relationship between public opinion, media representation, and Indigenous policy development in Australia. Before entering academic life, she worked in Australian politics and on the documentation of Indigenous oral history.

Mark Pedelty is Associate Professor of Journalism and Mass Communication at the University of Minnesota. He received his PhD in anthropology from the University of California at Berkeley. He is author of *War Stories: The Culture of Foreign Correspondents* and *Musical Ritual in Mexico City: From the Aztec to NAFTA.*

Mark Allen Peterson is Associate Professor of Anthropology and International Studies at Miami University. He has conducted fieldwork in Egypt, India, and the United States. He is author of *Anthropology and Mass Communication: Myth and Media in the New Millennium* and co-author of *International Studies: An Interdisciplinary Approach to Global Issues.*

Ursula Rao is Senior Lecturer in Sociology and Anthropology at the University of New South Wales, Sydney. Her most recent books are *News as Culture: Journalistic Practices and the Remaking of Indian Leadership Traditions* and *Celebrating Transgression: Method and Politics in the Anthropological Study of Cultures* (co-edited with John Hutnyk).

Adrienne Russell is Assistant Professor of Digital Media Studies at the University of Denver, where she researches emerging media tools and practices and their influence on activist media and journalism. She has published articles in *Critical Studies in Media Communication, New Media and Society,* and *Journalism: Theory, Practice, and Criticism.*

Christina Schwenkel is an assistant professor of anthropology at the University of California, Riverside. She is author of *The American War in Contemporary Vietnam: Transnational Remembrance and Representation,* and she has published articles on Vietnam, memory, and media in *Cultural Anthropology, American Anthropologist,* and the *Journal of Vietnamese Studies.*

Jonathan Skinner is Lecturer in Social Anthropology at the Queen's University Belfast. He is author of *Before the Volcano: Reverberations of Identity on Montserrat* and co-editor of *Managing Island Life: Social, Economic, and Political Dimensions of Formality and Informality in "Island" Communities.* He researches travel writing, the British Caribbean, tourism, and performance.

Debra Spitulnik is an associate professor in the department of anthropology at Emory University. Her research in Zambia and in the United States spans the areas of media theory, media ethnography, discourse circulation, critical epistemology, sociolinguistics, and the relationship between media and national publics.

Maria D. Vesperi is a professor of anthropology at New College of Florida, a trustee of the Poynter Institute, and a former *St. Petersburg Times* staff writer. Her publications include *City of Green Benches* and two co-edited volumes, *The Culture of Long-Term Care* and *Anthropology off the Shelf: Anthropologists on Writing.*

Karin Wahl-Jorgensen is a reader in the Cardiff School of Journalism, Media, and Cultural Studies, Cardiff University, Wales. She is author of *Journalists and the Public* and co-author of *Citizens or Consumers? What the Media Tell Us about Political Participation.* Her edited books include the *Handbook of Journalism Studies* (with Thomas Hanitzsch).

Leon I. Yacher is Professor and Chair of the Geography Department at Southern Connecticut State University. His most recent research trips to Latin America took him to Belize, Cuba, Mexico, Peru, and Venezuela. He completed a Fulbright to the Kyrgyz Republic (2003). He has published on a number of topics related to Latin America, Central Asia, and Connecticut.

Index

www.ingramcontent.com/pod-product-compliance
Ingram Content Group UK Ltd.
Pitfield, Milton Keynes, MK11 3LW, UK
UKHW021426090225
454829UK00015B/192